NEW FRANCE
1701-1744

DALE MIQUELON

NEW FRANCE

1701-1744

"A Supplement to Europe"

The Canadian Centenary Series

McClelland and Stewart

Canadian Cataloguing in Publication Data

Miquelon, Dale, 1940-
New France 1701-1744: a supplement to Europe

(The Canadian centenary series; 4)
Includes bibliographical references and index.
ISBN 0-7710-1533-X

1. Canada – History – 1713-1763 (New France).*
2. Canada – History – 1663-1713 (New France).*
I. Title.   II. Series.

FC370.M56 1987   971.01'8   C86-095077-8
F1030.M56 1987

Printed and bound in Canada by John Deyell Co.

McClelland and Stewart
The Canadian Publishers
481 University Avenue
Toronto, Ontario
M5G 2E9

A History of Canada

Ramsay Cook, EXECUTIVE EDITOR

VOLUMES STARRED ARE PUBLISHED

†ALSO AVAILABLE IN PAPERBACK

*Volumes I, III, VII, and XII of The Canadian Centenary Series
were published with the help of grants from the Humanities
Research Council of Canada.*

CONTENTS

New France 1701-1744

MAPS

The Canadian Centenary Series

Half a century has elapsed since *Canada and Its Provinces*, the first large-scale co-operative history of Canada, was published. During that time, new historical materials have been made available in archives and libraries; new research has been carried out, and its results published; new interpretations have been advanced and tested. In these same years Canada itself has greatly grown and changed. These facts, together with the centenary of Confederation, justify the publication of a new co-operative history of Canada.

The form chosen for this enterprise was that of a series of volumes. The series was planned by the editors, but each volume will be designed and executed by a single author. The general theme of the work is the development of those regional communities which have for the past century made up the Canadian nation; and the series will be composed of a number of volumes sufficiently large to permit adequate treatment of all the phases of the theme in the light of modern knowledge.

The Centenary History, then, was planned as a series to have a certain common character and to follow a common method but to be written by individual authors, specialists in their fields. As a whole, it will be a work of specialized knowledge, the great advantage of scholarly co-operation, and at the same time each volume will have the unity and distinctive character of individual authorship. It was agreed that a general narrative treatment was necessary and that each author should deal in a balanced way with economic, political, and social history. The result, it is hoped, will be an interpretative, varied, and comprehensive account, at once useful to the student and interesting to the general reader.

The difficulties of organizing and executing such a series are apparent: the overlapping of separate narratives, the risk of omissions, the imposition of divisions which are relevant to some themes but not to others. Not so apparent, but quite as troublesome, are the problems of scale, perspective, and scope, problems which perplex the writer of a one-volume history and are magnified in a series. It is by deliberate choice that certain parts of the history are told twice, in different volumes from different points of view, in the belief that the benefits gained outweigh the unavoidable disadvantages.

W.L. MORTON,
Executive Editor.
D.G. CREIGHTON,
Advisory Editor.

Executive Editor's Preface

W.L. Morton and D.G. Creighton, two of Canada's most distinguished historians, together conceived the Canadian Centenary Series, divided the work, recruited the authors, and presided over the publication of fifteen volumes. Regrettably, neither lived to see the final four books through the press. That responsibility has fallen to me. I intend to carry it through according to the letter and the spirit of the introductory statement written by the first editors, which will continue to appear in each volume. The series remains theirs, an appropriate reminder of the seminal contributions that they made to the understanding of Canada's past. Having served my apprenticeship as a historian with each of them, in different ways, it is a signal privilege for me to be able to oversee the completion of this fine series of Canadian historical volumes.

Professor Dale Miquelon's well-written study of the years when New France experienced its greatest success is strikingly new in the manner in which it is presented. Here social and economic development take centre stage providing a convincing picture of the fashion in which life was lived in the colony during the first half of the eighteenth century. And his revealing account of the complex story of contact between the original inhabitants of North America and the European intruders adds a highly significant dimension to this penultimate stage in the history of France's "supplement" in North America. War, diplomacy, politics and religion are all fitted into this rich social framework. This is a work of skilled synthesis.

RAMSAY COOK

PICTURE CREDITS

For material in the illustration sections of this book, acknowledgement is made to the following sources:

The Public Archives of Canada for Frédéric de Maurepas, Philippe de Vaudreuil, Charles de Beauharnois, Michel Bégon, Louisbourg, Canadian at War, Iroquois Warrior, Busy Beavers, The *Eléphant* Grounded, Gentleman, Bourgeois, Wealthy Woman of the Bourgeoisie, Woman in a Sleeveless Coat, Iroquois Youth, Micmac Woman in Traditional Cap, French Soldier *circa* 1725, Canadian Militia Officer, Canadian Militiaman, Sailor, Jesuit, Récollet, Sulpician, Charron Brother, Grey Nun, and Hospitaler.

Les Archives Nationales du Québec, Quebec, for Jérôme de Pontchartrain, Jean-Baptiste de Saint-Vallier, Pierre-Herman Dosquet, and Gilles Hocquart.

PREFACE

In early summer, 1975, the late W.L. Morton telephoned me to propose that I take on the writing of the present volume. I leapt at the chance and agreed that a deadline of 1977 would be quite acceptable: wishful thinking must have done strange things to our reasoning powers. Now, some dozen years later, this book at last reaches its public.

Some of the previously published volumes in the series had been written almost entirely from documents and were the summation of many years or even a lifetime of scholarship. These could not be my models; I had a Ph.D. dissertation and not much more behind me. While I made annual trips to archives to fill crucial gaps in the literature and to examine the documentary foundation of this or that argument, I relied to a considerable extent on secondary material. At first I assumed that this was a weakness, but I have come to believe that synthesis is a business quite different from the writing of monographs – that the synthesizer's job is to adjudicate the extant body of research and to bring its disparate and dispersed elements into fruitful juxtaposition. In the early stages of this project I read virtually everything I could find on certain topics, not because it was essential to the framing of the narrative, but because it seemed right to adjudicate all the materials. Later, necessity and right reason (mercifully) confined my research to the more strictly required materials. While, on the surface, history writing in Canada still has the appearance of being an individual and individualistic enterprise, beneath the surface even the writing of a monograph has taken on the character of a group effort.

In saluting the subterranean group, my primary obligation is to my mentor, W.J. Eccles, who put in a good word for me back in 1975 and who painstakingly reviewed the completed manuscript. (Indeed, this would seem an appropriate place to thank Professors Eccles, S.R. Mealing, and W.D. Farnham, who more than any others have shaped my understanding of history and the historian's craft.) I am also beholden to my editors. Dr. Morton was always supportive of my efforts and supremely understanding as our several deadlines slipped by. Ramsay Cook has been generous with his help – and has sometimes said no at just the right times. I knew that my copy editor, Janet Craig, would relieve my prose of errors and eccentricities. What I did not know is that she would also save me from real howlers in the realm of fact and argument.

I have made considerable use of unpublished theses and dissertations. More than twenty are cited in the notes. Here I wish to underscore my indebtedness to the dissertations of Peter Moogk, James Pritchard, and S. Dale Standen, three ground-breaking studies that have not yet been published in their entirety. The endnotes cite the many other historians on whose work I have relied; and as I cannot thank them individually, I wish to thank them here collectively. I will apologize in advance for oversights or failures in my reading of their works and also must absolve them of any responsibility for conclusions of my own with which they have reason to be dissatisfied.

Thanks are due to Professor Geoffrey Simpson, who many years ago in the Archives nationales passed on to me the document from which I have extracted my title. I am indebted to Keith Bigelow and George Duff for their skilful preparation of the maps, which do so much to clarify the text. Thanks are due to the Social Sciences and Humanities Research Council of Canada, which awarded me a release time grant for the academic year 1982-83. This made it possible for me to bring this project into the "home stretch." I have received much assistance from libraries and archives in both Canada and France and have enjoyed the support of my history department and university. To these institutions and the friends and colleagues who work within them, I extend my thanks.

Finally, I wish to thank my wife, Patricia, who has been able to put up with this obsessive literary entanglement. She is my witness that while the writing of this book has at times been burdensome, it has not been a solemn and grim undertaking. Rather it has been a privilege and great fun. My sincere wish is that the reader will learn from reading these pages as I did from writing them and will share in the fun too.

DALE MIQUELON
University of Saskatchewan
Saskatoon

DATES

Dates in the text are New Style – that is, eleven days have been added to all dates drawn from British sources and January 1 rather than

March 25 is taken as the beginning of the new year – excepting treaty dates, which are given Old Style/New Style, according to the practice of the time (for example, March 10/21, 1710/11). Old Style dates in footnote citations remain unchanged.

QUOTATIONS

English quotations from the period have been modernized in spelling and punctuation to conform to the style used in quotations from the French rendered in modern English.

CHAPTER 1

Introduction: "A Supplement to Europe"

On May 31, 1701, Louis XIV signed a dispatch to his Canadian officials announcing his intention to use New France together with his new colony of Louisiana as a military barrier to block the English from access to the North American interior. Canada was thereby given a new imperial mission quite different from its traditional and still continuing one of being a source of raw materials and a market for French manufactures. The barrier was intended to prevent the British colonies in North America from increasing in economic, political, and strategic value. In this way neighbouring French, and indeed Spanish, colonies (Mexico, the French and Spanish West Indies) that produced gold or sugar and were held in high esteem by mercantilists were to be protected. The new imperialism of cold steel and the old mercantilist imperialism of exotic cargoes would henceforth co-exist. As regarded the empire as a whole, they were complementary. But superimposing the new upon the old did introduce conflict and confusion concerning New France's role within the empire. Was it henceforth to be thought of as a march colony or military outpost – the mailed fist of empire? Or was it still to be thought of as a purveyor of raw materials and as a market – as an economic appendage with some obligation to pay its own way? Because of the advent of the new-style imperialism, the Canadian eighteenth century can be thought of as beginning in 1701, although we must go back to 1700 to put this date into perspective and even earlier to seek out the roots of ideas.

The new imperial policy was one element in France's preparation for the War of the Spanish Succession, which began in 1702 and ended with the Treaty of Utrecht in 1713. France survived that conflict a prostrate nation. By the treaty its empire of New France was stripped of Acadia, Hudson Bay, and Newfoundland. France was forced to recognize, or seemingly so, the right of British subjects to trade in the North American interior and of Great Britain to extend its protection to Canada's neighbours, the Iroquois Five Nations. From the wreckage of

1

Atlantic New France, Louis XIV salvaged Cape Breton and the right to dry fish along specified Newfoundland shores. The long shadow of Utrecht thus extended across all the remaining history of New France. France did its best to mitigate the most harmful effects of the treaty by finding substitutes for lost advantages and by disarming harmful clauses through reinterpretation.

In 1701 Louis XIV's newly minted imperialism had received the challenge of an ambivalent Canadian victory. The conclusion in that year of the Iroquois Wars that had long scourged the colony carried with it both an advantage and a danger. The West was more open both to Canadian initiatives and to the influence of Canada's enemy and the Iroquois' ally, the Province of New York. When the Iroquois had been at war with Canada and Canada's score of Indian allies, New York's Albany fur traders had found it impossible to penetrate to the tribes of the Great Lakes. With the advent of peace in the interior, that was no longer so. French influence in the West depended more than ever upon France's capacity to underwrite its imperial pretensions with the economic support of a thriving and competitive fur trade. At the beginning of the century, that trade was in an abject condition. When it revived in the 1720s, it fell into the hands of Canadian army officers at the western posts, who shared it with Montreal merchants. An imperial presence in the western interior was in one way a policy decreed by the mother country for its own strategic purposes, but it was consistent with Canada's historic quest for both furs and allies in the Great West. Throughout the first half of the eighteenth century, it was the officials in Canada who brought the imperial vision again and again to the attention of French ministers and bureaucrats and not the other way round. Thereon, no doubt, hangs a tale.

In mainland Acadia, on the frontiers of New England, where the French fur trade never had been sizeable, French influence was a matter of subsidies and of taking advantage of the inevitable falling out of the Abenaki Indians and their English neighbours. In peninsular Acadia, the building of the fortress of Louisbourg provided a defence and an anchor for the fishery. The governor of Louisbourg dispensed subsidies to the Micmacs, who combined complete independence with French sympathies.

The long War of the Spanish Succession was followed by an even longer Thirty Years' Peace, which was marked by strenuous Anglo-French competition for diplomatic leadership in Europe and for supremacy in world markets, a supremacy that to a large extent depended upon the successful exploitation of colonies. In 1744 in the course of the War of the Austrian Succession, at first a purely European conflict, France and Great Britain again declared war on one another and so involved the colonial world. In America, the war solved nothing, but by its end in 1748 it was clear there could be no long-term return to the policy triad that had been the rule since Utrecht: armed neutrality, vigorous competition in trade, and elaborate diplomacy among the Indian nations. Both sides saw that the issue of North American supremacy was to be settled on the battlefield. The peace that followed the Treaty of Aix-la-Chapelle in 1748 was only a breathing space, a phoney peace that was really a time of feverish preparation for the next war, which would begin in 1754 and was to destroy New France. In short, the Anglo-French experiment of peaceful but competitive coexistence came to an end in 1744. The remaining history of New France was a history of war and preparations for war. France's declaration of war on Great Britain on March 15, 1744, therefore marks one of the great watersheds in Canadian history. That date and some of the events of the troubled summer that followed rightly bring our narrative to a close.

The dates of economic history do not necessarily coincide with the alpha and omega of politics. In the history of the fur trade, the new imperialism brought metropolitan policy and colonial desires into shaky alignment and the Iroquois peace changed the rules of the fur-trade game. But the more fundamental, more purely economic turning points were the beginning of the years of glut and market collapse in the 1690s; the beginning after Utrecht of a period of modest growth, marked by the crystallization of a mature trading system; and the burgeoning of the trade beyond anything seen before in 1726-27. This dramatic turnaround was not confined to the fur-trade sector. Canadian economic life had unfolded in the context of a long depression, probably from the middle seventeenth century and lasting until the mid-1720s. Canada had had no market for its grain, had lacked capital, roads, and shipping, and had been lucky to attract the few French ships that it had. The troubled beaver trade had remained its economic mainstay. But from 1727, there was no looking back.

Canadian trade to the newly created market of Louisbourg and to the West Indies mushroomed from almost nothing in 1727. This was not an autonomous Laurentian phenomenon. Supplying the mother country with fur and sister colonies with lumber and provisions were roles to which Canada was called within the framework of empire. With astonishing precision, the beginning of growth in Canadian trade coincided with the revival of French metropolitan trade and with the stabilization of the French currency. The successful revitalization of the French trading system after Utrecht, sheltered as it was by the umbrella of the Anglo-French alliance, is a necessary part of our story.

Agriculture and lumbering were fundamental to Canada's new-found prosperity. Fields and herds were greatly expanded. Grist mills with improved sifting devices were built, and exporters began to use brands to identify their clean and merchantable flour. Sawmills in increasing numbers produced hundreds of thousands of board feet of lumber. Canadians were soon building their own ships. An iron mine and a smelter were opened. But beginning in 1736 there was a series of catastrophic crop failures. Wheat and dried cod bought with wheat had been the most valuable parts of Canada's mixed cargoes in the new trades. Without wheat, trade fell off to almost nothing in the last years before 1744. One can only speculate on the probabilities of recovery had war not intervened.

The period from 1713 to 1744 has often been called Canada's golden age. The prolonged peace was one obvious reason as was the unprecedented economic growth. But the description has seemed attractive and even compelling because a truly Canadian society has been thought to have come to maturity and flourished in those years. By 1701 Canadians had behind them almost a century of life on the edge of the wilderness. Many had experienced the life of the Indian – the paddle, the snowshoe, the campfire. They had moved from a country in which land was precious and ownership of land fundamental to the social structure to a country where land, if still valuable when broken, was nevertheless plentiful. Yet they continued to live within the orbit of French influences, which extended from the weight of imperial policies and the day-to-day acts of government to the imperial economic system to the thousand and one things they held precious, of which the familiar trilogy of laws, language, and religion is only the most general and familiar. Canadian society, in its originality and in its essential Frenchness, must also be an object of our study.

In summary, the forty-three years of Canadian history that are the subject of these pages can be organized around a number of themes that help us to make sense of the maze of persons, events, and "developments." The first of these themes is the policy of imperialism that runs through and serves as an organizing principle for the political history of the period. The second is economic development apprehended through the trace of a cycle of stagnation, boom, and bust. Canada's role within an increasingly vital French empire is a subsidiary theme related to both imperialism and economic development. A second subtheme more specifically related to economic development is the fashioning of Canadian material life. Finally, there is the capstone theme of the making of Canadian society (social structure, social habits, social ideas), which reflects the whole historical experience of Canadians.

Political history, story-like and familiar, comfortable reading, provides a framework and is specifically the subject of the opening chapters: this is the history of governors and intendants, of ideas and policies, and of discrete events. The history of economic policy fits well into this narrative. But to turn to the ups and downs of the economy itself, the slow accretions to the colony's material goods – more cultivated land, more farm animals, more houses – and the growth of economic and social systems, is to address history of a different order. This history has its protagonists and its important events, but it is even more the history of Canadians comprehended in the mass. Bringing together change, time, and causation, this history also has a narrative line. Its own economic and social "diffuse events" (the cumulative effect of thousands of occurrences) resist amalgamation with political story telling and so are the subjects of the several topical chapters that make up the second half of this book.

All of these themes, whether political, economic, or social, illustrate the profound and continuing influence of Europe on North America: the dominance of Europe's politics and Europe's mercantilist empires and, although North American originality was more and more in evidence, of European thought patterns. Canadian history in the first half of the eighteenth century, even where it displays its most considerable originality, is not the story of a North American rejection of Europe but of a particular development within the widening circle of European sway. Persistent and pervasive, this connection underlies and sustains the themes traced in these pages.

It is left to a contemporary of the history discussed here to encapsulate for us the nature of this relation between a mother country and a colony. In 1702, Guillaume Delisle, a geographer famous in his time, wrote that "the utility that the different nations of Europe established in America have drawn from that land has caused that part of the world to be considered as of consequence." He was ruminating upon the many discoveries that had been made in the Western Hemisphere, to which he would himself soon contribute by postulating the existence beyond the Great Lakes of a "Western Sea." He continued that none could deny that America was now important "to as great an extent as are Africa and Asia," and that it was, "as it were, a supplement to Europe."[1]

CHAPTER 2

France and New France at the Turn of the Century

I

While there may have been as many reasons for colonization as there were colonists, the state had only two such reasons: to gain wealth and to gain power. The spreading of the gospel had ceased to be a potent motive, although it continued to appear in state documents in the dried and empty husks of traditional formulae. Wealth was to be had from the trade with Canada – or Martinique or any colony. Power was the natural concomitant of wealth. The idea that even a poor colony could confer power by reason of a strategic geographical location alone was, of course, obvious and was basic to the new policy for Canada announced by Louis XIV in 1701. But for colonial administrators this idea went strongly against the grain; they continued to think of Canada and the other colonies primarily in terms of livres, sous, and deniers, as subordinate elements in the system of economic and political renewal that has come to be known as mercantilism.

Colbertism, as French mercantilism is called in deference to Jean-Baptiste Colbert's signal role in co-ordinating a system of mercantilist policies, made a common cause of the welfare of the people and the fiscal necessities of the king – in the words of Jacob Viner, it was intended to augment both power and plenty.[1] These aims had to be pursued under conditions of international rivalry, to which Colbertism in turn contributed, of dearth of money in a hard-money economy, and of low-level consumption patterns. From before the age of Louis XIV and Colbert until after the end of the Regency, including at least half the period covered by this study, Europe was in the grip of an economic recession intimately related to scarcity of bullion, marked by agricultural over-production, punctuated occasionally by famine. This was the background of mercantilism. The economic growth, prosperity, and optimism that are associated with the eighteenth century had barely begun to affect attitudes by the end of our period. Even at the end of the century, the French economy was characterized by archaic structures and regional compartmentalization. Conceived of as a machine, its motions were slow and fitful, frequently paralysed by breakdowns arising from the poor co-ordination of its parts.

The central mercantilist idea was that the level of production had to be raised and that this could be done only by government action – mercantilists had no dewy-eyed faith in an Unseen Hand. The under-utilization of resources and labour was everywhere evident. The lot of the poor was not one of toil alone but also one of idleness and boredom in crumbling country villages. Peasants lived in a world of circumscribed economic possibilities conditioned by the finite and unvarying land base of agriculture. The result was a fatalistic world view that the anthropologist George M. Foster has called "the image of limited good": "Broad areas of peasant behaviour are patterned in such a fashion as to suggest that peasants view their social, economic, and natural uni-verses – their total environment – as one in which all of the desired things in life . . . *exist in finite quantity* and *are always in short sup-ply. . . .* In addition *there is no way directly within peasant power to increase available quantities.*"[2] In an economy that promised only a subsistence and in which surpluses fell into the hands of tax collectors and landlords, work and thrift beyond the needs of subsistence were pointless. Yet Colbertists desired to prod the mainly rural masses to productive labour and self-improvement by establishing both urban and rural manufactures.

Economic growth through industry and international trade required the monopolization of the home market, the capture of external mar-kets and sources of raw materials (colonial status being the ultimate form of captivity), and the injection of a vivifying stream of bullion. Mercantilists have been pilloried for their *bullionism*, their obsession with creating inflows of gold and silver, which they defined errone-ously as *wealth*. While in many instances the charge is justified, it was more common, especially by the eighteenth century, for them to regard bullion as synonymous with *money*, the lubricant without which the economic machine would not go. Even though this identification ignored the role of bank credits and commercial paper, which increased considerably after 1700, it was to a large degree correct in an age when all debts were ultimately payable in coin and government paper had by no means earned the trust of the people.

Bullionism was in part responsible for the mercantilists' preoccupa-tion with maintaining a favourable balance of trade. Surplus credits abroad would be received in gold and silver. This concern also reflected the further mercantilist assumption that each nation's increase in bul-lion and trade implied a corresponding decrease in another nation's.

This is often said to mean that mercantilists believed the economy was static. But taking note of their lively awareness of the underutilization of resources and their determination to do something about it, we could correctly say that they recognized the existence of "limits to growth" and were exceedingly pessimistic about the extent of those limits. The implication is not so much that the mercantilists would have felt at home with the Club of Rome as that, for all their urban sophistication, they were in thrall to a vestigial "image of limited good" according to which trade (or the world economy) was as finite as the lands of a country village, where the increase in size of one farm implied the reduction in size of another. The spectacular growth of the European and colonial economies in the course of the eighteenth century would eventually weaken the belief in narrow limits. But mercantilist ideas, born in a time of economic difficulties, long remained a reasonable description, not of the world as it could be, but as it was: a world with a competitive state system in place, with nine-tenths of the population excluded from the market place, and with a rudimentary technology.

While the doctrines of mercantilism might have been devised originally by English merchants, early French mercantilists were not merchants; and Colbert never thought of himself as a sponsor of the interests of a class, certainly not of merchants, who in his words "nearly always understand merely their own little commerce and not the great forces which make commerce go."[3] The Colbertist programme was a national and royal policy based upon mercantilist assumptions about how the economy worked. Here are its main ideas:

1. International trade should be geared in such a way that bullion enters the country.

2. This bullion should circulate constantly and thereby make possible investment and commercial transactions.

3. Investment and trade would make use of France's considerable pool of labour and boundless resources.

4. If this circulation of money were spread as uniformly as possible across the country, prosperity would become widespread.

5. The surest avenue to the increase in national wealth lies in industry, and government should encourage its growth.

6. Tariff structures should be arranged in such a way that exports of manufactures and unique French products such as wine are encouraged and that the import of needed raw materials is also encouraged.

7. But, on the other hand, foreign manufactures should be kept out of the home market.

8. Colonies should be sources of needed raw materials and markets

for manufactures and are to be prized to the extent that they can fulfil these two roles.

9. The national market should be unified by the destruction of internal barriers to trade and the creation of a uniform French customs policy.

So far, our summary gives to mercantilism only the benign face of the patriotic benefactor of trade and industry; there is also the grim visage of the collector of taxes, fees, and rents. Widespread prosperity was to be fostered in part to enable people to pay their taxes. Regulations regarding the quality and flow of goods could be made to yield revenues in the form of customs duties, inspection fees, or fees from protected monopolies established to produce new, more, or better goods or services. These considerations provide us with a tenth point in the Colbertist programme:

10. The state's revenues will be increased by the country's increased ability to pay taxes and by various fees that the regulatory structure can be made to yield.

Colbertism thus had decidedly fiscal aims. It has even been described as nothing more nor less than the cartelization of the entire economy by the government in order to extract revenues to be shared by it with lucky and grateful monopolists as various as chartered trading companies, tax collectors, guilds, and the businessmen of towns with special trading rights.[4] Historians may argue forever about the "true face" of mercantilism. While the argument that fiscal exaction was the *point* of mercantilist policy (only masked by platitudes about the needs of trade and manufacturing) is an unconvincing one, there is considerable truth in the view that fiscal necessities *subverted* a system of regulation meant to restore the economy. If we are simply to describe what we see in the records of the time, all we can say is that the two faces of mercantilism stare back at us and claim our attention equally.

Colbertism was a great system concerned with increasing trade, manufacturing, and state revenues. It was not just a system of colonization, although colonies had their part to play. They were thought of in terms of maritime trade, which accounts for their being administered by the Department of the Marine, or Navy. Thus it was Jérôme Phélypeaux, Comte de Pontchartrain, Secretary of State for the Marine Department from September 6, 1699, until September 1, 1715 (succeeding his father in that office), who presided over the destinies of Canada at the beginning of the new century.

Jérôme de Pontchartrain was no Colbert. Historians have not been kind to him. His appearance, as reported by the waspish Saint-Simon, "heavy-jowled, very thick-lipped, unpleasant, ravaged by the small-pox, which left him blind in one eye," has been taken as the measure of the man and an adequate comment on his ministry.[5] Yet in new and fragmentary studies this rather unfortunate man is beginning to emerge as at least conscientious and humane, greatly concerned with the persons in his charge and caught in the toils of an overwhelming military and economic crisis.[6] Pontchartrain took office as a young man, and his youthful openness and desire to do his work well disarm us even while his penchant for solving all questions with mercantilist axioms warns us of his unpromising pedantry. On becoming minister, Pontchartrain asked his friend and former teacher, the Maréchal de Vauban, for his advice. Vauban professed a weakness for colonies, and Canada, in particular, was thus not without an advocate in the early days of Pontchartrain's administration.[7] In his replies and marginalia to Vauban's proposals Pontchartrain has left us his most candid reflections on colonization.[8]

There is no pigeonhole for Vauban. He echoed the best of the past and anticipated the most progressive views of the eighteenth century. Colonies as *la gloire du prince* and as self-sufficient in necessities – these are links with Talon and Colbert.[9] They are also glimpses of colonies as rising nations and willing trading partners. Within the framework of empire, Vauban's thinking had reached a laissez-faire position. The *pacte exclusif* had become unabashedly multilateral. Vauban's plan for the settlement of Canada by troops recalls the Canadian experience with the Carignan-Salières regiment in the 1660s as well as his classical education, but it is also a manifestation of scientific planning, complete with statistical calculations. His attention to Canada's strategic importance was altogether timely and an anticipation of La Galissonière.

Pontchartrain the administrator had to face realities that did not inhibit Vauban the memorialist. On one of Vauban's letters, he pencilled what became the refrain of his administration: "Would cost a lot," "Great expense," "Expense."[10] To Vauban's lyrical description of the "colonies of Canada" he rejoined with ill grace: "The worst of all. One gets nothing from them; they cost a lot, etc."[11] To Canadian administrators he was expressing not only a half-truth, not only a personal prejudice, but also the easily recognizable mercantilist view of the peasantry when he complained of the "idleness and sloth of the inhabitants that prevents this colony from being peopled," that Canada's slight utility came from "the debauchery of the inhabitants and from the little attention that has been given to inclining them to other things than the hunt," and instructed a Canadian intendant to encourage trade, "which enriches the people and draws them from an idleness that is often the cause of many misfortunes."[12]

In spite of his many negative sentiments, he was not entirely lacking in good will. "I assure you," he confided to Vauban, "that I would like with all my heart to be able to find sure and easy means to raise this colony from the infancy where you point out it has been these 160 years."[13] He understood strategy and consequently the necessity for better Canadian fortifications. His official correspondence shows that he was aware of a wide panoply of Canadian economic possibilities. At the same time, Pontchartrain could not ignore the waning of Canada's economic fortunes. As the colony's surplus of beaver pelts increased, so did his pessimism. He was distrustful of schemes for colonization by troops – usually an ill-assorted lot – and fearful that the mother country had already been depopulated by war, famine, and the expulsion of the Huguenots. For any Colbertist, Canada's need for population held a lagging third place behind the requirements of industry and the military. Although populationism became a national obsession only from 1756, the year in which Ange Goudar's *Les Intérêts de la France mal entendus* and the Marquis de Mirabeau's *L'ami des hommes* were published, fear of declining population had always nagged administrators. It played its part in preventing them from devising schemes of colonial emigration, although the high cost of such programmes, the bad reputation of colonies (particularly Canada), and the want of emigrants were probably more important factors.

Above all, Pontchartrain differed from Vauban, and indeed from Colbert, in his opposition to the notion of colonial self-sufficiency, which seemed to him contrary to the economic *raison d'être* of empire. He also gave a very limited acceptance to the idea of the multilateral benefits of empire. While Canada and the West Indies "could be of mutual assistance, and by the traffic they could establish between themselves could procure considerable advantages," he was opposed to the entry into that trade of any commodity that could be supplied by the mother country.[14] For him the veritable model of empire remained that of a series of bilateral trade relations between the mother country and each colony. He also very much doubted colonial abilities and so felt a continual need to intervene to steer the colonial economies on straight courses. Yet he could not rely on the King for funds; hence the importance in his thinking of monopoly companies, of which he established a number. There is, finally, in some of Pontchartrain's rejoinders to Vauban's enthusiastic propositions a feeling of alienation from Canada. That colony, he informed his friend, was a land of "another spirit, other manners, other sentiments."[15] The reliance that could be placed on the Canadians militarily had thus to be tempered by a consideration of their essential foreignness.

Pontchartrain set great store on regulation and on the desirability of

French national self-sufficiency. In a series of memoranda written in 1700-1701 by leading merchants from several French cities there is evidence of an older, humanist view that autarky was chimerical, that nations were meant to trade together, and that trade meant peace, not war. Most of all, the merchants demanded freedom of action, the oldest, most traditional merchant stance and one that even Colbert had recognized as basic. Historians have seen in these memoranda evidence of a liberal attack upon a rigidified post-Colbertist system, complaints that were still, however, in C.W. Cole's phrase, "imbedded in a matrix of thoroughly mercantilist thought."[16] But no historian has provided an adequate demonstration that Colbertism was in the throes of rigor mortis, and business freedom is so old a doctrine that it cannot be safely attributed to new liberal ideas. It is true that there were proto-liberals who criticized government policy and that by mid-century their ideas were making headway within the administration. In 1749 a rueful French monopolist complained of government, "The persuasion is that privileges are inimical to emulation."[17] That was the harbinger of a new age.

Colbertism was intimately tied to royal absolutism and state building, both of which encountered aristocratic opposition.[18] It was also mechanistic in its view of society and amoral both in its beggar-thy-neighbour stance in international relations and its the-end-justifies-the-means proceedings. Colbertism thus encountered the opposition of Christians who believed that the state too must live ethically and of humanists with a belief in universal harmony. Curiously, Jérôme de Pontchartrain, the arch-mercantilist, never could separate politics and morality. His belief that the people must be activated by "sheer volition" with "neither menaces nor constraints, but only suggestion and exhortation" and his willingness to relax his policies in the face of poverty and hardship stand in sharp contrast to his axiomatic Colbertist pronouncements.[19]

Many in aristocratic circles balked at Colbertism's centralizing tendencies and feared that the new policies would dislodge the French economy from its agrarian foundations for the benefit of urban businessmen. This opposition movement was manifest in Fénelon and the circle that surrounded the Duke of Burgundy, finding at least a feeble reflection in the Regency. In the eighteenth century the opposition movement absorbed the new utilitarianism, which saw mercantilism as a human meddling with a system that left alone would run in accord with natural laws. As early as 1695 there was an approving circle to greet Boisguillebert's "laisser faire la nature," and the circle grew wider. But the Marine Department was not run by reformers, with their mixed bag of liberal and reactionary ideas. The policies of its ministers from Pontchartrain to Maurepas and even beyond were largely Colbertist in inspiration.

Between 1699 and 1715 the office of Secretary of State for the Marine would have proved a burial ground for reputations far more brilliant than that of Jérôme de Pontchartrain. The financial state of his department in the War of the Spanish Succession could not have been worse. Its separation from the Contrôle Général on September 13, 1699, eliminated the easier access to funds that Jérôme's predecessor and father, Louis de Pontchartrain, had enjoyed. Of far greater importance was the fall of the navy from favour. According to President Hénault, whose lapidary summation of the matter is all too often taken as the last word, seafaring was simply un-French, and after the disappointing defeat of the navy at La Hougue in 1692, "one looked to the land for glory, and the word Marine was no longer spoken."[20] For Lapeyrouse-Bonfils, it was the failure to follow up the victory of Malaga by the capture of Gibraltar in 1704 that turned the French against their navy: "Its value was no longer believed in."[21] Together these dates frame the decline of the Marine from the favoured situation in which it had been left by Colbert and his son, Seignelay. The Nine Years' War (1688-97) was crucial. In that conflict, the navy's record was one of clever sea manoeuvres of uncertain value, of victories without issue, and of defeat. The fleet thus failed to prove its worth, perhaps because no one really understood how to use it. The result was that in 1694, a year of excruciating financial crisis, the Marine's budget was slashed, drastically and for the long term.[22]

In 1695 Vauban, that friend of colonies, published his *Mémoire sur la Caprérie*, arguing that grand naval strategy using warships, *la guerre d'escadre*, should be abandoned in favour of a pell-mell guerrilla warfare against trade, *la guerre de course*. In this new strategy, small French naval squadrons would tie down the bulk of the Dutch and British navies while privateers and naval cruisers wore down the enemy by destroying his commerce. The coast would be protected to a large extent by shore batteries, fortifications, and troops. Before Ryswick, Vauban's recommendation that privateers be supported by naval squadrons was not followed. The navy's ships were withdrawn from active duty or were outfitted as commerce destroyers, often by private capital. It was a policy that has aptly been described as spending the navy "in small change."[23]

France came out of the Nine Years' War having abandoned the ambition of dominating the seas, and this attitude was confirmed in the War of the Spanish Succession. Ships of the line continued to be built and used, but *la guerre de course* dominated French strategy. It was believed that a small navy was adequate because it could immobilize a large one, that the true aim of naval warfare was to destroy enemy commerce, and that naval battles were of their nature indecisive. It was not a policy that protected ocean-borne commerce or distant colonies, the very purpose of a navy as Colbert had conceived it.[24] Even in the spacious mind of Vauban, the connection was not made between empire over the seas and the empire of colonies. The sea was surrendered to traders, privateers, and the British navy just as Louis XIV proclaimed his North American colonies an affair of state vastly transcending the economic.

The year 1701 marked a turning point in France's North American policy from one wholly mercantilistic to a broader conception in which traditional economic aspirations were weighed against the purely political advantages of empire. The parallel economic development, admirable political cohesion, and conflicting commercial aims of France and England propelled the mother countries on a collision course. While the prospering and geographical extension of colonies in many cases revealed the two as rivals developing at cross purposes, they merely enhanced a confrontation of metropolitan origin that made of the most distant, economically unattractive possessions outposts of empire. North America's role in this imperial confrontation was brought sharply into focus in 1700 by the bequest of the Spanish succession.

On October 2, 1700, a month before his death, Charles II, the last of the Hapsburg kings of Spain, was induced by his advisers to will his kingdom to Philip of Anjou, Louis XIV's grandson. For years the great powers of Europe had bickered over this vast heritage, dividing it among themselves first on one plan, then on another. The unfortunate Charles's testament was intended to thwart this division. His councillors reasoned that they stood the best chance of keeping their empire intact with the support of Louis XIV. And they included a measure of blackmail in their offer by providing that in the event of a French refusal, the twenty-two crowns of Spain would be offered to the Emperor Leopold for his younger son. On November 16, Louis presented Philip to the court at Versailles as the King of Spain. He had not made his decision lightly, for the testament of Charles II brought to its legatee the very real danger of a far-flung and terrible war.[25]

It was implicit in Louis's decision that he take upon himself the task of guaranteeing the integrity of his grandson's realm, including the Spanish American possessions. His new colony of Louisiana became his first line of defence against possible English incursions. Ever since the Canadian explorer Louis Jolliet had ascertained that the Mississippi emptied into the Gulf of Mexico (1674), France had been interested in founding a colony at the river's mouth. The end of the Nine Years' War had made it possible to take up this project again.[26] Before Louis de Pontchartrain left the Ministry of Marine to his son and became chancellor, his last significant decision was to instruct the Canadian naval commander, Pierre Le Moyne d'Iberville, to search out the river's mouth, hidden amid the islands, tropical vegetation, and reefs of an extensive delta, and there to build a fort.[27] The venture had the usual mercantilist aims. The scarcity of money in Europe meant there was a great desire for the discovery of mines. And the Minister did not forget to direct that buffalo wool be tested by spinning and that it be ascertained whether mulberry trees grew there.[28] Scientific aspirations had also played a part. But the matter had been given urgency by the fear that the English would settle the area first.

Spain still held sway over the vast area that is now Florida, Georgia, and much of Alabama, and with justified suspicion founded Pensacola a short distance from where Iberville would found Fort Biloxi a few months later (April, 1699). But it was South Carolina that posed the greatest threat to the new French colony. From Charlestown, which was to the south what Montreal was to the north, the Carolinian traders walked into the west in groups of two or three with packhorses or Indian bearers, seeking slaves and deerskins. This gave the colony considerable sway over the four great tribes of the interior: the Cherokees, hill people in the last ranges of the Appalachian barrier; the Creeks, in the interior of what became Georgia, south and east of the last mountains; the Choctaws, dominating the lower Mississippi west of the Creeks; and the Chickasaws on the Mississippi, due west of South Carolina. In September 1700, Iberville smoked the calumet with the Choctaws, the best friends the French would find in a region where they would never succeed in establishing a widespread alliance such as rewarded their efforts on the Canadian frontier.[29]

Fear of English incursions was subsequently enhanced by the crisis of the Spanish succession. When in 1701 Jérôme de Pontchartrain announced to the authorities at Quebec that he was founding a permanent colony at the mouth of the Mississippi, he was moved by the necessity of protecting the route to Mexico.[30] The new colony was not expected to amount to much at first; there wasn't the money for it, and indeed, Louisiana proved to be something of a stepchild in the French Empire. But like that other stepchild of colonization, Acadia, it was a foothold that had to be retained.[31]

The ministry's Canadian policy could not have remained unaffected. Its long-term plan for colonial development, much honoured in the breach, was to prevent westward migration and involvement and to develop a strong and defensible "compact colony" in the St Lawrence Valley between Montreal and the sea. In 1701 the "compact colony

North American Neighbours, incorporating tribal relocations: Hurons, Ottawas to Detroit, c. 1700; Weas, Miamis southeast, c. 1712; Mingos, Shawnees northwest, post 1730.

policy" was being applied with something akin to passion, the bureau-crat's eleventh-hour attempt to ward off economic catastrophe with the bludgeon. To control the surplus of beaver pelts that years of over-trading had produced – more than enough for ten years were stock-piled – Louis de Pontchartrain had in 1696-97 closed the West and ordered most of its posts razed. Only four, Frontenac, Michilimackinac, Saint-Joseph-des-Miamis, and Saint-Louis-des-Illinois, were to be re-tained, and that for only as long as military necessity dictated. The fur trade was restricted to the central colony, to which the Indians them-selves were to bring their furs. Indeed, Michilimackinac and Saint-Joseph were abandoned by their garrisons, which could not support themselves without trade. Thus there remained in the Great Lakes basin only Fort Frontenac, which the Minister had decided to stock with goods as a concession to the Iroquois, and two posts that were abandoned by 1702, Saint-Louis (a private concession) and a post for the exploitation of a lead mine on the Mississippi. There were missions in the Illinois country, at Green Bay, St Joseph River, and Michili-mackinac. But although the garrisons had left, there remained in Indian towns and semi-abandoned posts the coureurs de bois, Canadians who had given up the routine hardships of a pioneer farmstead for the irregular and more exciting ones of an Indian-style life as traders. They constituted a French presence only to the extent that their interests dictated. To the north, on Hudson Bay, Iberville had captured Fort York at the same time that Pontchartrain was closing the West. To the east, along the lower north shore of the St Lawrence, there remained inviolate a string of trading posts belonging to the Crown and known as the King's Posts.[32].

Beyond the basis of economic desperation, there was in Pontchar-train's policy an attitude of disillusionment and even despair at Can-ada's linking of its fate to Indian alliances and embroilment for the sake of the fur trade with distant Indian tribes. Pontchartrain consciously renounced any French *imperium* in the interior or any monopoly of the fur trade. The logic of policy inherent in the acceptance of the Spanish succession was exactly contrary to that being followed. If the Mississippi were to be held, forts that were slated for demolition as soon as peace was secured would have to be retained. The allies would have to be supplied, by gifts and by trade, to prevent their adhering to the English. The renegade coureurs de bois suddenly were no longer seen as banditti flouting the King's ordinances in the Canadian hinterland but as agents of French imperialism in the hinterland of Louisiana.

There had been an air of unreality to the policy of withdrawal from the West concocted by the Pontchartrains and their clerks far from the scene of action among their maps and papers. The prohibitions of trade had been ignored with impunity by the governor and anyone who was his friend or creature. Illegal trade was encouraged by the Canadian revenue system that provided beaver be accepted at a fixed price by the holders of a beaver export monopoly no matter how un-favourable the market conditions. The new policy of holding the West was more in line with the main thrust of Canadian history, but it too had its share of mirage. It was supposed to be applied with only minor changes to the recent fur trade regulations, which inhibited the trade's

usefulness as an instrument of imperialism. While some provision was
made for underpinning the Indian alliances by legalizing the fur trade
at Frontenac and Detroit – a new post founded in 1700 as a kind of
minimal presence in the interior – a significant occupation of the West
was impossible without an expenditure on troops and forts that was
not forthcoming. This lack of funds was not only the result of the
financial strain of war. The contrary claims of mercantilism and the
new-style political imperialism continued to co-exist. The King, the
Minister, and France with them crossed this important watershed in
modern history without fully assimilating the implications or trans-
lating them into a consistent policy.

II

For Canadian merchants and Canadian administrators the new colony
of Louisiana was a source of anxiety and of complaint. Louis-Hector de
Callière, the rough-hewn, gouty career soldier who succeeded Frontenac
as governor in 1698 at the age of fifty, and Jean Bochart de Champigny,
the able and austere intendant of Canada since 1686, observed in their
joint letter for 1701 that "the *congés* [trading permits] were suppressed
because it was feared that too much beaver would be traded in the
woods." Nevertheless, they complained, "this country has the chagrin
of seeing that there are more merchants than ever in distant lands
without any of the profit returning to it" – the profits were draining
down the Mississippi.[33] They warned Pontchartrain that the coureurs
de bois, the chosen instruments of his new colonial foundation, could
not be relied on to do anything but swing the fur trade to a north-south
axis, ruining Canada, and that the adventurers to whom he had given
his confidence – Le Sueur, Tonty, Juchereau – whatever they might
propose, were interested primarily in the fur trade. The only way to
protect Canada's economic interests and prevent the coureurs de bois
from establishing treasonable liaison with Carolina, they argued, was
to establish a border between Canada and Louisiana at the Wabash and
to authorize the Canadian governor to build forts throughout his jurisdiction. Callière and Champigny also reported good news that, like
the founding of Louisiana and the new imperialism, marked a turning
point in the history of Canada. A treaty of peace negotiated the previous year had been ratified at Montreal by Canada, the Iroquois, and
more than a score of allied Indian tribes.

The Treaty of Ryswick, September 20, 1697, had concluded the war
between France and England, New France and the English colonies.
But the war with the Iroquois, the leitmotiv of Canadian history since

the 1640s, continued. The Iroquois question was among those to be settled by an Anglo-French commission established in accordance with Article 8 of the treaty, although in a strict interpretation problems in the Great Lakes region did not fall within the commission's terms of reference, "the settlement of the limits and confines of ceded or restored countries by both parties."[34] The French commissioners, Count Tallard and the Marquis d'Herbaud, the latter a Phélypeaux like Pontchartrain and a naval intendant knowledgeable about North America, were instructed to demand French sovereignty over the Iroquois or at least to see them declared a free and neutral people. Any agreement was to provide that neither European power support Indians attacking the other. If the commissioners were forced to concede English sovereignty, the French ultimatum required that the English agree to prevent the Iroquois from attacking Canada. The Iroquois question was subsumed under the boundary issue because the concession of French sovereignty over the Five Nations would have put the Canadian border to the rear of the Iroquois, whereas acceptance of English claims would have placed it on the south shore of Lake Ontario and would have encouraged pretensions to an even more northerly limit.[35]

Although the Ministry of Marine was not inclined to take seriously the English claim of sovereignty over the Iroquois, Tallard found that the English would insist on at least some species of suzerainty.[36] At the first meeting of the commissioners in London on March 2, 1699, he and his colleagues agreed that the Iroquois question above all others menaced the peace of North America.[37] In their view, hostilities had to be stopped immediately and claims of sovereignty dealt with later. The commissioners drafted letters to be sent to the governors of Canada and New York by Louis XIV and William III, ordering a cessation of hostilities.[38] The European view of the Iroquois in the two letters is uniformly myopic, and in this it is an accurate reflection of the correspondence of Tallard and d'Herbaud with the Pontchartrains. Louis de Pontchartrain had expressed the opinion that the war with the Five Nations resulted from interference in their trade by greedy coureurs de bois, a half-truth with the important part left out. He had even scolded Governor Frontenac for meddling in Indian quarrels.[39] Similarly, both French and English commissioners seem to have believed the solution to war in the North American interior lay in taking governors in hand and dealing sternly with savages.[40] The letters instructed the governors to cease all warlike acts and to join forces, if necessary, to prevent tribes from warring on each other or on either European nation. (These were both provisions that Callière would include in his treaty with the Iroquois, the second seemingly as an act of showmanship since the treaty was in no sense a joint project of Canada and

New York.) The letters also contained the order that the Indians were to be disarmed, evidence of a total ignorance of Indian life and of the relative strength of Europeans and Indians on the frontier. Callière prudently suppressed his own master's letter while with telling effect his diplomats among the Iroquois grossly misrepresented William III's identical order to the Governor of New York as a prelude to their extermination.[41] The final versions of the letters signed by the two kings, the French version dated March 25, 1699, were vague documents, phrases in the original French *projet* referring to a dispute over sovereignty and Iroquois neutrality having been expunged by the English commissioners as possibly injurious to English pretensions. The French commissioners were delighted that they had achieved as much as they had, "neutrality and neutrality with a species of offensive league to maintain it."[42] They turned to other issues, rightly fearing that further discussion of the Iroquois question would bring them to deadlock.

The London commission had not brought peace at the stroke of a pen. Peace was made in North America and in a manner not at all in keeping with the commissioners' understanding of North American affairs. The Treaty of Montreal was the result of three long years of negotiations with the Iroquois, from July 1698 to August 1701, the greatest achievement of Callière's brief governorship of only four and a half years ended by his death on May 26, 1703. "As every one knows," the bishop once wrote of him, Callière was a "man very devoted to his duty, personally brave, upright and well-bred, very capable of his position in the opinion of all those who know him."[43] It was Callière's task to make himself the indispensable agent of peace in the West. To this end, he had first to maintain his Indian allies' hostility to the Iroquois, preventing the Indians from making peace among themselves. He had to demoralize the Iroquois, convincing them that as he was the master of war, so also was he the master of peace. To fulfil this expectation, he then had to be able to stay the hatchets of his allies. At the same time, he had to sow distrust between the Five Nations and their ally and trading partner, the Province of New York. All this he accomplished in masterly fashion. At every stage of negotiation he was opposed by the Earl of Bellomont, Governor of New York, Massachusetts, and New Hampshire, commander of the militia of Rhode Island, Connecticut, and the Jerseys, who had taken office only a few months before Callière, and by Robert Nanfan, the acting governor in the crucial months after Bellomont's death on March 16, 1701.

Bellomont understood that it was in New York's interest to isolate the French by extending westward to the "Far Nations" (Ottawas, Hurons, and other allies of Canada) the "Covenant Chain" of alliance that bound the Iroquois to his province. This would entail admitting the western Indians to the trade of Albany, hitherto exclusive to the Iroquois. But Bellomont's bargaining position was weaker than Callière's, for he had no influence with the Far Nations that enabled him to act as peacemaker to his allies; rather, he looked to them as his agents of pacification. His plan was to consolidate his influence among the Iroquois by sending them Protestant ministers, building forts in their villages, and giving them presents. He also hoped to build a fort on Lake Ontario to circumvent them and secure a direct trade with the Ottawas. In Robert Livingston, the province's Indian Secretary, he had a sagacious lieutenant, the author of a remarkable series of memoirs on the Iroquois.[44] Plans abounded, but there was little Bellomont could do to effect them while he remained "so pinioned for want of orders, soldiers and money" by a distant British government and an uninterested and close-pursed lowland assembly that evinced little interest in the frontier.[45] The lack of support for his Indian policy is astonishing given the stakes, the Iroquois, as Livingston candidly put it to the Lords of Trade, "having fought our battles for us."[46]

The New York–Canada conflict was grafted into and aggravated wars between the Iroquois and their northern and western neighbours who were Canada's allies. These were disputes between parties divided by ritualistic and immemorial animosity. By 1670 many Iroquois, withdrawing from traditional homelands in response to attacks by the southern Andastes and attracted by the possibilities for hunting, trading, and the capture of prisoners, had established towns on the north shore of Lake Ontario at positions that gave access to strategic waterways. This had involved them in war with northern Indians and with Canada. From a date in the later seventeenth century, bands of Algonkian linguistic stock had been pushing their advantage against the weakened Iroquois. By 1700 they had displaced the northern Iroquois and had themselves occupied the territory that the Iroquois had won half a century earlier from the Hurons and other tribes. The Five Nations were anxious to maintain some foothold in these rich lands and to end the decimating war. Their fighting force having been reduced by half in the previous war, the Iroquois looked in vain to New York for some show of military support. It is not surprising that they also were taking measures, with apprehension and uncertainty, to save themselves by themselves. The Iroquois' one advantage was that they controlled access to Albany, one of the principal marts of the fur trade. As they had done a number of times in the past, by April 1700 the Ottawas and Iroquois were conducting peace talks on their own, the Iroquois *quid pro quo* for a sharing of the northern hunting grounds being that they would "open a path" to Albany.[47] It may be, as has been argued, that this understanding was an essential preliminary to the great peace that followed, which would, in that case, constitute its ratification.[48] Yet there were undoubtedly cross-currents in Iroquois thinking on this point. Subsequent to these talks, the Ottawas were still afraid to visit Albany.[49] Bellomont believed, assurances to the contrary notwithstanding, that the Iroquois would "rob 'em of their peltry and then knock 'em on the head that they may tell no tales."[50]

Callière did his best to maintain the ancient and smouldering enmity that lay between the western tribes and the Iroquois. "The French had as good be in open war with us as to set their Indians to war upon us continually," the Iroquois complained.[51] French diplomatic pressure was concentrated on the Onondagas and the Senecas, among whom Canadian representatives, Father Jacques Bruyas, Paul Le Moyne de Maricourt, and Louis Chabert de Joncaire, confronted the ambassadors of Albany. Renewed Ottawa efforts to negotiate with the Iroquois on their own were stopped by the cajolery, bravado, and sheer force of character that were the only weapons at Callière's disposal.[52] It was because Callière was successful in maintaining his ascendancy over his allies that the Iroquois, except for the recalcitrant Mohawks, on September 8, 1700, finally signed a treaty at Montreal with Canada and such of Callière's allies as he could muster.[53] As a prelude to ratification, Callière again sent his emissaries to the Iroquois villages, this time to round up French and allied prisoners who were to be exchanged. In September his ambassadors, Augustin Le Gardeur de Courtemanche and Father Jean Enjalran, loaded with Onontio's wampum belts, began their journey to Michilimackinac, from where Courtemanche proceeded to the countries of the other allies, abandoning his canoe for snowshoes when the waters froze, everywhere exhorting the Indians to descend to Montreal, preventing the formation of war parties against the Iroquois, or, in the case of the Ottawas, thwarting their persistent plans for a separate peace.[54] The Iroquois found themselves in the age-old dilemma of border peoples. "You both tell us to be Christians," the Onondaga chief, Teganissorens, said to New York and Canadian officials. "You both make us mad; we know not what side to chose."[55] The Iroquois did ratify the treaty. Some thirteen hundred Indians representing thirty-one nations or distinct groups descended upon Montreal near the end of July, 1701, and the ratification was signed on August 4.[56]

The two most important clauses of the treaty provided that the peace was to be given substance by a mutual exchange of prisoners and that if any party to the treaty committed an aggression against another and refused just settlement, the governor of Canada would side with the aggrieved party to punish the aggressor, even inviting the governor of New York to assist him. The governor of Canada was thus elevated above the turmoil of intertribal strife and made to appear the disinterested guarantor of a *pax gallica*. Hunting rights were a kind of subtext not mentioned in any clause of the treaty or ratification, that is, not covered by the exchange of wampum belts. Yet they were a fundamental grievance. The Iroquois complained of encroachments. Disputes over hunting territories broke out even during the lengthy negotiations. Callière, whose limited authority in the matter permitted little else, simply enjoined the tribesmen to accommodate one another, something that peace would at last permit.

Callière believed that the treaty had put the four Iroquois nations that signed it – the Mohawks as usual were absent – in such a position that they would accept his proposals for neutrality.[57] Indeed, they did so at a special conference between Callière and themselves on August 7.[58] Even the Mohawks eventually sent delegates to ratify the treaty and agree to neutrality.[59] But the border people had hedged their bets. Before leaving Onondaga, they had promised their commercial alliance to whoever would sell to them on the best terms. Some sachems had been sent to ratify the treaty at Montreal, but others had gone to Albany, where they had conferred with Lieutenant-Governor Nanfan from July 23 to August 1. On July 30 (19 O.S.) they took the unprecedented action of deeding in trust to William III the vast hunting ground between Lake Huron and Lake Erie and the entire circumference of Erie – an area that included the new Canadian fort at Detroit. Their aim was that the King should protect it for them in perpetuity.[60]

Robert Livingston is believed to have drawn up the document and to have been influential in devising it. If so, he must have congratulated himself on his cunning, for the surrender could be extremely useful as a foundation for English claims of suzerainty in the interior. It was also subtle diplomacy on the part of the Iroquois. Since they had already lost control of the area to the Hurons, Ojibwas, and Mississaugas, they gave up nothing. By accepting the deed, Nanfan (and Great Britain) would find it quite impossible to argue against the Iroquois talking peace with Canada unless willing to take the lead in the struggle for the interior that would have been thrust upon them. The gift of suzerainty was only the bait on a hook. The Iroquois diplomats demanded that Livingston carry the trust deed directly to the King. "We fear, if he does not go," they said, "there is much business, this will only be read, laid aside, and forgot, but if he goes, we are sure of an answer."[61] The Iroquois thus made two covenants, one at Montreal and one at Albany, and waited on events. The English demonstrated their own subtlety by their equivocal response. Livingston did not go to England; the Iroquois deed was received by the Lords of Trade, duly read, and, as the Iroquois had feared, filed. There was no show of rejection, but the document was not forgotten. Yet it did not precipitate any action. Only the treaty with Callière had substance.

In reporting the ratification of peace to the Minister, Callière and Champigny wrote as though Iroquois neutrality were anything but assured. They referred to the necessity of retaining their own allies and of making allies of the Iroquois, or at least "of rendering them neutral in case of war."[62] Neutrality was not a clause of the Treaty of Montreal, but of a separate agreement of dubious value. But as long as the relations of power expressed in the treaty remained the same, the treaty tended to maintain neutrality on Callière's terms. An anonymous memorandum in the Marine archives makes the point:

> This Peace places all the Indians in the French interest and prevents the Iroquois uniting with the English in case of a rupture; otherwise, should they do so, all the other Indians would unite together to make war on the Iroquois, who would soon be overpowered by the multitude. The Five Nations can muster only 1,200 warriors at most. It would be easy to organize a corps of 6,000 men from among the other Indians, which conjointed with a detachment of 500 of our troops would annihilate, and forever, the Iroquois.[63]

New York's inability to defend itself or assist its allies lay behind the Iroquois negotiation of neutrality. The Iroquois were not displeased with neutrality as such, only with Callière's terms. Iroquois neutrality in turn implied New York neutrality. It was this simple reality and not the commercial aims of the politically negligible Albany fur traders that made possible the gentleman's agreement that Canada and New York should remain at peace in the event of war.[64] At the end of 1701, Canada's western frontier was thus to some extent stabilized.

The Five Nations had failed to wring greater support from their English allies by the questionable gift of their hunting grounds. In spite of this, they continued to renew the Covenant Chain, which bound them to assist New York if it were attacked, and in their councils they continued to debate the idea of forging new links with the Far Nations independently of the French by opening the path to Albany.[65] "Where we find goods cheapest," some Algonkian Indians told the new governor, Lord Cornbury, at Albany, "thither we will bend our course."[66] The Iroquois were not moving fast enough for them. A request that the creeks be cleared of obstructions may have been a metaphorical reference to Iroquois hostility. The Iroquois dilemma over sharing the Albany trade was undoubtedly made worse by the depressed state of the fur market and the high price of manufactured goods in the immediate post-war economy, conditions common to both New York and Canada.[67] In 1702 many Iroquois were still very distrustful of allowing the western nations to trade at Albany, reasonably fearing that an increased supply of beaver would cause the price to fall, rendering goods more costly. Cornbury, of course, argued the opposite – more beaver, more goods.[68] In his talks with the western Indians that year, he promised that obstructions would be cleared from the creeks and that they would have goods as cheaply as the Iroquois.[69] By 1704 the Iroquois were giving some western Indians access to Albany.[70] The argument of economic exclusivity that had its support among certain sachems and factions in all the Five Nations and was persistently opposed by New York authorities was overridden by the political argument that Iroquois safety and independence necessitated changing the ground rules of neutrality, taking the hatchets of the Far Nations one by one from Onontio's keeping.

III

To the east lay another frontier zone, between the Saco and St John rivers in what is now Maine and New Brunswick, the land of the Abenakis. The area was most often reached from Canada by mounting the Chaudière River and, after a considerable portage, descending the Kennebec. The name "Abenakis" has in common with "Iroquois" that it was a collective name for a group of kindred peoples, but unlike "Iroquois" it did not designate a confederacy. While the nomenclature of the different tribes or groups is confused, they are generally known in historical literature by the names of the rivers and bays they inhabited, the Saco, Androscoggin, Kennebec, Penobscot, and Passamaquoddy. The tribes to the south in Massachusetts are now thought also to have been Abenaki; in any case, in the tribal dispersals of King Philip's War (1675-76) they migrated to Canadian Abenaki villages or to Abenaki lands east of the Saco where they became absorbed. The inhabitants of the northeastern bank of the St John, named St John's Indians after the river or called Maliseets, were never described as Abenakis although they may have been kin. Their eastern neighbours, extending into the Acadian peninsula, were the Micmacs, who are thought to have had a different origin. At the turn of the century, the Micmacs and Maliseets were still distant from the Anglo-French frontier.[71]

While the Abenakis traditionally traded with New England rather than New France, the pressure of English settlement upon their lands and the incomprehension and fear with which the English viewed them had brought the Abenakis to war with Massachusetts in 1675 and 1688. As France also contested Massachusetts's influence in Maine, the

Abenakis and New France found themselves allies in the Nine Years' War. The Abenakis, rightly distrustful of French motives, maintained their independence as much as possible, made their own peace in 1693, and when it failed continued the war until 1699, two years after Ryswick.

Aside from their military co-operation in the war, the Abenakis and the French had many ties of friendship and religion. Abenakis converted to the Christian faith at Sillery in 1646 were among the first apostles on the Kennebec. By 1683 there was a special Abenaki mission, Saint-François-de-Sales, on the Chaudière, and by the end of the century there were many Jesuit missionaries among the Abenakis. The fathers were useful interpreters of the Europeans' ways, and the religion they brought was a strong support in a world in which traditional values were collapsing under the pressure of unprecedented change. Among the Penobscots, French prestige was merged in the personal ascendancy of Jean-Vincent Abbadie, Baron de Saint-Castin, who as a young French officer of twenty-two had come to live with them, having escaped from pirates. He had married the daughter of a chief, Madokawando, and become something of a Grey Eminence to his father-in-law. Although he returned to France in 1701, he left three sons, two of whom successively bore the title of Baron de Saint-Castin, a strong support to the French presence in continental Acadia.[72]

Canada could not equal nearby Massachusetts as a source of trade goods, especially given the collapse of the Canadian fur trade at the turn of the century. The Abenakis hoped that peace would bring them stable relations with New England and a good trade. At Casco Bay, however, on June 3/14, 1701, they refused the English offer of protection from the French, a new home in New York, and education New England-style for their children. They also refused to give up their Catholic religion or to sever their relations with Canada. Their wishes were plainly expressed at a conference in Boston the following December, that "if there should happen to be war between England and France, we would have all calm and quiet in this Land . . . [and] not have it affect us."[73]

Abenaki neutrality was quite acceptable to Massachusetts governor Joseph Dudley, who even encouraged it. The Jesuits were in favour not only of neutrality but also of the renewal of trade links with New England, which would give the Abenakis a greater measure of economic stability. French officialdom would not go that far. Callière limited himself to telling the Abenakis not to strike the first blow against the English. Louis and Jérôme de Pontchartrain instructed two successive governors of Acadia – for the jurisdiction over the Abenakis was divided between that colony and Canada, much to Callière's disgruntlement – to prevent any military incidents between the French, English, and French Indian allies. Those Indians in the border region were to continue to receive royal presents of guns, powder, and shot even in peacetime, while this largess was no longer to be extended to the peninsular Micmacs.[74] Jérôme de Pontchartrain was willing to contemplate the neutralization of North America, but only if this constituted a strategic advantage to France. His instructions to the Governor of Acadia in 1701 include comprehensive directions for the negotiation of a treaty of neutrality with Massachusetts but conclude with the advice that should the Governor find it possible to preserve Acadia from harm and still injure New England trade, then he was to drop the notion of a treaty. As for the Abenakis, it was important that the Governor "gain the friendship of these Indians in order to employ it usefully in case of war."[75]

East of the St John, following the arc of the shores of Fundy, lay the Acadian settlements from Beaubassin to Minas and the smaller but original concentration at Port Royal: totally dependent upon New England traders, ever prey to New England pirates, almost ignored by government. John Bartlett Brebner has written: "There were, in effect, two Acadies, each important in its own way. The one was the Acadie of the international conflict, the other the land settled and developed by the Acadians."[76] It was the former that focused the attention of Acadia's succession of governors and commanders. Thus continental Acadia was generally more important to them than the peninsula; the Abenakis were their comrades in arms, the Acadians a problem population, at once vulnerable and stubbornly independent – "republican" was a favourite epithet.

The character and structure of the Acadian files of the Ministry of Marine are themselves a telling comment on the history of the colony. Many of these volumes do not constitute a *fonds d'archives*, the steady and orderly accumulation of papers testifying to a steady and orderly colonial development; they are instead collections of copies of originals patched together years later to serve as proofs in boundary disputes with Great Britain. The volumes are full of plans and proposals for forts never built, new political divisions never created, a great company of mercantilist inspiration never chartered.

The most significant commercial undertaking in the region was that of the Compagnie de la pêche sédentaire de l'Acadie (the Acadian Company). This was an example of the time-honoured combination of an entrepreneur, in this case a La Rochelle merchant named Bergier backed by Parisian financiers, and a well-connected nobleman, exploiting a monopoly under letters patent from the Crown. The original rather unassuming company, founded in 1682 on the basis of a shore concession for a fishery, had been transformed into a more grandiose instrument of state by Colbert, who had improved its financial position by bringing into it the Marquis de Chevry and granting it an enlarged monopoly of fishing and trade in its letters patent of December 1683. Eventually, the company's concession included the Strait of Canso and an extent of Atlantic shore, Cape Breton, Ile Saint-Jean, and the Magdalens. But war blighted its operations, and in 1703 its concessions were reunited with the Crown.[77]

In 1690, a Canadian officer, Joseph Robinau de Villebon, returned to Acadia to find Port Royal sacked and its governor carried off a prisoner to Boston. The following year, Villebon was named commandant in Acadia. He was domineering and dissolute but had the requisite toughness and was esteemed by the Abenakis. He gathered up the public papers at Port Royal and retreated to Jemseg and then Nashwaak on the St John, where he established his capital in safety among the Maliseets. Short shrift for peninsular Acadia! Upon Villebon's death in July 1700, another commandant with a good reputation among the Indians, Sébastien de Villieu, took his place. It was Villieu's successor, Jacques-François Monbeton de Brouillan, named commandant in March 1701 and governor in February 1702, who returned the capital to Port Royal. The French salient moved eastward again.

When Brouillan took command of the colony in 1701, he was as impressed with its possibilities as he was disheartened by its actual backwardness.[78] He was optimistic concerning the quality of the land, masts, and timber, the prospects for mining, and the fishery. The latter he thought better than that at Placentia, where he had served as governor, or St Pierre. He regarded the fur trade as not only nearing its end but, by the mores it encouraged, also inimical to economic development. He believed that French authority in the peninsula should be concentrated in fortifications at La Hève on the southeast coast, an excellent centre for the fishery that would be safe from pirates once the natural defences were crowned with a fort, and a strategic location from which corsairs could swoop down and break the trade link between New England and Old. By the turn of the century, prevailing opinion seems to have been that Acadia should be fortified at La Hève and on either the Penobscot or the St John – the fishery and the Indian frontier – and perhaps divided into two governments accordingly. The one spot that was never mentioned in this regard was the locus of Acadian settlement at the bottom of the Bay of Fundy.

While the arguments in favour of development by monopoly were acknowledged by Brouillan, he preferred development by the King "for his own glory," knowing that the population feared and hated monopolies. He wrote that they would refuse to help rebuild the fort at Port Royal if they thought that the colony was to be granted to a company. The Acadians vexed Brouillan. If they were not so lazy, he argued, they would produce more. They would cultivate the highlands now left to trees rather than lazing about their diked marshlands. He asked for the immigration of Placentian fishermen, people who knew how to work and who would be a good example. He was not the first administrator to regard marshland farming as indolent in spite of the considerable labour required to build and maintain the dikes. And of course, as in the case of Pontchartrain's complaints about Canadians, we recognize in his voice the Old Regime administrator, exaggerating the nonchalance of a pre-industrial workforce.

Brouillan's other complaint about the Acadians was their lack of martial prowess, their being "very unwarlike" in spite of lives lived in a theatre of war. The central concern of a governor was war. Brouillan was uneasy about contacts between the New Englanders and the Abenakis. They had met, he reported, in an allusion to Casco Bay, and buried the hatchet, "a very significant thing among them." The English were opening trading posts where they offered goods at giveaway prices. Not all the priests seemed reliable – Father Vincent Bigot among the Kennebecs made no effort to prevent their reaching an understanding with the English. The Baron de Saint-Castin was trading with Boston. But Brouillan had himself met with the Abenakis and given them, all at once, the presents for 1699, 1700, and 1701 as well as muskets, sabres, and flags. Of the latter he reported, "They accepted them, which is an infallible indication that they are completely for us." Brouillan thus believed that the Abenaki alliance was secure, and although he stood in need of arms, ammunition, and better fortifications, he had completed his fort at Port Royal. Acting in accordance with Pontchartrain's instructions, he had earlier proposed neutrality to New England. Now he was ready to cast that mask aside. His instructions encouraged this stance provided that Brouillan thought his position secure. But at Quebec Callière still hoped North America might be neutralized. He was alarmed when Brouillan tried to stir up the Abenakis and even asked the Minister that Abenaki affairs be dealt with from Quebec only.[79]

The location of the border between Acadia and New England was another matter of controversy under discussion by the commissioners meeting in London in 1699. Tallard demanded that the border be set at the Kennebec, cutting the English off from the mouth of the St George River, where Iberville had destroyed their fort of Pemaquid. The English held that the border should be farther northeast at the Penobscot (to the French, Pentagouet) River, which would place the French fort of the same name in a demilitarized zone. Eventually both sides agreed on the St George, but any conclusion of the matter was made impossible by their failure to agree on fishing rights. The French insisted that English fishermen must remain four leagues from the Acadian shore, that being the distance perceptible with the naked eye, and not enter the bays, harbours, and river mouths of that coast.[80] The issue of the Acadian border, ultimately left unresolved, was one of many before the commission; others were Newfoundland, of which France coveted complete sovereignty, the renewal of the Treaty of Neutrality of 1686, perhaps the negotiation of a trade treaty, and, as we have seen, the Iroquois. All of these were held to rank behind the main reason for which the commission had been established by Article 8 of the Treaty of Ryswick, that being the adjustment of the claims of both powers on Hudson Bay. Article 7 stipulated a return to the status quo ante bellum in all colonial areas. This required that posts on James Bay built by the Hudson's Bay Company, captured in peacetime (between 1682 and 1686) by the Franco-Canadian Northern Company, and recaptured during the war by the English company, be returned to French possession. Since the French occupation had not been legitimate, the Hudson's Bay Company refused to comply. Another post originally built by the Hudson's Bay Company, Fort York (or Bourbon), on the Hayes (or Ste Thérèse) River, had been captured by Iberville, recaptured by the English, then captured again by Iberville – alas for the French – during the treaty negotiations. While the treaty required the French to give up the post, the French questioned the legitimacy of the English claim since the terms of their own surrender to the English had never been honoured. The treaty-makers' solution to these northern problems – turning the clock back – proved to be no solution at all.

Pontchartrain wanted both Hudson Bay and James Bay to give Canada a monopoly of the fur trade. If division were necessary, he would prefer to keep Hudson Bay proper, abandoning James Bay to the English company. His view, which French commissioners had espoused as early as 1686, was that whoever held the Nelson-Hayes river system would not only have access to the best northern furs but could cut off trade to James Bay on the inland rivers. He also believed the English would find this the path of least resistance as they then held Fort Albany on James Bay and the French held Fort Bourbon.[81]

The commission recessed from June 1699 until after the new year. By then the English were insisting on an exchange of Albany for York. Pontchartrain had in the meantime changed his mind and decided this was more advantageous, Albany (Ste Anne) being much closer to New France.[82] The English commissioners, "warned from Quebec" in the same sense, then tried to make the French pay for the post that until that time they had been trying to force them to accept. "Thus Monsieur," an exasperated Tallard concluded a letter to Pontchartrain, "whether for these reasons or because no one in this country worries about finishing anything nor wants to decide anything, I do not flatter myself that a treaty will be agreed upon. . . ."[83]

*   *   *

None of the North American issues that divided France and England at Ryswick were resolved at the opening of the War of the Spanish Succession. The only area that had been neutralized was the Iroquois frontier, and that neutrality was most uncertain. The ratification of the Treaty of Montreal and the parallel renewal of the Covenant Chain at Albany constituted only one of the contradictions in which Canada was caught up. Canada had confirmed its ascendancy over its Indian allies, but the Canadian fur trade remained in an abject condition. The Abenakis had confirmed their friendship toward Canada and Acadia but remained economically dependent upon New England. France had both given up and not given up the compact colony policy. It had framed an aggressive imperial policy for North America and at the same time had abandoned control of the Atlantic. The Canadian future was still wide open.

CHAPTER 3

New France and the War of the Spanish Succession, 1702-1713

The maritime powers of Holland and England were not so much fearful that a Bourbon should sit on a Hapsburg throne as that the prophecy of the French journal the *Mercure galant* should be made good: "What joy! The Pyrenees no longer exist. They are laid low, and we are now but one."[1] The claim was newspaper hyperbole, but the policies pursued by Louis XIV could not but appear threatening to his enemies. While Philip of Anjou was on his way from Paris to Madrid in February 1701, letters patent recognizing his rights to the French throne were registered by the Parlement. French troops occupied the barrier fortresses in the Spanish Netherlands on Philip's behalf, sending home the surprised Dutch garrisons. In August a Franco-Spanish treaty conferred upon a French company the monopoly of supplying slaves to the Spanish colonies (the Asiento). With considerable gusto, Louis XIV took upon himself the task of reforming and governing Spain by remote control: ". . . we are now but one . . ." On September 7, 1701, a Triple Alliance of the Emperor Leopold, England, and the United Provinces (Holland) was concluded at The Hague. England still hung back from a war that William III and the continental allies saw as inevitable. But on the sixteenth, Louis gave an unequivocal response to the Hague treaty. On that day James II died at Saint-Germain-en-Laye, and Louis recognized James's son, the Old Pretender, as James III, *de jure* King of England, a challenge to the Protestant succession. William took advantage of the resulting wave of loyalist emotion, dissolved parliament, and saw the election of the pro-war Whig party to a majority. After his accidental death in March 1702, his successor, Queen Anne, and her ministers had no recourse but to continue his policy. When the Triple Alliance declared war on France and Spain on May 15, hostilities had already begun. On June 13 Spain in turn declared, followed by France on July 3. Ahead lay eleven years of war, not the less terrible in their consequences for their leisurely pace. From this war the colonial world could not be isolated. North America was too strategically important not to become a theatre of war, because access to Spanish American markets was one of the war's major causes. North America was also, quite simply, an area where France and England could hurt each other. New France would escape the worst; there would be no Canadian Malplaquet. But the war would be felt, even in the wilderness.

I

While Canada had on the eve of war neutralized the interior by treaty, the means at hand to enforce this policy were pitiful. The Marine companies were seriously under strength, and the West was no longer garrisoned. But the situation was about to be revolutionized by the plans of an adventurer, Antoine Laumet de Lamothe Cadillac.[2] Wherever this picaresque character travelled, strife and turmoil were not far behind. It was true in Acadia, where he had first appeared in the light of history, and at Michilimackinac, where as commandant from 1694 to 1697 he had made a small fortune by illegal brandy trading and tyrannical exactions from traders. He had also maintained a constant fusillade against the Jesuits who stood in his way, parallel to an attack on the clergy of Port Royal that had marked his stay in Acadia. In 1698 Cadillac returned to France. There, on the high seas, or perhaps still at Quebec, his fertile mind conceived the grandiose scheme of making the whole trade of the interior his alone. At Versailles he presented Jérôme de Pontchartrain with his plan for the founding of Detroit. The idea of founding a post on the river between Lake Huron and Lake Erie was nothing new; the place was of obvious strategic significance. New York's Indian Secretary, Robert Livingston, had urged building a fort there; Denonville, the Governor of Canada, had actually done so in 1687.[3] Cadillac's scheme went beyond that. Detroit was to be not just a post but a bona fide colony with a strong garrison and a seat of government, a nucleus around which all the French Indian allies would settle. Once the Indians were gathered there, no reason would remain for coureurs de bois to penetrate farther into the wilderness. A well-regulated trade, based on the revival of the *congés*, would be possible. But the best part would be that because of the diversion of energy to the necessary tasks of settlement, no furs would be taken from Detroit to Canada in the first three years. Most of Cadillac's memorandum concerned an exceedingly fanciful scheme to Europeanize the Indians, adducing that a great many of them already spoke French better than Canadians and that the Métis were pillars of the colony. Cadillac's intention was to obtain permission to found Detroit himself and to use his position to monopolize the Canadian fur trade.

To judge from his subsequent actions, the rest was prettification.

Whatever he may have thought of the trimmings, Pontchartrain at once saw the scheme as reconciling the economic and social aims of a limited fur trade and a circumscribed colony with the necessities of an imperialism depending on a French trade and presence among the Indians. The alacrity with which Pontchartrain seized upon the Detroit scheme is the plainest evidence that in edging toward the new policy of 1701 he was not giving up the policy of 1696. But instead of giving carte blanche to Cadillac, the Minister referred the matter to Callière and Champigny. Unlike the Intendant, Callière saw some merit in the scheme, although he held it less desirable than the re-establishing of the *congés* and of a network of garrisoned posts. Both officials' objections, formulated after discussions with Canadian notables, included fear that the plan would offend the Iroquois, with whom peace had not yet been made, and that the Allies would be brought too close to the Iroquois – there a *cordon sanitaire* was highly desirable. Champigny also feared outbreaks of fighting if the allied tribes were made to live close together; he doubted that the settlement could subsist if the fur trade were stopped altogether for a few years. He poured cold water on Cadillac's vision of Frenchified Indians and schools and hospitals in the wilderness and he pointed out what seemed to him the heart of the matter, that the commandant of such a post would be able to carry on a very lucrative fur trade while everyone else was busy building houses and barns.

Another pilgrimage to Versailles enabled Cadillac to counteract Champigny's lack of imagination. The King's memorandum of May 5, 1700, instructed Callière and Champigny to found the post if at all possible and to make Cadillac its commandant. The details were left to them, but the royal intent was clear: "The possession of the lakes can be made secure, the English prevented from establishing themselves there, and the Indians kept friendly towards us by selling them goods at low prices; and at the same time men are prevented from ranging the woods. His Majesty still looks upon this last as the cause of the misfortunes of the colony."[4] On June 4, 1701, Cadillac left Montreal with one hundred soldiers and settlers, two priests, and the paraphernalia of trade and settlement. On July 24 Detroit was founded. Callière sent Cadillac in haste via the Ottawa River so that when the Iroquois arrived to ratify the treaty of September 3, 1700, Detroit would be a *fait accompli*.

The following year the new post as well as Fort Frontenac was turned over to a new, all-Canadian fur company known as the Colony Company, a project that had become the focus of Canadian economic aspirations. Cadillac was transferred to the employ of the company at

an increased salary. He now had a new master, and his duties precluded his making a fortune in private trade, the only reason for his
having come to Detroit. He therefore intended to make the post as
unattractive to the company as possible. Cadillac's own malfeasance
combined with Detroit's limited trade made the post from the start a
financial liability. Yet Cadillac sent the Minister a mendacious balance
sheet showing profits of 200 to 700 per cent. In 1704 the company
sent a clerk to investigate Cadillac's management. After imprisoning
the clerk, Cadillac hurried to Quebec, probably intent on another
pilgrimage to the feet of Pontchartrain. But once at Quebec he was
himself promptly jailed. He successfully challenged the right of his
judges to try him on grounds of conflict of interest. It would have been
rather difficult to find a judge in Canada, from the governor down,
who would not have suffered this disability in a fur trade case. What
saved Cadillac, however, was that *deus ex machina* of colonial history,
the Minister. Cadillac was, the court dispatches of 1705 announced,
the new proprietor of Detroit, for which favour compensation to the
company was in detail specified. It was a solution that the company, *in
extremis*, had itself suggested. The primary reason behind the decision
was not that Pontchartrain favoured his protégé but that the company
did not wish to maintain Detroit except as a modest commercial outpost. Cadillac was on the side of the imperial angels.

Detroit had been intended by its founder to be the locus of Indian
settlement in the West. While many Indians could not be persuaded to
abandon their traditional homes, enough of them did settle at Detroit
to make it a trouble spot. The Hurons and part of the Ottawa tribe built
their own forts near Cadillac's Fort Pontchartrain. This brought them
into close proximity to a number of other tribes, notably the Miamis
on the St Joseph River southwest of Detroit, some of whom had also
established a village at Detroit. Callière, obedient to his instructions,
had himself encouraged them. His successor, Philippe de Rigaud de
Vaudreuil, governor from October 20, 1703, to October 10, 1725, had
little use for Cadillac and even less for his Indian policy. Nevertheless,
he too obeyed his instructions, urging Indians to settle at Detroit and
to listen to Cadillac. At the same time he explained his misgivings in his
letters to Pontchartrain.[5]

Just at the time that Cadillac received his proprietorship, events at
Detroit were fulfilling the dire prophecies of knowledgeable observers. In 1706 a party of Ottawas fell upon a Miami village near the French
fort, killing a half-dozen inhabitants. Most of the Miamis got into the
fort and from there, following the orders of the commandant, Ensign
Etienne de Bourgmond, they exchanged fire with the pursuing Ottawas, some thirty of whom were killed. A Récollet and a French soldier

were also cut down in the cross-fire. The Miamis then attacked the Ottawa fort. When Pontchartrain heard of the incident, so dangerous to the policy founded on the treaty of 1701, he had no recourse but to order an investigation. No doubt it is impossible to be entirely confident in assigning blame for obscure, frontier killings. The report, tendered in November 1708 by the investigator, François Clairambault d'Aigremont, an incorruptible career bureaucrat serving in Canada, did point to poor French leadership at Detroit.[6] If the Ottawas' evidence as collected by d'Aigremont is to be believed, they had by an intricate chain of reasoning decided that the French were plotting against them.

Upon his return to Detroit, Cadillac attempted to deal with the situation. His first gambit was to ask the Senecas to join him in punishing the Ottawas. Fortunately, they refused. Next, he decided to imprison the fugitive Ottawa war chief, Le Pesant, who was held responsible for the mischief at Detroit. The Miamis and Hurons were angered by the chief's presence, even as a prisoner, and were enraged when Cadillac connived at his escape in an effort to calm the situation. In a rampage of protest, they killed three French settlers and one of Cadillac's cows. He thereupon led a military expedition against the Miamis of St Joseph River, obtaining hostages and furs.[7] While all of Cadillac's actions could be justified by a literal reading of the Treaty of Montreal, French weakness in the West dictated the use of diplomacy and tact rather than violence and bombast. In the midst of war, French policy in the West was left in shambles. It was all duly reported by d'Aigremont.

According to d'Aigremont's report, there was nothing much to Detroit itself: a few hundred arpents of poor land growing Indian corn, most of it belonging to Cadillac or the Hurons; a few settlers, namely twenty-nine of the soldiers who had married and had among them forty-nine arpents; small houses of stakes set in the ground with thatched roofs; a rotting palisade with two bastions "so small and of such extraordinary shape as to be unrecognizable." Cadillac was revealed as a tyrant, exacting fees on every pretext, giving the soldiers short rations, controlling to his profit the brandy trade that had become the post's *raison d'être*. Battles among the Allies, new treaties negotiated by the Hurons and Miamis with the Iroquois, and a brisk trade in beaver to Albany were the results of founding Detroit. "The Iroquois," d'Aigremont observed, "will win all these nations to the English side by the cheapness of their goods and will engage them to bring them all their beaver, and by means of these trade goods that they obtain from the English, the Iroquois do a part of this trade on their own behalf." He also argued that the migration of the remaining Michilimackinac Indians to Detroit would leave the trade north of Lake Superior to the Hudson's

Bay Company. Conclusion: "Detroit is a post very burdensome to the colony of Canada and will achieve its complete ruin if it continues to be sustained." He believed that if it were not for the illegal trade carried out at Michilimackinac, there would be no beaver in Canada, parenthetically noting that this trade was in part supported by the illegal trading activities of Vaudreuil and other officials. He ended his report with a strong plea for the re-establishment of Michilimackinac as a garrisoned post and for the distribution of *congés*.

Pontchartrain was fortunate in having the former Canadian intendant, Jean Bochart de Champigny, close at hand at Le Havre to annotate Canadian dispatches. Champigny was a scion of the Paris magistracy and manifested its combination of piety, austerity, and prickly dignity. His intellect was sharp and reflective. His acerbic comments on Cadillac's letters make hash of them, but Champigny drew the line at telling his chief he was being made a fool. The Minister's marginalia on Cadillac's glowing accounts of Detroit, "so much like a novel," "a romantic description,"[8] indicate that he at least detected a penchant for hyperbole in Cadillac. He was clever enough to label "self-love"[9] Cadillac's consistent identification of the King's interest with his own. He had seen that Cadillac's original high-flown plan for Detroit was to a large extent unrealistic. But these appear to have been lapses of clarity in an otherwise credulous reading of Cadillac's dispatches. With apparent equanimity, Pontchartrain read and passed on to others Cadillac's memoranda couched in the form of dialogues between the two of them in which the Minister as the Platonic straight-man Glaucon feeds the appropriate lines to Socrates-Cadillac. Pontchartrain seems to have had no will to break the spell. That he placed his trust in Cadillac for so many years is a sad commentary on his ability to judge men; his reaction to the d'Aigremont report is a study in absurdity. D'Aigremont was censured, and Cadillac was defended with the lame assertion that "in a new country, new maxims are sometimes necessary."[10] Worst of all, the King's next letter to d'Aigremont commented on Detroit's considerable progress under Cadillac, fairly clear evidence that Pontchartrain had spared His Majesty the details. He was covering his tracks and made the job complete by promoting Cadillac to governor of Louisiana on May 5, 1710. The commandant of Detroit was got rid of without bureaucratic scandal, and a new French province in the midst of war was delivered to his proven incompetence. From this point on, the historian asks himself if he is dreaming . . .

Cadillac or Harlequin or Scapin – whatever alias we should give Laumet – goes not to Louisiana but to Quebec and Paris, intent on squeezing the last sou out of Detroit before it is taken from him. At Paris he finds the lucrative trade of Louisiana-Eldorado is to be given to a rich bourgeois (Antoine Crozat). Outraged at being cut out, he protests against the bourgeois's unscrupulous propaganda. Completely out of character, he tells the truth, that Louisiana is no Eldorado. This untimely honesty results in his being thrown into the Bastille. But his dotty master (Pontchartrain), with woollen cap pulled tightly over his eyes, relents, gives the fast-talking prodigal his blessing, and sends him off to Eldorado as governor after all. Then a new just ruler appears on the scene (Louis XV). The dotty master in the woollen cap, degraded to the rank of candle snuffer to the council that succeeds him, is bundled off the scene and Scapin is recalled in disgrace. His clever tricks in the end win him the consolation prize of being mayor of a sleepy little town. The Cadillac story simply slips beyond the limits of normal experience and degenerates into pure farce.

The founder of Detroit manipulated for his material gain every situation in which he found himself. He was a habitual liar: indeed, in his campaign against the Jesuits, whom he blamed for the failure of Detroit and pictured as the enemies of the royal power, he practised what would now be called the technique of the big lie. He was interested in power, but in his psychology it ran a poor second to lust for wealth. Of the many unflattering descriptions of Cadillac left by his contemporaries, the most telling and also the most moderate in tone is that of Jean-Baptiste Duclos, his close associate in the government of Louisiana: "He must really be a very uneasy and a very restless man."[11]

When, at the start of the war, Philippe de Rigaud de Vaudreuil, then Governor of Montreal, had languished in the shadow of Callière, he had argued hotly for an attack on Albany, showing all the rashness of a subordinate officer bent on distinguishing himself – a behaviour pattern that would be repeated by his successor in that post, Claude de Ramezay.[12] In inheriting Callière's office, Vaudreuil also inherited his greater responsibilities and much of his more cautious attitude. Rashness, in fact, was no part of Vaudreuil's character. He was cautious and conservative, giving little evidence of imagination. But he was not afraid of action and was deliberate and forceful, determining his policies with great clarity and acting on them. He had none of the "glitter and *panache*," as his biographer says of him, that leave an obvious impression for later centuries, but he had a rock-like solidity that eased the minds of his people. The fundamentals of his policy can be reduced to three axioms: that concerted military action by the English colonies was not to be feared; that the Iroquois were Canada's most redoubtable enemy; and that Canada could control the Iroquois only by retaining the power to unleash the western allies against them.

Translation of this third axiom into policy was hindered by the new liaisons of the Hurons and Miamis with the Iroquois, just as the negotiation of the Treaty of Montreal had earlier been endangered by Ottawa and Mississauga diplomacy. The founding of Detroit facilitated this disintegration, while Cadillac's application of his own Indian policy fragmented and obscured Canada's authority in the wilderness. The second axiom explains Vaudreuil's perpetuation of Callière's pragmatic neutrality toward New York, which until 1709 was gratefully reciprocated. Vaudreuil even maintained a secret correspondence with Kiliaen Van Rensselaer, a member of New York's provincial council.[13] The first point, the most personal element in Vaudreuil's policy, was also its weakest point. It explains his aggressive stance in the Acadian theatre, which first raised opposition to New France and where finally most was lost.[14]

In the execution of his western policy, Vaudreuil had the backing of Pontchartrain. The closing of the western posts and the founding of Detroit and Louisiana were policies forced on Canadian governors by ministerial fiat. The conduct of Iroquois policy during the war, in startling contrast to the disposal of the question at the peace, was primarily the fruit of Canadian experience. The Minister's contribution tended to reflect the views expressed in Canadian dispatches. Pontchartrain's letters of 1701 and 1702, for example, contain optimistic magnifications of Callière's slight hope that the Iroquois would become Canadian allies; those of 1703 bear the more realistic expectation that they could at least be kept neutral.[15] The Indian situation in the West was particularly delicate. If there were instances of Iroquois-Allied fraternization, there were the equally dangerous occurrences of armed attack on the Senecas by the Miamis and Ottawas (1704) and the Miami-Ottawa brawl at Detroit (1706) already considered. In each case Vaudreuil had to secure a remedy by diplomatic means. Were he to have resorted to arms against an ally in these cases, the Iroquois might have joined him, as they had every right to do under the treaty of 1700. Had they in the process destroyed a major allied tribe, the balance of power would have been so altered that it would have been possible for them to have turned on Canada itself. The treaty articles governing such police actions had been framed to promote the policy of *pax gallica*. By elevating the governor above tribal strife, it encouraged the notion that he dealt with all tribes with equal disinterestedness. In fact, Callière and Vaudreuil only envisaged actions against the Iroquois and not with their assistance.[16] Vaudreuil had a staff of four agents among the tribes to carry out his western diplomacy. Jesuit missionaries are known to have been useful in stopping Indian raiding parties.[17] Still, the means at Vaudreuil's disposal were slight, even negligible, compared with the garrisoned posts and the expanding fur trade of the past. And policy was almost negated by Cadillac, who, Vaudreuil claimed, kept him in the dark about affairs at Detroit.[18]

Once war had been declared, Callière had authorized the Abenakis to attack the English: "I will no longer stay your hatchet." But even in 1703 the Abenakis still maintained their desire "to be as Neuters."[19] Vaudreuil, in common with Governor Brouillan of Acadia, feared that the Abenakis would be lost to the English. Accordingly, he raised a party of Canadians and mission Iroquois who recruited as many Abenakis as possible and fell upon the towns of Casco and Wells in August, 1703. Before the first snow, many other hamlets of the New England frontier had been the subject of guerrilla raids. Only a minority of Abenakis had joined the forays, but on August 18, 1703, Massachusetts declared war on them; the raids had served Canada's purpose. On March 16, 1704, a body of 200 Abenakis and mission Iroquois and 50 Canadians fell on the Massachusetts town of Deerfield, killing 47 and carrying off 111 prisoners. It was characteristic of the guerrilla or commando warfare that had become as Canadian as it was Indian: a small force and a small objective, stealthy approach, complete surprise, immediate retreat, no follow-through, no real strategic gain, and a legacy of horror and bitterness. The only large undertaking of the campaign, Berthelot de Beaucours's expedition against New England, miscarried. The body of 800 men, mostly Indians, was large by Canadian standards and could not be kept in discipline.[20] Pontchartrain approved of this aggressive approach in the East.[21] Neither he nor Vaudreuil seems to have feared the English response.

Warships, transports, and 550 militia sailing up the Bay of Fundy were New England's answer. Benjamin Church, who had ravaged Beaubassin in 1696, led this new expedition that attacked Penobscot, Passamaquoddy, and the settlements at Minas and Beaubassin, where the dikes were broken. At Port Royal, Brouillan had rebuilt the fort that had fallen into decay during the Acadian government's long years of retreat on the St John. Church's forces decided not to attack it and returned to Boston. Once again, the peaceful settlements of Acadia, not those of Canada, had been made to pay for Canada's attacks on the settlers of the New England frontier.[22]

In 1705 there came an interlude. A Massachusetts request for a prisoner exchange blossomed into a proposal of neutrality. Vaudreuil was not blind to the advantages for Canada. Throughout the summer an English vessel lay in harbour at Quebec, while Samuel Vetch, the "particular friend" of Massachusetts's Governor Dudley, awaited an answer, incidentally spying out the land and probably conducting a contraband trade.[23] Dudley's plan was useless because it made no provision for any English colony except Massachusetts and for any French colony but Canada, leaving open the invasion routes to Canada from Connecticut, New Hampshire, or New York and isolating Acadia. It was commonly suggested at the time that Vaudreuil was being duped by Dudley, who was gaining time for New England. It is equally possible that both governors assumed any neutrality treaty would be the result of tough negotiation and that neither expected the other to do his work for him. Be that as it may, the 1705 dispatches from Versailles revealed that financial anxieties had converted Pontchartrain to neutrality.[24] Given this encouragement, Vaudreuil sent Vetch home with a counter-proposal. The Canadian plan was ultimately rejected at Boston, and Vaudreuil's deadline of March 1, 1706, slipped by unheeded.

As the war progressed, the Abenakis suffered considerable deprivation. Thoroughly alienated from New England, they had no choice but to throw in their lot with the French. Many of them were even moved to Canada. This had originally been a plan of the Jesuit missionaries, who saw it as a means of extricating the Abenakis from the quandary of their economic need for New England and their religious affiliation with New France. Vaudreuil had been converted to the plan in November 1703, thinking the Abenakis would serve as a reliable buffer against the Iroquois, while Versailles eyed this denuding of the Acadian frontier with misgiving.[25] When war was taken up again after the failure of the neutrality negotiations, Abenakis and other domiciled tribes were used in stepped-up raids on New England. The Abenakis had lost the initiative in their own affairs and gained little by fighting Canadian battles. Many disliked their Canadian villages and were soon returning home. Some, feeling neglected by the Canadian authorities, even settled among the Senecas.[26]

Peace and neutrality in the West, guerrilla warfare in the East – Vaudreuil's policy had returned to its classic form. For an increasingly hawkish Pontchartrain, it was not enough. It was true that two attacks on Port Royal in 1707 had failed. A new and highly capable governor, Daniel d'Auger de Subercase, who had earlier replaced Brouillan as governor of Placentia and now succeeded him at Port Royal, strengthened the fortifications and was so successful in his encouragement of privateering, a repetition of his policy at Placentia, that Port Royal was becoming known as the Dunkirk of America. But Subercase could do nothing to assist the other Acadian settlements. He had all he could do to fend off famine at Port Royal and to keep morale from breaking altogether. Pontchartrain was convinced that to preserve Acadia, New England had to be kept on the defensive.[27] He also made a complete about-face in his New York policy. A French business group that had taken over the export monopoly and the debts of the Colony Company in 1706 was not receiving its required amount of beaver. Contra-band shipments of pelts from Detroit to Albany were being sup-plemented by an increasing trade between Montreal and Albany on the Richelieu River–Lake Champlain route, the mission Iroquois acting as carriers. This trade, which had sprung up after Ryswick, was contin-ued because of the low French price for beaver and the high price of French trade goods.[28] To stop it, Pontchartrain ordered Vaudreuil to attack Albany. The Governor, with the support of the father-and-son team that shared the intendancy of Canada, Jacques and Antoine-Denis Raudot (1705-10), resisted this instruction that would either have raised the New York Iroquois against Canada or, perhaps worse, not have been obeyed by the Canadian mission Iroquois necessary for its execu-tion. Vaudreuil made some effort to comply with his chief's wishes regarding the eastern theatre. The result was the destruction of the town of Haverhill in 1708, for the Indians a heartening victory that encouraged further raids on the New England frontier. But Vaudreuil's primary motive was not the same as the Minister's. His aim was to involve his mission Iroquois in the war on New England at a time when New York had almost succeeded in neutralizing them.[29]

That Vaudreuil did not perceive that his renewed attacks on New England would affect New York's policy is understandable. The English colonies were a byword for disunity, as the Board of Trade in London described them, "crumbled into little governments."[30] New Yorkers could remember how New England had taken advantage of destruc-tion along the Mohawk River to attract the fur trade to itself in the last war and how Massachusetts had disregarded royal orders to vote funds for forts on the New York frontier. Indeed, even the lowlands of New York were not much concerned with the frontier. A history of hanging back did not, however, imply a positive desire to see kith and kin suffer. Albanians collected military intelligence for New England. In 1704, Peter Schuyler, Albany diplomat, politician, and Indian Commis-sioner, had attempted to have New England included together with New York in a formal truce. It was his considerable influence that had brought the Caughnawaga Iroquois to the threshold of neutrality.[31]

New England and New York were finally goaded into action against Canada itself. In 1690 Boston had sent a fleet against Quebec under Sir William Phips; the expedition had failed, but the idea remained, ready to be taken up again. The catalyst was Dudley's "particular friend" who had carried his neutrality plan to Quebec in 1705.[32] Being in London on personal business in 1706, Vetch began to lobby for the mounting of an expedition that, like the 1690 plan, should provide for an attack on Quebec by sea and a concurrent attack on Montreal from Albany via Lake Champlain and the valley of the Richelieu. Vetch

brought to a traditional plan original formulation and forceful lobbying. In "Canada Surveyed," a paper prepared for the Board of Trade in
1708, he argued that a populous empire was letting itself be blighted
by an absurdly small number of Frenchmen and that Canada was a
prize great in proportion to the cost of its capture. He pointed out that
the English colonies in North America provisioned the sugar islands,
were a potential source of naval stores, and constituted a significant
market for British goods, all points that tended to be forgotten in
London. Canada was the incubus that weighed upon America, from the
Atlantic fisheries to the plantation colonies; it was no local problem
for the Albany Indian commissioners. On December 10, 1708, the
board approved his plan and recommended it to the Queen, stressing
the connection between the northern colonies and the West Indies.
The Cabinet in turn supported the plan, hoping that victory in Canada
would distract attention from their bogged-down Iberian campaign
and lend *éclat* to its administration. This was fast work for the machinery
of empire, which would later demonstrate its legendary slowness.

Concerted action did not come easily to the English colonies.
Nevertheless, amid the bickering over costs and controls, they did
manage to begin preparations for a fleet in Boston and to send a
motley army beyond Albany. Nothing, of course, could be done until
the main invasion force, both army and navy, arrived from England.
All the Iroquois but the exposed Senecas were pressured into participation. In Canada, Vaudreuil was expecting the worst, aware of preparations at Albany and warned of the fleet preparing at Boston. Yet the
summer of 1709 passed without its arrival. Finally, on October 22
dispatches reached Boston announcing the government's decision of
the previous May to call off the expedition. The reason – none was
given to the colonial governments – appears to have been that peace
conferences had begun in Holland and had they been successful would
have called for the restitution of colonial territories. The expedition
under such circumstances would have been money down the drain.
The land army, which had been collapsing under the weight of its task,
disintegrated completely in jealousy, English-Indian conflict, looting,
and sickness.[33]

The English fiasco was, of course, wonderful propaganda for Canada. There was a return to Franco-Iroquois friendship and neutrality,
although this was accompanied by sober Iroquois warnings that they
would not stand by and see New York attacked and by Canadian
warnings to the Iroquois that if necessary the Ottawas would be loosed
against them.[34]

Vetch's efforts to salvage as much as possible from the miscarried
enterprise, in particular by using men and ships at hand to attack Port

Royal, came to nothing. The colonies soon reverted to their customary bickering and penny-pinching.[35] But Vetch was not long idle, nor
was his ally Francis Nicholson, a former governor of Virginia who had
commanded the abortive overland campaign. Nicholson went immediately to England, and by March 29, 1710, his lobbying had produced
500 marines, munitions, a bomb ketch, and orders to use these together
with colonial levies to attack Port Royal.[36] In the meantime, Peter
Schuyler had brought four Indians to London advertised as the "Kings
of Canada." Whether these men were really Iroquois sachems is uncertain, but they were politically sound.[37] In their speeches to Queen
Anne they said all the right things: they had for years been a bulwark
against Canada; without a British expedition to assist them, they would
have to leave their lands or become neutrals; they were in danger of
being corrupted by Catholicism. Belts of wampum were presented; it
was a tremendous show.[38] The Four Kings were a great sensation in
London, and their embassy helped to shape thinking by drawing attention to a neglected theatre of war.

At Versailles, Pontchartrain was quickly apprised of the Nicholson
expedition against Port Royal. He vainly urged Vaudreuil to rush aid to
Acadia, something the Governor could not do without leaving Canada
exposed, while the Minister himself could send no aid because of the
virtual bankruptcy of the government.[39] The Anglo-American expedition left Nantasket on September 29, 1710, and appeared before Port
Royal at noon on October 5. They were some two thousand men
against Subercase's two or three hundred, their morale now further
broken by the ravages of an epidemic. After a siege of a week, the
garrison surrendered and marched out of the fort with the honours of
war – "their arms and baggage, drums beating and colours flying."[40]
Renamed Annapolis Royal, this oldest of the French towns in America
was put into the hands of its new governor, Samuel Vetch, who was
now beginning to reap the rewards of his patriotism.

Vaudreuil learned of the surrender of Port Royal only on December 6, when the news was brought to Quebec by the Baron de Saint-
Castin, an Acadian officer and eldest son of Jean-Vincent, and John
Livingston, son of the New York Indian commissioner and Vetch's
brother-in-law, the envoys of Subercase and Nicholson. As Vetch had
done in 1705, Livingston made his mission an occasion for espionage,
as the manners of the time gave him considerable freedom. "I had the
Governor's sleigh," he wrote in his final report, "and paid a visit to
the Intendant, who very handsomely received me, and so did all the
gentlemen in town."[41] The best Vaudreuil could do for Acadia was to
send back Saint-Castin to raise a resistance among the Abenakis and
Acadians. With a nucleus of French soldiers and officers, an attack on

Annapolis Royal could conceivably have been arranged; but when Vaudreuil was at last able to contemplate such a move, he received word that another English fleet was on the seas, this time destined for Quebec.

Throughout the summer of 1710, Queen Anne was transforming her mixed Whig-and-Tory ministry into one purely Tory. In the subsequent elections, the voters proved themselves the Queen's friends by electing the largest Tory majority in English history. The party of continental strategy and the implacable slogan ''No peace without Spain'' was replaced by a party that chafed at the expenses of war, balked at continental entanglement, and preferred a more wholly naval strategy. As the Whigs had once been tempted to prepare an expedition against Quebec to counterbalance the lacklustre Iberian campaign, so now, on the heels of the visit of the Four Kings and the capture of Port Royal, taking Quebec appealed to the Tories as a dramatic way to eclipse the already-waning star of Marlborough and to bring the war to an end.[42] It was all the more attractive as the French navy had evidently abandoned the Atlantic.[43] Nicholson brought Boston the news of a new expedition on June 19. There was not time for the elaborate preparations of two years earlier. By July 31 the van was on the seas. Since 1709 the people of New York had fallen back on the old defence of Iroquois neutrality, in the words of their frustrated Provincial Secretary, ''contented under this precarious security, without even so much as raising any money for presents.''[44] The province's new governor, Robert Hunter, hitherto as ''pinioned for want of orders, soldiers and money'' as ever Bellomont had been, jumped at the opportunity for a new offensive and led the Anglo-Iroquois land expedition himself.[45]

September 2 found the British flotilla lost in fog on the lower St Lawrence. That night, seven transports and a supply ship were driven on the rocks with a loss of nearly a thousand lives, including thirty-five women and some drummer boys. The operation had been mismanaged from the start. Neither the admiral, Sir Hovenden Walker, nor the brigadier, John Hill, had any heart for the assignment. Shortage of provisions, poor piloting, and the admiral's uncertain seamanship contributed to a failure of nerve under the strain of that stormy night.[46]

In Canada the summer of 1711 was one not only of waiting but also of some tense, last-minute diplomacy among the Indians. At a great meeting of Allied tribes and Iroquois observers in the second week of August, Vaudreuil barely succeeded in keeping his allies faithful. He visited missions, retrieving wampum belts sent by Governor Hunter. By the time he felt free to return to Quebec from Montreal, the Walker expedition had already begun its retreat. But it was not until October 17 that the first witness of the wreckage of the lost ships appeared at Quebec. By that time Vaudreuil had already surmised what had happened and returned to Montreal to face the land army. But it too had vanished, leaving boats and canoes for the burning at the head of Lake Champlain.[47] News of the failure of the sea expedition had reached the New York–Iroquois force on September 30. An appropriate epitaph to the whole misadventure was set down by one participant, the Reverend John Buckingham, in his diary: "An awful frown on New England in particular. . . . But God governs."[48] Canadians thought so too. On October 25 Father de La Colombière gave the same sermon in the Quebec cathedral that he had pronounced in 1690 on the occasion of the defeat of the Phips expedition, ascribing Canada's salvation to the intervention of the Virgin Mary. After the war the church of Notre-Dame-de-la-Victoire in Lower Town was renamed Notre-Dame-des-Victoires, thus consigning the Walker and Phips expeditions to a shared infamy.[49]

Canada was fortunate that the war was effectively over. In the West, the alliance system was crumbling in confusion. Intertribal battles flared up constantly. Raids on the Senecas had become an Allied pastime. The most portentous of many flareups was the Battle of Detroit (late May, early June[?], 1712), the beginning of the Fox Wars that were to trouble the West for decades to come. In the 1660s the French had found the Foxes living in what is now the State of Wisconsin. In 1709 Cadillac, manifesting his usual bad judgement, had persuaded many of them to move to Detroit, overlooking their bad relations with many tribes allied to the French, their robbery of coureurs de bois, and their friendliness toward the Iroquois even during the last years of the Iroquois Wars. Vaudreuil was of the opinion that the Foxes seized this opportunity to relocate, the better to have access to English merchandise. Indeed, they soon concluded new alliances with both the English and the Iroquois. At Detroit they indulged in threatening bluster that prompted Vaudreuil to suggest that they should return to their old homeland, where many of the tribe had remained.

The war that broke out in 1712 was in part the predictable result of tribal animosities intensified by proximity.[50] Sometime in the early spring, a band of Ottawas under Chief Saguima ambushed a party of Mascoutens. The latter sought refuge within the Fox stockade at Detroit, the Foxes being their kin. The Ottawas, Hurons, and warriors of a number of other tribes soon arrived in hot pursuit, intent on destroying both the Mascoutens and their hosts.

In the Battle of Detroit the tribal feud was also fused with Anglo-French competition. While most of the Detroit Hurons, Ottawas, and Potawatomies were yet at their winter hunting grounds, the paltry French garrison posed a tempting target for the Foxes, their habitual warlike resolve strengthened by the Iroquois alliance and an abundance of English goods. The commandant, Jacques-Charles Renaud Dubuisson, had already undertaken preparations to defend his fort against a possible Fox attack when the Allied war party arrived on the scene. Dubuisson broke out the ammunition and took command of the Allies. According to Dubuisson's account, the Foxes covered their palisades with English scarlet blankets, hoisted them as flags and shouted to their besiegers that they "had no father but the English."[51] On the nineteenth day of the siege, the starving Foxes and Mascoutens, men, women, and children, escaped under cover of rain and darkness only to be caught in a hastily thrown up fieldwork on Lake St Clair. Some thousand were killed or enslaved.

It has been argued that Dubuisson acted wrongly and weakly by failing to keep an intertribal quarrel in check. But it is not clear that he was in a position to do more than channel an unleashed force. While Fox provocations might not have been sufficient to authorize the Crown's representative to clamber down from the lofty perch of mediation to which he had been consigned by the Treaty of Montreal, he was undoubtedly faced with a crisis transcending the usual frontier feud. Vaudreuil not only approved of his action but recommended him for promotion. This is not to say that the event was less than a tragedy. Latent hostilities had broken the surface of events. The numerous Foxes, Mascoutens, and kindred Sauks and Kickapoos had a *casus belli* in the destruction of their brothers. A policy of French occupation of the West concentrated only at Detroit and the concomitant abandonment of the western posts could not continue. On September 25, 1712, Vaudreuil sent a party to garrison Michilimackinac. He also sent agents to live among the Illinois and the Miamis. He did not wait for ministerial approval, although that would be required for the thorough revamping of policy that had by then become a necessity.

As to the East, by 1710 Vaudreuil admitted he had lost control of the Abenakis. These unfortunate people had been buffeted by drunkenness and poverty, warfare and displacement. For them the war was purely destructive. After peace had been ratified by the French and English crowns, the Abenakis were left to make their own peace with Massachusetts, a colony they apparently could not live with and could not live without. On July 13/24, 1713, Dudley and members of the councils of New Hampshire and Massachusetts signed the Treaty of Portsmouth with the Abenakis and Maliseets – all the Indians between the Merrimack and the St John. The Indians accepted blame for the war as rebels. They vowed that they were British subjects and friends and that their relations with the English were to be governed by English laws. They renounced "treasonable conspiracy" with the French. The land clauses were ambiguous; although the Indians were to have "their own ground," the English were to enjoy their "rights of land" in the eastern region. Indian liberty to hunt and fish as formerly was confirmed. The Indians put great store on Dudley's promise, covered by a somewhat ambiguous clause, to revive the truck house policy of 1699. Finally, the Indians were to be confined east of the Saco.

The Treaty of Portsmouth was a thoroughly unsatisfactory foundation upon which to build. The clause of exile drew no true boundary, for the English meant to cross the Saco themselves in due time. The land clauses were menacingly vague. The promise of truck houses was not followed up – the cheese-paring ways of the Massachusetts House of Representatives ensured that. And it is doubtful that the Indians clearly understood the claim regarding their subject status, a claim that in any case the English could not make good.[52]

There had been little other fighting in North America. In 1709 a private-enterprise expedition, in which Vaudreuil invested, failed in its attempt to capture the beaver stock of Albany post on James Bay. In 1710 Mobile in Louisiana had been raided by pirates – the isolation and paltry character of the event eloquent testimony of how little that region had counted in wartime strategy.[53] There were military actions with greater verve in Newfoundland, where the French fishery continued on a very reduced scale. Several outports were captured by Subercase in 1705, and in 1708 Philippe Pastour de Costebelle, Governor of Placentia, captured all three forts at St John's, a victory that the Ministry of Marine did not have the financial capacity to follow up.[54]

Privateering, to which the French naval offensive had become reduced in the course of the war, had its counterpart in the colonies. The small vessels required by this seaborne guerrilla warfare could be financed by colonials. There is record of seven prizes being brought into Quebec, eighteen to Acadia, and sixty-three to Placentia, which thus, more than Port Royal, deserved the title of the Dunkirk of America.[55] But the war had not unfolded as expected. Fought largely for the trade and treasures of the West Indies and Spanish America, it had had the New World as its intended focus. But the British recognition of Emperor Leopold's son as Charles III of Spain in 1703 transformed a war for a new plan of partition into a war for Hapsburg restoration and mired down the opponents in an Iberian campaign.[56] The war had thus been fought on European soil.

II

The war in Europe had been a procession of French defeats: Blenheim (1704), Ramillies, Turin, and Madrid (1706), Oudenarde (1708), and Malplaquet (1709). Early in December, 1710, the English army in Spain

Jérôme de Pontchartrain, Minister
of Marine, 1699-1715: more
handsome here than in
Saint-Simon's malicious pen
portrait

Frédéric de Maurepas, Minister
of Marine, 1723-49: a portrait
revealing none of his great
charm

Philippe de Vaudreuil, Governor of Canada, 1703-25: deliberate and forceful

Charles de Beauharnois, Governor of Canada, 1726-47: an impenetrable countenance, with no revealing tension and only the hint of a smile

Jean-Baptiste de Saint-Vallier, Bishop of Quebec, 1688-1727: painted in old age, disdaining the vanity of a wig

Pierre-Herman Dosquet, Bishop of Quebec, 1733-39: unpopular and foreign, but the very image of an eighteenth-century divine

Michel Bégon, Intendant of New France, 1712-26: swathed in the sober dignity of the Robe

Gilles Hocquart, Intendant of New France, 1729-48: a paid bureaucrat from the age of twelve

GILLES HOCQUART

Louisbourg: New France's newest town and busiest port

Canadian at War: snowshoes, moccasins, and the Canadian winter are
beyond the ken of the French artist

Iroquois Warrior: authentic paraphernalia on a male figure from the
European artistic tradition

The Cataract of NIAGARA some make
this water Fall to be half a League while
others recken it no more than
a hundred Fathom

ABOVE Busy Beavers: fantasy embraced. BELOW The *Eléphant* grounded, September 1, 1729: no one has lost his hat in this forerunner of news engravings and photos

was defeated at Brihuega, demonstrating that Philip v could not be dethroned. This precious victory and the formation of the new Tory government in England brought Louis xiv the peace that the most humiliating compliance had not gained him from the Whigs and the intransigent Dutch. The Tories hoped that by being peacemakers they would save themselves in office and that by making a peace favourable to English commercial interests they would build their own following in the Whig City.[57] "They find themselves," a French spy reported, "exposed to the rage of a people weary of taxes and little contented with the Government."[58]

On January 21, 1711, the French foreign minister, the Marquis de Torcy, received a verbal message from the English ministers through an Abbé Gaultier, Count Tallard's former chaplain who had remained in London as a French agent after the commission of 1698-1701. As Gaultier shuttled back and forth across the channel, a plan was woven. England and France would negotiate the peace secretly and then bring Holland and the other powers to heel at a general conference.[59] Talks, which began at London on August 26, 1711, dealt with numerous matters of strictly European concern. But the questions of trade and colonies constituted the meat of negotiation and the bones of contention.

Louis's original proposals lumped all such issues together in a vague offer of "sureties" for English trade in Spain, the Indies, and the Mediterranean.[60] The English ministers who negotiated directly with the French envoy had a much clearer idea of what they wanted. While the capture of Port Royal was Great Britain's only significant victory west of Europe, they looked to the New World to repay their bloody and costly European campaigns. The French negotiator, Nicolas Mesnager, wrote in a confidential report to Torcy that "it is likely that the English want . . . to get themselves the means to make use of their power in America, which is already great, to make off with a part of the rich states that Spain there possesses."[61] The British made heavy demands on Louis to force from him concessions with regard to Spanish colonial trade. They were also moved by a motive no more complex than getting as much of the spoils of war as possible from an enemy at their mercy. Most important, every gain in America was an improvement to English trade and brought England a step closer to its commercial domination of Spanish America. This France feared even more than the loss of its American empire as such, as a French strategy paper of the time reveals:

> Finally, if the English were in possession of Canada, having chased us from our settlements, they would easily conquer the Mississippi, which they have hitherto attempted without success. [This is] because of the lakes above the Saint Lawrence of which we are today the masters but

which would belong to the English were we to cede them Canada. From there it would be easy for them to proceed to Mexico and to become, little by little, the masters of the New World.[62]

The writer argues that Canada, with its bulwarks of Acadia and Cape Breton, constituted what the geopolitical theorists of the 1920s would have called a "heartland," whereas Hudson Bay and Newfoundland were peripheral areas that could be given up, provided that rights to the fishery were maintained. From the heartland, one could reach out and limit or even destroy the minimal settlements of the periphery.

On September 9 the British produced a list of demands. These, with French replies written in the margin, signed by both sides on October 8, constituted the "Preliminaries of London" on which subsequent negotiations in the Dutch city of Utrecht were based. France agreed to all but the last demand. By this, the English ministers requested Newfoundland, Hudson Bay, and Hudson Strait as "restitutions," together with whatever colonial possessions Great Britain might have in its possession at the time the ratification of a final peace were published in those parts. [63] Should British arms have been so fortunate as to have conquered Canada, the British ministers wanted to keep it.[64] In vain did Mesnager argue, with cold Canadian winters in mind, that "Canada could be of no use to England, which has no wine to sustain its inhabitants."[65]

The Utrecht conferences began on January 29, 1712. Regulations drawn up the previous day provided that delegates would meet in the town hall "without ceremony" in a room "where there will be neither upper nor lower end, but they will be mingled together, pell-mell and without distinction." Most of the regulations governed "the coachmen and other lowly domestics" who had to be prevented from causing international incidents by street fighting.[66]

The Anglo-French struggle at the bargaining table was from the first the heart and soul of the Utrecht negotiations. Britain's allies in the war were quite aware that they were being shut out and that the British were "running away with the trade."[67] They were therefore keen on continuing the war and not losing their initiative. But Anglo-French negotiations at Versailles had arranged a secret two-month truce in Flanders. Marlborough, the bellicose British generalissimo, had been relieved of his command at the end of December, 1711, and his successor was now ordered to avoid battle. After the new commander left Flanders to occupy Dunkirk, his French counterpart, Marshal Villars, took advantage of the moment to defeat the army of Prince Eugene at Denain (July 14, 1712), demonstrating to the Austrians and Dutch that without the help of Great Britain the war could not be continued. From that point it was clear that peace was imminent and that Great Britain would quit Utrecht with all the prizes.

As negotiators threaded their way through the paperwork and posturing of diplomacy, the British remained constantly ready to break off negotiations. To the French, the Englishmen appeared fickle, taking back one day what they had given another. But the British, unlike their French counterparts, were subject to the political pressures of a party system.[68] At moments of stress, French negotiators had to remind themselves of Louis XIV's advice, "Profit by this occasion and by all other means you have to settle with England, because there is nothing more important than to try and detach this crown from the league. . . ."[69]

On August 21, 1712, the two-month truce was replaced by a universal Anglo-French armistice to run from August 22 to December 22 and in America, "beyond the line," from February 22 to June 22, a lag in keeping with the transportation difficulties of the time. At the beginning of December, the truce in Europe was extended to April 22, 1713. Arrangements were made in November for a renunciation of the French crown by Philip V and of the Spanish crown by the dukes of Orléans and Berry. Philip's renunciation was utterly void in French law, but the British, who had either a blind eye for the facts or a good one for propaganda, derived comfort from it all the same. On April 12, 1713, the plenipotentiaries wrote to Louis XIV, "Yesterday afternoon and tonight we signed the peace treaties with the ministers from England, Portugal, Prussia, Savoy and Holland and the commercial treaties with England and Holland."[70] The negotiation at Utrecht and Versailles, the latter involving the King himself, can be endlessly fascinating for the leisured armchair diplomatist. A general history such as this must confine itself pretty much to the results – to the disappointment of that ideal reader.

Article 10 of the Treaty of Utrecht "restored" Hudson Bay and Strait to England.[71] It made provision for the appointment of a commission to determine the exact boundary between Hudson's Bay Company territories and those of Canada as well as of other colonial boundaries at issue between France and Great Britain in North America. Article 11 gave the commission jurisdiction to decide long-standing Hudson's Bay Company claims for damages sustained during peacetime (i.e., the capture of the James Bay posts and related incidents in 1686), evidence of the company's assiduous lobbying.[72] Article 13 ceded Newfoundland with all adjacent islands, including St Pierre and Miquelon, and defined what in future would be known as "the French shore," an exclusive right to fish by and to dry fish on the Newfoundland shore from Cape Bonavista by way of the north to a Pointe Riche of dubious location.[73] Cape Breton and the islands of the Gulf of St Lawrence were recognized as French possessions. It is a measure of French desperation that Louis XIV had been prepared to accept the loss of both Acadia and Cape Breton even though, in his own words, "Canada becomes useless, its entrance is closed up, all fishing stops and the French navy is absolutely destroyed."[74] That Cape Breton was saved, it was thought, secured both the fishery and the route to Canada.

Article 12 ceded to Great Britain, St Christopher's in the West Indies, Sable Island, and "all Nova Scotia or Acadia," endowed with a thirty-league fishing zone. Pontchartrain had toyed with a rather elaborate plan to divide the colony by an east-west line that would have given the Strait of Canso to France as an additional protection to the approaches to Canada and would have retained the coastal area once the fief of the Acadian Company. The plan had come to nothing, but in a memorial presented to him by the son of the Acadian Company's Duret de Chevry, Pontchartrain found an idea that was to have a long life and to complicate the question of identifying the limits of Acadia. This was the notion that *Acadia* properly speaking referred to the peninsula and only by extension to the mainland.[75] An even more drastic minimization of what the English had accomplished in capturing Port Royal was dredged up from Acadia's murky past. Port Royal, it was claimed, was not even in Acadia, which was only a region in the south of the peninsula. British diplomats, uncertain of geography and fearful of being bamboozled, devised the treaty's description of their conquest as Acadia "with its ancient boundaries, as also the city of Port Royal." The palm would go to whoever could turn this diplomatic obfuscation to best account.

In the Atlantic region, France had salvaged the essentials: the fishery itself and the security afforded by possession of Cape Breton. Both the cession of an Acadia of "ancient boundaries" and the possible implication that Port Royal was not within them were seized upon to provide creative arguments that could minimize territorial loss. A special appeal to Queen Anne led to the inclusion of the provision that French subjects who remained in the ceded territories and became British subjects were to be permitted to enjoy the exercise of the Catholic faith "as far as the laws of Great Britain do allow," a phrase of beguiling ambiguity that thus makes its first but not its last appearance in Canadian history.

One question that arose rather late in the treaty negotiations, the significance of which the French appear not to have really understood, was that of the Iroquois, which had been so important a question at the time of Tallard's mission. To it was attached the question of interior trade. These issues were governed by the omnibus Article 15 that carpentered together a host of contradictory notions. It opens with a recognition of British sovereignty over the Iroquois and of Great Britain's legitimate influence among other Indian nations yet unnamed. The Iroquois, of course, would have vehemently denied any such claim of sovereignty, but the treaty was not meant for their eyes. This is followed by a similar protection for French interests that Louis XIV and the Marquis de Torcy had insisted upon.[76] Next comes what must be regarded as the plenipotentiaries' own masterpiece. The trade question was separated from the political and solved by the creation of a quasi-free-trade area in the North American interior. Both French and British subjects were to be free to enter the area and trade. Indians were to be free to go to the colonies of either power. It was a solution that Pontchartrain had earlier denounced, a sin against mercantilism and a transgression of the many boundaries he was wont to chalk upon the maps that passed back and forth between Versailles and Utrecht.[77] Nor can it be laid at the door of Louis and Torcy. It was introduced by the British and must be presumed to have reflected a supreme confidence that they could win the contest to which it was an obvious invitation. The article closes by providing that the commission established by Article 10 determine all frontiers and questions of sovereignty, a provision that was Pontchartrain's own particular contribution[78] and that tends to weaken all that goes before it.

The contradiction between the first and last sentences of Article 15 renders its meaning obscure. In the years that followed, the French behaved and wrote, even in the most private communications, as though the article were completely governed by the findings of the proposed commission. The British presumed their right to trade throughout the interior and trumpeted the recognition of their sovereignty over the Iroquois, which they did not consider liable to re-examination by anyone. This, indeed, seems to be the more logical interpretation of the article. By its failure to mark out clear-cut spheres of influence and by its encouragement to both sides to engage in competitive trade in the interior, Article 15 ensured that the decades to follow would be marked by an Anglo-French struggle for Indian trade and imperial dominion.

*   *   *

In 1701, anticipating a war over the Spanish heritage in North America, the object of which he described some years later as "the trade of the Indies and the wealth that they produce," Louis XIV had redefined Canada's role. Its *raison d'être* was henceforth to be imperial and political. Together, Canada and the new colony of Louisiana were, by extensive alliances with Indian tribes, to hold the Great Lakes, the Mississippi, and the route to Mexico, confining the British colonies to their Atlantic beachhead. In fact, the principal theatres of war came to be Spain and Flanders. Scarcely a sou or a soldier was contributed to add strength to purpose in Canada, and Louisiana was left a moribund, lame-duck outpost. Nevertheless, an American "heartland" strategy still governed French thinking at the beginning of the peace negotiations. Yet if there is some possible trace of it in the retention of Canada and the sacrifice of footholds on the maritime periphery, it is completely undone by the Treaty of Utrecht's Article 15. With the signing of the treaty on April 12, 1713, French imperial policy for North America, pursued from the beginning with much ambiguity, lay in fragments.

CHAPTER 4

Trade, Finance, and War to 1713

"The loaders place the earth upon the tails, and trample it to make it hold . . . those which are loaded march quite upright drawing their tails behind them. They unload near the masons, who, having their materials, begin to arrange their sticks one above another, and make of them a bed . . . others bring handfuls of earth which they place upon it, packing it down . . . they hammer it with the tail." Such was Nicolas Denys's description of the building of a dam by "as many as two, three or four hundred Beaver," written in 1672. The European reading public was as happy to swallow such tall tales as frontiersmen were to concoct them. Over forty years later, Denys's upright beaver, loaded with mud or sticks "According to ye French Accounts," marched comically across Herman Moll's "New and Exact Map" of North America.[1] An animal that had become the source of so much wealth could not escape the fabulist.

I

The years from the turn of the century to Utrecht were difficult ones in the history of Canadian trade and finance. The fur business, founded primarily on the demand for beaver, could not market its product and attempted to deal with the problem by corporate restructuring. The colony's finances were thrown into disarray, partly because they depended upon a healthy and taxable beaver trade, partly because they depended upon direct transfers of funds from the Marine, itself proceeding inexorably toward bankruptcy under the stress of war. The French shipping that Canada depended upon varied directly with the shrinking demand for beaver and inversely to the increasing risks resulting from the war at sea. Consequently, grain could not be exported. The only bright spot in the period was the beginning of shipbuilding and Canadian-based trading to the West Indies, attempts to fill the gap left by French traders who had turned their backs on the colony.

The European demand for beaver pelts, which dated from the beginning of the seventeenth century, resulted from the fact that the beaver's soft underfur – beaver wool or *duvet* – which grew beneath a protective layer of guard hair, was the only fibre that could be felted to "permit the manufacture of a hat with a large and durable brim."[2] This was achieved through the interlocking of tiny barbs on the fibre. Europeans may have found the example of broad brim and beaver felt, as has been claimed, in the Swedish army. But their immediate acceptance of that mode resulted from its consonance with the egotism, extremism, and "theatrical exaggeration of reality"[3] that marked the period. High crowned, its brim wide and stiff or wide, floppy, and plumed, the baroque hat in its outlandish splendour had meant money in the purses of Canadians. The broad-brimmed model was replaced by a smaller hat in the 1670s and then in the eighties by a positively diminutive version that did not detract from the flowing ringlets of a wig – something that unfortunately could not be made from beaver. Hats did become larger by the turn of the century, as the classic tricorne took its shape, but they never regained their former size.[4]

The vogue for smaller hats with brims turned up and fastened in place also made possible the use of fibres of poorer felting quality such as vicuña wool or rabbit fur. Attempts were also being made to improve the felting quality of various fibres. What was required was a process that would break down the smooth, hard fibre to produce rough surfaces that would cling together. Even natural beaver could be improved upon. The high value of *castor gras*, beaver pelts that had been sewn into robes and worn by Indians fur side inside, resulted not only from the removal of the unwanted guard hair by wear and tear but also from the breaking down of the wool by aging, smoke, and sweat. In France felters attempted to duplicate the process by boiling beaver wool with fat and nitric acid.[5] This treatment was partially successful and may have been applied to other fibres – there must be some such technical explanation for the successful manufacture of the Caudebec hat, for example, which was supposedly made from vicuña and rabbit without admixture of beaver. The common method of making cheaper hats was to mix beaver wool with other fibres, resulting in either an adulterated beaver hat or an upgraded wool or rabbit hat, depending on one's point of view. Either way, the official view was that mixed-fibre hats, *demi-castor*, were a threat to the Canadian beaver trade, and they were forbidden by legislation in 1664, 1666, 1673, 1690, and 1699. As the repetition suggests, the laws were not obeyed. In 1700 the law was therefore changed to protect the integrity of the true beaver hat and encourage the legal use of beaver in cheaper hats by recognizing the *demi-castor* as a hat half of beaver, half of vicuña or vicuña with rabbit and goat hair, as well as the *mêlé*, which might be of a less exacting mix.[6] In addition, the Canadian beaver market was protected by increased tariffs and other restrictions on the import of foreign beaver and hats in 1685, 1687, 1689, and 1693.[7]

Historical knowledge of the vicissitudes of the beaver hat market remains fragmentary. Both England and France were in search of new markets in the three decades from 1682 to 1715 and increased their exports to Russia through the agency of Dutch shippers.[8] The Russians used the pelts to make trimmings for coats after having first combed out the beaver wool by a secret process and sold it back to the Dutch for hatting. The prime pelt for the Russian trade was a top quality *castor sec d'hiver* – that is, the pelt from an animal killed in winter, very carefully prepared because the skin with guard hairs intact was to be used as well as the wool and therefore could not have been made into a robe and worn. In years in which the Russian market was more important than the domestic, *sec* was more sought after than *gras*. This and the mixing of beaver wool with other fibres by French hatters meant that the two-to-one ratio of *gras* to *sec* traditionally used in making felt[9] no longer governed the market. Selling beaver had become a complicated business.

There is no proof that the European market for beaver and hats was as a whole declining, although it was clearly being restructured. The trade with Russia was an example of this. And if French demand for beaver did drop, Russian demand may have made up for it. The importance of changes in fashion and technology is not known with any precision. If there was less beaver in a hat and the hat itself was smaller, it is also possible that more hats were being made. The effect on hatting of the Revocation of the Edict of Nantes in 1685 also has not been ascertained. We know that the Revocation disrupted the industry in the short term; long-term results such as the loss of French export markets by a wider dissemination of the hatting technique remain matters of controversy.[10] It was the development of a market for Canadian furs other than beaver that gave breadth and stability to the Canadian export sector in the earlier eighteenth century. The course of the rise of this market has never been charted. Finally, behind marketing difficulties lay the general economic malaise that marked most of the reign of Louis XIV; still something of a mystery, it is usually explained by the dearth of monetary metals that undeniably coincided with it.

European marketing problems appear to have been considerable at the turn of the century, but they should not be allowed to obscure the beaver trade's most fundamental problem, which was not declining demand but overproduction. The average annual output of beaver in the decade 1675 to 1685 had been 89,588 pounds, and between 1685 and 1687 it rose to 140,000 pounds. Because of war, production fluctuated wildly in the years that followed, but the trend was clearly upward, with output for 1699 being 296,000 pounds.[11] One reason for such a dramatic increase was the opening of the trade out of Hudson Bay by the English Hudson's Bay Company, founded in 1670, and the Canada-based Compagnie de la Baie du Nord, or Northern Company, founded in 1682. Another was the very great expansion of Canadian trade south of the Great Lakes. Canadian expansion into new fur-producing regions can in particular be linked to the maintenance by the French government of a fixed price for any amount of beaver delivered at Quebec – whatever it might be. This arrangement had been made in 1674 when overcompetition was resulting in the dumping of Canadian fur on the French market at less than cost price. There was a clear necessity for some mechanism to provide for orderly marketing. The fixed price had been suggested four years earlier by the prominent Canadian merchant Charles Aubert de La Chesnaye. In the years that followed, Canadians had simply conformed themselves to his ingenuous prediction that the fixed price "would encourage the various habitants of the country to penetrate farther inland and up the rivers to seek beaver, as they would be assured of having money in France or merchandise at reasonable prices."[12]

The state of the beaver trade was not only a commercial question but also a financial problem of crucial interest to the government. The *privilège exclusif* of exporting beaver was one of a number of lucrative rights in Canada and the West Indies regularly leased to private companies by the French government and known collectively as the Domaine d'Occident (the Western Domain).[13]

Louis de Pontchartrain's closing of the Western Posts was intended to protect both the Canadian staple trade as such and the financial system that depended on it. The impending necessity of finding a new lessee for the Western Domain was uppermost in his mind in 1696. From 1684 the domain had been included among the General Farms of the kingdom leased by a syndicate of Farmers General. In 1696, however, the farmers refused to include the domain in their new lease. It was taken instead by a new group acting under the name of a Parisian financier, Louis Guigues. The new lease was signed on March 18, 1697, and was to run from October 1 of that year to September 30, 1709.[14] Guigues gambled that he could match open-ended supply with open-ended demand. Along with the domain he leased the tax of the mark on hats, giving him the right to inspect them for quality and to mark any that were to be sold. Created in 1690, the tax of the mark was a characteristic mercantilist device; it was at once a regulatory mechanism and the source of a handsome revenue.[15] Guigues easily turned it into an instrument of monopoly by marking only his own hats, which the hatters were to sell at retail. The assumption behind monopoly was that unified control of quality, price, and distribution would increase sales. In this instance, the hatters simply rebelled. Hats were clandestinely made without beaver or with smuggled beaver, and the hats that came from Guigues's "manufacture" were talked down in the market and lost their reputation.[16] According to Savary des Bruslons's *Dictionnaire du Commerce* (1726), Guigues also attempted to market cloth and stockings made of wool and beaver: "This manufacture, which was established in the Faubourg St. Antoine in Paris, succeeded rather well at first; and given the French genius, novelty gave some vogue to beaver fabrics and stockings. But they went out of fashion abruptly, because experience showed that they wore poorly. And aside from the fact that they faded considerably, once they had been wet, they became dry and hard like felt."[17]

When the Guigues group's financial resources failed, they sublet the entire domain; and when the sublessee also failed, they sublet the Canadian farm alone on April 21, 1700, to yet another syndicate under the name of Nicolas Bailly.[18]

Guigues had already decided in 1698 that the supply of beaver had to be curbed and the price reduced, but Canadians would have none of it. He therefore obtained a decree dated February 24, 1699, stating that his representatives and the Canadian traders were to agree to a new schedule of prices or the matter would be evoked to the King's council and settled by ordinance. Guigues made the significant suggestion, perhaps echoing views expressed to his agents by disgruntled Canadians, that the colonists might "in future take on themselves the selling and distribution of their beaver as might seem best to them, paying nevertheless the tax of the *quart. . . .*"[19] Louis de Pontchartrain rejected the idea out of hand and ordered Champigny to get on with the negotiation of the new schedule of prices. In words that Colbert himself might have penned, the Minister instructed the Intendant not to pander to the merchants, "who speak only for their badly understood interest and in no way for the good of the country."[20]

In 1699 the farmers sent their representative, Villebois, to Quebec to argue their case to the colonial traders. There was no meeting of minds. On October 10 the two parties signed an agreement subject to the King's pleasure that was in accord with Guigues's wishes but contrary to the letter of the decree of February 24. The colonists were to have the freedom to form a company to take over the beaver export monopoly, paying the *quart* to the farmers. The discerning Champigny reported to the new minister, Jérôme de Pontchartrain, "It is very doubtful that the inhabitants can make a success of a company. . . . Guigues, knowing this farm and having established workshops, can run it better than another and must have more insight concerning the consumption of beaver."[21] In the colonists' acceptance of this burden was not only the naïveté and rashness of the frontier but the frontier's deeply ingrained belief that the metropolis grows rich at its expense. To colonial merchants, impatient of subordination, it was natural to suppose that in their own hands their affairs would take a turn for the better.

With high hopes, the Canadians delegated two of their number, Antoine Pascaud and Charles Juchereau de Saint-Denys, to participate in a three-cornered negotiation with the Minister and the farmers. They convinced the government that freedom for the colony to export its own beaver would be of little use to Canadian traders were they to find themselves competing in the French market with Bailly, the possessor of the vast stock of beaver that would be replenished annually by his receipt of the *quart*. The government also had to consider the rights of the farmers as well as those of the Northern Company and the Acadian Company, the latter having long enjoyed the freedom to export a small quantity of beaver to France free of the *quart*. The King in Council issued a decree on February 9, 1700, that confirmed the Quebec agreement of October 10, granted the colony a monopoly of the beaver market in France and northern Europe as well as control of the existing stock of beaver, and provided that Bailly might turn his beaver into manufactures for Spain, Italy, and other southern markets. It further directed the colony to buy out the Northern Company and not only confirmed but enhanced the modest rights of the Acadian Company.[22] Within this framework, Guigues, Bailly, and the Canadian representatives negotiated a final agreement that was deposited with a Paris notary on June 9.[23]

Bailly retained the tax of the mark, but for the first time since 1663, the colony controlled the export of the beaver staple. The farm of Canada was turned over by a sub-sublease to the colony itself for 70,000 livres a year, the price of the first year to be paid by instalments of 10,000 livres in each of the seven succeeding years. The colony left a part of the beaver inventory to Bailly but acquired most of it, 776,250 pounds with a nominal value of some million and a half livres, for a cash payment of 350,000 livres. The money for this was borrowed from three Parisian financiers, Pasquier, Bourlet, and Goy, who became the colony's agents. They would honour the drafts that the colony would be obliged to issue at Quebec for beaver received.

The high interest rate of 10 per cent on the financiers' loan, their commission of 5 per cent, and the arrangements they demanded for expenses, while commensurate with the risks involved, could be crippling to Canada. There was no evidence that beaver could be advantageously sold.

At Quebec on October 10 an assembly held in the presence of Callière, Champigny, Bishop Saint-Vallier, his predecessor, Laval, and the heads of the religious communities ratified the agreement with the farmers while rejecting (to no effect) the onerous terms of the contract with Pasquier, Bourlet, and Goy. The minutes record, with that calm assurance in social matters that characterized the Old Regime, that those present with the officials in the great hall of the Château St-Louis were "the better part of the people of the other estates."[24] They set their names to the agreement, "acting in this assembly for all the said colony of this country of Canada." The body politic had acted with what majesty a colony could muster. The way was cleared for the formation of the Colony Company. On October 15, in a second assembly, the colony proceeded to forge this instrument of its economic salvation, observing in the preamble to its constitution that "the preference given the farmers had always been damaging to the good of the colony because of their slight application to the problem of beaver consumption and because of the considerable reductions they made in the price of this merchandise."[25]

Canadian merchants intended to make the most of their liberation. Membership in the new company was to be limited to Canadians or French merchants already present in the colony, and only shareholders were to participate in Canadian trade. There was to be a ceiling of 4,000 livres on the value of shares held by non-Canadians. These provisions did not, however, survive review by the French government. A decree of May 31, 1701, provided that the shareholders' monopoly of trade would be confined to fur. While initial purchases of stock, including a new issue planned for three years hence, were limited to inhabitants of Canada, after the first three years stock could be resold to any French subject. With these changes, the Crown gave the approbation by letters patent necessary for the formation of a joint-stock company.[26]

There were few joint-stock enterprises in the world in 1701. Almost all businesses were partnerships, and most of these had no more than half a dozen partners. Even the General Farms was a partnership, although composed of forty members. Joint stock was the mark of a very great enterprise, usually, as in the present case, the exploitation of a royal monopoly and always founded by a legislative act. Its chief characteristic was that it could raise a considerable capital fund by the issue of shares and that it was given a life of its own independent of its shareholders by the shares' negotiability. It did not enjoy limited liability status unless this was specifically conferred.[27] In the case of the Colony Company, it was not. Share value was set at fifty livres, and to vote or hold office an investor had to own at least twenty shares. An edict of January 10, 1700, had dissolved the Northern Company because it was intended that all the fur trade of Canada be concentrated in one hand. Seven of the defunct company's nine Canadian directors were now awarded shares in the Colony Company as required compensation. Most of the top shareholders in the new company had been leading investors in the old; five of them were elected to the first board of directors.[28] A capital of 339,000 livres was subscribed by over two hundred shareholders. But a small band of eleven investors held about one third of the shares. Hardly any of these investors – it is a title of courtesy only – put up anything more than his signature. This is hardly surprising, given Champigny's remark two days after the drafting of the company's articles that "by being deprived for only one year of the capital they have tied up in last year's beaver, they are considerably inconvenienced, that money being the prime mover of their trade."[29] Finally, to the company's many other burdens were added a year later the unprofitable posts of Detroit and Fort Frontenac, to be maintained for *raison d'état*.[30] A difficult economic and political conjuncture misconstrued through the distorting lens of a self-righteous sense of grievance, an irresponsible attitude given free rein, and the absence of any financial base: the Colony Company weighed anchor and unfurled its sails to the storm.

Pontchartrain would not permit Canada to renounce its contract with Pasquier, Bourlet, and Goy, although the arrangement negotiated by Pascaud had been provisional on ratification. The Minister's sole concession to the Canadians was a reduction in the interest rate from 10 to 8 per cent. The new machinery was set in motion. Canadian traders brought their furs to the company's office at Quebec, where they were bought for bills of exchange on the Paris agents. The traders sent the bills to their French correspondents to cover the cost of trade goods, while the company sent the furs to its agents. The tally of honoured drafts mounted; but as the bales of unsold beaver mounted also, the total in bills constituted a debt owed to the agents. The colony had long desired the abolition of the tax of the mark, believing that it burdened the hatting trade and reduced sales. But the Colony Company's problems were actually increased by the suppression of the tax on September 20, 1701. According to the contract with the tax farmer Bailly, the colony now owed him an additional 25,000 livres a year to compensate him for non-enjoyment.[31] In Canada, the new intendant, François de Beauharnois, made state loans to the company on two occasions to enable it to pay the *état des charges*. Beauharnois, it may be said in passing, was a relative and protégé of Pontchartrain, an affable and capable man. His term of office in Canada was brief (1702-5), not because of ministerial displeasure, but because the superior post of Intendant of Naval Forces awaited him farther up the bureaucratic ladder.[32]

That part of the Canadian financial system that reposed on the Canadian economy was collapsing. The *quart* had become worthless, and the farm was showing a loss. No wonder Pontchartrain was interested when the company's representatives, de Lino and La Chesnaye, proposed the abolition of the *quart* and the taxing of the Canadian population by an assembly of their own estates, the conversion of the colony into a *pays d'états*. The plan must have encountered opposition elsewhere, for the most that was done was the suspension of the *quart* by a decree of April 18, 1702. Before leaving for Canada, Beauharnois had been instructed to investigate what taxes could replace the lost revenue so that the tax could be abolished altogether. But no other taxes were levied in its place. Although the *quart* was never revived, in 1706 the Minister still refused its outright abolition.[33] In 1702 there also occurred a considerable sale of beaver in Holland. While its long-term effect was to saturate the Russian market, it provided momentary cheer and considerably helped de Lino to produce a Panglossian balance sheet to convince everyone that all was for the best.[34] The most knowing were not deceived.

By 1703 Pasquier, Bourlet, and Goy could sustain the trade no longer. Goy brought together a new combination, Goy, Dumoulin, and Mercier, that negotiated a tougher contract with the company's new representative in France, Denis Riverin. The new agents were granted a beaver monopoly in Europe. They raised the interest rate to 10 per cent and restricted the company's credit, even specifying how much of this credit was to be used for the purchase of beaver and how much for expenses. They refused to accept any further *castor gras*. The Colony Company's articles had from the very first forbidden trafficking in *gras* (article 22), but the provision had evidently been ignored. The prohibition was now seen as an outrage. By signing the contract, Riverin brought down on his head the wrath of his fellow shareholders. But Pontchartrain stood firmly behind the contract, as he had the earlier contract negotiated by Pascaud, refusing to let the company dismiss Riverin. He had taken a liking to this practical man, whose memoranda on the beaver trade he found persuasive and invaluable.[35]

Figures presented by Riverin in 1705 suggest the company was indebted for more than one and a half million livres with no assets to offset it except unsaleable beaver. He demonstrated that every beaver skin sold brought less than the cost of delivering it to market, in addition to which, of course, pelts sold were only a small portion of the company's inventory. At the same time, the company had borrowed heavily to maintain the trade to Hudson Bay, thus increasing the flood of furs. Greed, ignorance, and corruption were Riverin's chief explanations for the company's troubles.[36] There was much truth in his charges. The Canadian shareholders included all the fur traders. They were content to sell furs and services to the company and cash their bills of exchange. If the company eventually made a profit, they would be grateful; if it failed, they lost nothing, since they had never paid for their shares. The company's shipping of furs direct to Hamburg, circumventing the Parisian backers to whom it owed a fortune, shows how little it cared about business obligations.[37] While the Colony Company was a large business for its time, accountable to shareholders and creditors and responsible for Canada's economic welfare, its papers, according to Beauharnois, were in complete disorder.[38]

In 1705 Pontchartrain sent two intendants to Canada, Jacques Raudot and his son Antoine-Denis, a kind of junior partner. Both were men of penetrating intelligence, the father a jurist and the son a specialist in finance. In another way they were complementary: Jacques's mercurial disposition and hot temper were balanced by Antoine-Denis's equable temperament and self-possession.[39] Their first priority upon arriving in Canada was to deal with the company. Prior to leaving France, they submitted a report to the Minister. They planned a severe restriction of the fur trade; only the question of security and Indian alliances dissuaded them from wanting to suppress it entirely. *Castor gras* and *castor sec d'été* were to be excluded from trade, and trade was to be ended at Detroit, Fort Frontenac, and Hudson Bay. Finally, the company's administration was to be greatly simplified, a reflection of the belief they shared with Pontchartrain that corruption was the company's basic problem.[40]

To the nuns of the Hôtel-Dieu, Jacques Raudot may have appeared an amiable old raconteur, fond of children,[41] but he had an autocratic disposition in the best of circumstances and appeared to the company as absolutism personified. With no regard for the company's constitutional forms, he dismissed the directors and replaced them with two men of his own choosing. His embarrassed choices, Georges Regnard Duplessis and René-Louis Chartier de Lotbinière, did as they were told, but argued in favour of their deposed colleagues. Soon the Raudots were won over to the belief that difficult circumstances, not the least being the government responsibilities that had been foisted upon the company, were more significant problems than maladministration. Drastic changes were postponed. A proper election of directors was held. But at that juncture, affairs at Quebec were suddenly eclipsed. L.F. Aubert, an Amsterdam merchant and cousin of the late Charles Aubert de La Chesnaye of Quebec, had joined with J.B. Néret and J.B. Gayot, Parisian financiers, to buy out the Colony Company. On May 10, 1706, Riverin negotiated the transfer on behalf of Canada. Royal approbation followed on July 24 and Canadian ratification on October 12. The Colony Company ceased to exist.

Aubert and Company, whose contract was retroactive, running from October 1, 1705, to October 1, 1717, took over the export privilege, the inventory of beaver, the Canadian import duties, and an outstanding debt of 1,823,000 livres. The remaining domaial dues and the export taxes on moose and beaver (the defunct *quart*) were returned to Bailly and eventually reunited to the Western Domain. The price at Quebec for *castor sec* was reduced to a very low thirty sous a pound, and no *castor gras* was to be accepted for the first six years. The great problem now was to ensure that enough beaver reached France. Legislation that proved spectacularly ineffectual was passed to prevent smuggling pelts to Albany.[42]

The history of the new "beaver company" bore at least a family resemblance to that of the Colony Company. While vastly superior to the Canadian merchants in capital and business sophistication, they too depended upon credit. As the economic crisis of the war intensified, they reached the end of their resources. In 1709 Dumoulin and Mercier reappeared on the scene, accepting the bills of Aubert and Company as they had those of the Colony Company. In 1714 two surprising things happened: the supply of *castor gras* ran out and the debt of the Colony Company assumed by Aubert and Company was paid. The following year the Paris hatters complained that if they did not get a shipment of beaver from Canada, they would be ruined.[43] It was a turning point, but one that must have been barely discernible in the economic shambles of post-war Canada and France.

Over the tortuous history of the Colony Company and its successor Louis and Jérôme de Pontchartrain had presided. Other men contributed plans, diplomacy, and money, but it was up to the Minister to say yes or no. Neither was at first a strong supporter of the idea of a colonial company, but they were not presented with a wide choice of reasonable alternatives. Even Champigny, for all his sagacity, was no help, arguing that either Guigues or the Crown should take the fur trade in hand when Guigues had already demonstrated his incapacity and royal funds were fast disappearing.[44] So the Pontchartrains twice had recourse to monopoly companies. But upon expiry of the Aubert and Company contract, Jérôme decided, the beaver trade would become free. Suspension of trade in *castor gras* was a necessary step toward that end because it would result in the entire inventory being used up, enabling the Canadians to make a fresh start.[45] The Minister, who was no original thinker, probably took the idea from Riverin. The latter argued that the monopoly, with its fixed price, had produced the economic crisis and caused the Crown needless headaches and expense, that the overblown trade was a source of divisions, an encouragement to lawlessness, and diverted men from useful occupations. Pontchartrain's decision also meant he had given up trying to balance the needs of the Indian alliance system with the needs of trade; it is certain that he did not decide to accept Riverin's solution, which was to export to Albany the beaver surpluses produced by unavoidable overtrading.[46]

The history of the Colony Company provokes two final comments. The first is that founding the company was a serious business error. Mistakes of this kind must always seem unaccountable in retrospect. In fairness to the Canadians, it should be remembered that they did not have the assistance of accountants and economists and that they were doubtless encouraged by the support given them by experienced Parisian financiers. The second point is that the company was so poorly managed. La Rochelle's deputy to the Council of Commerce pointed out in 1701 that the proper starting point for the company should be to burn more than half the stock of beaver. Riverin made a similar suggestion, but only as a rhetorical flourish.[47] Instead, the company held on to every pelt, keeping the market overstocked with a commodity the quality of which was being diminished daily by rot and vermin. Part of the explanation for the irresponsible conduct of the company directors was the absence of any body of law or any regulatory agency to govern the company's operations. In the early eighteenth century, a public company operated in an institutional vacuum. Perhaps it is not too hazardous a generalization to say that the eighteenth-century Canadian mind had not yet grasped the notion of accountability to abstract entities: shareholders, corporations, even the community. If an explanation in terms of frontier mentality helps to explain the rashness of the Canadians' decision to found the Colony Company, the further argument of intense individualism is illuminating regarding the company's operations. But it would have to be thinly stretched to cover all the knavery and foolery that seem to compete for first place in the company's history.

II

The crisis of the fur trade was not the only problem to bedevil the Canadian economy. The War of the Spanish Succession taxed the resources of the French monarchy to the limit; and the Marine, which was by no means a favoured department, felt the pinch of hard times. Most costs of government in Canada were met by the Marine – some three or four hundred thousand livres a year, compared to the eighty or ninety thousand livres contributed by the domain.[48] Like the receipts of the domain, this direct transfer of funds from France to Canada was drastically curtailed during the war. Canada was virtually abandoned. Naval strength was concentrated in the Caribbean to protect the Spanish treasure fleets, and after 1707 the department could not afford to send a single ship to Canada. Dispatches were sent on private ships; private parties outfitted naval vessels. In 1709 and 1713 even these expedients failed.[49] Shipments of flour to garrisons in Acadia and Placentia in 1710 had to be paid for in gunpowder, the department being out of money.[50] For a time Pontchartrain even tried to get together a private company to recapture Port Royal, a task that the Marine could not afford to undertake.[51] By the end of the war, the Canadian intendant confessed himself "hard put to it to provide the soldiers with the clothes which are absolutely necessary to prevent them from freezing this winter, for they are all almost naked."[52] But even suffering is relative. Pontchartrain's wartime letters to the Controller General conjure up a worse scene of destitution, starvation, and incipient revolt in ports of France.[53]

Marine finances were in the hands of three Treasurers General, *officiers* who owned their positions and rotated in office. There were three of them because the sale of three offices netted more than the sale of one. Under the stress of war the system also proved to be advantageous because three treasurers had more credit than one. Fontanieu, the treasurer in office in 1701, was the first to receive orders from the Marine to disburse monies he had not yet received from the treasury.[54] This set the precedent for the entire eighteenth century: by 1703 treasurers were borrowing on their own credit and advancing money to the state at interest.[55] For example, between 1710 and 1713 the Marine estimates totalled 56 million livres while the central treasury forwarded to the Marine treasurers only 17 million – and of course, expenditures were well in excess of the estimates.[56]

At Quebec, as everywhere that the Marine Department was active, the treasurer had a clerk who received monies from his master and disbursed them on the orders of the intendant, the system thus providing a rigid separation of the accounting and executive functions. In the four-cornered relation of treasurer, clerk, intendant, and Marine controller, the accounts of each were a check on those of the others. The intended use of funds was spelled out in an annual *état du roi*, which the intendant was supposed to keep secret from the clerk so that the latter could not juggle his accounts in conformity with it, ruining their value as an independent reference.[57] The Old Regime was not unfamiliar with checks and balances. The *état du roi* was a pared-down version of a proposal submitted to Versailles by the governor and intendant. The more elaborate contained as many as fifteen "chapters" or headings of designated expenses such as "Fortifications and buildings," "Indians gifts," "Army pay." There was always a final chapter covering unforeseen expenses, one that was subject to considerable expansion.[58] The whole of French government financing was based on such *états*, but no one thought of them as more than guidelines.[59] Given the regular way in which expenses exceeded estimates year after year, we are unable to escape the conclusion that Canadian officials produced a plan slightly more costly than they thought Versailles would accept and that from it the Marine Department produced an *état* suitable to a wholly imaginary state of affairs. By a bookkeeping convention, the inevitable excess expenditures were charged to the following year so that they would not prevent the accounts from balancing.[60] The procedure was ritualistic and quite uninfluenced by fiscal realities. And the administration of funds was so casual and negligent[61] that once again, as in the case of the Colony Company, we are confronted with the mentality of another era: the same weak sense of stewardship and, perhaps, an attitude to numbers different from our own.

The chaotic budgetary system, which occasioned much Canadian special pleading, ministerial scolding, and all-round wringing of hands, was not responsible for the financial strain of war, but it aggravated the situation by making impossible departmental control or cognizance of expenditures. In Canada too officials were forced to the most ingenious devising to pay escalating war costs. In the 1680s and 1690s the intendants de Meulles and Champigny had resorted to the manufacture of paper money from playing cards to cover their shortages between annual shipments of specie from France. From 1686 Champigny had also authorized the treasury clerk to draw bills of exchange on the treasurer in office payable from the funds of the next year, these being negotiated at Quebec to pay the upkeep of troops.[62] In 1691, the treasury clerk, not being authorized to draw bills, had made promissory notes to cover expenditures. The Marine Department rivalled the ingenuity of its Canadian officials when in 1693 it substituted shipments of trade goods for shipments of specie and set up shop at Quebec. This enabled it to pay bills by emptying its accumulated stores at Rochefort and to hope for some profit, while the devices of card money, bills, and notes enabled the intendant to expand the local money supply to suit his needs.

Card money kept the war machine going and by facilitating government loans kept the Colony Company afloat. Ultimately it was responsible for spiralling inflation. As early as 1705, it was clear to Claude de Ramezay, the Governor of Montreal, that "there are here many more cards than there appear to be funds to retire them, which some day will cause much trouble and confusion."[63] Here was a second problem for the Raudots. Holders of cards were expecting to exchange them for drafts on the treasurer. Ramezay mentions the treasury clerk's refusal to accept over a hundred thousand livres in cards for such drafts. The bad effect of the refusal is obvious from Jacques Raudot's ordinance two weeks later reminding the public that cards were legal tender that could not be refused in trade.[64] While cards and bills were still treated in official correspondence as distinct alternative financial expedients, here is a first indication of the development of a system whereby cards enjoyed credit because of their convertibility into bills.[65] In 1707 the arrangement failed at the Paris end when the hard-pressed treasurer was reduced to paying matured bills with promissory notes. The value of cards dropped by 50 per cent.[66] When Raudot was forbidden to issue any more cards, he too resorted to notes. "These are new cards you are making under another name," the Minister complained.[67] Receiving no *états* or instructions in 1709 and 1710, the Intendant again resorted to cards. The marriage of cards and bills had not lasted, and these cards were issued because of the absence of "any individuals who were willing to take bills of exchange."[68] Although he did not attempt to carry on the war without card money, Pontchartrain continued to voice his disapproval of the expedient, peppering his letters with querulous remarks about the burdensomeness of Canada.

The issuing of fiduciary paper was creating a large state debt. As the war drew to a close in 1712, the liquidation of this debt became a central preoccupation of the Marine Department. In an "entirely secret" dispatch Pontchartrain now proposed to accept cards in exchange for drafts on the treasurer convertible into *rentes sur l'Hôtel de Ville*, annuities that had originally been based on the credit of the city of Paris, hence their name.[69] The proposal was addressed to a new intendant, Michel Bégon, who had received the reins of the intendancy from the Raudots in 1712. He is always remembered as the intendant who lost his fortune and barely escaped with his life when the intendant's *palais* burned to the ground in that first winter at Quebec and as one who busied himself with a private trade and, perhaps, mixed the King's money with his own a little too freely.[70] His sparring with the Minister over what kind of monetary settlement would be acceptable to Canada provides a good example of the role an intendant could play in the elaboration of policy. He pointed out the obvious flaw in the Minister's scheme that merchants who depended upon cash flow could not see their capital permanently immobilized. His own solution was to use the Crown's considerable bargaining power to usurp the role of supplier to the Canadian merchants. If the Crown sent all the funds to Canada as merchandise, the considerable profits would be sufficient to redeem all the cards.[71]

Heavy seas prevented the annual naval vessel from reaching Quebec in 1713. The bulging mail pouch of the following year thus contained two years' official dispatches and draft ordinances, which were a faithful reflection of the confusion and desperation that reigned at Versailles. First there were the dispatches of 1713 according to which Bégon's scheme was rejected. Annuity conversion remained official policy. Cards were to lose value at a regular rate but more rapidly if they were kept as currency than if they were exchanged for treasury drafts. Next were orders to suppress the draft ordinances of 1713; new ordinances authorizing greater reductions; then news that a small sum in bills sent by Bégon in 1713 could not be redeemed even in annuities, that source of credit being exhausted. There followed orders that, alongside the annuity conversion scheme, implemented a second idea submitted by Bégon – the redemption of cards at half their face value. Finally, the ministerial capitulation came in a letter of May 23, 1714: full approval of this second of Bégon's suggestions with cards having a face value of 320,000 livres Canadian to be received each year for five years. The annuity schemes were to be dropped entirely.[72] But while plans were made for the retirement of all outstanding issues of card money, the bankrupt French government could not extricate itself from the necessity of issuing new cards. Pontchartrain himself planned a new issue for 1714, the first time that the initiative had come from Versailles. His plan was that new cards marked with a special stamp were to circulate at face value alongside the remaining old cards circulating at a 50-per-cent discount.[73] Instead, Vaudreuil and Bégon simply saved the required amount from cards turned in at half value to spend the following year at face value.[74] "You derange the plan entirely," scolded Pontchartrain, while Bégon replied with a spirited defence, minister and intendant reading each other lessons in monetary policy.[75]

Meanwhile, for the Canadian traders, half a loaf was better than none. In the first year, Bégon retired the allotment of cards for the second year as well, giving for the latter bills maturing in two years.[76] Although these drafts would be heavily discounted, traders could make use of them immediately to purchase goods in France. But the traders were doomed to greater disappointment. Although the treasurer in office, Pierre Gaudion, accepted bills drawn on him, he could not meet his payments. Like any businessman defaulting on a bill he had accepted, he was to be arrested by order of the Consular Jurisdictions – the Canadians' French creditors saw to that. "Canada ruined by this

default on payment and besides that a treasurer of the Marine condemned to be arrested, which causes a dreadful scandal,'' so wrote a
very frustrated Pontchartrain, appealing to the Controller General.[77]
Canadian card money and Gaudion's acceptances had become near
worthless paper of interest only to speculators. Not Pontchartrain, not
the Marine treasurers, certainly not the Raudots or Bégon: none of
these men were in a position to solve the problem of the Crown's
indebtedness in Canada. That was part of the larger crisis of the bankruptcy of the French state, and the solution lay beyond the death of
Louis XIV in the draconian measures of the Regency.

After the first reaction of panic, French shippers learned to live with
the dangers of war and with increased costs. Nantes and La Rochelle
even increased their traffic to the West Indies – perhaps the explanation lies in the development of Saint-Domingue or new trade opportunities in the Spanish West Indies.[78] For Canada it was otherwise: shipping between colony and metropolis dropped by almost half. The
phenomenon is not a simple one. In Table I the first column, "Long-
term Movement," shows that the decline in traffic had set in well
before the British declaration of war in 1702. As the figure for 1709-13
suggests, improvement did not occur in 1713 in spite of a truce "beyond the line" that began in February; only four ships came to Canada
from La Rochelle and Bordeaux in 1713, but ten came in 1714.[79]
When these figures are considered alongside the contrary record of
the West Indies trade, the inescapable conclusion is that, more than
anything else, they reflect the fortunes of the fur trade, although reinforced by the physical dangers and fiscal chaos of the war. Of course,
strictly economic and strictly military factors converged as a potential
shipper in La Rochelle or Bordeaux balanced danger and rising costs
against potential return.

The table also isolates war-related changes to the extent that this is
possible. During the war the triangular trade between La Rochelle,
Quebec, and the West Indies (usually Martinique) suffered a much
greater decline than the bilateral trade between La Rochelle and Quebec. Here, perhaps, the game was not worth the risks as ships drop-
ping south before the wind ran the gauntlet of the long, hostile coast
of English America. Placentia was an additional port of call often
included in voyages to Canada. As Champigny explained, "Ships bound
for Canada do not ordinarily always find cargo at Quebec for their
return voyages, so take on flour, peas and other provisions for Placentia and there load dried fish that they bring to France."[80] Only some
captains sailing from La Rochelle to Quebec specified before setting

Table I
The Decline of Franco-Canadian Shipping in the
Early Eighteenth Century

		War-related Changes		
		Eleven Pre-	Eleven War	
Long-term		war Years	Years	Per cent
Movement[1]		Breakdown	1691-1701	1702-12	Change
1689-1693: 13.2	All voyages to	9.7 p.a.	5.1 p.a.	−47.4
1694-1698: 8.6	Quebec[2]			
1699-1703: 6.8	La Rochelle to	7.1	3.9	−45
1704-1708: 5.4	Quebec[3]			
1709-1713: 5.2	La Rochelle to	2.0	0.7	−65
1714-1718: 7.8	Quebec-W.I.[4]			
1719-1723: 6.6	La Rochelle to	5.1	3.1	−39.2
1724-1728: 10.2	Quebec-Nfld.[5]			
1729-1733: 10.8	La Rochelle to	0.86	1.18	+37.2
1734-1738: 9.6	Nfld.[6]			
1739-1743: 12.8				

[1]Average number of ships per year by five-year periods by all routes from all French ports based on tables 2, 4, and 10, J.S. Pritchard, "Ships, Men and Commerce," Ph.D. dissertation, University of Toronto, 1971, pp. 488-89, 491, and 496.
[2]Based on ibid., table 2, pp. 488-89, table 4, p. 491.
[3]Ibid., table 2, pp. 488-89.
[4]Ibid.
[5]Ibid., and M. Delafosse, "Le trafic maritime franco-canadien, 1695-1715," International Colloquium on Colonial History, Ottawa, 1969.
[6]Based on Delafosse, ibid. The pre-war average is based on the shorter span, 1695-1701.

out that they would stop at Placentia on their return journey,[81] but all these vessels may be considered potential supply ships for Newfoundland. The decline in shipping to Quebec therefore meant fewer French supply ships for Newfoundland. This is reflected in the increase in ships sailing direct to Placentia from La Rochelle, but the increase by a third of a ship annually does not compensate for the decrease of two potential carriers a year from Quebec.

For the Canadian trader, the conjuncture had changed dramatically. The traditional staple trade was stagnant, and this together with the derangement of the currency was ruining the traditional trade with

France in French bottoms. But while the price of wheat in Canada was falling steadily from 1702 to 1707,[82] Placentia and Martinique remained chronically under-supplied with provisions. Canadians were encouraged to their first seaborne adventures by the lure of these two markets and the promise of even greater profits from privateering. Governor Vaudreuil was enthusiastic, "not finding a more glorious nor a more suitable way to occupy youth."[83] This line of business was within Canadian means as it could be undertaken with small vessels of limited firepower, provided that they were supplied with large crews to act as boarding parties.

The first step in trade or privateering was the purchase or building of ships, for there was no Canadian merchant fleet to fall back on. A Quebec baker and innkeeper, Louis Prat, distinguished himself as the leading spirit in the revival of Canadian shipping, which had fallen into decay after the departure of Jean Talon from the colony in 1672.[84] Prat's *Joybert* (1704) was probably the first Canadian ship built by private enterprise and was followed by his *Pontchartrain* in 1709. Denis Riverin launched his *Notre Dame de Victoire* in 1706, and in the following year the Port-Royal-built *Biche* was put to sea by a Canadian business group headed by Denys de la Ronde. In addition some ships were bought, for example, the *Hollande*, a leaky old naval vessel that Riverin and three associates acquired, repaired, and sent to Martinique in 1706.[85]

The Canadians' trade to Placentia appears to have begun in 1703 using small boats. Privateering followed in 1704 and the trade to Martinique in 1706. While the pirate's trade conjured up visions of wealth and was exciting – the descent on Bonavista or the capture of the *Pembrooke Galley* in 1704 were no doubt stirring stuff – it does not seem to have produced the profits.[86] It was virtually abandoned when in 1708 the Intendant lifted the ban on the export of flour that had been imposed to protect Canadians from shortages.[87] From that date the big profits lay in the trade to Martinique. The following year several French ships arrived at Quebec to load wheat for the West Indies because of the failure of the harvest in France. With their cargoes of scarce French manufactures to trade, they easily dominated the Quebec market. It was a minor flexing of the economic muscle with which they would shoulder Canadians aside after the war. While the *Pontchartrain* sailed to Martinique in 1711, 1712, and 1713, Canadian attention was henceforth concentrated on Placentia, as the ministry wished.[88] In 1712, the last year before the loss of that colony to England, there were seven Canadian ships in its port.[89]

To some extent, the Marine Department disposed the trade of Canada according to the needs of imperial policy. Generally, such dispositions were governed by mercantilist principles. The production of raw materials that did not compete with French commodities was always encouraged. The Ministry was especially interested in the production of naval stores, pitch and tar, hemp and masts, for which it depended on the Baltic countries.[90] All ministers, even Pontchartrain, also conceded that the building of ships in Canada was desirable, an infraction of the mercantilist rule against colonial manufacturing dictated, once again, by France's dependence upon foreigners for ships and shipbuilding materials. Intendants Beauharnois and Antoine-Denis Raudot, while still newcomers to Canada, wrote enthusiastically about shipbuilding, but they soon had to agree with more experienced hands that it was yet too expensive in Canada to be a practical undertaking.[91] Wartime shipbuilding was a special case that arose out of pressing necessity and was accomplished with considerable cost and difficulty. Raudot and Pontchartrain looked forward to the day when Canadians would be able to build their own ships to carry their low-value exports to the French market as no French shipper would find a sufficient profit in fetching them.[92]

Even with regard to other manufactures, Pontchartrain was not always unbending. In 1704 he sent two potters and a spinner to Canada in response to a request from Vaudreuil and Beauharnois. At a time when there was little money to spare in the Marine coffers, he also authorized an annual gratuity for Madame de Repentigny in recognition of her establishing a weaving factory.[93] Pontchartrain's attitude was probably softened by the experience of war. He felt keenly the misery of the towns and persons relying on his hamstrung department. Two years running he warned Raudot against colonial manufactures, only to add, "This ought to be the general view; however, their establishment in Canada ought not to be absolutely prevented, especially among the poor."[94]

Pontchartrain's restrictive views on intercolonial trade were also challenged by the altered circumstances imposed by the war. In contrast to previous ministers, he was originally distrustful of trade between Canada or Acadia on the one hand and the West Indies on the other, fearing that the colonies would exchange sugar and flour, cutting into the trade of the French Atlantic ports.[95] As we have seen, Canadian–West Indian trade had always been an adjunct to La Rochelle's trade with Canada; but it attracted little attention, and Pontchartrain does not appear to have been well informed on it. In 1708, however, Canadian flour was being exported, Canadian ships were in port at Martinique, and a Canadian trader named Pierre Peire had produced a glowing memorandum on the prospects of Canadian trade in the Caribbean, his purpose being to have the duties levied on Canadian produce at Martinique abolished.[96] The local intendant, Vaucresson, sent the memorandum to Pontchartrain, who in turn passed it along to the chambers of commerce of Nantes, Bordeaux, and La Rochelle, the deputies to the Council of Commerce in Paris, and the Intendant of Rochefort, Michel Bégon, father of the Canadian intendant of the same name. Pontchartrain was unfavourable in his response to Vaucresson, but to these others he pointed out that the trade was perfectly legal. What was at stake was the abolition of customs duties and the placing of the trade on a firmer footing. When these advisers reported that they saw no harm in the trade, Pontchartrain went so far as to recommend to d'Aguesseau, head of the Council of Commerce, the abolition of the duties, a matter outside his own jurisdiction. He advised that in case of need the duties could be restored or officials could refuse permission for trading ships to sail.[97]

A second letter to d'Aguesseau, written the following year, after the French harvest failed, is particularly revealing of Pontchartrain's views.[98] Contrary to the advice of the deputies, he was willing to permit foreign ships to carry foreign flour to the West Indies. French merchants he wrote, would starve the colonists to have their monopoly or starve the kingdom to make profits from scarcity in the West Indies. But a minister had to guarantee the subsistence of both Frenchmen and colonials. Here is the mercantilist dilemma. The colonists, Pontchartrain pointed out, "are not of a more lowly condition than others that they should be so roughly treated." As far as Canada was concerned, he drew attention to the weakness of its agricultural economy:

> [The deputies] also say that Canadian flour can be sent there [the West Indies]. That is what has been done this year and will continue to be done as long as the harvest in that country permits it. But it is never very great, and we would be fooling ourselves if to feed the islands we relied on the grain of that colony. It will be doing well if it can feed itself and the other northern colonies. If it can send a few small cargoes to the islands, shipments by foreign vessels can be diminished by as much.[99]

Here Canadian flour exports are put into a better perspective than in many of Pontchartrain's earlier dispatches. Far from being considered a threat to French exports, they are seen as small and highly unreliable.

Pontchartrain was now concerned to assure that Canada have on hand a sufficient supply of grain to make it a supplier in times of emergency, even sending Vaudreuil and Raudot a memorandum on methods of grain storage used in Brittany. This fitted well with his desire of long standing that the Canadian economy be diversified and its reliance on the beaver trade be reduced. The supply problems of the war had made Canada appear the natural provisioner of the Newfoundland colony, although Pontchartrain had also called Acadia to that role in 1707. His dispatches of that earlier time show him more caught up in the toils of mercantilism, fretting that the self-sufficiency and surplus production necessary to make his own plan work were "entirely contrary to the general principle of colonies, which is to draw all their needs from the State."[100]

With the loss of both Acadia and Placentia, the Crown decided to establish a new colony on Cape Breton Island, renamed Ile Royale; and Canada was to be the supplier to the soldier-fisherman population of that barren highland. The King had learned with pleasure of the Quebec traders' abundant provisioning of Placentia, so read the King's memorandum of 1713. The governor and intendant were in future "to leave navigation between Quebec and Ile Royale entirely free." The King admonished that "they must even encourage the traders as much as possible and never suspend this freedom without significant reasons for which they must account to His Majesty."[101]

*   *   *

The long years of war and of economic travail had tried Canada severely. Never since Louis XIV had taken the colony under his wing in 1663 had Canadians been so cut off and alone. The port of Quebec had seen fewer than half the number of ships from France that it had seen in happier days. Canada's monetary house of cards had collapsed utterly. For a time, it had seemed that the mountain of unsold beaver would crush the life out of the colony. Yet at the end of the war there was not only loss but hope, not only hope for the re-establishment of the fur trade but hope that Canada's first significant initiatives in ocean-borne trade would yet bear fruit. News of the peace of Utrecht reached Canada by the first ships arriving at Quebec at the end of June, 1713. It was not good news unalloyed, but, wrote the annalist of the Hôtel-Dieu of Quebec, "It cannot but give us hope for better days and hope that by peace all our past losses will be made good."[102]

CHAPTER 5

The Reclamation of Empire, 1715-1744

The same annals that report the Treaty of Utrecht so hopefully confide, after an interval of only a few lines, "the peace just made did not
procure us that swift succour all Canada desired." They explain that
"the state of French affairs permitted the court no thought of us."[1]
Optimism has given way to a worldly-wise resignation.

The derelict colony was a matter of secondary concern in the mother
country – demoralized, bankrupt, its institutions shaken. The death
on September 1, 1715, of Louis XIV, the king who had loved war too
much, completed the picture of disarray. But it also provided a release
from a past gone sour and an opportunity for new beginnings. By
restoring the right of remonstrance to the *parlement de Paris*, Louis
XIV's nephew the Duke of Orléans identified himself with the magistracy and was declared sole regent, in defiance of the late king's last
will and testament. He was the rallying point of a circle that saw
themselves as the party of reform. Reflecting the views of the late
Duke of Burgundy and his preceptor, Fénelon, Orléans humbled the
secretaries of state and the controller general upon whom the absolute
government was founded by transferring their powers to councils that
gave full scope to the governmental pretensions of the nobility and the
princes of the blood. This conciliar system, or *polysynodie*, together
with the unshackled *parlement*, constituted what to contemporaries
seemed a representative system of government. Libertine, some of
them high-minded, frequently seeking the patterns of the future in an
idealized past, those now put to the task of restoring France and
reclaiming its empire were a fascinating group.[2]

No problem facing the Regent and his councils was more difficult
than that of the state's wrecked finances, mired in a stagnant economy.
The years 1689-90 had been a turning point after which government
was carried on in an atmosphere of chronic financial crisis. Expenses
were always greater than the estimates, and the available money often
less. There was no central control over finances except the King him-

self, who was unequal to the task, and it was never clear whether the controller general was in charge of financial policy or was simply a purveyor of funds. There was no budget that co-ordinated the expenditures of the various departments. The departmental *prévisions* were but the roughest forecasts, which no one accepted as final, a point worth remembering in connection with expenditures in Canada.

Between 1708 and 1715, the state had spent 1,564.5 million livres and taken in a revenue of only 461 million. A variety of government paper engaging a wide array of funds circulated at considerable discounts. War was only one cause of this bankrupt condition. It aggravated a basic tendency of the Old Regime monarchy, which, in the words of Marcel Marion, "administered its affairs as grand seigneurs administered their patrimony, with prodigality and carelessness" – obviously a problem with which the new Finance Council was ill equipped to deal.[3] The conversion of state debts into interest-bearing annuities, the disallowance of many debts accompanied by the terrorizing of creditors and a debasement of the coinage had by the end of 1717 reduced the national debt from 3,300 million to just over 2,000 million.[4]

Given the circumstances, we should feel no surprise that the Regent was susceptible to a beguiling plan of fiscal and monetary reform put together by the Scottish card-sharp, adventurer, and monetary theorist John Law. That Law should conceive a banking project of revolutionary character and vast scale was not in itself so unusual. This was the beginning of a great century of promoters.[5] France had already had experience of Vauban and of Boisguillebert, who "said repeatedly that if his schemes were adopted the financial and economic ills of France would be cured in a few hours."[6] And *polysynodie*, what was that but the Regent's own *système*? Law's plan for a central bank and its implementation have never ceased to elicit controversy. Placed in the context of its time, the plan astonishes us by its penetration and audacity. It cannot be denied to Law that "in short, he conceived the first co-ordinated 'system' of economic expansion, the first 'general theory' in the Keynesian meaning of the term," while at the same time one recognizes that his theories were a "mixture of correct perceptions and illusions."[7] It was Law's view that the quantity of money available determined the volume of economic activity; an increase in the quantity of money in circulation would increase the volume of transactions, the total of production, and the level of employment. The mechanism for this was the falling rate of interest. As Law considered the value of money to be symbolic rather than intrinsic, he recommended the use of paper money rather than gold or silver. A bank of issue was the beachhead from which Law would attack the fiscal

problems of the state by centralizing the government's financial operations and taking over payment of the national debt. Law also envi-
sioned equality of taxation (as had Vauban and Boisguillebert), the
abolition of taxes hindering circulation of goods and money, the abolition of privately owned offices and of tax farming.[8]

Thus began the remarkable adventure of the *système*. By letters
patent of May 2, 1716, Law was authorized to create the Banque
générale, which offered banknotes in exchange for government promissory notes, thus retiring the debt. This ingenious but dubious scheme
was a popular success. On December 14, 1718, the bank became a
state institution under the name Banque royale. In the meantime, Law
had undertaken a second scheme with the same immediate end in
view of retiring the national debt. This was the founding of the Occident Company in August 1717, to take in hand the colonizing of
Louisiana.[9] The Mississippi colony had been one result of Louis XIV's
imperialist designs in North America. But its history had thus far been
one of vegetation. True to Old Regime form, in 1712 Pontchartrain
had turned it over to an entrepreneur, Antoine Crozat, in the hope that
Crozat would develop it in the interest of his own profits. Crozat had
found Louisiana a drain on his resources and suggested, as did many
others, that it should be put into the hands of a joint-stock company,
the shares of which could be purchased with government promissory
notes. It fell to Law to put together such a company, which received
the monopoly of trade with Louisiana and the proprietorship of its
lands and mines, all for twenty-five years. Designated tax farms and
the monopoly of the Canadian beaver export were added to provide it
with a capital fund, while a monopoly of the Guinea slave trade was
intended to complement the economic needs of the new colony. The
company excited much good will, but it could not amass a sufficient
capital to colonize Louisiana, nor could it and the bank together retire
the national debt. Hence a remarkable series of stock issues and market
manipulations, a shameless propaganda campaign on the virtues of
Louisiana, and the spectacular corporate mergers and takeovers engineered by Law to increase the strength of his company and his control
over it.

The Occident Company had taken over the beaver monopoly from
Néret and Gayot in July and the Senegal Company in December 1718.
The China Company and the East India Company followed in May
1719, when the Occident Company became the Compagnie perpétuale
des Indes (the Indies Company). The opposition of the Farmers General,
themselves a "rudimentary state bank,"[10] to Law's schemes led him to
buy up the minting privilege and take over the lease of the tax farms
for the Indies Company, which was to enjoy its monopoly until 1770.

Law became Controller General on January 5, 1720, and on February 22 he merged his bank with the company. Under the impetus of these events, speculation mounted to a frenzy, and stock prices reached absurd levels. Foreseeing the inevitable bursting of the speculative bubble, Law took steps to reduce the speculation that he had unleashed. Heavy-handed methods that included twenty-six monetary manipulations destroyed all confidence. On November 1 banknotes ceased to have currency, and in December Law fled France for Brussels. Theoretical errors, imprudent banking practices, the use of falsehood and force, the opposition of financiers, and the naïveté of the public all combined to bring about disaster. The national debt was neither increased nor reduced. But in the easy-money period of 1716-19, with interest as low as 2 per cent, a great burden of private debt was paid off, and both trade and industry experienced fresh starts, the revivifying effects having been clearly discerned in Rouen, Nantes, and far-away Marseilles. Certainly, there was no return to the dolorous state of France at the beginning of the Regency.

The victim of an already inflated colonial currency, Canada did not share the financial state of grace France enjoyed until the collapse of the *système* unleashed a new inflation in 1720. In that year Canadian merchants and merchants trading to Canada found themselves with quantities of worthless banknotes in hand. They were soon complaining of the rapid increase in the cost of French manufactures, which placed them at an even greater disadvantage than usual in the competitive trade with the Indians.[11] The most important result of the Mississippi Bubble for Canada, as for France, was long term and negative. The experience destroyed confidence in banks and banknotes and thus retarded business modernization and more particularly government finance, which fell back upon its antique system of tax farming. Reform *manqué* was worse than no reform at all, and it is not farfetched to see links connecting Law's failure to the financial chaos of the ensuing hundred years and the loss of Canada by a bankrupt state in 1763. Another important result for the history of Canada was the fillip given the development of Louisiana. Many concessionaires, as well as Law's company, recruited the poor, the crippled, or the criminal for the colony, much as Roberval had done for Canada nearly two centuries before. The Indies Company had two corps of recruiting troops that aroused horror by their press-gang activities, fully supported by Church and State. With purchased Swiss, German, and Italian immigrants, Law founded forty villages of twenty families each. Thus was Canada's sister colony on the Mississippi developed by the most expedient and often brutal methods for ends entirely mercantile.[12]

The *système* left behind it the Indies Company, with a fleet of over a hundred ships, considerable assets, and an active, ongoing trade.[13] It had inherited the beaver *exclusif* from the Occident Company, but by a decree of May 16, 1720, this was converted into customs duties on beaver entering France that were payable to the company.[14] At the same time, the government forbade the export of beaver to foreign countries. The plan pleased no one. Canadian and Rochelais traders welcomed the freeing of the trade but claimed they could neither give good prices to the Indians and still pay the tax nor receive good prices for the furs in France as long as prohibition of export left the Paris hatters in control of the market. Vaudreuil and Bégon supported their contentions. The Farmers General revealed that the beaver trade would be double taxed under the new scheme, since they already collected customs duties under the tariff of 1664. The Deputies of Commerce declared the tax burden insupportable. Thereupon, the government reversed its stand and on May 30, 1721, re-established the monopoly! Its response to the predictable hue and cry was to suspend the new decree and ask for more information. All the arguments against monopoly were again rehearsed, but the monopoly was confirmed by a definitive decree of January 28, 1722. To meet traders' complaints, the price of *castor sec* payable at the company's office at Quebec was raised from thirty-four sous to two livres the pound and that of *castor gras* from three livres to four. Canadian and Rochelais traders, observing events from the outside in – and up – saw corruption as the only explanation. It is indeed a striking example of the Indies Company's almost effortless exertion of influence. "Canada must be thought utterly stupid and blind," wrote Mme Pascaud, the La Rochelle merchant, "if it is imagined that without knowing why and after having lost considerable sums on banknotes received in payment last summer, it will still confide its property to the care of this company."[15] She predicted that rather than send their beaver to France, Canadians would hide it in the woods until such time as they could smuggle it to Albany. The decree stood, but the widow was right; and in the years that followed an increasing volume of beaver fur entered the contraband trade. It was once again an example of Regency reform *manqué*.

Meanwhile, the Marine Council that had replaced Pontchartrain settled the question of Canadian paper money. The minutes of April 12, 1717, record three decisions. First, there were to be no more cards issued except for the expenses of that year. Second, cards were to circulate at half face value, which was indeed their value on the market. Third, the old distinction between money of Canada and money of France was to be abolished. What should always have been clear was now spelled out, that the distinction had "nothing real about it, and, strictly speaking," dwelt "only in the imagination," as prices invariably rose with the nominal increase in the value of money.[16] The council decided that card money could no longer be used because it had lost its credit. These decisions were embodied in a declaration of July 5, 1717, registered at Quebec on October 11.[17] On a theoretical level the council might have accepted cards, and later in the year they sent to Canada printed bill of exchange forms, a convenience that a later intendant, Gilles Hocquart, would ask for again and again without result.[18] The government that swept aside the mass of Canadian paper had in fact an openness towards its use not shared by the government that had produced it.

Financial problems caused the postponement of the redemption of the card money until 1719.[19] In that year, the *Chameau* arrived with a precious cargo: coined money and pay warrants for the expenditures of 1718 and 1719 plus an advance for the expenses of 1720. In addition, there was a shipment of stores valued at over a hundred thousand livres. Thus after the departure of the last vessels of that year, Treasurer Gaudion's clerk, Monsieur Petit, was able at last to turn his attention to the tallying up of all the turned-in cards.[20] Only the bookkeeping remained. Canada moved into a new period of its monetary history, the paper-free interlude of 1720-28, a veritable monetary famine after which, once again, the indispensable cards would appear on the scene.

After the Law episode there was, of course, another of the customary, covert bankruptcies by which the national debt was reduced to what it seemed possible to pay. This included the despoilment of a select list of Indies Company shareholders from which high nobles and princes of the blood were carefully excluded. By the end of 1724, the debt was reduced to 1,500 million livres converted into life and perpetual annuities. Having experienced the rough procedures used to reduce the debt in 1717, the public knew better than to complain.[21] It seems that the liquidation of the *système* struck more terror into the hearts of Frenchmen than the *système* itself, for in 1721-22 the Bank of Amsterdam recorded its highest deposits of the period 1600-1800, a result of the momentary flight of French capital.[22]

On February 16, 1723, Louis xv achieved his majority, and the Regency was over. Before the end of the year, Cardinal Dubois and the Duke of Orléans were both dead. There was thus little overlap between the Regency and the new regime headed by the Duke of Bourbon, with financial power in the hands of the man who had been Law's principal opponent, Pâris-Duvernay. Although traditional in his thinking, Pâris-Duvernay was also a reformer. Of his many efforts to improve the finances, only one was fruitful and of long-term significance for France and Canada. This was an attempt to control inflation by returning the *livre tournois* to a proper relation with silver. The nominal value of the livre was decreased through successive decrees from August 1723 to December 1724. This brought the livre's nominal value more or less into line with the market value of the bullion it represented. Financial pressures were responsible for inflationary increases in nominal value in January and May 1726, but by then good times made further manipulation unnecessary; and long-term stabilization of the coinage was the result.[23] In June 1726, the Duke of Bourbon was dismissed by the King. Bourbon had become unpopular for many reasons, not the least of which was his attempt to impose a system of equitable taxation on the privileged classes. The remainder of the period covered by this study is dominated by Louis XV's teacher, the Cardinal Fleury (a prime minister in all but name), and by two controllers general, Le Pelletier Desforts (1726-30) and Philibert Orry (1730-45). Under Le Pelletier Desforts, the Farmers General plundered the state treasury.[24] They had no such opportunities under Orry. From March 1730 until December 1745, one must imagine in the background of Canadian history this man with "more good sense than imagination . . . the conviction that the first rule of financial administration was economy. . . ."[25] French finances were never better in the entire Old Regime than in the years 1736 to 1744 in spite of the demands of the wars of the Polish Succession, 1733-36, and Austrian Succession, beginning in 1740.[26] Much thanks were due to Orry, but he was himself the beneficiary of a new economic climate.

The depression of 1650-80, coinciding with Colbert's struggle for economic improvement, had been the worst years of a century of economic stagnation.[27] In the advanced economies of England and Holland, there was a marked reversal of the trend after 1680, and there was some indication of renovation in France as well: a much-increased trade with the Far East and considerable activity in the Atlantic ports, enough to inspire France's enemies to a war on her commercial fleet. French businessmen were confident and expansive at the turn of the century and favoured the acceptance of the Spanish succession that increased the possibilities of their trade in the Spanish Empire. This dynamism was not destroyed by the war effort but subsisted in the "great hospital, desolate and unprovided"[28] that, as Fénelon would have it, France had become by 1693. Pierre Goubert has pictured the condition of France at the death of Louis XIV as one in which productive forces were waiting, ready to accept the challenge of improved conditions.[29] The stabilization of the livre in 1726 and the upward turn of prices in 1733, both having their counterparts throughout Europe, marked the reversal of the trend, the metamorphosis of the seventeenth-century world into that of the eighteenth.[30]

The economic growth of the eighteenth century stands in remarkable contrast to the grim realities that had preceded it. In the seventeenth century, markets had remained small and inelastic, equipment and institutions of trade minimal, while difficult weather conditions had exacerbated the problem of feeding the people, limiting population growth. The contrast with the eighteenth century is dramatic. For example, the glutted market for Canadian beaver in the seventeenth may be compared with the relatively trouble-free marketing of beaver in the eighteenth, a pattern repeated with regard to sugar and other exotic commodities. There was evidently an expanding market, probably explained by greater wealth in better distribution and better marketing techniques, something of which we know next to nothing. The fortuitous improvement of the climate and better grain prices caused a modest increase in agricultural output, which, combined with the transfer of money to the countryside by putting-out manufacturers, permitted an increase in the population. All indications point to France's trade and a related increase in industrial output, especially after 1730, as the dynamic elements.[31]

Behind this was a great increase in the import of bullion. Most of the seventeenth century was a hiatus between the early bullion imports from Mexico and Peru and the discovery of gold in Brazil after 1680, which influenced England via Portugal, and of silver in Mexico after 1710, affecting France because of its trade with Cadiz. The flow of metal was a life-giving stream; but it flowed because its increasing price made men search for it, and the European economy was sufficiently dynamic to attract it, just as the supply had dried up after 1620 when its price was lowest and as Spain collapsed and ceased to have power to attract bullion or to organize the search for it. France also witnessed a considerable and rapid expansion of fiduciary paper that helped to answer the needs of trade. The dynamics of development thus appear to have been the new availability of bullion and secondary means of payment coupled with a great complex of psychological and physical factors that might best be described as a capacity to need money.[32]

Beginning in the 1720s, but following earlier indications, there was thus a great revival of commerce, marked by the eastern trade of the Indies Company and by the rise of the trade of the Atlantic ports with the sugar islands and Canada. From the imperial point of view, Canada's part was modest; from the Canadian point of view, the creation of this context of prosperity was crucial. For the generation after Utrecht, it was the envelope of Canadian existence. But with the revival of trade came its concomitant, an intensification of Anglo-French rivalry.

The hostility of France and Great Britain has been described as the most persistent, stable characteristic of eighteenth-century Europe.[33] The growing economic competition, the striking ideological divergence, the very nearness to one another of these two countries reinforced this traditional rivalry. Yet the years of the reclamation of empire that were so beneficial to Canada were made possible by the alliance of France with Great Britain and the peace that it procured. Frenchmen wanted a Spanish alliance; anything else seemed to make nonsense of the War of the Spanish Succession, but two things prevented it. The first was Philip v's willingness to replace Orléans as regent and even to accept the crown if Louis xv, a delicate five-year-old, should die. This raised the prospect of civil war, since a great many Frenchmen supported Philip in his pretensions. Secondly, Spanish foreign policy soon fell into the hands of Philip's wife, Elizabeth Farnese, who was willing to undertake any political adventure to settle Italian duchies on her two sons. France would have followed the bizarre paths Elizabeth Farnese traced out at its peril. On the other hand, Great Britain had as much need of peace as did France. The Jacobite rebellion (September 10, 1715, to February 5, 1716) had just been put down, and the Hanoverian dynasty was by no means secure. A general Anglo-French agreement was worked out at Hanover in October, 1716. In the fifteen years that followed, it was this union of great rivals, driving "in tandem" with "constant competition as to which should be the leader," that dominated Europe.[34]

Yet Frenchmen continued to feel that a Spanish alliance was the natural one. Orléans had attempted to secure it in 1721 by betrothing Louis xv to the Infanta. His successor at the helm of affairs, the Duke of Bourbon, fearing that Louis xv might die before his child bride had produced an heir, returned her to her outraged parents in 1726 and married Louis to a Polish princess. The resulting family quarrel was eventually patched up by his successor, Cardinal Fleury. Together with his English counterpart, Robert Walpole, Fleury maintained the English alliance and hence the peace long after the original dynastic motive had been eclipsed by the birth of a dauphin (1729). He also continued to woo the Spanish sovereigns and negotiated the first Franco-Spanish Bourbon "Family Compact" in 1733. The Anglo-French alliance was over and done, but the peace held even after war had broken out between Great Britain and Spain in 1739. It lasted, indeed, until British attacks on the French merchant marine and a general European war, which brought with it British interference with French policy in Germany, made its continuance impossible. When that happened, in 1744, a generation of peace and of social and economic development in Canada came to an end, and the train of events was unleashed that led to the fall of New France.

The administration of Cardinal Fleury, the stingy, canny old man who took office in 1726 at the age of seventy-three, stood for peace, economy, and trade.[35] There was, of course, nothing new in solicitude for trade. It characterized the administration of Colbert and was particularly marked from the beginning of the new century, when the government began the renovation of its institutions of economic management. A decree of June 29, 1700, created a Conseil (later Bureau) de Commerce to co-ordinate the policies of the Marine and the Contrôle Général and provide continuity of policy. Deputies from the great trading cities constituted one element of this advisory body, and chambers of commerce were established to elect them – for example, at Rouen in 1703, Bordeaux in 1705, and La Rochelle in 1710.[36] The Bureau de la Balance du Commerce was founded in 1713 to monitor the level of imports and exports. The Regency made two notable contributions to maritime trade legislation. Letters patent of April 1717 consolidated a mass of earlier customs legislation governing trade in the American empire, including all the exemptions from duties and other privileges. A further decree of December 11 specified that the edict applied to Canada and not just to the West Indies. A complementary *règlement* of January 12, 1717, provided for the establishing of admiralty courts with jurisdiction over maritime trade in the major colonial ports, the court at Quebec being established in 1719.[37] In 1717 the Marine Council granted permission to Quebec merchants to meet as a body on matters of mutual concern and to lobby the government.[38] It was a manifestation of the same spirit that created the chambers of commerce. In 1727 the Fleury administration produced new letters patent intended to stop contraband trade within the empire, a landmark statute. The following year, it renewed and improved the system of *classes maritimes* that provided a continuous supply of sailors for the navy.[39]

After Utrecht, few denied the equation of trade with national power. But France had not the freedom of England that came from the complete identification of the latter's national interest with its navy and maritime trade. French policy, like that of the Dutch, was marked by a division of money and interest between trade and security. No doubt there were plenty of Frenchmen, especially nobles, critical of Fleury's pacific policies and hot for war. But the age saw the decline of *la gloire* as a major aim of foreign policy and was perfectly conscious of it: witness Dutot's clarion cry, "Away, then, with those victories acquired by ruinous efforts! Let glory rest!"[40] The gift of the great peace was economic growth, particularly evident in maritime trade, with the greatest rate of increase in colonial trade.

The wars of France and England between 1688 and 1713 had made it impossible for French overseas trade to enjoy sustained growth. But activity in the peaceful interlude 1698-1701 had been such that the merchant marine was slightly larger in 1701 than in 1688, 763 ocean-going ships as opposed to 750. According to Voltaire, there were only

300 big merchantmen left in France at the arrival of John Law, but the number had increased prodigiously to 1,800 by 1738, the eve of the War of Jenkins's Ear.[41] That these figures are half statistic, half guesswork is true, but the general impression they give is trustworthy. The same may be said of the estimated values of trade, the total of French imports and exports.

The trade figures with the greatest claim to accuracy are those of the Bureau de la Balance du Commerce. These record an increase from 87 million livres in 1716 to 263 million in 1720, a figure influenced by both the inflation and the increased activity of the Law period. The figure for 1726, the beginning of the era of stable money, is 200 million livres, and this increased to 300 million in 1739. For the period 1716 to 1739, the increase was nearly three and a half times.[42] Colonial trade with "America" – Canada and Louisbourg included but primarily the French West Indies – is estimated to have multiplied about six or seven times, from a high of 25 million livres for the reign of Louis XIV, through a drop to 20 million just after Utrecht, to 140 or 150 million in 1739-44.[43] When it is considered that a very large part of French exports were really re-exports of colonial produce and that these re-exports are thought to have multiplied by eight between Utrecht and the Revolution, it is clear that colonial trade was the leading edge of commercial expansion and probably of economic growth in general. As Frédéric de Maurepas, Minister of Marine, argued in a memorandum of 1745:

> The great number of ships and seamen employed in it, the multitude of merchants, labourers, winegrowers and tradesmen of all kinds that it occupies, the abundance of money that it attracts to the Kingdom and causes to circulate therein, are an inestimable boon, providing a livelihood for some, enriching others and increasing the King's revenues. Indubitably, these revenues have increased considerably in proportion with the increase in colonial trade, which consequently is the principal cause of their augmentation.[44]

In England the growth of French trade from a very low level to a position equal with that of England was seen as cause for alarm. England temporarily experienced a drop in its trade with its own colonies, which hit bottom in 1731-35, thereafter increasing steadily. English exports to all countries dropped alarmingly from £13.5 million in 1735 to £9 million in 1740. Competition from France was sharply felt in India, in the woollens trade to the Levant and Portugal, in the success of the Ile Royale fishery, and most particularly in the loss of England's sugar markets in Europe.[45] There was, of course, constant fear that the reconciliation of the French and Spanish branches of the

House of Bourbon might result in the French being granted special trading rights in the Spanish empire while those of the British were cancelled. The tone of Sir Matthew Decker's *Essay on the Causes of the Decline of the Foreign Trade*, published in 1740, is an accurate reflection of a large and influential body of English opinion and its nervous, aggressive spirit: "Because the Incumbrances on our Trade at present have given the French so much the Start of us in times of Peace . . . War seems absolutely necessary to obstruct their growing Power."[46]

II

The various jurisdictions over ports, ships, galleys, maritime trade, and colonies had been brought together under a single jurisdiction by Colbert in the creation of the State Secretariat of the Marine on March 7, 1669.[47] It was from the offices of this department on the Rue des Bons Enfants at Versailles that the destinies of Canada were governed. It had been a creaking and irrational structure, this first bureaucracy, divided into its sections of Ponant, Levant, and Funds, with Canada and the West Indies governed by different offices. The jurisdictional boundaries between the Marine and the Contrôle Général regarding expenditures and trade had only been definitively drawn on September 13, 1699, when it had been determined that the two departments, which had twice been held by the same person, would be permanently separated. The Marine had been given jurisdiction over the commercial affairs of colonies, the defence of their territory, general instructions to governors, and details of their interior administration, but had lost jurisdiction over the tariff and over chartered trading companies. This was the status of the ministry under Jérôme de Pontchartrain. On January 1, 1710, he reorganized the department, creating a colonial office (*bureau des colonies*) under its own chief clerk, or *premier commis*. By 1715 there were four distinct offices, each with its chief clerk, and the number had grown to eight by 1740, with a complete staff of probably no more than fifty. A civil service thus provided continuity of administration from the last days of Louis XIV through the Regency, when the minister was replaced by the Marine Council, to the return to the old system with the nomination of the Count of Morville as Secretary of State for the Marine on March 23, 1723, followed in office on August 14 by Maurepas, who was Pontchartrain's son.

The chief clerks, who might be compared to modern Canadian deputy ministers, were individuals of great power and wide influence. They were granted patents of nobility, generous salaries and bonuses, wielded power and patronage, and followed the court. Historians have pointed out but so far scarcely investigated the importance of the chief clerks: Monsieur de La Touche of the Bureau du Ponant until July 1, 1709, and subsequently the chief clerks of the newly created Colonial Office, Augustin Moise de Fontanieu, November 23, 1710, to February 3, 1725; Pierre de Forcade to June 17, 1738; and Arnaud de Laporte to January 27, 1758. It has been argued that after Jérôme de Pontchartrain it was they who really controlled colonial affairs, although it is scarcely credible to argue that the Count of Toulouse, head of the short-lived Marine Council, or Maurepas, the latter with a particularly long tenure of office, did not play a significant role in policy formation.[48]

While Canada and the West Indies were never more important to France than in the first half of the eighteenth century, the Department of Marine was then relatively neglected. In Chapter 4 we have already seen how underfinanced the department was during the War of the Spanish Succession and how the Treasurers General of the Marine, supposedly accountants handling funds received from the Controller General, were reduced (or as it turned out, promoted) to finding money on their own credit and advancing it at interest to the department. Thus debts never grew old; they just grew. The financial chaos ran through the Marine offices, the fleet, and to Canada and the other colonies. After Utrecht, this department in particular was subjected to the pruning knife. Its annual *prévision*, which had been 14 million livres a year during the war, was reduced in 1716 to an unheard-of 8.5, this being increased to 9 in 1725. Two and a half million of this was for colonies. For the next fifty years, the navy could not even put a ship to sea without calling upon "extraordinary" funds that depended upon the good will, first of the Finance Council, and later of the restored Controller General. For some years between 1715 and 1739 that meant no sailing at all. The level of naval expenditures for this period can be compared with that of the 1650s, although after 1739 it was increased under the threat of war. Undoubtedly, the Marine Department was denied money it wanted and needed, not only for the navy but for colonial development.[49] It was from this distorted view at the centre of empire that stemmed the entire through-the-looking-glass character of colonial finances so important in the Canadian history of the period. Of course, the financial exigencies and continental defence commitments of France must be weighed in the balance. The Duke of Newcastle saw this clearly when he wrote of his country's enemy, "France will outdo us at sea, when they have nothing to fear by land."[50]

The Regency's reduction of the Marine department's *prévision* was partly a result of penury, partly of policy, a policy aimed at conciliating England. It ought not to obscure for us that the Marine Council was a body of real talent. Its chief, the Count of Toulouse, had inherited the bureaucratic taste of his father, Louis XIV. Methodical, hardworking, disinterested, honest, he presided over Marine policy until 1723. The council became imbued with his own spirit and had as its stated policy the "aggrandizement" of colonies. Colonial administration was to be made more uniform and regular. To this end, surveillance over colonial officials was increased by encouraging denunciations from subordinates and requiring naval commanders to report on colonial justice in their ships' logs. The uniform currency of money throughout the empire, the new seats of admiralty, new legislation, and masses of documents collected to pinpoint needs for reform are all indications tions of this. Engineers were sent to the colonies to draw up plans for improved fortifications, which were henceforth to be of stone. Efforts were made to improve the conditions of the troops. But in spite of talent and enthusiasm, the results of the council's work were meagre. There was a ruthless streak in the new administration. Gone were the humanitarian dicta that peppered the correspondence of Jérôme de Pontchartrain. In pursuing a "utilitarian policy," the council agreed to the forcible emigration of salt smugglers, vagabonds, foundlings, and libertines whose families had lost patience with them. Some vagabonds and foundlings were enrolled in the troops sent to Canada, also a favourite post for recaptured army deserters.[51]

Frédéric de Maurepas held the office of Secretary of State for the Marine from 1723 to 1749: twenty-six years, including half the period covered by the present work. He was only twenty-two when he took office but had been associated with the work of the department since he was fifteen. At the outset, he may or may not have been, as a detractor described him in 1725, "a young man . . . with a good mind who has very good intentions but wouldn't recognize the sea if he saw it."[52] In the course of his ministry he revealed considerable ability in many areas. To intelligence and a phenomenal memory, a taste for work, and complete honesty he joined the considerable charm and finesse that enabled him to survive so long at the court of Louis XV. On the debit side, his pleasant amiability degenerated into frivolity, often quite out of place, a characteristic that caused many contemporaries and historians since to mistake his measure.[53] Maurepas understood the great importance of the navy and the colonies in French affairs and never ceased to plead the case of his penurious department. But he never succeeded in obtaining substantial increases in the Marine *prévision*. He was responsible for scientific expeditions; he advanced naval construction and improvement in medicine and cartography. But while his best qualities appear in the realm of policy and advocacy, he was not a tough administrator. During his tenure, the Marine offices were marked by corruption and incompetence, the navy by indiscipline.

Maurepas was no less a mercantilist than Colbert, only less dogmatic than Jérôme de Pontchartrain. But the dogmas had changed. The economic *raison d'être* of empire remained, and Maurepas's view of the *pacte colonial* was rigid. There is no better evidence of this continuity than the Letters Patent of 1727, which reiterated legislation of 1670, 1698, and 1720 prohibiting foreigners from trading within the empire and adumbrating precautions to be taken to that end. The scheme apparently originated with the Bureau de Commerce – a council of officials and businessmen that advised the government on trade matters – as did the tax of one-half per cent on colonial trade that was intended to provide bonuses to colonial officials successful in enforcing the new regulations.[54] But within the framework of the *pacte coloniale*, Maurepas aligned himself with what was becoming the prevalent view, that commerce must be free: "Regulation should be occasional, temporary and only when absolutely necessary"; "Encouragement is the only method that can be used, and success waits upon time and the industry of men."[55] What a contrast to the homilies that left the Marine offices in earlier days! But to an even greater extent than his father, who always paid heed to moral considerations, Maurepas was a protagonist not for colonies but for the possession of colonies, not of colonials but of metropolitan traders.[56] He understood that through multiplier effects colonial trade had a profound influence on the French economy; indeed, in 1745 he declared it the most important single factor contributing to the kingdom's economic growth.[57] But given the colonies' need for a strong parent state – this was especially true of Canada and Ile Royale – Maurepas was in effect their advocate vis-à-vis an administration always in danger of losing sight of them. Maurepas's attention was particularly drawn to Canada because to enforce the Letters Patent of 1727 some substitute for the illegal trade of the Lesser Antilles with the English colonies had to be found. The department's outward correspondence during the Maurepas years abounds with exhortations that intercolonial trade be stepped up, in particular that the shipment of Canadian wood, flour, peas, and horses to Martinique in return for molasses and tafia replace the illegal trade of the island with New England. Tariff exemptions were provided to encourage the desired traffic.

The administration of Maurepas coincided with the term of office (1729 to 1748) of one of the ablest Canadian intendants, Gilles Hocquart. It was Hocquart's misfortune, along with that of a new bishop, Pierre-Herman Dosquet, to be shipwrecked in the lower St Lawrence when the ship *Eléphant* ran upon a rock on September 1, 1729. When he clambered ashore from a boat a few days later at Quebec, short, fat, and wheezing and probably not looking his best, his welcomers might well have underestimated the man they were getting. The son of a Marine bureaucrat and himself a paid bureaucrat since the age of twelve, Hocquart was a man of experience. He was also diligent, intelligent, and a politician. It was not immediately apparent that he had any imagination or that he was to be the creator of great projects of economic development. What was probably known of him, and what was very soon apparent, was that he was a first-rate accountant. After the purposefully loose bookkeeping of Bégon and the chaos twice confounded left by Bégon's successor, Claude-Thomas Dupuy, an accountant was in order.[58]

During the Maurepas-Hocquart administration Canadian finances assumed their definitive form. One element of this was the transfer of the *Domaine* in Canada to the Marine on August 5, 1732, effective September 1, 1733. Thus it ceased to be a tax farm. But within the structure of government bookkeeping it retained its identity, taking its Canadian staff into the royal bureaucracy.[59] More important was the department's attempt to deal with the Canadian monetary crisis by authorizing, beginning in September 1730, a constant circulation of 400,000 livres in card money and the annual redemption of 250,000 livres of cards with drafts on the Treasurers General of the Marine. The total circulation was increased to 600,000 in 1733 and to 720,000 in 1742, while the ceiling on drafts was raised to 350,000 a year in 1735.[60] Although in the past the issue of cards had invariably been an expedient to find relief from an impossible financial situation, the new arrangement was seen at first solely as an improvement of the monetary system.[61] But the chronic underfinancing of Canadian government by the Marine naturally affected the question of monetary policy. The system was no sooner established than Hocquart and the new governor, Charles de Beauharnois, appointed in 1726, were asking permission to issue more cards and were using a new fiduciary money that escaped the direct control of their superiors, the *ordonnances* or *orders* on the treasury at Quebec.[62] Government promissory notes and government receipts for goods and services accepted but not paid for circulated alongside the orders and cards. Throughout the period, the cover in bills of exchange became increasingly smaller in comparison to the paper in circulation.

In 1731 Beauharnois and Hocquart had issued 60,000 livres in cards beyond the authorized level to pay the troops and men working on the Montreal fortifications, but they had been required to retire these cards and burn them. Orders were the obvious answer to a ceiling on cards, and in 1733 the Governor and Intendant issued an ordinance obliterating the distinction between cards and orders, which they said was "being made only by ill-informed persons."[63] It was Hocquart's view that if orders, receipts, and notes were not given a common standing with cards, the feebleness of the treasury would become evident, and the credit of paper money as such would decline.[64] By the expedient of drawing bills against the funds of a following year, a growing burden of debt was being thrust into the future.

The demands of Canadian administrators for more cards and greater drawing privileges were justified in terms of the colonial economy's need for a larger money supply, but this was a kind of code. Administrators simply wanted more to spend themselves and knew that direct appeals for budget increases fell on deaf ears. Flooding the marketplace with orders, receipts, and notes also facilitated a blackmail tactic from Canada. "There is nothing I wish as much, My Lord, as to see this multiplicity of paper abolished," Hocquart wrote to Maurepas in 1741. "You should permit us to make an issue of 120,000 livres of new card money."[65] This was one of the few times that Maurepas agreed. While his ordinance authorizing the issue of 1742 featured the usual arguments about the good of trade, his private letter to Hocquart explained, "but it is particularly for restoring easy conditions in the colonial treasury and thus putting you in a position to restore order" that the increase had been made.[66] Far from restoring order, Beauharnois and Hocquart soon reported "with pain" that the increase in their budget (which is what a new issue of cards was) had all been spent; the deficit for 1739 to 1741 superseded the value of the new issue. They suggested another issue – or rather they stated that they would not dare suggest it, which is the same thing.[67] A few days later they admitted resorting to promissory notes throughout 1742 and that they had few cards left to finance their operations for the next twelve months.[68]

The Marine Department never came to grips with the budgetary and monetary problems of Canada. Its hectoring correspondence unaccompanied by substantial reforms was no solution. In Canada financial turmoil remained a considerable brake upon the reclamation of empire. Of course, the Canadian predicament was only a minor manifestation of the financial problems faced by the French government at home. And these were part of the illness of a regime that could not heal itself.

Maurepas, looking back on these years in 1745, saw two particular reasons why the Marine continued to be neglected after the end of the Regency.[69] The first was the obvious one, that the controllers general had had no wish to increase its budget, given the great financial problem with which they daily struggled. The second, a debatable one that ties up a final strand in this survey of imperial outreach, was the existence of an alternative navy operated by the Indies Company.

Control over the company had fallen into the hands of career administrators answerable directly to the Controller General. It was almost a
department of government. Its officers and men were therefore more
experienced than those of the navy proper; and because of the company's sovereign role in India, its ships were large vessels equipped for
military purposes. The ships and men were available to the state in
time of war. In effect, the Controller General had his own navy.[70] It is
a telling example of how in the Old Regime policy was shaped, and
inevitably deformed, by various expedients, precluding rational, overall
planning.

*   *   *

The story of the reclamation of empire is a chapter in the history of
mercantilism. The theme easily accommodates the histories of Saint-
Domingue, Martinique, Guadeloupe, the other, smaller French West
Indian islands, and even Ile Royale, the centre of the fishery. The sugar
islands' greatest prosperity began in this period and reached such
dizzy heights in the second half of the eighteenth century as to make
them quite impervious to anticolonial arguments. Their growth could
only enhance the importance of the fishery. It was quite otherwise
with Canada, or for that matter with Louisiana. That Canada increased
in prosperity between 1701 and 1744 is certainly true. Maurepas and
Hocquart bent their best efforts to make Canada capable of fulfilling
the role assigned it in the imperial economy. But in mercantilist terms,
Canada remained a frustration, a colony that always fell short of the
promise it seemed to hold. Its role in the story of empire, which was
only beginning to be appreciated, was to be not so much economic as
political. In the War of the Spanish Succession Canada had been swept
into the vortex of the Anglo-French struggle for the empire of trade
and colonies. It was a strategic area, the possession of which conferred
an advantage over the neighbouring English colonies. In this lay its
ultimate contribution and sacrifice.

CHAPTER 6

Utrecht and Acadia, 1713-1744

I

In June, 1713, the court was at Rambouillet. From there Pontchartrain wrote to Vaudreuil and Bégon that he found no papers regarding the borders of Acadia among their most recent dispatches. They were to search out evidence that would limit it at the St Croix River or even to the peninsula. Their opinions on the matter were welcomed.

The response from Canada was a long memorandum and a map. The latter was the work of Joseph Aubery, an experienced Jesuit missionary among the Abenakis, and the paper was either his alone or written jointly with Bégon. It argued that the ceded province had to be confined to the peninsula terminating in the Isthmus of Chignecto because the continental coastline from Beaubassin to the Kennebec could not be given up without exposing Canada to invasion. The rivers emptying into the Atlantic rose in the highlands so close to the St Lawrence that a border based on the height of land principle would bring the English frontier dangerously close to the river's south shore. Equally important, were the French to withdraw from this area, the Abenakis would be won over by the English and inevitably become enemies to Canada. To forestall this, the Abenakis would have to be declared French subjects by the commissioners to be appointed under Articles 10 and 15 of the Treaty of Utrecht.[1] These Indians regarded themselves as independent and their territory as their own. This was not a notion that came easily to Europeans, although its usefulness would become apparent.

What *was* the Acadia that had been given up at Utrecht? The distinction between Canada and Acadia had been of small importance when both were French, the Governor of Acadia was the subordinate of the Governor of Canada, and Acadia was thought of primarily as a coastline, the vast territory between the Atlantic and the St Lawrence being *terra incognita* to most Europeans. Early governors' commissions show that Canada was conceived of primarily as the St Lawrence drainage

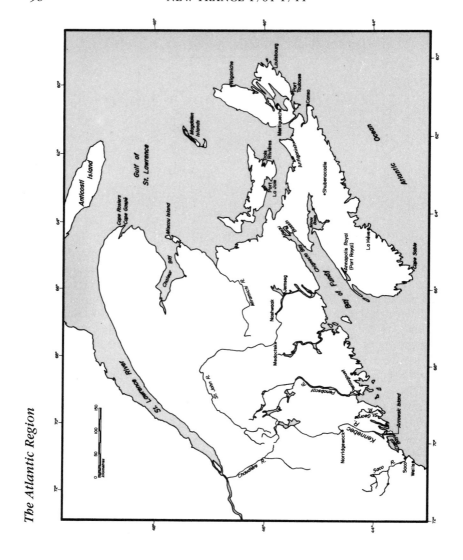

The Atlantic Region

basin and the Gulf of St Lawrence. Definitions of Acadia in seventeenth-century documents are vague and variable, but there is no doubt that it was held to include both continental and peninsular components. Its coastline was variously described as running, in the north, from Cape des Rosiers, Cape Gaspé, Percé, or Miscou south to the Kennebec, a major river and a natural frontier with New England. Cape Breton and Ile Saint-Jean were included, and it was a major triumph of French diplomacy at London and Utrecht that the English did not understand this.[2]

In 1670 Acadia had been returned to France in accordance with Article 10 of the Treaty of Breda after some fifteen years in English possession. Its English proprietor, Sir Thomas Temple, in the tradition of his French predecessors, had accepted the Kennebec as his western boundary. But Massachusetts had not agreed, and eventually Temple had withdrawn the border to the St George, a smaller river that at one point comes very near the Kennebec, making it possible to draw the boundary along the St George to this point and then to transfer it to the larger river. It had been a good compromise. Both the English Act of Cession (1670) and the Temple-Grandfontaine Treaty (1670), named for the retiring English and incoming French governors, limited specific mentions to the names of the forts being transferred: Pentagouet, St John, Port Royal, Cape Sable, and La Hève. Although the boundary had not been named, Grandfontaine had clearly understood that he had acquired Acadia with its frontier at the St George.[3]

In 1700 this new border came its closest to acceptance by way of two independent initiatives. The boundary commission meeting in London pursuant to the Treaty of Ryswick agreed on the St George in principle, but a definitive final agreement was prevented by continued dispute over the fishery. At the St George itself, in a more concrete action, De Villieu, "commandant in Acadia," met, under orders from Callière, with Captain Sandrick, delegate of the Governor of Massachusetts; together they raised the arms of France and England on a point of land in the mouth of the river.[4] Had it not been for the fall of Port Royal in 1710, this boundary settlement would probably have been consecrated by treaty, but the cession of Acadia put all in flux again. The French were once more tempted to think of the Kennebec as the boundary – no longer as the boundary of Acadia, which was to be confined to the peninsula, but of an ill-defined French sphere of influence.

London talks on the implementation of the Anglo-French commercial treaty began early in 1714, but the death of Queen Anne on August 12 revolutionized British politics and temporarily sundered the delicate Anglo-French connection. While the death of Louis XIV and the careful diplomacy of Cardinal Dubois brought about rapprochement and even alliance, colonial affairs constantly strained relations. The earliest postwar incident was the Canso affair of September 1718. Under instructions from Governor Samuel Shute of Massachusetts, Captain Thomas Smart of H.M.S. *Squirrel* expelled French fishermen from the island of Canso on the grounds that it was a dependency of Acadia, taking boats, cargo, and prisoners back to Boston.

In these years the Marine Council, alerted by the Canadian authorities, was also growing alarmed at New England's efforts to settle the coastline of the Abenaki territory, synonymous with a large part of mainland Acadia, by means of land companies. Thus on May 5, 1719, Dubois requested the appointment of British commissioners to consider the American questions.[5] The commissioners met in December, but after a brief British exposition of claims on Hudson Bay, talks were suspended. The French negotiators subsequently collected a vast amount of material on the various questions outstanding. It seems that almost everyone who knew anything about New France became a memorialist: Father Aubery, Cadillac, Riverin, and so on. Father Charlevoix, the Jesuit historian who had once taught at Quebec, laboured ten months on American problems at the request of Dubois and the President of the Marine Council, the Maréchal d'Estrées. The most curious paper was that of the Abbé Jean Bobé, a priest attached to the royal chapel at Versailles and an amateur geographer. With regard to the boundaries of Acadia, Bobé argued: "The Government of Acadia must not be confused with Acadia properly speaking and according to its former limits, which are two very different things. . . . Acadia, not according to its new limits, but according to its old ones, certainly does not include all these lands, but only the southern part of the peninsula."[6] The name *Acadia* in common with the name *Canada* had once referred to a specific locality but with the passage of time had come to signify a whole province. Thus the phrase "with its ancient boundaries," which the English had insisted be used to describe Acadia at Utrecht to prevent French trickery, was turned against them. A general memorandum on Acadian boundaries prepared for the French negotiators explained without expressing a preference both the Bégon-Aubery and the Bobé arguments.[7]

At English insistence there was another meeting of the commission on September 10, 1720.[8] The sole subject of debate was Canso, and the unsuccessful session was followed by a letter from the Regent in which he stated the unalterable French position that Canso Island was not a part of Acadia. In view of continued English settlement along the Abenaki coast, the Marine Council asked Dubois to intervene with the English a second time in 1721. Dubois informed the British govern-

ment that if settlement did not cease, Louis xv "could not refuse protection" to the Abenakis.[9] A reply was to be received by March 1722.
The recipients of this stern diplomatic note made the correct analysis
that it was a bluff, and the deadline passed unheeded.

In other matters the French tried to be conciliatory. French troops
on the disputed West Indian island of St Lucia were evacuated. Indians
who attacked English installations in Acadia, including Canso, were
repudiated, and restitution was promptly made. This was contrasted
with the British fortification of Canso and failure to make restitution
for the pillage of 1718. In 1722 the British Privy Council gave £800 to
one Hiriberry, the principal sufferer from the Canso affair, but this
was regarded as grace and favour. Captain Smart's action was upheld.
The new prime minister, Lord Carteret, in the same year bestowed St
Lucia upon a supporter, an outrageous action in view of the French
evacuation in good faith two years earlier. The Regent believed he had
no choice but to order the eviction of the English from St Lucia,
which was accomplished in January 1723.

Undoubtedly, there was at first a measure of good will on both sides.
The extensive preparation of the French for the conference indicates
that they, at least, anticipated lengthy negotiation. That the sessions
should have fizzled out after two brief encounters almost a year apart
must be explained by the mounting competition of the two powers
that rendered colonial and mercantile affairs impervious to the influence of the Anglo-French alliance that was so useful in the managing of
European affairs. In particular the rise of Law's Indies Company aroused
fear and jealousy in the British American colonies and in London.
"Some of them," a French agent wrote of the London merchants, "say
openly that if it continues to exist it will entirely absorb the trade of
this country, and that soon war with France to stop the course of a
prosperity so dangerous for England would become unavoidable."[10]
"The fortunate success of the arrangements that are reviving France
inspires an unbelievable jealousy in this country," wrote another
informant, "and certainly without the union that exists between His
Royal Highness and the King of Great Britain, England would not long
wait to manifest it."[11] While there is more than a little irony in a
Frenchman writing from England on the eve of the Mississippi Bubble,
"The love of gain . . . is here more than in any other country the main-
spring of hearts,"[12] this nevertheless reflects the perception of Englishmen as aggressive, grasping traders that was common coin among
other nations in the eighteenth century. It was a view of the English
spelled out at great length and with examples in instructions for the
French ambassador to the Court of St James's written in 1724.[13] At
that time it was still anticipated that the commission might reconvene,

and the ambassador carried with him a memorandum on all the points at issue. In this, the restrictive interpretation of the boundaries of Acadia inspired by Bobé – Cape Canso to Cape Sable with Port Royal – is the only one mentioned. The French position had hardened. When the commission finally did reconvene in 1751(!) as an act of pre-war diplomatic showmanship, this was still the French claim.[14]

Caricature images of one another, mutual distrust, real imperial ambition, and real conflict of interest precluded any settlement of important colonial issues at the conference table. The great issues of the continuing history of Acadia – possession of its continental component, the transformation of Cape Breton Island into fortress, factory, and fishery, the fate of Indian and Acadian – these were questions born of the answers given at Utrecht, questions to which contemporaries could find no satisfactory response short of war.

II

From King Philip's War in 1675 until the Treaty of Portsmouth in 1713, the Abenaki world experienced the first great upheaval arising its contact with Europeans. After the death of the Indian leader King Philip, Indian refugees from southern New England appeared in New York, at Sillery, and especially among the Abenakis. Throughout the Nine Years' War and the War of the Spanish Succession, the various Abenaki tribes carried out a continuous guerrilla warfare against New England, not only from Maine and Canada but from refuges in New Hampshire and the remote town of Koes at the present site of Newbury, Vermont. Abenakis west of the Kennebec appear to have been dislodged in the early eighteenth century, from Koes and Anmesokkanti on the Sandy River in 1704, from the Saco in 1708. Thus the period is marked by migrations and tribal mixing. After Utrecht a number of Abenaki settlements still existed in Canada at Missisquoi on Lake Champlain, at Chambly, and in the mission villages, or reserves, of Saint-François, Saint-François-de-Sales, and Bécancour.[15]

In New England west of the Saco, Abenaki life was finished. But to the east, where Dudley had banished the tribes at Portsmouth, the diaspora had been returning since 1710 to reconstitute the focus of Abenaki life. The years of exile in Canada had sharpened their attachment to their ancestral lands. While aware that their lot was ultimately thrown in with that of the French, they had cause for complaint in the subordination of their interests to those of the French in the late war and their abandonment at the peace. Relations with the English, their closest neighbours, promised no better, given the weaknesses of the

Treaty of Portsmouth. But the abject state of the French fur trade made trading relations with New England essential. Friendship and religious fraternity with Canada, peace and trade with New England, independence in Abenakia: this was the ideal. But the political and economic pressures of every day meant that the Abenakis were continually faced with making pro-French or pro-English decisions, and the tribes were soon rife with faction.[16]

After Utrecht Pontchartrain informed Vaudreuil that he was no longer free to incite the Abenakis or any other Indians to attack the English. He was, however, to encourage them to have dealings with Canada and to avoid the New Englanders. When *polysynodie* replaced the ministries of Louis XIV in 1715, the Governor was on hand to brief the new Marine Council on Canadian affairs. He obtained their consent to a frankly expansionist policy in the West, but their concern for the Anglo-French entente led them to concur in Pontchartrain's pacific instructions of 1713 regarding Acadia. France had no stomach for war, a fact that underlay the formation of policy in the post-Utrecht era. "War is in no way suitable to the colony," Vaudreuil was informed in 1716. The following year this observation was evidently raised to the level of a principle: "War is definitely not suitable in *a* colony."[17]

After a brief dalliance wth the impractical plan to move the Abenakis to Cape Breton Island – one nipped in the bud by Father La Chasse, the Jesuit missionary among the Penobscots – it was agreed that they should return to their own land, where they might still serve as a buffer. Vaudreuil suggested they should be secretly abetted in any war to drive the English from the Abenaki coast. In time this was the view that prevailed.[18] It was the last of four elements in Canada's policy as it took shape after Utrecht – a policy formulated by Vaudreuil but dependent upon the *oui* or *non* of the Marine. First, the "wavering" Abenakis and their eastern neighbours, the Maliseets, had to be attached diplomatically. Beyond fair words, medals, and the mobilization of the Jesuits, that meant money to build churches at Medoctek and Norridgewock and the revival of the Acadian gift fund, both in 1716.[19] Next, the nature of Canadian-Abenaki relations had to be formulated in terms compatible with the overriding imperative of the Anglo-French alliance. This Vaudreuil did in two steps, comprising the second and third elements of policy. In 1716 he pronounced the Abenakis who had returned to their ancestral rivers and shore French allies rather than subjects, "having always observed to call them such so as not to be responsible for their conduct."[20] This would seem inapplicable to the "domiciled" Abenakis and, in spite of the "always," would earlier have been inconsistent with Vaudreuil's preference for settling all the Abenakis on Canadian reserves or Cape Breton Island. Not until two years later does he leave us documentary evidence of his acceptance of the obvious counterpart of the pronouncement – that the land of the Abenakis was not French but Indian. "I will not cease maintaining all these Indians in the sentiment that the land where they are is theirs," he wrote in 1718, "and that they ought not to permit the English to take it from them."[21]

At first sight Vaudreuil's Abenaki policy thus consorts uncomfortably with Paris's stand on Acadian boundaries – that from Chignecto (at least) to the Kennebec was French territory. But the two arguments were in use at different levels, that of Paris primarily intended for consumption in London, Vaudreuil's offered to the Governor of Massachusetts and to the Abenakis themselves. They converge in the notion of a French protectorate over the Abenakis not very different from the English relationship with the Iroquois, in spite of the divergent uses in the two cases of *ally* and *subject* to describe native status. Indeed, the Iroquois/Abenakis parallel must have been apparent long before Vaudreuil put it to paper in 1721:

> Article 15 of the Treaty of Utrecht states that the inhabitants of Canada and other subjects of France will not trouble the Iroquois Five Nations and that similarly the subjects of Great Britain will behave peaceably towards the friends of France.
> The English contravene this article with regard to our allies the Abenakis.[22]

It was on March 22, 1719, that the Marine Council first asked Cardinal Dubois to expedite the convening of the boundary commission that the dispatches from Canada, particularly those of Bégon, had for so long requested. The next day the King's Memorandum for Canada was signed and dated, authorizing the secret military aid to the Abenakis that Vaudreuil had suggested in 1715. The language is veiled, but it was no doubt clear enough to the Governor: "As he understands the importance of preventing the English from becoming established in these lands, [His Majesty] relies on his prudence in preventing it either through the medium of the Indians or by some other means that, however, must not produce any cause for a rupture with England."[23] Vaudreuil replied that the Abenakis would not lack the munitions of war.[24]

In the years after 1689 war had forestalled the advance of the New England frontier of settlement beyond the confines of Connecticut, Rhode Island, and Massachusetts. The spread of English population was lateral, filling empty spaces within the old colonies. Now a dynamic New England society, driven less by indigenous population pressure than by capitalist enterprise, prepared to make good its conquests west of the Saco and to extend along the coasts of New Hampshire and Maine to the Kennebec and beyond. A tenuous outreach of settlement had extended to the Kennebec in the seventeenth century, and vague claims remained. Land companies with Massachusetts charters and colonists imported from Ulster now founded new settlements in the shadow of English forts. Speculative interests dominated the Massachusetts assembly, thwarted the efforts of Governor Dudley to frame a policy in line with the promise of truck houses given at Portsmouth, and even envisaged, in the words of the assembly's land committee, that settlement would "dislodge the Indians from their principal fishery, keep them from chief carrying places and be possibly a means of removing them further from us, if another war should happen."[25]

With no support from the House of Representatives, Governor Dudley was unable to re-establish the truck house system. Trade fell instead to farmer, fisherman, and itinerant; rum flowed; Anglo-Abenaki relations became tense; and at Norridgewock, the principal Abenaki town near the frontier, the rift between French and English factions grew sharper. In the fall of 1716 Dudley was replaced by Samuel Shute, an altogether unsuitable incumbent, contemptuous of Indians and, as Thomas Hutchinson described him, "somewhat warm and sudden when provoked . . . void of art."[26] His conference with the Indians at Arrowsic Island in August 1717, marked by his hectoring and plain bad manners, was a failure of communication. But in the end a treaty provided rather vaguely that the English might settle where their forebears had. It was a strategy devised by the pro-English party among the Abenakis to appease, but the result of it was that the land question continued to fester unattended. Border incidents continued, now including Abenaki slaughter of English cattle.

Throughout this period New Englanders were continually suspicious of the Jesuit missionaries among the Indians: Father Pierre de La Chasse, promoted from his mission to the office of Superior at Quebec in 1719; Joseph Aubery at Saint-François; Jean-Baptiste Loyard, who had replaced Aubery at Medoctek; Etienne Lauverjat, the missionary among the Penobscots; and Sébastien Rale, the oldest of the missionaries, at Norridgewock. Rale, in particular, stands out as the very model of a missionary. He was dedicated to his chosen people and able and articulate in their defence. Inveighing against English encroachments, he echoed the thunderous disapproval of an Old Testament prophet whom, one suspects, he must have resembled. He was not free of the missionary's arrogance. "Any treaty," he once wrote, "is null if I don't approve it, though the Indians have consented, for I bring them so many reasons against it that they absolutely condemn what they have done." In time of peace when there were no French officers in the Abenaki country, these men were the messengers and interpreters – literal and figurative – interposed between the Château St-Louis and the Abenaki villages. Before the war of 1702-13, some Jesuits had hoped for a fruitful trade link between the Abenakis and New England that would provide social stability. During the war they supported the removal of the Abenakis to Canada. In the post-war years their majority opinion was that the Indians should remain in their own country, which, if the boundary could be established and the English kept out, would provide an economic base and a quarantine from the most unsettling results of white contact – French or English.[27] The missionaries became able and articulate spokesmen of the Abenaki position with a Catholic frame of reference. The memorials of Aubery (1713, 1720) and Loyard (1722) and the letters of Rale clearly explain the interconnectedness of Canadian, Abenaki, and Catholic interests: that without Canada, the Abenakis' Catholic faith would be lost; that while New England expansion into the area might have a variety of outcomes in detail, in general it posed a triple threat to the Abenakis as a people, to the Church among them, and to Canada. The corollary of this was that instead of passively benefiting from Abenaki resistance to New England, Canada ought actively to support its allies by a final settlement of the boundary and by coming to the aid of any Indians attacked.[28]

Following the example of the first Jesuit among the Abenakis, Gabriel Druillettes, these missionaries earned respect and a place in Abenaki society by learning the language, becoming allied with kin-groups, and working within the structures of Abenaki society. The avowal of Rale has become famous: "As to what concerns me personally, I assure you that I see, that I hear, and I speak, only as an Indian."[29] French and Canadian officers demonstrated a similar bent by lobbying their points of view in councils as equals. The Baron de Saint-Castin is the most extreme example, marrying among the Penobscots, he and his sons becoming powerful and respected among them. This was the path that the pioneers of New England could not follow. They dealt with the Abenakis from the outside, never participating in their politics, and, some outstanding individuals aside, never understanding Indian society. "A clear refusal to see and hear the Abenakis as persons," an inability to "conceive of meaningful relations with members of minority groups" and "the creation of a myth of joint French and Abenaki conspiracy" are a recent historian's considered judgements of the New England mentality. Father Rale, on the sensitive Kennebec frontier, toiled at his writing desk not only keeping Vaudreuil informed but also time and again remonstrating with the authorities at Boston. What Rale had to say New England was not willing to understand, and for his pains he came to be seen as the creature of the Canadian governor and the evil genius behind Abenaki hostility.[30]

In 1720 the Kennebecs asked Vaudreuil for help in resisting continued English encroachments on their land. His instructions forbade his sending them the armed French troops that Father Rale had led them to believe would be forthcoming in such an emergency. Rale's very life was endangered by this loss of faith and loss of face that appeared to vindicate the pro-English faction. It was blustering Shute himself who enabled Rale to overcome this serious setback to French interests. Shute had in hand four Kennebec hostages. When these were not returned at a conference at Arrowsic, July 28/August 8, 1721, a conference the Governor did not bother to attend, the disappointed Abenaki audience was not a friendly one. Vaudreuil and Rale had packed the conference with Canadian reserve Indians. Joseph d'Abbadie de Saint-Castin, Father Rale, Father La Chasse, and a French officer constituted a rallying point for pro-French opinion. Arrowsic became a French triumph, Shute being sent an ultimatum by the Norridgewock headman, Wowurna, to clear Abenaki lands of English settlers or suffer the consequences.[31]

Settlers began to flee the frontier while the government of Massachusetts, far from reducing the tension, named seven Abenaki headmen to be seized and put a price on Rale's head. Saint-Castin was captured by trickery and carried off to Boston, and in the winter of early 1722 an armed force reached Norridgewock in search of Rale. Pursuers came within a few paces of the tree behind which Rale was hiding and although it was leafless, they failed to see him and passed by "as if they had been driven away by an invisible hand."[32] The capture of Saint-Castin and the pursuit of Rale resulted in acts of controlled violence by the Indians – the killing of cattle, an attack on a fishing boat, the capture of settlers. While the Massachusetts assembly debated its response, events took their own course. In July 1722, first blood was drawn in the ambush of eighteen Abenakis, and on July 25/August 5 Shute declared war.[33]

In 1721 Vaudreuil had for the first time written to the Marine Council that "if his Majesty permit him to adjoin some French with the Abenakis the English will be forced to abandon all their settlements on the lands belonging to the Indians."[34] This was the background of Cardinal Dubois's warning to the British government, described above in relation to the boundary question, that if the English settlers did not retreat from Abenaki country, the French "could not refuse protection" to the Indians. But one looks in vain in the dispatches of 1722 for any protest at the British failure even to reply to this note by the specified March deadline. Sabre rattling having had no effect, France would continue to shoulder the burden of peace with Old England, however vexatious, while the Abenakis would do their part by shouldering the burden of war with New England. From 1719 to 1725 the government reiterated its support for this division of labour in its letters to Vaudreuil; and in 1726, Canadian reports being favourable, this policy was contained in instructions to Vaudreuil's successor.[35]

Governor Shute left Boston for England in January 1723, committing New England to the keeping of the Lieutenant-Governor, William Dummer. The war dragged on, a model of mutual incomprehension that passed into New England memory as "Dummer's War." It was New England that was winning, destroying a number of Abenaki towns, whose inhabitants fell back on the reserves in Canada, from where they continued the war. The turning point was the destruction of Norridgewock on September 3, 1724. Instead of the twice-attempted, twice-failed overland winter march, there was a quick ascent of the Kennebec in whaleboats. Less than thirty people were killed, but among them was Father Rale; and some have claimed he died gun in hand.[36]

Vaudreuil now took a position of benign neutrality, given that Dummer was in a stronger position than himself, and offered to mediate the war. His covert aim was to prolong it. Vaudreuil would not have been against peace to French advantage, but there was little likelihood of that. In March 1725, he convened a conference at Montreal between a Massachusetts–New York delegation and the Abenakis. He urged upon the Indians terms he knew the English would not accept: reparations and an extravagant land claim. The talks collapsed. Perhaps this first conference could not have been successful, for the basic cause of the war, the land question, was unavoidable and insurmountable. In any case, this was a hollow victory for Vaudreuil, eighty-three years old, ill, and soon to die. For from this time the initiative in Abenaki affairs was permanently lost by Canada.[37]

It was the Penobscots who began picking up the pieces. Four of their headmen, Sauguaaram, Alexis, François Xavier, and Meganumbe, signed terms of agreement at Boston, December 15/26, 1725, claiming to act in the name of all Indians.[38] They gambled that they would be able to rally the villages behind this *fait accompli*. Before the assembled General Court of Massachusetts, the Penobscot delegates exchanged the principal "articles of submission and agreement" for written terms or promises, these two documents being the basis for peace with Massachusetts, New Hampshire, and Nova Scotia and even including reference to New York, Connecticut, and Rhode Island. At the same time the Indian delegates also made secondary treaties with Lieutenant-Governor Wentworth of New Hampshire and Paul Mascarene, delegate of Lieutenant-Governor Lawrence Armstrong of Nova Scotia, who, as he explained to his superiors, had sent Mascarene with "some articles to be demanded of the Indians; that by a separate peace, we may not be left alone to the fury of their insults."[39] This treaty was to be ratified at Annapolis Royal. On August 5-6 (16-17 N.S.), 1726, the Penobscots ratified the main treaty at Falmouth on Casco Bay with Dummer, Wentworth, and Mascarene. The following year on July 21 and 25 (August 1 and 6 N.S.), the Kennebecs and Canadian Abenakis also adhered to the treaty. It was the first time, Dummer noted, that the Canadian Abenakis had "submitted" to the British Crown.

In 1725 the Penobscot ambassadors at Boston had argued, "We think it would be better to come wholly upon a new footing, for all those former Treaties have been broke because they were not upon a good footing."[40] But for Dummer, who dictated the terms, the old footing served well enough, although he was determined upon an improved trade policy. The Boston/Falmouth Treaty was thus essentially the same as the Treaty of Portsmouth. The only really new clause created an Anglo-Abenaki defensive alliance whereby the Indian signatories were to join the English to put down any "refractory" Indians and the English were to join Indian signatories attacked by other Indians. For the rest, the old footing, unfortunately, was no more suitable than it had been in the past for governing the relations of two peoples. The treaty was wholly fanciful in its attribution of all war guilt to the Indians, its subjection of them to British sovereignty, and its provision that Abenaki fight Abenaki to protect New England. It took no account of the Indians' special relations with Canada on the ground of religion, a fact that was not going to disappear. And by perpetuating the traditional policy that the land disputes of English and Abenaki were amenable to solution by English laws and New England courts, it confirmed the continued expansion of New England at the expense of the Indian. The difficulty of negotiating the treaty may have been further complicated by faulty translation, a subject about which much remains to be learned. While the English minutes of the conference suggest a perfect understanding and while all parties were given true copies of the treaties, there are suggestions worth consideration that the Abenakis included in the treaty oral statements made at the signing, as Father Lauverjat wrote to La Chasse from Pentagouet: "The Abenakis have told the English that they are making peace with them only on condition that they would definitely not trespass on Abenaki lands; and that in case of a rupture between France and England, they would reserve the right always to take the part of the French. But these two conditions are only verbal."[41]

An impotent and, given the disregard of his advice by the Abenakis, a piqued witness of the Anglo-Indian negotiations of 1726-27 was the new governor of Canada, Charles de Beauharnois, who had arrived at

Quebec in August 1726 aboard the *Eléphant*. Beauharnois, who had considerable experience in the "service," was the brother of the Marine intendant at Rochefort and of Mme Bégon, wife of the departing Canadian intendant. He was consequently familiar with Canadian affairs. In accord with his instructions, he attempted to maintain the war, sending raiding parties from the reserves and lobbying against the treaty. But it was soon clear to Beauharnois, whom the Indians were always careful to inform and to court, that a watershed had been crossed in Acadian affairs. A vigorous effort was called for just to maintain the historic connection with the Abenakis by diplomacy, including the maintenance of the gift fund at wartime levels, good trade, and religion.[42] As in the days immediately after the War of the Spanish Succession, it was once again thought that the Indians would best be held to the French interest by keeping them on the Canadian reserves. To discourage the resettlement of Norridgewock, no missionary was sent there until 1730, at which time the movement of some Kennebecs back to their homeland caused the Governor to give in rather than risk losing them.[43]

There were two very divergent aspects to Abenaki–New England relations after 1727. On the one hand, a smoothly functioning truck house system was finally established, supplying Indian wants at fair prices and staunching the flow of rum. On the other hand, the New England frontier entered a period of rapid expansion as the Massachusetts government granted blocks of townships to speculators, pushing the Abenakis to the margins of their own country.[44] When war at last broke out in America between France and England in 1744, Canada once again drew military strength from among the Abenakis, but the coast of Maine was not again a major theatre of war. The whole history of the Abenakis since the later seventeenth century had unfolded around a central theme, one that had been expressed by the Marine Council, from interested motives, of course, some twenty years before: "Make them see the number of people there are in the English colonies and how few the French are and that it is, nonetheless, these French who keep them in freedom."[45]

III

"Canada becomes useless, its entrance is closed, all the fishery comes to an end, and the French Navy is absolutely destroyed": that had been Louis XIV's prediction if France should fail at Utrecht to maintain some foothold in the American North Atlantic, be it part of Acadia, Newfoundland, or Cape Breton.[46] It was Cape Breton that was saved and there that in the decade after Utrecht France established a new fishery and began the fortress of Louisbourg. Compared to many of the Corps of Engineers' other fortresses that may still be seen in replica at the Musée des Plans en Relief at Paris, Louisbourg's defences were modest. But there had been nothing else like them in the colonial world; they were dazzling ornaments set against the humble cloth of colonial experience.

In 1712, before the Utrecht settlement had been agreed upon, Pontchartrain was already investigating new locations for fishing posts in Labrador and Cape Breton to replace Placentia, Acadia, and St Pierre and Miquelon. The criteria for selection were an abundant and long-season fishery and a good, easily defended harbour. By April 1713, when he revealed his plans to the Controller General, Labrador had been eliminated and it had been decided to move the population and garrison of Placentia and St Pierre to Cape Breton, where modest fortifications would shelter a settlement devoted to fishing and trade. The consensus of colonial reports was to select a site known as Baie des Anglais (English Harbour).[47] In July an aging vessel, the *Semslack*, with a detachment from Placentia, and a ship from Quebec carrying a Canadian detachment made a tour of all the ports of the island before agreeing that Baie des Anglais was indeed the best choice. On September 2, the expedition's chief, Joseph Monbeton de Brouillan *dit* Saint-Ovide, king's lieutenant at Placentia, the nephew of the Brouillan who had successively governed Placentia and Acadia, took possession of the island for the King and returned to France, leaving the engineer, Jacques L'Hermitte, to begin preparations to receive the evacuated population. In January Pontchartrain wrote to L'Hermitte that the King had approved the choice as the best for trade and fishing and had named it Louisbourg. Sainte-Anne was now Port Dauphin, Saint-Pierre Port Toulouse, and Cape Breton Ile Royale. New names on the map: a new colony had come into being. The migration from Placentia was completed by a straggling flotilla of merchant ships with fishing shallops in tow that left Newfoundland on September 25, 1714, and arrived at Louisbourg on October 2.[48]

From the first the idea of Louisbourg embraced more than fishing. A resident fishery required supplies and marketing facilities and hence a trading town. For protection it required a garrison and some kind of fortifications. Of all this Placentia was the model and the miniature.[49] Yet more ambitious ideas surrounded the birth of the new colony. In 1705-6, Antoine-Denis Raudot, the junior intendant of Canada, and Denis Riverin had written lengthy papers in favour of establishing a great commercial entrepôt on Cape Breton that would link the fishery with Canada, France, and the West Indies and by its strategic location guarantee French hegemony in the gulf and in the Atlantic fishery. It is fair to conclude that Pontchartrain had in mind something like this, but neither he nor anyone else yet contemplated the building of the great fortress.[50]

In February 1715, Pontchartrain announced that the principal establishment at Ile Royale was not to be at Louisbourg but at Port Dauphin. Explaining this to the Controller General, he stressed that Port Dauphin was "a very good port easily fortified with a much less considerable expense." Anxiety over cost accompanied the realization that fortifications more extensive than originally planned would be required:

> I will not expand, sir, on the urgent indispensable necessity of solidly fortifying this new establishment since you understand its importance. The English are already unsettled by it and are certainly not unaware that beyond the advantages French commerce will derive from it, this establishment will be very prejudicial to their own, being in time of war capable of attacking all their ships arriving from ocean crossings; and it is certain that at the first rupture, they will do everything to try to become its masters, something at which they will not succeed once it has been well fortified. If France were to lose this island, it would be irreparable; and as a result, it would be necessary to abandon the rest of North America.[51]

Behind this ministerial somersault were both the bankruptcy of France and the momentary collapse of good relations with Great Britain. In 1714 talks on the ratification of the Anglo-French commercial treaty were abandoned, Queen Anne died, and George I arrived in England. As the Canso affair, the English occupation of St Lucia, the English response to Law's schemes, and the failure of the boundary commission demonstrate, the alliance of Great Britain and France of three years later did nothing to reduce Anglo-French imperial rivalries; rather it provided the framework for the first recognizable cold war of modern history. By the end of 1714 the problem of fortifying Ile Royale was thus cast into high relief; there it remained, undiminished even by the permanent slashing of the Marine budget in 1716.

When the Marine Council replaced Pontchartrain, the members again took up the question of where the principal establishment of Ile Royale should be. In 1718 they decided to return the capital to Louisbourg, concurring in the opinion of their own expert, Jean-François Verville, an engineer whom they had sent to Ile Royale. There he had found Governor Philippe Pastour de Costebelle and almost everyone but Saint-Ovide in favour of Port Dauphin – the colony had had its own little controversy. The primacy of the fishery and Verville's argument that the selected port should not be subject to blockade prevailed.[52]

The Fortress of Louisbourg was the only project in North America built by metropolitan fortification contractors under the supervision of the Corps of Engineers. The difficulties were enormous: building in a harsh and unfamiliar climate, using local building materials of unknown qualities, importing others from France, maintaining a skilled labour force in a remote setting, and, for the Marine, the necessity of keeping financial control from a great distance. Roofs leaked, walls bulged, stones cracked, and mortar melted away. No wonder one officer wrote home (in jest?) that moonbeams were destroying the fortifications![53]

Building was begun by Verville, but the principal architect of Louisbourg was his successor, Etienne Verrier, who between 1724 and 1745 left his mark on everything from the grim walls and bastions to the elegant clock tower, the gates and public buildings. Most construction was completed between 1723 and 1745, by which time some three and a half million livres had been spent. (Repairs after the English siege and occupation of 1745-49 and a reprise of building activity under the engineer Louis Franquet in 1754-58 added another million.) For its money the Marine got more than walls and guns. Government buildings, warehouses, a hospital, wharves, a lighthouse, a dike to make a lagoon safe for fishing craft, and roads – all were built by the military engineers and their contractors.

Why did the French build so great a fortress? One historian has argued that the engineers and contractors, the latter with no doubt labyrinthine connections in the world of French finance and government, constituted a phalanx of vested interests in favour of continued building.[54] Another points to a French obsession with fortresses that played the key role in an essentially static and defensive strategy.[55] Both observations are probably true. To them it is sufficient to add that Cape Breton/Ile Royale had long been pinpointed as of crucial strategic importance both to Canada and to the fishery and that the building of the fortress was simply the extension to North America of a type and scale of defence common in Europe where the stakes were no greater.[56] Louisbourg was considered the key to French strategy in America because it would guarantee to privateers, who did most of the French fighting at sea, a safe haven unequalled in the past by Placentia or Port Royal and because an enemy naval expedition against Quebec could not risk leaving an unsubdued Louisbourg in its rear. In 1727 Governor Beauharnois voiced his sceptical opinion, which was then very much the minority report: "I do not know, My Lord, who could have given the Court to believe that Ile Royale was the rampart of this country. The entire English Army could come to Quebec without anything being known of it at Ile Royale; and even if they did know about it there, what could they do about it?" To this Maurepas replied that Louisbourg was indeed the rampart of Canada, a view with which the

English appear to have concurred, since they threw their forces against it in 1745 and 1758 rather than bypassing it for Quebec.[57]

The château within the massive King's Bastion, which has been painstakingly reconstructed for modern visitors, was the heart of official Louisbourg. The apartments of the governor, the council chamber, and numerous sumptuous rooms are in one wing that terminates in the chapel at the centre, where a portrait of Saint Louis above the altar blends the royal with the divine in one suggestive image. From there a second wing, housing the squalid barracks of a tattered soldiery, finishes the straight line of the building.

In the period 1713-44, there were only two governors of importance at Louisbourg: Costebelle, who had been the governor of Placentia, and Saint-Ovide, with the longest tenure in the history of the colony, 1717 to 1739. In addition to being head of government, nominally under the Governor General at Quebec, the governor also commanded the local Marine companies, the garrison of some four to six hundred men who were his near and disadvantaged neighbours. Next to the governor in the civil government was the commissaire-ordonnateur, an intendant except in name, since he too was nominally subordinate to his counterpart at Quebec. Of these ordonnateurs only François Bigot, who took office in 1739, has become well known and that for lining his pockets, a proclivity that was not unusual. The nucleus of the officer corps consisted of men who had been officers at Port Royal before 1710 or Placentia up to 1713, men who with their wives and children constituted a caste. These officers and civil officials have claimed the attention of historians, not because of their individual importance, which in most cases is slight, but because their lives tell us so much about values and realities in the age of the great fortress.[58]

From dates early in the sixteenth century, the fishermen of the French Atlantic and Channel ports had come to the banks, to Newfoundland, Acadia, and the Gulf of St Lawrence, to participate in both the green and the dry fisheries.[59] In the green fishery, the fishermen remained on their sailing vessels, catching fish by hook and line. The cleaned fish were salted in the hold and carried home for the French market. The dry fishery was carried on inshore in shallops manned by three men, also using hook and line, the boats and crews either being local or having been brought by large 150- to 350-ton mother ships. By a long and exacting process the split fish were dried on clean gravel beaches, on brush, or on wooden *flakes*, producing a well-preserved fish especially suited to export markets in warm climates.

Canadian Types of the Old Regime:
A Portfolio of the Historical Paintings of Henri Beau

Gentleman

Bourgeois

Wealthy Woman
of the Bourgeoisie

Woman in a
Sleeveless Coat

Iroquois Youth

Micmac Woman in
Traditional Cap

French Soldier
circa 1725

COMPAGNIES FRANCHES DE LA MARINE vers 1725

Canadian
Militia Officer

Canadian
Militiaman

Sailor

Jesuit

JÉSUITE   ancien costume 17+18ᵉˢ

Récollet

RÉCOLLET   ordre éteint

SULPICIEN XVII= S.

Sulpician

FRÈRE HOSPITALIER de la CROIX (CHARRON)

Charron Brother

Grey Nun

SOEUR GRISE de L'HOPITAL de MONTRÉAL.
Mod. d'YOUVILLE XVIIIme S.

Hospitaler

HOSPITALIÈRE de la MISÉRICORDE de JESUS (HOTEL
DIEU de QUEBEC)
- 1639 -

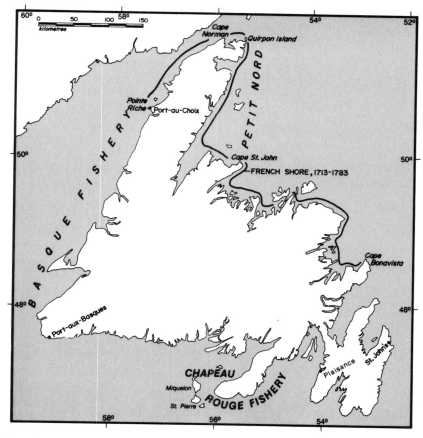

Newfoundland

Before Utrecht the French dry fishery had been located along the great extent of Newfoundland coast: the Petit Nord from Cape St John along the east coast of the northern peninsula to Cape Norman on the Strait of Belle Isle; the French Basque fishery along the west coast, with centres in the north at Port-au-Choix and in the south at Port-aux-Basques; on the south coast, the fishery of Chapeau Rouge on both sides of the Burin Peninsula; and the fisheries of St Pierre and Miquelon and Placentia with their own resident populations. After 1713 the southern fisheries were ceded. French sovereignty over the Petit Nord was replaced by the fishing and drying privilege of the French Shore, which extended along a much greater coastline from Cape Bonavista to a Pointe Riche of indeterminate location beyond Cape Norman. If Pointe Riche really existed, it was somewhere on the west coast where the Basques continued to fish after 1713, undisturbed by the English. The one established continental fishery remaining to the French was Gaspé, and now to it were added Ile Royale and Labrador.

Although suitable beaches for drying were not numerous in Labrador, a profitable fishery was established on the south coast between Phélypeaux Bay (now Brador Bay) and Red Bay. The area had long been shunned by Frenchmen because of their fear of Inuit attacks, but the establishment of a permanent post at Phélypeaux Bay in 1704 by a Canadian officer provided some protection and, especially, a place to store fishing shallops safely over the winter. Across the gulf, the fishery of Gaspé occupied the coastline from Matane almost to the Restigouche and included Ile Saint-Jean. Before the war of 1744, Gaspésie was almost uninhabited except for a few Indians in the interior and insignificant fishing villages at Pabos and Grande-Rivière on the south coast. But at Gaspé, Bonaventure, and Percé in any given summer there were several hundred French fishermen; and at Percé, in particular, there gathered a rough community of fishermen, fugitives, and Indians centred on the cabaret.[60] The Labrador and Gaspé fisheries were related, a bad fishing year in one being a good year in the other, ships moving accordingly between them.

After Captain Smart's attack on Canso in 1718, the French fishery in that area, once dominated by the Acadian Company, was limited to the Ile Madame side of Chedabucto Bay, while the New Englanders monopolized the Canso fishery proper. The main Ile Royale fishery was between Louisbourg and Scatarie Island, and the most northerly was at Niganiche, the island and adjacent mainland harbour at present-day Ingonish. It was at Ile Royale that between 1720 and 1723 the French first adopted the New England schooner. Because at Ile Royale the cod followed the caplin and herring away from the coasts to the banks in the course of the fishing season, they escaped the shallop fishermen. But the schooner could follow them and return with a catch that had been given a preliminary salting and was still in good condition. The fish were then washed and dried on flakes in the traditional manner. Thus a new kind of fishery was born. Small size (about forty to sixty tons), good lines, and lateen sails made the schooner swift and manoeuvrable with a small crew. It was a ship of grace and economy. Neither the hulking mother ships of the dry fishery nor the ninety-ton square-rigs of the green could have filled its role. Both shallop and schooner were used by the resident fishermen who came to dominate the Ile Royale fishery, their share of the catch rising from half in 1718 to about two thirds by 1744.[61]

In most harbours where the dry fishery was carried on, the first captain to arrive was designated admiral, chose his own drying space on the shore, and parcelled out the rest to those who followed. But at Louisbourg the beaches had been reserved for the Placentian exiles; this privilege came to be conceived of as ownership, and soon these "fishing rooms" became the object of trade, being sold and rented. Labour was scarce at Ile Royale and commanded a high wage. Many of the fishermen were *engagés*, indentured labourers brought from France by Basques or Malouins who sold the *engagés'* labour for the price of their passage. Frequently fishermen were persuaded to break contracts and sign new ones, being plied with alcohol or offered other inducements. Thus custom and regulation (of which there was a lot!) gave way at Louisbourg, where usufruct became ownership and cash defined the relation of man to man.[62]

Interesting rhythms have been perceived in the history of the fishery after Utrecht. The French moved decisively away from the Petit Nord and into the new continental fisheries in 1717-20. Then a disaster in the continental fisheries in 1733-34 speeded a return to Newfoundland. (The New England fishery at Canso was virtually abandoned by 1744.) Not until 1748 did the continental fisheries again improve. While overfishing and competition for beaches may have played their role in these movements, it is now suggested that they were principally due to changes in the Labrador current that sent the cod migrating in search of warmer waters. It is a hypothesis that seems confirmed by related movements in the English fishery at Newfoundland and on the Grand Banks.[63]

The fishery was crucial to the French Empire. It was the training ground of sailors, fed the people, provided a valuable export, and reduced the French West Indies' requirement for foreign foodstuffs. It was a large and increasing sector of the economy. Between 1725 and 1735, for example, over 300 ships left France annually for the fishery, carrying between 7,500 and 10,500 men. Evidence for St Malo shows a doubling of that port's ships in the fishery between 1713 and 1755 and a trebling of crews. Although the green fishery of the Grand Banks accounted for half of all French ships in the fishery, these were smaller vessels. The dry fishery was responsible for three quarters of the tonnage and three quarters of the men.[64]

State expenditures and the fishery were the first pillars of trade and a class of traders at Louisbourg. The community of exiles that came from Placentia in 1714 already contained within itself a body of traders and fishing entrepreneurs. This was the nucleus of the trading class at Louisbourg. It was common for former Placentians such as André and Philippe Carrerot, Michel Daccarrette, Guillaume Delort, and Joseph Lartigue to both manage fisheries and become involved in trade. Many added to this the holding of public office (A. Carrerot, Delort, and Lartigue were all councillors) or some civil service employment. To this group were added numerous French merchants, often with the same Bayonne origins or connections characteristic of the Placentians. They too combined fishing, trade, and government service in various combinations. In the 1730s there were some fifty merchants at Louisbourg, but this included both shopkeepers and important traders. About half of them were involved in the fishery, accounting for over a third of the cod taken. Finally, there were the French fortification contractors such as Michel-Philippe Isabeau, François Ganet, and David-Bernard Muiron, representatives *par excellence* of the government-business connection. As many who were primarily government officials also became active in trade, there was no neat division of classes between the two spheres.[65]

In the trade that developed at Louisbourg, France supplied wine and the bulk of required manufactures, taking in return the lion's share of cod, much of it for re-export to Spain and the Mediterranean. Canada, in good years, was able to supply the flour, biscuit, and dried peas Ile Royale needed together with some lumber, primarily in exchange for cod to be carried to the West Indies.* But this by no means provided for the needs of Ile Royale. From as early as 1714 when Pierre Arsenault of Beaubassin sold ten sheep at Louisbourg, the Acadians of Nova Scotia provided Ile Royale with most of its livestock as well as some grain. And two New England sloops Arsenault saw at Louisbourg were the harbingers of a brisk trade with Boston based upon the exchange of New England provisions, building materials, and ships for French West Indian molasses, rum, and sugar.[66] Louisbourg quickly moved beyond the simple exchange of cod for imported goods to an entrepôt trade on two levels. The first was the exchange of imported goods procured with cod for other imported goods, as in the exchange of cod for rum and its subsequent exchange for New England bricks. Secondly, two foreign products in no way tied in with Ile Royale's cod staple might be exchanged: a French West Indian cargo of sugar and molasses for a New England schooner laden with bricks and lumber – a purely entrepôt trade that could have been handled by a port with no productive hinterland. The significance of this entrepôt function (a third pillar of commerce) can be seen in Louisbourg's trade figures of the last few years before the war of 1744, which show an increase in trade although the fishery was in decline.[67]

---

*Canada's role is discussed further in Chapter 7 below.

The New England and Nova Scotia trades were, from the French point of view, illegal except in cases of "the most pressing and indispensable need."[68] But even after the Letters Patent of 1727 were registered by the Superior Council at Louisbourg (a leisurely three years later!) the local government of traders in office and officials in trade did not manage more than the most sporadic enforcement, perhaps when interested motives dictated. As for Massachusetts, the assembly was dilatory, the customs service a shambles, and the most usual imports, molasses and rum, were not prohibited, although after the Molasses Act of 1733 they were dutiable, a complication that made some subterfuge necessary.

In 1716 the Marine Council decided that Ile Saint-Jean should be developed as an agricultural hinterland to Ile Royale.[69] The island thus began to emerge from the historical shadow to which it had long been consigned. The first attempt at development was by means of a company, the island being granted to the company's principal member, the Comte de Saint-Pierre. Although the company failed, it left a residue of settlement. In 1726 the island was reunited to the royal domain, and a little detachment of soldiers was assigned to its capital of Port La Joie, near the site of modern Charlottetown. Acadian settlers began to trickle in, while at Trois-Rivières (Brudenell Point) in 1732 the imaginative and energetic Jean-Pierre Roma, whose company had been granted a concession along the lines of Saint-Pierre's, was building harbour works, roads, and buildings and clearing fields. Over the years, at Trois-Rivières, Port La Joie, and the fishing ports of the north coast a small population was being built up: more than 200 in 1720, more than 400 in 1740, and probably about 600 by 1744. But the island never did serve as the bread basket of Louisbourg, a role that fell, more or less, to Canada.

In 1737 there was a census of Ile Royale. Louisbourg had grown to a town of about 1,500 civilians with a garrison of about 600 officers and men. Around the Placentian nucleus had gathered a motley population from every corner of France, from Canada, Acadia, and the West Indies: soldiers, fishermen, merchants, tradesmen of every kind, domestics, slaves, salt smugglers and other transported convicts.[70] Louisbourg was more than four times as busy as its sister port of Quebec: nearly 150 ships a year compared to over 30.[71] Since what trade statistics there are have yet to be subjected to rigorous analysis, generalization beyond this comparison is pointless. The fishery had entered a period of difficulty from which it never fully recovered. As a consolation to local fishing masters, it would fall almost entirely into their hands in the post-war period. And if the trade of Louisbourg would come to depend more and more on its purely entrepôt function and upon New England cargoes, it would also become greater than ever.[72]

Among the 2,500 colonists outside of Louisbourg, there were few who were not fishermen. A small colony of Acadians had settled at Port Toulouse, where they practised trades and agriculture. On the Petit Bras d'Or (St Andrews Channel), Louis-Simon de La Boularderie had formed a small settlement in his concession. And at Port Dauphin, for a time the capital, a small population had remained. Ile Royale's agricultural potential, most of it on the unknown western coast, remained undeveloped. It was difficult to farm this marginal land while provisions were to be had from elsewhere, even given the uncertainty of supply.[73] Only a major programme of assisted emigration could have turned Cape Breton forest into farmstead, but the only initiative of that kind in the period was the impressment of the poor for Louisiana. Ile Royale was to the end of its history to remain the narrow crescent of the eastern coast: rock, swamp, and thin soil; cold, wind, and fog; the island of trade, fortress, and fishery.

IV

"It is absolutely necessary," Pontchartrain wrote to Vaudreuil in 1713, "to persuade the French and Indians of Acadia to go and settle the island of Cape Breton."[74] In this way the new fishery was to have been provided with an agricultural base and the Indian guerrilla force was to have been kept on French territory and under close French control. This policy was framed in the light of a rather theoretical understanding of the possibilities, in line with the Minister's penchant for clear boundary lines demarcating areas of indubitable sovereignty. It was rejected by Indians and Acadians alike. Nor was Pontchartrain's idea consistent with the advice from so many quarters that Canada's southeastern flank must not be exposed to New England aggression. The policy that did emerge accommodated itself to these realities. Only the foundation of Louisbourg and Ile Royale was new, radical, and clear cut. In all other respects French policy was rooted in the past, all the more accepted on that account but dangerous in its ambiguity. The refusal to give up continental Acadia and the covert support given the Abenakis in their wars with New England, all the while maintaining the Anglo-French entente, was one – quite successful – element of this policy. But France had also to take account of its allies the Micmacs, most of them living in English territory, and their neighbours the Acadians, former French subjects, to whose stories we at last must turn.

The Micmacs were a widely scattered people; their small population (one thousand? three thousand?) was distributed throughout Nova

Scotia, Ile Royale, continental Acadia east of the St John watershed, Ile Saint-Jean, and along the coast of the gulf through Gaspé. They moved from shore to upland forest according to the bounty of the seasons, the large coastal villages of summer breaking up as the bands separated for winter hunting. For them emigration to Ile Royale would have been an imprisonment on short rations; besides, they argued that even if Queen Anne had conquered the Acadian lowlands, "for themselves, they had the forests from which no one would ever be able to expel them."[75] Certainly the English presence was not imposing: a small and poorly equipped garrison, a handful of civilians, the seasonal appearance at Canso of New England fishermen with no taste for trouble, and the only military works the rotting fortifications of Annapolis Royal.

Thus the Micmacs, joined at times by eastward wandering Maliseets, constituted a hostile force within Nova Scotia, one over which the French were at pains to maintain some ascendency. As with the Abenakis, the missionaries were here fundamental to the French connection. In 1716 the Indians agreed to Father Antoine Gaulin's plan to found a permanent mission village at Antigonish and in 1722 to the establishment of a second centre at Shubenacadie, nearer the Acadian settlements. Under the stress of Dummer's War, in 1724 the Antigonish mission was moved to Merligueche near Port Toulouse and was at last on French soil. These and later missions became, not agricultural settlements as the missionaries may have hoped, but "places of resort" where hunters often left families.[76] The gospel message preached by Gaulin and his successors, men such as the scholarly Pierre Maillard, who perfected Micmac hieroglyphics, and Jean-Louis Le Loutre, then and since the object of much English criticism, was melded with heady French loyalism but was not bereft of a sense of the common humanity of French, Indian, and English.

Payments for missionary stipends and for building churches were only one way in which the French Crown attached the Micmacs; half the old Acadian gift fund was administered by the governors of Louisbourg, who dispensed their largess annually at Port Toulouse and Port La Joie, much of it in the potent form of guns, powder, and shot. To this were added the customary giving of medals and military commissions, the provision of surgeons and gunsmiths, bounties for enemy scalps, and participation by the French in councils, feasts, and, from 1744, fighting. The French management of Indians has been described as "the most consistent and most successful military activity at Louisbourg."[77] At the same time, the governors of Nova Scotia, their hands tied by a Board of Trade that saw no profit in gifts and subsidized trade, were at a loss to compete and were out of pocket when they did.[78]

The French were able to maintain the friendship but not the obedience of the Micmacs. Early Micmac acts of hostility – the sack of Canso in 1720 is notable – were contrary to French policy, although by the time of Dummer's War such acts were encouraged. In the course of the war the Micmacs captured vessels and cruised the Nova Scotia coasts, terrorizing fishermen. With the Maliseets they attacked Annapolis Royal in 1724. The year following, they again raided Canso. But Micmac and Maliseet hostilities were tied to the Abenaki resistance and ended with its collapse. On June 4/15, 1726, even before the ratification of Falmouth, a number of Indians ratified at Annapolis Royal the agreement they had made with Mascarene. This treaty declared the Indians British subjects as a result of the Treaty of Utrecht. The Indians submitted to King George I "in as ample a manner" as they had "formerly done to the Most Christian King," and one cannot but wonder if the English understood just how ambiguous a submission so described was. The treaty also differed from Dummer's in recognizing the Indians' right to practise the Roman Catholic religion and to have approved missionaries among them. In other matters, such as the integrity of the Indians' "persons, hunting fishing and planting grounds," it was traditional and traditionally vague. John Doucett, the commander at Annapolis, reported to the Lords of Trade that the Indians appeared tired of the war and that many assured him "they would never take up arms against either of the two Crowns but that they would live neuter & friends to both." He also added plaintively that "they have cost me near three hundred in presents and feasting."[79] For a number of headmen, the ratification meant a dressing down from Saint-Ovide, but the peace held. Whatever the treaty said, however, it was not an English pacification. In the upland forests and on the south coasts, the bands retained their old dominance and their old independence.

At the time of Utrecht there were some fifteen hundred to two thousand Acadians farming the drained marshlands of the Bay of Fundy. The centre of population had shifted from its point of origin around Annapolis Royal up the bay to Minas and Beaubassin, pushed by fear of pirates (and perhaps of government), drawn by the prospect of better lands. Beyond Beaubassin, in continental Acadia, there were scarcely a hundred white inhabitants. Only a fraction of the 75,000 acres of Fundy marshes, the only really excellent soil in Acadia, had yet been diked and farmed. The Acadians traded a farm surplus to New England. Some of the goods obtained were then traded to the Micmacs, whose long-standing friendly relations with the Acadians were not threatened by the marshland agrarian frontier. In the image of Acadian plenitude that has come down through the centuries, two elements are fundamental: the blossoming apple and the protective dike. The traveller Dièreville describes the dikes as he saw them at the turn of the century:

> Five or six rows of large logs are driven whole into the ground at the points where the tide enters the marsh, & between each row, other logs are laid, one on top of the others, & all the spaces between them are so carefully filled with well-pounded clay, that the water can no longer get through. In the centre of this construction, a sluice is contrived in such a manner that the water on the marshes flows out of its own accord, while that of the sea is prevented from coming in.[80]

Article 14 of the Treaty of Utrecht gave the Acadians the right to leave Nova Scotia with their moveables within one year and gave to those who elected to remain a vague guarantee of religious freedom. Queen Anne, in a subsequent letter, guaranteed their rights to hold or to sell their landed estates.[81] Their legal position was thus identical with that of the Placentians. French policy regarding both groups was also identical. The Acadians were to sell out (it was hoped with better luck than the Placentians, who found no buyers) and to be moved to Ile Royale with government assistance and supervision. To that end, two French officers visited the settlements in the summer of 1714, and no less than 302 of 355 heads of families declared their intent to emigrate. They were, however, canny enough to send delegates to examine the proffered lands. Governor Francis Nicholson, not wanting to be responsible for depopulating the country, seized on the technicality that a year had already elapsed since Utrecht, thus invalidating all the privileges given by treaty and letter. He also forbade the transport to Ile Royale of livestock and grain. In this Nicholson had the support of the Board of Trade, to whom Samuel Vetch, who had masterminded the conquest of Nova Scotia, had argued in mercantilish fashion that "as no country is of value without inhabitants" the Acadians should remain: "The removal of them and their cattle to Cape Breton would be a great addition to that new colony so it would wholly ruin Nova Scotia unless supplied by a British colony which could not be done in several years, so that the French inhabitants with their stocks of cattle remaining there is very much for the advantage of the Crown."[82]

Given the perilous conditions of Anglo-French relations after the death of Queen Anne, the weakened French state was in no position to offend English opinion by sending a flotilla to evacuate the Acadians.[83] Nevertheless, it was neither English obstruction nor French timidity that accounted for the Acadian decision to remain at home. Rather, in the light of continued freedom from interference by the Nova Scotia government and the reports of the delegates to Ile Royale, it was

Acadian good sense that would not exchange hearth and home for a year's rations and a lifetime supply of stony ground. Only sixty-seven families are known to have emigrated to Ile Royale, where most settled on the marginally good land near Port Toulouse. Most of them were from the area around Annapolis Royal with its English garrison, and a high percentage were tradesmen rather than farmers.[84]

The Nova Scotia government that dealt with both the Micmacs and the Acadians was a sorry affair. Militarily it was weak to the point of being laughable. It was penniless because under its constitution, granted in 1719, it could not collect taxes without an assembly, and it could not have an assembly without Protestant voters and members. Richard Philipps, governor from 1717 to 1749, was also governor of Newfoundland; he preferred Canso when in residence and preferred London most of all. But there were always lieutenants at Canso and Annapolis Royal. From 1710 the Acadians treated with the government through elected delegates (elections were held each year on the anniversary of the conquest of Port Royal) who also constituted what local government there was. Under this shadowy government, the Acadians continued to prosper. Their numbers probably reached 5,000 by the early 1730s and 10,000 by mid-century. The extension of settlement throughout the marshes continued. To the traditional trade with New England, more vigorous than ever, was added the trade to Louisbourg, most of it across the Isthmus of Chignecto to Baie Verte, where ships were waiting, a route that involved no more than four miles of land carriage. It was living thus, almost a law unto themselves, under a government no more capable of stopping their contraband than of controlling the Micmacs, that conditioned the Acadian response to the one great political question of the period: the oath of allegiance.

Neither Commander Doucett in 1717, Governor Philipps in 1720, nor Lieutenant-Governor Armstrong in 1726 was able to exact from the Acadians an unqualified oath of allegiance. They proposed to Doucett that they would subscribe to an oath that included exemption from military service, the first appearance of the idea of Acadian neutrality. Armstrong inserted such a clause in the French translation but not in the English original of his oath; and when a junior officer returned from the outlying settlements with a qualified oath in 1727, the qualification was annulled and the unqualified oath was held to subsist. This pointless duplicity was preferred to the disappointed young man's pragmatism. In 1730 Philipps tried again and soon reported a complete submission. But it is almost certain Philipps worked his miracle by adding a verbal promise of neutrality to the written oath of loyalty. Certainly, in the years that followed, it was taken for granted by everyone that the Acadians were neutral.

Acadian history leads, of course, to the Expulsion, "le grand dérange-ment" of 1755, a rejection of the idea of neutral status in law and a loss of faith in Acadian willingness to remain neutral. That tragedy arose, no doubt, from circumstances peculiar to the moment, but it is useful to remember that administrators had always considered the possibility of deportation. On the whole they considered it only to reject it. The exemplary conduct of the Acadians in the war of 1744 consigned it temporarily to the back of the mind, but no one banished it to the realm of the unthinkable.

*   *   *

The history of the Atlantic region after Utrecht was that of a restructuring on the grand scale. Stripped of their traditional fishery in Newfoundland and of the Acadian peninsula, the French succeeded in accommodating the fishery along new shores. Louisbourg was a new and greater Placentia. To the empire of politics and military force it contributed the great fortress that protected both the fishery and the approaches to Canada and the distant heartland. To the empire of trade it gave a unity and wholeness hitherto lacking. The Acadians continued to increase and multiply in their precarious Eden, and the Micmacs could still brush aside the pretensions of their would-be English masters. It was on the southern frontier that the structure first gave way in the subordination of the Abenakis to New England's will. In the end, none of this new construction, admirable and successful in so many ways, would be proof against conflicting imperial aspirations, the unfin-ished business of the negotiators "mingled pell-mell and without distinction" in the Utrecht town hall.

CHAPTER 7

Quebec and the Atlantic

There was no convenient site farther down river – no place where a real town could rise and domicile the tradesmen that ships and shipping depended upon, the body of merchants that would manage the exchange of inland and Atlantic cargoes, speeding turnaround time and taking in hand the debts and untied ends left behind, no place where law courts could be established, where provisions could be bought; in short, Quebec was the first site on the St Lawrence for a proper colonial port. Here the gargantuan St Lawrence shrank to the proportions of just a great river. Beyond was unmistakably Inland, a place for freshwater sailors in small boats. The Laurentians loosed their grip on the river and gave place to the ribbon of lowlands that supported a farming population.

The voyage to Canada was a hard one. It was difficult to reach Quebec before mid-July, and arrival was often enough in August or even September. In November the river would begin to freeze over, and Quebec's role as a link between Europe and America would come to its seasonal end.[1] The durations of known crossings bear out the estimates of Lahontan: two and half months east to west against the prevailing westerlies and thirty to forty days west to east, carried along by these same winds. Crossings of over four months were common misfortunes to be endured.[2] In the letters and journals of travellers, certain images recur: for all but the most advantaged passengers, a cramped existence between decks and the assaults of legions of vermin; the breaking of masts and spars in Atlantic storms; eating newly caught fish on the Grand Banks, the first fresh food tasted in weeks; the sailors' "baptism" or fining of those crossing the banks for the first time; then, coasting Acadia, the visit of Micmacs bringing gifts of game to exchange for powder and shot; finally, the appearance of a shallop to bear away dispatches or distinguished arrivals, a sign that Quebec was near.

At the end of the long journey, hidden by the bulk of Ile d'Orléans until the last moment, was the town, scattered carelessly across its splendid site. Newcomers admired the topography, the spacious and protected harbour, and the view of the St Lawrence from the cliffs. The town itself did not much impress them. A cramped business quarter was squeezed between high tide and the black face of a cliff. On the height above, Upper Town, the governor's fortified house (the Château St-Louis) and numerous religious institutions and single-storey houses, work yards, and gardens provided an open townscape only partially subdued to *bon ordre* by a street grid. At the outskirts of the town to the north and west near the bank of the St Charles River stood the intendant's large house, called the "palais" by reason of its being the seat of the Superior Council. Around that nucleus a new quarter developed in the first half of the century.[3]

In 1701, Upper Town was surrounded by rotting palisades, eroded earthworks, and a few stone redoubts, including one on Cape Diamond, the height of land south of the town. Lower Town was protected by batteries. During the first two decades of the century, the construction of new defences, first on one plan, then on another, occasioned much moving of earth and spending of money before the government tired of the project and consigned Canada's defence to Louisbourg and the forts of the Richelieu. Not until 1745, when both the government and the local people were a good deal shaken by the fall of Louisbourg, was work begun on more substantial fortifications.[4] Between 1701 and 1744 the town itself grew considerably. Stone continued to replace wood; increased prosperity, frequently abetted by disastrous fires, stimulated the erection of new and better buildings. Twenty-five hundred people were enumerated in a census in 1716, and this population had approximately doubled by 1744.[5] Small as it was, Quebec was the colony's port and political capital, and therein lay its importance. "You find in it a small number of the best company," wrote the Jesuit scholar and traveller Father Charlevoix, "where nothing is wanting that can possibly contribute to form an agreeable society."[6]

Quebec was the beachhead of metropolitan business. There independent Canadian importers or the clerks or junior partners of French shippers received incoming cargoes of French goods and shipped out the colony's exports, which by value were mainly, but by no means entirely, fur. The transatlantic link was the beginning of a vertical chain attaching metropolitan creditors to colonial debtors.[7] Links of credit extended from French shippers to Quebec importers to local traders, entrepreneurs, retailers, and their customers and, in the case of the all-important inland fur trade, to Montreal outfitters, fur traders, and Indian hunters. As the agent of this metropolitan dominance, Quebec basked in its reflection. Its role was more than mere reflection when the Quebec-metropolis link was founded on a transatlantic partnership. It might shrink to almost nothing in cases where trade

was undertaken by Montreal-metropolis partnerships. Quebec therefore occupied a somewhat insecure niche in a vertical system that was
itself an enduring structure of the metropolitan-colonial relation. The
many personal exceptions tend only to prove the situational rule. The
successful merchant – an importer at Quebec or an outfitter at Montreal – who became the equal of his metropolitan correspondents or
partners characteristically joined them, making the understandable
move from colonial backwater to metropolitan city. The move to the
metropolis may have been commoner at Quebec, where so many of
the traders were Frenchmen. These were usually young men for whom
colonial exile provided an initial access to a trading system within
which they aspired to higher position. What remained typical of Canadian business was the chronic indebtedness of those left behind.

Except during the brief and unsuccessful career of the Colony
Company, the export of beaver was in the eighteenth century in the
hands of European monopolists, the Indies Company being the most
notable. In the seventeenth century it had similarly been in the hands
of monopolists. This meant that a significant portion of the profits to
be made from Canadian trade (sale of beaver on European markets) was
permanently outside the control of Canadians or the private French
traders who became involved in Canadian trade. It was thus an impoverished trade that in the years after 1650 had fallen into the hands of La
Rochelle merchants and their Canadian partners, a secondary trade for
secondary traders, plagued by an insufficiency of return cargo items.[8]
In the largely Huguenot port of La Rochelle, the Canada traders were a
small Catholic group dependent upon Protestants or Parisian bankers
for capital. In the sixteen-eighties and nineties military activity in
Canada had made the trade more profitable, and even some Huguenot
Rochelais had begun to take an interest in it. Protestant traders from
many cities became increasingly involved in the Canada trade in the
eighteenth century and, as the trade was concentrated in Bordeaux
and other cities of the southwest in the forties and fifties, may even
have come to dominate it.[9] During the second half of the seventeenth
century, many traders had come to Canada, formed partnerships with
Canadians from either Quebec or Montreal, and married into their
families, so that there emerged Franco-Canadian business families with
members on both sides of the Atlantic. This can be seen in the extensive Gaigneur-Grignon connection, which married into the Canadian
families of Jolliet, Le Ber, and Fleury Deschambault; in the marriage of
François Viennay-Pachot into the Juchereau family; in the marriage of
the children of Simon Mars into the Jolliet and Riverin families; in the
marriage of Le Moyne de Serigny to the daughter of the Rochelais merchant Antoine Héron; and so on.[10]

The classic example of the founding of a Rochelais house in the trade of Canada is that of Antoine Pascaud. He came to Canada in the 1680s, married a Canadian, became a prominent merchant, and moved to La Rochelle in 1709 or 1710. Until his death in 1717, he sent two ships annually to Canada. Trade with Canada was continued by his widow down to 1728 and by his sons, Antoine and Joseph, down to 1748. Pascaud's was the most prominent La Rochelle house trading to Canada, and until 1738, when it initiated a trade with Louisiana, Canada was its only market. The second house was that of Simon Lapointe, who sent his first ship to Quebec in 1727 and thereafter sent one each year to 1744. At Quebec he was represented by Jean-Baptiste Soumbrum, who became his son-in-law and, moving to La Rochelle, succeeded to the business in 1744. The third trader in importance, Charles Policarpe Bourgine, sent a ship to Canada each year from 1725 to 1732 and seems, like Pascaud, to have lived for a time in Canada. The last of the Rochelais big four trading to Canada was Charles de Fleury Deschambault, a Canadian by birth whose brother, Fleury de La Gorgendière, remained a merchant and government official in Canada. These four houses were responsible for sending more than a third of the tonnage that sailed to New France during its history, nearly three quarters of La Rochelle's share.[11]

The Rochelais traders to Canada, headed by the redoubtable Widow Pascaud, argued in 1734 that it was "notorious" that Canadian merchants owed the growth of their trade to credit extended by French merchants, especially those of La Rochelle, that advances to Canadians at 8 per cent had become a "usage" of commerce, and that the merchants of Quebec and Montreal admitted their dependence on French credit.[12] Although Rochelais traders had failed to extend the arena of their activities when the Indies Company was given the beaver monopoly in 1720, their role in providing outbound cargoes remained secure when in 1723 the company abandoned its short-lived attempt to send its own ships laden with cargo to Canada.[13]

The years from the mid-1690s to the earlier 1720s were not good ones for the Canadian economy. The collapse of the fur trade, the difficulties of war, and monetary problems were all reflected in a falling off of shipping between Canada and France. This decline and the subsequent recovery were summarized in Table I and are reflected in the totals of Table II. This table confirms that Canadian trade had little to attract new shippers and new ports until after 1720. "La Rochelle alone . . . undertakes the trade to Canada," the town's chamber of commerce declared in that year.[14] If that was an exaggeration, it was a pardonable one. A glance at Table II, which shows decennial averages of the number of ships sent annually to Quebec from La Rochelle and

Table II
Decennial Averages of the Number of Ships per Year
Sailing from France to Canada

Decade	La Rochelle	Bordeaux	Other Ports	Total
1650s	2.0	No data	No data	3.1
1660s	4.5	"	"	5.75
1670s	4.6	"	"	4.8
1680s	5.1	4.8	"	9.9
1690s	7.4	2.4	"	9.8
1700s	3.9	2.2	0.0	6.2
1710s	3.9	1.8	0.7	6.4
1720s	3.8	1.9	3.2	9.2
1730s	4.3	2.6	2.8	9.7
1740-44	3.0	5.4	2.4	12.2

Source: J.S. Pritchard, "Ships, Men and Commerce," Ph.D. dissertation, University of Toronto, 1971, Tables 2-10. Totals column includes additional Basque ships.

elsewhere, reveals that city's ancient ascendancy in the Canada trade, particularly when it is realized that the strong input from the port of Bordeaux in the 1680s and 1690s included a great many ships sent there from La Rochelle for wine.[15] But in the first two decades of the new century a portion of the departures from Bordeaux represents a new current of competition. Jean Jung, whose father had sent ships to Canada before the war, had himself lived in Canada and from the beginning of the century to 1730 was responsible for outfitting about half of Bordeaux's shipping to Quebec.[16] Many ships outfitted at Bordeaux were owned by Canadians – even some that never called at Quebec. Bordeaux was becoming a great colonial port because of its West Indies trade; it was undoubtedly a great source of capital, facilities, and skill. For whatever reason, perhaps because of the smallness of its own stake in Canadian trade, it was hospitable to Canadian traders.[17] The Canadians, for their part, were filling a void attributable to metropolitan lack of interest.

There was very little change in the volume of traffic from La Rochelle and Bordeaux in the 1720s; the stability of the first three decades of the century is indeed remarkable. It can only be explained by positing that the two ports had all they could do to manage the great expansion of their trades to the West Indies and that Canadians (who turn up in Bordeaux figures) had little capacity to expand. The market was there. The gap between the expansion of the Canadian market and the low level of servicing it received from these traditional ports was filled, as the table shows so clearly, by "other ports," these being Nantes,

Table III
La Rochelle's Bid for Ascendancy:
Averages for Designated Periods of the Number of Ships per Year
Sailing from France to Canada, 1720-1739

Years	La Rochelle	Bordeaux	Other Ports	Total
1720-28	3.3	2.1	2.8	8.2
1729-32	6.0	1.25	3.5	10.75
1733-39	4.0	2.8	2.75	9.55

Source: J.S. Pritchard, "Ships, Men and Commerce," Ph.D. dissertation, University of Toronto, 1971, Tables 2-10.

Marseilles, and St Malo. But none of the outfitters of these ports established a continuing relation with Quebec. Their ventures constitute a series of speculations, many of them unique entries in a big shipper's accounts, never to be repeated.[18] The twenties were marked by increased competition between the ports, beginning in 1722, and by overall growth beginning in the following year, reminding us of the economic recovery in both colony and metropolis. It is interesting to see La Rochelle try harder in the 1730s and the way in which Bordeaux moves with it. The 4.3 figure for La Rochelle in Table II alerts us to a second burst of activity in that port, which may be examined more readily in Table III. La Rochelle's recovery of its trade is concentrated in 1729-32, finding its parallel in "other ports" if not in Bordeaux.

The heartening growth of Franco-Canadian trade in the context of expanding colonial trade in general and growing optimism in commercial circles undoubtedly was responsible for drawing to Canada La Rochelle's greatest competitor of the 1730s and early 1740s, Robert Dugard and Company of Rouen, with ships outfitted at Le Havre and Bordeaux. For if the figure for "other ports" drops in the 1730s, it gains in stability from this large company with its permanent presence at Quebec in the persons of its factors, Havy and Lefebvre, its programme of shipbuilding, and its vast trade, which in 1741 accounted for around one fifth of Canada's imports.[19] In the years just prior to the War of the Austrian Succession (1744-48 in America) there was a third burst of activity that is reflected in Table II by the increase of Bordeaux's figure to 5.4. This renewed growth at Bordeaux begins in 1738, continues to the end of our period, and is indeed a new pattern in the commercial history of New France. For the years 1738 to 1743, comparative annual averages for La Rochelle, Bordeaux, and Other Ports are respectively 3.3, 5.5, and 2.1. Bad harvests, a veritable collapse of Canadian agriculture, had created a dependence upon the vast agricultural hinterland of Bordeaux, a dependence that would be perpetuated after 1743, as the student of these port records has put it, "owing to the demands of war and an altered government policy which saw New France transformed from an agricultural and trading community into a large military fortress and garrison."[20]

The picture for the period 1702-43 is thus clear: the persistent relation with La Rochelle; Bordeaux always dabbling, a favourite with Canadians on the make; the challenge of Rouen; these three giving rise to the establishment of factors, agents, partners, or principals at Quebec; and the spate of "seekers," ships bearing cargoes on speculation in the care of their captains or supercargoes, *marchands forains* from Nantes, Marseilles, or St Malo. This was the transatlantic relation.

In Quebec's Lower Town, metropolitan and colonial met, sometimes head-on. The *marchand forain* (the *itinerant*, not foreign, merchant) was the particular object of the Canadian merchant's spleen. A supercargo or sea captain, the *forain* was the natural enemy of established middlemen, bringing in goods that he sold to both retailers and the general public at the same price, buying up crops and flooding the rural parishes with his cheaper goods in barter transactions, often enough dumping the remainder of his cargo when the approach of freeze-up forced him to leave the colony. The Canadian merchants' complaints against these unequal competitors regularly found their way to the Marine Department, for example in petitions in 1719, 1724, and 1727. In 1730 Governor Beauharnois and Intendant Gilles Hocquart were ordered not to forward any more petitions on the subject.[21] Nevertheless, Hocquart continued to plead the Canadian cause in his letters, and the Minister had to spell out for him government policy on the question: "In a word, trade cannot be too free."[22] Hocquart, at first critical of Canadian business for its fur trade fixation and lethargy, came to appreciate the many difficulties under which colonials laboured. Much of the trade was in the hands of their French brethren, and they were themselves too poor to break into this trade or to diversify their investments for the benefit of the colony. There was no colonial pool of capital. French competition began to seem unfair to Hocquart. He conceived the idea of fostering the development of a nucleus of Canadian businessmen by encouraging their trade and putting into their hands both lands and industrial projects. The times were ripe for a grand strategy: the Marine demanded it; internal stability and external market demands made it appear a not impossible dream.

The difficulty facing Canadian enterprise was not one of dealing with itinerants. The significant metropolitans at Quebec were not the *forains* but the factors. They too complained about the *marchands forains*.[23] Hocquart argued that the problem was the stranglehold of this respectable body on the Atlantic trade link: "A great many of the merchants owe considerable sums in France, and without fear of contradiction I can say that these still amount to more than 250,000 livres. Today the Canadian traders don't profit from half the trade conducted here. Merchants at La Rochelle and Rouen send their clerks here with a great quantity of merchandise. . . ."[24] The Quebec merchants had been given the right in 1717 to assemble for business purposes and to elect a syndic to represent them vis-à-vis the government. A glance at their election of a syndic in 1740 is instructive of the makeup of the merchant community. Of the seventeen persons involved, ten were definitely Frenchmen, and the syndic elected was a Canadian who moved to France seven years later![25] Feeling against *forains*, which might spill over to include resident Frenchmen, was intensified by the fact that shopkeeping was a very overcrowded profession[26] and that while there were many Canadians at the top, there were only Canadians at the bottom.

It was not easy to be a successful Lower Town merchant in the Franco-Canadian trade.[27] He must rightly assess the needs of the Canadian market, tie a good clientele to his parent house through the shrewd extension of credit, and grade and price the "returns" of fur. Making up cargoes for France that would return as much as possible of his principal's capital was his constant preoccupation. The shortage of export commodities in Canada that put a premium on the long-term business connections most apt to provide a steady supply of return cargo combined with the shortness of the Canadian navigation season to make local representation essential for any French house desiring a continued trade with the colony. In short, the very difficulty of the representative's task was his *raison d'être*.

The status of representatives varied. The most significant among them were factors – *préposés* or *commis* (they used these two terms interchangeably) – sent out from La Rochelle, Rouen, or Bordeaux. They were Europeans who saw the advancement of their careers in terms of a return to the Continent, although they often stayed long years at Quebec and achieved a high degree of identification with Canadian society.[28] These factors might be employees working for salary, commission agents earning 5 per cent on sales of incoming cargo and 2.5 per cent on returns, or partners on some such basis as one third or one half of profit and loss.[29]

There was nothing extraordinary about the profits earned on French goods sent out, except perhaps that the invoice prices were always 5 or 6 per cent higher than they should have been. Except when war or monetary instability interfered, mark-ups were usually 20 to 30 per cent of the inflated invoice price, making a total of 26 to 36 per cent. Wine and brandy were treated differently, with prices as high as the traffic would bear – and it traditionally bears a lot. In 1743 white wine was marked up 160 per cent and red, 128 per cent. It was the high price of alcohol that gave outward voyages some prospect of profitability. Indeed, whereas the dry goods, which made up the bulk of French exports to Canada, were sometimes shipped to Canadian customers for freight and commission alone, wines and spirits were invariably sold in Canada by the shipper himself, who could not afford to forgo the large profits they earned.[30] How freely market prices were established remains a matter of conjecture. There seems to have been a certain pressure to maintain prices at a level determined by the Quebec community.[31] The presence of the *marchands forains* probably kept prices down; indeed, these traders would have a better historical reputation had there been consumer groups as well as the mercantile bourse and its syndic to memorialize the administration.

The Lower Town merchant always stocked a wide variety of goods; his was a general store. The big customer, a fur trader, a Montreal outfitter or retailer, bought everything from one dealer. In return for his undivided custom, the dealer gave him credit. When Intendant Hocquart came up with the notion of favouring some of his protégés by granting them a monopoly of the sale of metals, Governor Beauharnois was quick to point out that credit facilities, "of which the trade of this country has more need than others, could no longer be found if our merchants were obliged to buy woollens and linens from some and metals from monopolists."[32]

The 8 per cent that La Rochelle business houses charged Canadian businessmen for merchandise advances was a high rate. The usual level of interest in France was one-half per cent a month, 6 per cent annually.[33] This too was the rate in Canada, but it is not always easily discerned, being hidden in the face value of promissory notes, of which considerable use was made in Canada, and of obligations signed before notaries by major debtors, instruments routinely signed by fur traders. Nevertheless it is always in the invoice. Thus, when the Widow Monfort came down from Montreal to purchase an outfit for her post of St Joseph River, she was given an invoice in which her blankets, various woollens, tools, and smallwares were listed at their original inflated French invoice price. The mark-up of 20 per cent was added at the bottom, making a total of 10,684 livres 10/7 and to this was added interest of 641 livres 1/5. The grand total of 11,325 livres 12/ – appears in the obligation simply and laconically as "for merchandise furnished and delivered to the said lady."[34] The term of credit granted Mme

Monfort was characteristically elastic, ending the following September "or earlier if the canoes for the said St Joseph River are back at the said Montreal before the said month of next September." The debt was payable in furs from the post at the rate current at the time of delivery. The obligation constituted an encumbrance on Mme Monfort's furs as well as on her property in general.

There was always a great rush of business in the Lower Town in the autumn. Like the ships from Europe, canoes from the West were late arrivers. One group was usually waiting on the other for a matter of weeks. Lenders of capital had to wait a year, perhaps two, for payment in furs. There were undoubtedly some holders of fur beholden to none, free to freight their packs with whomever they chose, consigned to whomever they thought fit. But the majority were tied by debt to a Lower Town merchant or directly to a French house. The price for fur was set in Lower Town in accordance with the exigencies of the European market – except for the price of beaver, which was set by statute. The going rate was set for a standard pelt; a certain number of lower-quality pelts were equivalent to one good one. Suppliers of furs appear to have had little influence over the price they were paid. The Lower Town dealers, who as creditors were difficult to argue with, passed on added costs to the suppliers. "It wouldn't be fair if I paid you the same price as in previous years since freight and insurance have increased considerably" was the chiding advice of the dealer Jean-André Lamaletie to his Montreal supplier, Pierre Guy, after war had altered the conditions of trade in 1745.[35] Nothing speaks more eloquently of the colonial relation than this exception to the general rule that costs are passed on to the consumer.

Canada almost invariably had an adverse balance of payments; 1739 and 1741 were exceptions.[36] The colony experienced every difficulty in finding exports suitable for the French market beyond its reliable base of fur; yet its growing population boosted consumer demand. There were certainly numerous efforts to find new exports or at least to cut imports by increasing self-sufficiency. Lumber, flour, seal oil, tobacco, and even ships were at various times in the period exported to the metropolis. Naval stores were produced to supply the local market. But only fur and bills of exchange resulting from government expenditures seemed wholly reliable, year in, year out. The result, Hocquart estimated, was chronic indebtedness to French merchants for some five to six hundred thousand livres, which increased and diminished but could never be done away with entirely.[37] It can readily be seen on the level of the individual firm, for example Havy and Lefebvre, for whom tardiness in payment left an ever-growing pool of outstanding debts.[38] Yet the scale of Canadian operations was small by international standards and trade debts were not spectacular. "These debtors," the Intendant observed, "make satisfaction little by little."[39]

Quebec had its own fur trade, distinct from the trade of the Great West. This was the trade of the "King's Posts" or the "Traite de Tadoussac," the scattered posts north and east of Quebec that collected the furs of the harsh uplands of the Montagnais. The entrepôt of this trade was the ancient port of Tadoussac, from which furs were sent up-river to Quebec for export. In the middle of the seventeenth century there were only the waterfront posts of Godbout and Tadoussac, the latter drawing directly on the two inland posts of Chicoutimi and Lac Saint-Jean.[40] By 1700 the coastal post of Moisie had been added, together with five more posts inland. Seven more coastal and two more inland posts were set up by 1733, when the domain extended from Les Eboulements, opposite Ile aux Coudres, to Cape Cormorant below Sept Iles, nearly four hundred kilometres along the shore, extending inland to the height of land.

The King's Posts were part of the Domaine d'Occident, or Western Domain, and were generally sublet to merchants in Canada. At the turn of the century, the lease was worth 15,200 livres a year. Between 1701 and 1714, the posts were held by a succession of traders at 12,700 livres a year.[41] Profitability declined so much that when Charles Guillimin's lease expired in 1714, he declared that he would not renew it again for more than 1,000 livres. This decline has been attributed not only to the collapse of the fur market but also to the ruining of the *ferme* by a previous lessee, Denis Riverin, by overhunting, abandoning posts, alienating the Indians, and importing large amounts of brandy all in the interests of short-term profit. As the trade was thought to be no longer worth leasing, it was run by the Western Domain down to 1733. François-Etienne Cugnet, the domain's agent from 1719, was an imaginative businessman who came to share Hocquart's hopes for Canada and his friendship. He was given the task of nursing the trade of the posts back to health, and it was during his administration that many new posts were founded. When the domain in Canada was returned to the Crown in 1733, Cugnet's *régie* continued; he simply became a civil servant. As the trade showed a profit of 33,000 livres between 1733 and 1737, Cugnet leased the posts himself for the next ten years at 4,500 livres a year. Later, more substantial offers made for the lease suggest that the trade may have been more profitable than Cugnet let on.[42]

Quebec business interests were also active beyond Cape Cormorant. This period sees the lower North Shore and the coast of Labrador

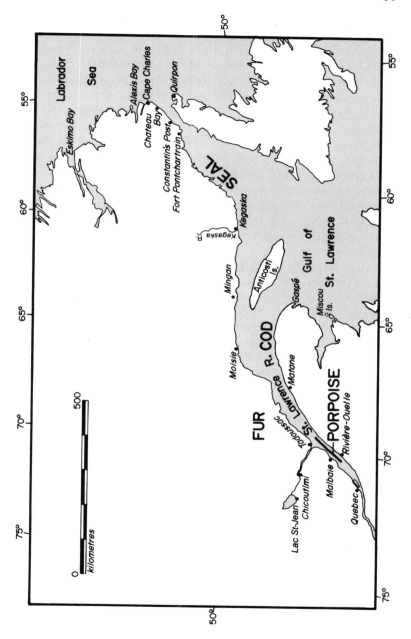

Quebec's Own Empire

brought into the purview of Quebec trade. Every vessel that had ever cast anchor before Quebec had sailed along this familiar coast. French fishermen had frequented it from time out of mind; even in 1534 Cartier encountered a fishing vessel "lost" one hundred miles into the Strait of Belle Isle.[43] In the later seventeenth century, there had been a number of attempts to turn to commercial account this area so often seen from the ship's rail. The earliest was the granting of the seigneury of Mingan to François Bissot and shortly afterwards the grant of the Mingan islands to Lalande and Jolliet and the grant of Anticosti to Jolliet. In 1689 a company was formed by Riverin to exploit the fur trade at Belle Isle and another by Aubert de La Chesnaye to undertake fishing and sealing as well as trade at Blanc Sablon.[44] The formation of the Northern Company and the Colony Company diverted entrepreneurial energies and capital and was closely followed by the war, the derangement of the currency, and the King's default. Yet it was during the war that the first steps were taken towards establishing a permanent Canadian foothold in the area.

Two Canadians of widely different background were willing to make their homes in the region. The more prominent was Augustin Le Gardeur de Courtemanche. A military man, the same who had acted as a frontier diplomat for Callière in 1701, Courtemanche had married into a Quebec business family. He was granted an immense concession from the Kegashka River on the North Shore to Hamilton Inlet (then known as Eskimo Bay) on the Atlantic coast.[45] The concession was subsequently reduced in size, and in 1714 Courtemanche was given a life grant of Baie Phélypeaux, where he made a considerable establishment and persuaded thirty or forty Montagnais families to settle. In the same year, he was made the King's Commandant on the coast of Labrador "to settle and adjust the disputes which arise between His Majesty's subjects in connection with the situations of fisheries on the said coast." After his death in 1717, the post remained in the hands of his family, and the title of commandant passed to his stepson, Martel de Brouague.[46] The other precursor in the region was Pierre Constantine, described in a concession as simply an "Habitant of the côte and seigneury of Maure."[47] He was for a time in the employ of Courtemanche but ultimately had his own establishment on the Strait of Belle Isle. Both he and Courtemanche had visited the coast all the way to Eskimo Bay and produced either sketch-maps or information on which maps were later based.[48]

The North Shore–Labrador coast was not easily won. By nature it is inhospitable. A low-lying coast of rock along the river and gulf is fronted from Mingan to the strait by a vast archipelago, confusing and hazardous to navigation. Beyond the strait, past the ancient landmark of Chateau Bay, at Cape Charles the coast turns north to front the

Atlantic. Here is the coast of enormous swells, of ice-clogged harbours and drifts of icebergs, rocky headlands of increasing height, sombre mountains, high beach terraces, a landscape barren of vegetation but for the scrub, black spruce in the milder climates of deep-set bays.[49] But all of it is the natural habitat of migrating seals, of whales and walrus, sea birds, salmon and cod. In its own way, it is a region of great richness.

In the period under review and much later, Inuit frequented these coasts and were encountered as far west as Anticosti. They were regarded as savage and hostile. It was always a major point for suppliants demanding concessions in the region to claim that they had established, or intended to establish, good relations with them.[50] Inuit were certainly responsible for the near desertion of this northern coast by French fishermen, who resorted to the Newfoundland shore. They constantly harassed the sealing stations set up in this period. It has been alleged that the Inuit had been lured so far south in the seventeenth century by trade goods and that their hostility resulted from the bad treatment they had received from both Frenchmen and Indians.[51]

In spite of difficulties, a large number of posts, primarily sealing stations with ancillary trade, were established in this period, half of them in the 1730s. Six new concessions were made between 1710 and 1730 and seven more between 1733 and 1740.[52] In 1742 it was decided in order to conserve the seal population to make no more concessions.[53] A cursory examination of the recipients of concessions shows them to have been for the most part Quebec businessmen and civil servants, the persons best situated to ask for them. In the official category were Lafontaine de Belcour, Foucault, Boucault, Pommereau. Hazeur, Bazil, Marsal, Fornel, Havy, Lefebvre were all Lower Town merchants, not necessarily Canadian, but long established and resident. In many cases, there were ties of marriage between these two groups.

Sealing was an exploitation that was a particular outlet for Quebec business, something within the reach of colonials that increased their buying power in the trade with France by providing, in seal oil and skin, exports acceptable to the French market. It was thus dependent upon the trade with France, and those who undertook it were themselves usually involved directly in that trade. The sealing stations were invariably run by partnerships and staffed by employees. The buildings, ships, and payroll required a large investment. Often the partnerships represented the union of a concessionaire and a capitalist, privilege and money.

By the eve of the War of the Austrian Succession, the coasts of the North Shore and Strait of Belle Isle were provided with a string of human habitations, beginning with the posts of the Traite de Tadoussac from Malbaie to Moisie and the private stations starting at Mingan. Several major stations marked the foggy strait ending at Chateau Bay. There was little activity beyond. From Cape Charles to Alexis Bay was the last concession, held by Antoine Marsal. Four hundred kilometres from the strait, north along this coast, lay Eskimo Bay, visited, known to fishermen, perhaps the site of intermittent trade.[54] But it had not in any permanent way come within the Canadian sphere of commercial activity. An expedition to Eskimo Bay was a costly undertaking, and while different persons had asked for a concession there, no one did anything about it in the 1730s. "The costs have seemed to all of them to be too considerable, let alone the other difficulties and risks to be contended with in such an enterprise," the local authorities explained.[55]

In 1743, when there were no more concessions being granted nearer to hand, the Quebec merchant Louis Fornel, probably spurred on by competition, undertook the journey to lay claim to the site. It was a frugal and merchantly voyage of discovery, starting on a ship belonging to a company in which Fornel was a partner while on its regular run to Chateau Bay, continuing on a schooner rented at Quirpon for the last leg to Eskimo Bay, with the return made again on board the company ship to Quebec, where Fornel arrived on August 25, 1743. Hocquart, however, was most reluctant to make the concession. As the lessees of the domain, François-Etienne Cugnet and Guillaume Estèbe, explained to him, the Northern Indians "by way of the Kitche-chatsous River [the Churchill?], as wide and as deep as the Saguenay, could . . . easily visit the establishment that Sieur Fornel was proposing, provided that they were brought birchbark to make the necessary canoes."[56] Eskimo Bay was a potential Tadoussac of the north. Hocquart temporized; war broke out; Fornel died. There were no more new concessions until 1748: six between then and 1750. It was not the equal of the burst of activity in 1730s but is sufficient to remind us that the Quebec merchants were still capable of increasing their interests in the area. Most of the new posts were in familiar territory in between earlier concessions. Eskimo Bay, however, did go to Fornel's widow in 1749.

Fishing on a commercial scale was undertaken in the lower St Lawrence and gulf in this period, but it did not answer expectations. At Kamouraska, Rivière Ouelle, and Pointe-aux-Trembles there was an initial flurry of activity in porpoise "fishing" between 1701 and 1708, all of it inspired by Quebec merchants. The aim was the same as that of sealing, to provide oil for export. There was renewed activity after the war, including habitant initiatives. In 1721 there were fourteen porpoise fisheries; in 1724, seventeen; and in 1725, twenty-one. But in the 1730s yields declined, and the industry became negligible. Cod fishing was undertaken primarily from French ports or from Ile Royale. Canadian efforts were confined to the St Lawrence below Matane and to the Gaspé region. Quebec merchants did play a role in the cod fishery, but it was a small affair.[57]

Louisbourg became in this period a major market for Canadian agricultural and forest exports. Throughout the period studied here, the colony was provisioned from Canada.[58] Previously there had been a Canadian trade to Placentia, but nothing to compare with the trade to Louisbourg, where a large garrison, a sedentary fishery, and a trading town came to constitute a large market. Louisbourg had no agricultural hinterland, and even before the town was built, Canadian flour and biscuit were needed there. The link was not established without awkwardness and trouble. In 1714 trade to the West Indies left no surplus for Cape Breton. A special effort was made to supply the colony in 1718, although to stretch the food supply, two hundred of the garrison had to be sent to Quebec for the winter.[59]

The major problem in establishing the Canada–Ile Royale link was not one of will, nor even of capital, but of the availability of provisions for export. As agricultural conditions improved, the situation stabilized. In 1727 no less than thirty-one Quebec merchants claimed an interest in the trade; in 1728 Canada was officially entrusted with the task of supplying Louisbourg's garrison to the extent possible. A new economic structure had been put in place.[60] The traffic grew abruptly. From 10, 12, and 15 ships respectively in the previous three years, in 1727 the number of ships giving Louisbourg as their destination rose to 27 and from then until 1736 averaged 24.3 vessels a year. The traffic faltered badly in 1737 – down to 5 – rallied to maintain an average of 16.3 over the next three years, and then trailed off to the eve of war: 6, 9, 7.[61] For much of this period the volume of shipping between Quebec and Louisbourg, measured in tonnage, was larger than Quebec's trade with France itself.[62]

The small boats that provisioned this market flitted back and forth, up and down the St Lawrence and gulf, shuttles weaving a fabric of trade. It was a delicate fabric. Ile Royale was a small market, easily glutted. Sudden gluts shared the same historical canvas with dramatic moments of dearth. In the case of the latter, after a good deal of delay and awkwardness accompanied by price-fixing ordinances, supplies could usually be brought from somewhere around the rim of the Atlantic. Even under the best market conditions (enough wheat to export but not enough to produce glut) prices did not rise to compensate for bad years (those of glut or crop failure). Profit margins remained low. "Nevertheless," wrote Beauharnois and Hocquart, "as it is the principal market for the produce of this country and the most accessible for small ships," it was a significant trade that Canadians could not forgo.[63]

When Louisbourg rose on the shore of Baie des Anglais and into the consciousness of traders, there was a very small trade already in existence between Canada and Martinique, to which Saint-Domingue and other islands were added in due time. To read, even cursorily, the correspondence of the Minister and other Marine officials at Versailles with their governors and intendants is to see what great store government put in the development of these trades, which would provide markets for Canada, support its merchants, and at the same time feed Ile Royale and provide the sugar islands with food, lumber, bateaux, horses, and a market for their tafia and molasses, all without leaving the empire open to Anglo-American interlopers. West Indian administrators were always a little guarded in their acquiescence, perhaps because they profited from smuggling, but certainly because they knew the best interests of the islands lay in a sure and steady flow of goods from English America and the low prices of plentiful supply.

As we have seen, Quebec traders had secured a foothold in this trade during the War of the Spanish Succession. Carried on by both Canadian and French shippers, it burst into vibrant life just when the Louisbourg trade did, in 1727. According to port statistics it occupied 9 ships that year and an average of 8.6 yearly – based on an incomplete count – to the end of 1739, when it too trailed off in disappointing fashion: 5, 8, 5.[64] Viewed in the aggregate of island trade, Canada's input was small. Intendant Blondel of Martinique can be pardoned for having missed the take-off of this trade in 1728 – most of the impact was at Saint-Domingue that year. He wrote that the trade never had become well established, that two Saint-Pierre de la Martinique merchants who had attempted it the previous year had failed, and that they were the only ones in his colony capable of trying. But the major pitfall, he argued, was inherent in geography. Because food would not keep in the tropics, Martinique could not be provisioned on a once-a-year basis; and Canada was so far from the West Indies and the Canadian navigation season was so short that it was impossible to make two trips a year from Quebec.[65] Sixteen years later, one of Blondel's successors, de La Croix, echoed the complaint of colonial incapacity, writing that it was difficult to form a company for an ambitious trade in "a land of colonists who consider themselves transients, who have as the object of their sojourn prompt and rapid fortunes."[66] But in the interval Blondel's second obstacle was overcome. As early as 1731, another intendant of Martinique, d'Orgeville, noted that trade with French North America had increased, but he pointed out that merchants from his island did not usually go all the way to Quebec. They stopped at Louisbourg, which served them as an entrepôt. With luck, two voyages a year were at last possible.[67]

There was more to Louisbourg's role than halving the distance ships were required to sail to link the markets of Canada and the West Indies. A portion of the Canadian grain carried to Ile Royale was sold for cod by either Canadian shippers or Louisbourg purchasers for shipment to the West Indies. Let Hocquart explain it:

> The cargo of a 200-ton ship coming from the Iles du Vent with molasses, sugars, syrups and other goods would be worth 40,000 to 50,000 livres. The Canadian produce that the same ship could carry to the islands in wood and provisions would total at most 15,000 livres. Thus the trade of the islands with Canada cannot be balanced except by the shipments of flour and biscuit made to Ile Royale, there to be converted into cod that goes to the islands or to France. Almost all the ships from France after having made their sales at Quebec go to the Iles du Vent via Ile Royale. Those that go directly from Canada to the Iles du Vent can only make a part of their return cargo in the produce of that colony and the rest in bills of exchange.[68]

As Hocquart put it in another dispatch, if Ile Royale hadn't taken Canada's biscuit (this was the way of disposing of inferior stuff) and "rough flour," it would not have been possible for Canada to continue its trade with the West Indies in high-quality flour.[69] Cargoes of Canadian produce were also sold at Louisbourg or in the Indies for promissory notes used to purchase French wares. In this way produce unsuitable to the French market was used to pay for the importation into Canada of manufactured goods.[70]

The presence of the Louisbourg entrepôt and of the fishery made possible many different patterns of trade. Canadians had the option of sailing only as far as Louisbourg, where their cargoes could be sold to Creole shippers, probably through Louisbourg middlemen. Or Canadians could stop at Louisbourg to "enrich" their cargoes with cod and proceed themselves to Caribbean waters. Or French ships returning to metropolitan ports could stop for "enrichment" and proceed to the islands or to southern European ports where there was a market for cod. Because of the variety of possibilities offered, port statistics are rather difficult to interpret. Many or all of the small number of ships reported as leaving Quebec for the West Indies may have stopped to trade for cod at Louisbourg or elsewhere along the coasts of Ile Royale. Some of those reporting Louisbourg as their destination may have proceeded on to Léoganne or Saint-Pierre.

The rise of Quebec's Louisbourg trade gets part of its significance from the fact that it was originally a relatively easy trade for native Canadians to enter. "It is only since the establishment of Ile Royale that maritime trade has acquired some favour," wrote Beauharnois and Hocquart in 1733. "Before that time it was limited to fishing and the sending of one or two ships to the islands."[71] But if this trade was a great boon to Canadian merchants, it was one that they had perforce to share with competitors. In 1732 Hocquart believed that metropolitans dominated the export of Canadian flour, that is, the trade to Louisbourg and the Indies.[72] In the 1720s the percentage of La Rochelle ships, for example, that plied the triangle route may have been as high as 18, rising to 44 in the thirties, before making the characteristic descent that we have learned to anticipate to 16.7 per cent in the last four years before the war.[73] We can see a closeup of this merchant activity in the history of Robert Dugard and Company of Rouen, the only firm trading to Canada for which we have detailed knowledge over an extended period of time. The company undertook thirty-nine voyages involving Quebec, Louisbourg, or both. Twenty-eight per cent of them were triangular. Of the thirty-four voyages that involved Quebec, 20.5 per cent were triangular, the difference being made up by triangular voyages to Louisbourg that did not include Quebec. But either on a triangle route or as a stop on a return west-east voyage, fully 38 per cent of Quebec voyages included a stop at Louisbourg.[74] Dugard and Company were rather special because of the scale of their operations. Many of the stops at Louisbourg on direct returns were synchronized with voyages of other company vessels coming from the Caribbean which were thus afforded the quickest possible turnaround time at Louisbourg.

Contraband made it increasingly difficult for Canada, whether by ᵗhe agency of native Canadian or of French shippers, to maintain any share at all in Louisbourg's trade. In 1729 the director of the Domaine d'Occident in Martinique complained that the "Canadian" lumber got from Louisbourg was really from Boston.[75] Complaint was thereafter continuous. This is not surprising because contraband had always been a part of island trade, had for long periods been its very substance. Louisbourg was a good locus for smuggling because of its proximity to New England and its entrepôt trade with Canada, which afforded cover in a period when the government was attempting to tighten controls. It was complained of not only by government and tax farm officials but also by French and Canadian traders, who found the Anglo-American competition unbeatable, given the plenty and the cheapness of its commodities, whether English manufactures or colonial produce. As Maurepas put it, "the necessity we are in of tolerating in certain cases the admission of English ships to Louisbourg" made it easy for them to smuggle goods to French ships.[76] Such fraud, which required the connivance of local officials, was added to the injury wrought by discriminatory regulations that forced Canadians to dispose of all cargo they had brought to Louisbourg before getting permission to leave – no matter what the price.[77]

The inner history of the trade of Louisbourg is still a closed book. But the surface of events suggests that both officials and merchants (the link was close, identity sometimes the same) found in the trade with New England more advantage than in the trade with Canada. As Louisbourg became an important entrepôt rather than a dependent colony on the fringe of things, there was less and less place within its economy for the Canadians of the shuttle traffic.[78] In years when the Canadian economy was in disarray and few ships left Quebec laden with lumber and produce, Louisbourg remained a busy port; and the link between northern and southern economies remained intact.[79]

Canadian trade needed little outside pressure to falter. Canadian traders were dealing in new commodities, the products of forest and farm. Often the product was of a rough, backwoods quality, and the demands of export markets necessitated improvement. For example, government regulation and the introduction of sifters were necessary before merchantable flour could be produced.[80] More important, agriculture was by nature precarious. On a number of occasions the wheat supply failed, greatly disrupting the trade and giving Canada a reputation for undependability. The Lower Town traders Havy and Lefebvre well expressed the pessimism that had come to prevail wherever the possibilities of Canadian trade were considered: "It is worthy of notice that if provisions are abundant for two or three years running, they become rare and dear for two or three years too."[81]

The new trades cannot be left without a comment on their scale and weight in economic life. They were bound to be ancillary to the traditional trade with France. The straggling, one continued village that was really Canada – lying in a short and narrow parallelogram of arable soil, all of which endured a rude and extreme climate – was in no position to satisfy the wants of the sugar islands in the heyday of their opulence. Nor, with the best will in the world, could its people make use of the available quantity of the base products from which rum is distilled, all that the plantation economy had to exchange for basic necessities. It could not send the horses so much in demand on the long journey to Saint-Pierre de la Martinique and deliver them healthy and alive. But in the Thirty Years' Peace, it could and did provide a good and welcome share of what was needed, thereby balancing its own trade and buttressing its commercial development.

*   *   *

The trade of Quebec with the ports of the Atlantic had thus increased remarkably between 1702 and 1743, both in size and in new directions. Growth was particularly marked in the decade of the thirties. The scale of economic life in the eighteenth century must, of course, be kept in mind; an active colonial port was a small affair. From humble beginnings, the number of ships that might be found in Quebec harbour in the course of a shipping season averaged no more than thirty-one in the twenties and thirty-six in the thirties.[82] Trade statistics collected by the intendancy can be used to supplement shipping statistics, although no high degree of accuracy can be claimed for them. These figures attribute to Canada average annual exports valued at 1,633,554 livres and imports valued at 1,863,885 livres for the 1730s with corresponding figures of 2,229,341 livres and 2,247,988 livres for 1740-43. The trade deficit was chronic, and the two years of favourable balance, 1739 and 1741, were so unusual as to become celebrated. But the deficit was decreasing, from equalling 14 per cent of exports in the thirties to less than 1 per cent in 1740-43. New export commodities were replacing bills of exchange in Canadian "returns." The *rate* of increase for exports throughout the Thirty Years' Peace was greater than the imports rate, reflecting the growth of intercolonial trade.[83]

After the war, Quebec's provisioning trade to Louisbourg would not be revived, and the trade to the sugar islands – with rare exceptions in 1748 and 1752 – would return to the modest scale of the twenties. The question of trade with France is more complicated. This trade would increase considerably, but much of the growth would be related to government expenditure for war and war-related activities, not the least being the considerable import of flour and grain into the colony. The metropolitan traders of the new war machine would tend to shoulder aside many of the lesser merchants of the economy of free and private enterprise. All this would mean an increase in Crown expenditures in Canada, the "invisible export" that had always kept the imbalance of trade from being calamitous. There would be short-run gains for many, even for Canadians.

CHAPTER 8

Montreal and the Inland Rivers

I

The islands of the Hochelaga archipelago lay at the confluence of two great rivers, the Ottawa, flowing from the west into the Lac des Deux Montagnes, and the St Lawrence, bringing the waters of the Great Lakes into Lac Saint-Louis, the lakes themselves separated by Ile Perrot and the garden-like expanse of Montreal Island, crowned by its sentinel mountain. Bateaux and barques could go no farther west. The rapids of Lachine barred the interior to the questing trader. At the foot of the island's eastern slope was a deep and protected anchorage. Here the boatmen could land their cargo and merchants take it into their care to sell at the fairs to visiting Indians or to send by cart to Lachine and then by canoe to the Great West. Here, around the original mission, grew up the town of Montreal, the inland centre of the fur trade. A few miles overland to the east, at Chambly, the Richelieu cut through the plain on its way to the St Lawrence, providing the smuggler with an open road to the New York fur-trading capital of Albany.

By means of a stout plank extended from the side of the small bateau or a dinghy lowered from a larger vessel, passengers and cargo alike were delivered to a stretch of shore referred to as the *quai aux barques* from which it was a short walk to the market square surrounded by the houses of merchants. The town was really two long streets intersected by numerous cross streets in which, for the most part, officers, soldiers, merchants, artisans, and labourers lived cheek by jowl. At the beginning of the century, only about 1,300 people occupying fewer than two hundred houses lived in the city. A spurt of growth in the postwar period raised the population to nearly 3,000 by 1731. Ten years later, 3,575 people occupied 457 houses. The many public and conventual buildings gave a certain urban substance to a town consisting mostly of small wooden houses. Partly a result of the cumulative effect of prosperity, partly in response to disastrous fires in 1721 and

1734, more and more stone houses were being erected. Still, there were not enough of them, even in the 1740s, for the local stone to impart to the townscape that sobriety that would engulf it at the end of the century. A rickety old palisade was being replaced by a stone wall, begun in 1717 and finished in 1741. Within, plenty of open garden space, the practice of keeping pigs and chickens, and the use of horses meant the streets were just one remove from the congested farmyard. But mud, garbage, and smells did not greatly perturb those who were used to them. "The town of Montreal has a very cheerful appearance. It is well situated, well laid out and well built," wrote Charlevoix. "The charm of its countryside and its views inspires a certain gaiety that everyone feels."[1]

Beyond the town, the island offered the best soil and the warmest climate in Canada – for Charlevoix, sailing from Quebec to Montreal was like crossing the Loire to the sunny Midi. There were four rural parishes in 1700, and six more were added by 1741. Communities of Christian Iroquois at the mouth of the Ottawa (Two Mountains) and across the St Lawrence from Lachine (Caughnawaga) gave an Indian presence to Montreal even after the decay of the fairs and provided defenders for this frontier of settlement and carriers in the smuggling trade between Canada and New York.

Montreal had come into existence as a mission, and its churches, schools, hospitals, and convents were the continuing evidence that the Church's outreach to the world remained vital to it. To serve as an entrepôt for the fur trade of the inland rivers, to organize that trade and house its participants quickly came to overshadow this original purpose. It provided the same supply function for military posts in the West and was the meeting place for the governor, his western commandants, and the ambassadors of the western tribes.[2]

At the beginning of the century, the Canadian beaver trade was still suffering from that crisis of oversupply that had led to the closing of the West by the King's Declaration of April 28, 1697. But there was still a fur trade. In those years, traders were turning their attention to the *menues pelleteries*, the whole gamut of furs from small animals such as martin, muskrat, and mink, as well as to the furs of wolves, bears, and lynx. And there was always a trade in the hides of moose and deer. Reduced quantities of beaver continued to be traded, and the English market, in particular, showed some resiliency. As a measure to regulate the trade, the declaration of 1697, although buttressed by a continued output of decrees and regulations, had proved a failure. It had two effects. The first was to surrender by default a great part of the fur trade to the English either at James Bay or in New York, who received pelts from the hands of Indian traders including the "domiciled'' Indians living near Montreal. The second was that Canada was left with a much diminished trade, a legal one at the fairs and at Detroit and Frontenac, where it fell into the hands of self-seeking commandants, and an illegal one at Michilimackinac in the hands of Governor Vaudreuil and his creatures. Much of this illegal commerce was founded on the smuggling trade between Montreal and Albany in which the domiciled Indians, once again, were the carriers. French influence among the ''nations'' in the course of the War of the Spanish Succession was at its lowest ebb. After the recovery of the beaver trade in the 1720s, hides and furs other than beaver may still have accounted for as much as half the value of skins exported from Quebec, but beaver may have predominated in the sizeable smuggling trade to Albany. In that case, the restructuring of the trade may not have been as dramatic as Quebec export and La Rochelle import figures would indicate.[3]

Although beaver and the other small fur-bearing mammals were everywhere, the richest trapping country bordered the Canadian Shield from south to west – the Great Lakes forest, the lakes and marshes of Wisconsin and Minnesota, the Rainy Lake–Lake of the Woods country, the parklands west of Lake Winnipeg – and then north across the Saskatchewan, Beaver, Athabaska, and Peace and down the Slave and Mackenzie to the sea.[4] In the first half of the eighteenth century, the Great Lakes were still the heartland of Canada's western fur trade. From Montreal voyageurs paddled west along the Ottawa, Mattawa, and French rivers and Georgian Bay to Michilimackinac, the inland depot of the northern lakes.[5] The St Lawrence was the road to Detroit and the southern trade. While the country beyond the Lakes was not unknown to Canadians in 1700, it cannot be said to have been consolidated into the Canadian trade and alliance system. The beaver glut that began in the nineties had been a disincentive to expansion, and carrying the trade west of Lake Michigan and west and northwest of Lake Superior becomes a major part of the Canadian story in the years after Utrecht. This is one half of a diptych; the other is the story of the re-establishment of Canadian interests south of Detroit in the inverted triangle between the Mississippi and the Ohio. Along the line of the lower lakes and in the Ohio triangle, as in Acadia, the Canadian presence was as much political as economic. There a number of Indian nations found themselves in a zone of conflicting French and English pretensions.

In previous chapters, the Abenakis, Ottawas, Iroquois, and numerous other tribes have already appeared as crucial participants in Canada's history. Until about 1775, native peoples were the majority, both within the present boundaries of Canada and in the various territories that once constituted the sphere of French influence.[6] Without that population's previous adaptation to the environment – their geographical knowledge and sketch maps, linguistic and hunting skills, techniques of warfare, wilderness clothing, snowshoes, toboggans, and canoes – and their willingness to accept French goods and the French themselves, Canada would not exist. Yet the Indians revealed to the French societies, values, even personality structures in many ways alien and baffling to them.

The Indians saw themselves as a part of nature and all nature as animated by spirits. In the manner of hunters for millennia before them, they respected and honoured the spirits of the animals they killed. For the Frenchman, the environment was matter to be exploited. The French were acquisitive to a degree and reserved voluntary poverty for nuns and friars. Indians, even agricultural ones, retained the hunter's principle of sharing everything and thinking little of property.

While the French lived in a society based upon inequality, subordination, and force mirrored in the developing modern state, Indians gloried in the equality of sovereign individuals organized into bands or tribes whose government was indistinguishable from or modelled on the close but non-coercive links of kinship: family, lineage, clan. Indian headmen persuaded and were followed as long as a consensus lasted; French magistrates commanded and enforced obedience as best they could.

Indians held their societies together by trying not to give offence and by hiding negative or anti-social feelings, even to the point of voicing agreement when they did not agree or withdrawing from council or community rather than blocking the search for consensus. Coercion not usually being an option, Indians enforced community norms by playing on the tribesman's sense of honour, responding to deviations with ridicule and shaming. The Frenchman, on the other hand, had no corresponding fears for the fragility of his society. He felt free to be quarrelsome and offensive and frequently exhibited the irresponsibility of the underling. In his case, conformity to social norms was secured both by force and by the cultivation of a sense of sin, one of the worst sins being disobedience.

The French nobleman was a soldier and a sportsman, and his virtues were a model to French society. The French were thus in a position to appreciate the courage and endurance of the Indian warrior-hunter, although his guerrilla tactics at first struck them as cowardly and they never ceased to denounce him as wantonly cruel in war. Cruelty may have been dialectically related to the repression of negative feelings in daily life. It was certainly an outcome of the code of retributive justice of which the warrior was the instrument. "Their character is such and their manners are so odd and so little governed by ordinary sense, that they throw away on the impulse of the moment all the advantages which they have long enjoyed and sacrifice them to the recollection of some past wrong for which they will plan vengeance," complained Governor Beauharnois.[7] Blood feud and vengeance weren't much in keeping with French *realpolitik* and frequently upset French campaign plans.

The French thought of the Indian as a man in a state of nature (a savage) who had yet to be subdued and disciplined by the civilizing process. "It will necessarily be a task of infinite time to break through these people and compel them to take on our manners and customs," wrote one anonymous observer early in the century. "It will be only by continual attention to them that little by little we will succeed. I assure you this will be the work of centuries."[8] Missionaries and men of cultivation have left us a large body of ethnographic works that testify to considerable admiration of the Indians described as savages in the best sense, that is, unspoiled, or as savages only in name. Many people, in both Canada and the English colonies, shook the dust (and shoes) of civilization from their feet and went to live with the natives. But we have little evidence that most Canadians admired their Indian neighbours. Perhaps the crucial idea to be discerned is the French and Canadian notion of the relation between European and Indian. The explorer La Vérendrye in one of his journals refers to Crees and Assiniboins as "barbarians" whom he feared might "shake off the French yoke, which in truth makes for their well being."[9] Beauharnois used the same expression to describe French-Indian relations, and both it and similar metaphors can be found in English sources. It seems a long way from the traditional idea that the French "cherished" the Indian.

It was with the Indian, and in the Indian way, that the Canadian had perforce to trade. From ancient times Indians had traded. Trading was thought of as the exchange of gifts, and trading partners were described as kin. Trade was therefore a social or political act that knit together separate people or peoples. It was not, however, all politics and no economics. Even the Christmas present is economic redistribution and, frequently, well-calculated trade. In the eighteenth century, the fur trade still incorporated an exchange of gifts and a ceremonial that confirmed a friendly relation, but it was nevertheless a marketplace exchange. The Indian exploited competition, whether between the Hudson's Bay Company and Canadians or Canadians and the New York traders, to improve his bargaining position. His attitude toward the prices of all the Europeans seems best summed up in the words of the Ottawa trading at Albany, quoted in an earlier chapter: "Where we find goods cheapest, thither we will bend our course."[10] The Indian also insisted on quality, frequently showing traders the superior goods available from their competitors. The well-known French search for better trade woollens to meet English competition was a result of this insistence.

In one way the price mechanism did not work as expected, and the Indian proved to be an odd customer. His demand for European goods was so fixed and unbudgeable that if the value of his furs increased, he brought fewer of them to trade rather than enlarging his shopping list. One way the fur trade could be expanded was by bringing into it more *Indians*. While much has been made of the necessity to increase the geographical extent of the fur trade to counteract the decline in animal populations and, later in the century, to provide new territories for increasing numbers of Montreal traders, this counterpart to geographic expansion has gone unnoted. The Indian acted as a middleman in the trade in addition to his role as hunter and consumer, but, once again, in an Indian way. Present research suggests he passed on his own cast-off goods and while intent on getting the best price for them may have made little attempt to bring extra goods to trade or to enlarge his market. As there was a definite ceiling on his notion of consumption, so was there on his notion of profit. His trade, while accomplishing desirable redistribution of goods, may have been more political than economic in his eyes.

The political dimension of gift exchange with the French was concentrated in the exchange of presents of fur for the King's presents, comprised primarily of arms and ammunition, and had an English counterpart in exchanges at Albany that were conducted at the same time and place as the trade with private individuals. The King's presents were sufficiently substantial that they must be considered in economic as well as political terms. Many of the Allies were as surely Louis XV's clients as any Rhineland princeling. Certainly the French regarded the Indians as dominated purely by their own interests rather than by ancient obligations and kinship ceremonials. In a Canadian merchants' petition, they are "these Indians governed only by interest."[11] In the words of Intendant Hocquart, "There is no fear of saying that the Indians, a few excepted, love neither the French nor the English; they know that both need them."[12]

Cloth, clothing, and blankets made up the greater value of a Canadian fur trader's outfit. Unbleached linen and hemp were the major non-woollen fabrics. Shirts of these and such woollen clothing as capots, sleeves, and leggings were made up in Montreal. Much gunpowder was purchased there from the royal magazines. Few guns were traded, given their important place among the King's presents. Copper kettles and all manner of edge tools, needles, and awls were traded. Tobacco was essential. Beads and baubles, the trade goods of popular imagination, were necessary to the assortment and may have borne more than their share of the profit margin, but in total value had a modest place. Table IV shows a purchase of trade goods made at Quebec in 1742 for the post at St Joseph River. Add gunpowder and tobacco, have some of the cloth and thread made up into clothing, and the result is a well-assorted outfit.[13]

Brandy requires special comment. While it was used by the most unscrupulous traders to debauch tribesmen and facilitate the pillage of their furs, even responsible traders wanted liquor in their stock of goods. It attracted customers away from English competitors, and as it was both much desired and speedily consumed, it had the effect of raising the Indian's overall level of consumption. It was easier to increase sales by trading brandy than by seeking more Indian customers who, with regard to durable goods, could not be persuaded to deviate from a fixed pattern of purchases. By a host of edicts, ordinances, and regulations, the King and local officials sought to suppress or control drunkenness of White and Indian alike.[14] Although Indians continued to consume their share of brandy in the colony – Montreal's taverns with their "Indian barrels" of adulterated liquor were infamous – in 1679 the trade in brandy at the posts had been forbidden. Brandy could be taken west only for personal use. If much of it in fact was drunk by Indians, perhaps as a ceremonial preliminary to trade, the quantity was limited. But in 1727 the brandy trade was authorized where necessary to compete with the English. As a result, the Canadian bishop, Pierre-Herman Dosquet, in 1730 reserved to himself absolution of penitents directly or indirectly guilty of selling strong drink to Indians. Although he returned the power of absolution to the priests in 1738, he did not back down on the main issue, which remained a source of contention between Church and State throughout the colony's history.[15]

While the question of alcoholism *per se* remains poorly understood, all of the mystery cannot be dispelled from the special case of Indian alcohol abuse. The eighteenth-century missionary and superior of the Sulpician seminary, François Vachon de Belmont, in his *Histoire de l'eau-de-vie en Canada* related alcoholism to the Indian's personality structure, in which he discerned a build-up of repressed emotion behind a façade of utter calm and sang-froid. Belmont was careful to point out that most Indians were upright men and women and that there were really few who drank. Those who did, he believed, sought "to get outside themselves" and had done so before alcohol was available by smoke intoxication, by enacting dream fantasies, and through festivals that Belmont compared appositely to carnival:

> It must be understood that the people are naturally impassive, and the women shy and bashful – this coldness coming either from the climate or

from education; that they never fight unless they lose control; that they quarrel little; that excess and imprudence are decried among them; finally, unless drawn from their cold temperament by an external agency, or bolstered by some custom, they can scarcely overcome a sense of shame.[16]

His conclusion, expressed without benefit of a modern scientific vocabulary, opens the door to psychological explanation. It was a remarkable insight for a man of his era who never suspected any psychological reasons for drinking among Whites. Even after 1727 the fur trade continued to be based primarily on durable goods, but desperate French-English competition, the relaxation of control of the liquor trade, and, perhaps, new psychological pressures unknown to Abbé Belmont

Table IV
French Trade Goods for the Post at St Joseph River

Items	Quantities	Values (livres sous/deniers)	Per cent by Value
Woollens and worsteds			
Blankets, from "cradle" to 3-point size – mostly 1 1/2-point	490	2337 10/	
Molton, a warm, napped blanket cloth, in white, blue, red, and violet (the most popular)	889 aunes*	2210 19/	
Cordelats, esp. from Dourgne, cheaper and coarser in blue and violet (the most popular)	282 aunes	530 2/6	64.7
Others, very costly or very cheap (Flanelle rayée, calamando, polimy rayée, carizet, camlet, cadix)	396 aunes	692 17/11	
Toiles			
Trade, Beaufort, and Mesly, mostly canvas-like hempen cloths in various widths and prices	774+ aunes	815 4/	11.6
Cottons and silk	75+ aunes	216 13/	

* 1 aune = 1.88 metres

Items	Quantities	Values (livres sous/deniers)	Per cent by Value
Smallwares			
Thread, lace, white wool, false gold braid, silver galoon, silk handkerchiefs, scissors, pins, and 2,000 needles		165 3/6	6.6
Other items of Indian decoration			
Box and horn combs, seal rings, round bells, mirrors, vermilion, beads		426 12/	
Tools			
200 axes, 12 gross knives, awls, gimlets, and files		368 16/4	6.4
Kettles (½ lb.)	115	198 2/6	
Arms			
6 guns (4 ft.), 4,000 flints, 700 lbs. shot		299	3.3
Brandy	4 kegs (76 1/2 veltes)	533 15/	6.0
Miscellaneous			
Pressing irons, paper, pewter, vinegar, playing cards, stockings, toques		126 13/7	1.4
TOTALS:		8,921 10/–	100

Source: Invoice, Havy & Lefebvre to Mme Ve Monfort, Quebec, 13 Oct. 1742.

tended to increase brandy drinking among the Indians and make that date seem in retrospect the sinister turning point Dosquet and his missionaries knew it was.

No one has traced with exactitude the fortunes of the Montreal fur-trading fair that flourished for a time in the second half of the seventeenth century and maintained a tenuous hold on life in the early 1700s. In 1721 Charlevoix could write of Indians who still came down to trade "now and then."[17] The locus of trade had shifted decisively to the interior, and the fur trader had become an itinerant. His vehicle, the birchbark canoe, increased in size over the years in response to the needs of the trade. Whereas in the early eighteenth century the canoe carried three or four men west to trade, in the years just before the war of 1744 it carried six to eight men.[18] Yet as early as 1705, a Jesuit reported seeing a thirty-two-foot canoe that carried eight paddlers. He remarked:

> I have not yet ventured to ride in these sorts of conveyance and it seems to me I would be hard pressed to resolve to. I am assured, however, that few perish. Our Canadians have not yet reached that point where they can construct them with the finesse of the Indians, but as for paddling them I would be fully as confident in them as in the natives of the country. In addition, it can be said that they begin this exercise from the cradle and that they have no greater pleasure than finding themselves paddle in hand.[19]

Trading in the Indian villages and encampments had become the avocation of the Canadian coureurs de bois, men as much, or more, attached to the West and the Indian life – or their version of it – as to the colony. Long hours of arduous paddling, months of sleeping on river banks in all weathers, monotonous rations, the real danger of drowning, starving, breaking bones, or being killed by enemy Indians all were the lot of these canoemen. The closing of the West, which it had been thought would have brought them home, only encouraged an existing tendency for them to lose their ties with the colony. Antoine-Denis Raudot summed up the attractions of the West in three words: "Idleness, independence and debauchery." In his portrait of the coureurs, "independence," by which we may understand freedom from authority, is just another vice:

> They are in perpetual idleness when they are among the nations. They do nothing but smoke, gamble and drink brandy, whatever the price. They debauch the wives and daughters of the Indians and live in complete independence.
>
> Formerly, they continued nearly the same life on their return to the colony. As long as they had money, they were at the tavern. They made every foolish expense imaginable. They gave an écu to the first one who happened along to light their pipe, not wanting to take the trouble themselves. Soon they saw the last of their profits and then sought the means to make a new voyage in search of the beaver skins that have always been the prime object of the trade with the Indians.[20]

There remained in the West while it was nominally closed and even after the return to a licensed trade an unnumbered corps of coureurs de bois, well armed and a law unto themselves, often in advance of the westward movement of legitimate traders. For example, in 1737 Beauharnois passed on to Maurepas the contents of a report from one of his western commandants: "In the vicinity of his fort there were nearly thirty coureurs de bois armed with swords, guns, and pistols wherewith to fight those who might oppose their passage; that those people had many Indians on their side, and that as he is not strong enough to stop them, he causes a careful watch to be kept. He writes that nothing that he could say would represent the fact as bad as it is."[21] The Illinois country, with its hospitable climate, became a centre for them, and it was reported as late as 1745 that their "numbers increase yearly."[22] Governor La Galissonière suggested in 1747 that as they could not be controlled they should be sent to the West Indies. "They might be employed to advantage on the privateers," he suggested, "as the majority are resolute men."[23]

The revival of legitimate trade after Utrecht meant that alongside these outlaws estranged from the colony was a new body of legitimate Indian traders, originally called *voyageurs*. With them came canoemen, hired under contract and originally referred to as *engagés*.[24] The voyageur was himself, if not a man of merchant mentality in the classic sense, yet a trader and a specialist. Typically, his was a family long devoted to Indian trading from Montreal Island, the adjacent seigneuries, or Trois-Rivières. But officers and Montreal merchants also put their sons to school with experienced voyageurs. At any time from the last quarter of the seventeenth century to perhaps 1720, two hundred of these men could be found; thereafter, a smaller number of voyageurs hired an increasing number of *engagés*. The Colony Company had made considerable use of hired canoemen. The increasing use of *engagés* in the twenties is the direct result of predictable business concentration. This effect was undoubtedly enhanced by the participation of the commandants of the western posts in the trade, both developments reducing the terrain of the independent voyageur. Indeed, the designation *voyageur* was a depreciating currency that became synonymous with *engagé*. The trader sought refuge in the refinement *marchand voyageur* and was known to his men as the *bourgeois*.[25]

The canoemen were typically illiterate young farm boys. Some rented out their muscle for a summer of hard paddling to and from the entrepôts of Detroit and Michilimackinac. Others, for 150 to 300 livres, a new pair of leggings, a breechclout, and a cotton shirt, wintered in the West. Some of them the West claimed permanently for its small French communities in Illinois and at Detroit or for the Indian tribes. But most returned to the farmsteads of the St Lawrence with much to remember and to tell.

A demographic "sounding," which lumps together voyageurs and *engagés*, suggests that about 18 per cent of the Canadian males born from 1680 to 1719 and surviving beyond fifteen years made fur-trade journeys west, participants in the trade during the first half of the eighteenth century. The participation rates that reflect the revived trade of the thirties and forties are in the range of 20 to 25 per cent. From this study emerges an image of the man going west: young, and usually a younger son who delayed marriage until his late twenties and then, most often, renounced the fur trade.[26] Can we not conjecture that the one third who continued to go west after marriage included a large proportion of *marchands voyageurs* and fewer *engagés*? For most participants, was not the trade a transitory occupation to overcome an economic necessity that postponed marriage and settled life? And were not transitory sexual liaisons or perhaps family life in the Indian country an integral part of the trade's attraction?

Numbers: the records of legitimate trade provide annual figures for Canadians going west of about 100 in the second decade, about 140 in the twenties, and after a sharp increase in *engagements* in the thirties, 300 to 500 in the early forties. The actual number of departures was probably higher, and some think much higher. As many voyageurs stayed in the West eighteen months or even longer, the exodus of one year overlapped with that of another, and at a given time there could have been twice as many Canadians in the West as these figures indicate. The highest standards of proof limit the historian to affirming that the numbers given are minimums and that departures increased substantially from the years just after Utrecht to the years just before the war of 1744. The increasing participation rate and size of the canoe are the confirmation of this tendency.[27] "Thus a part of the Youth is continually voyaging," wrote Charlevoix:

> And although they no longer [1721] commit the disorders that have so discredited this profession, at least not so openly, they still contract from it an habitual libertinism of which they can never completely rid themselves: at least they lose their taste for work, they exhaust their strength, they become incapable of the slightest constraint, and when they are no longer up to the fatigues of these voyages, which happens soon as these exertions are excessive, they remain without any resource and are no longer good for anything.[28]

Thus the life of the western waterways and the presence there of Indian role models from whom Canadians made highly selective borrowings continued to bear an influence on the social evolution of the colony. The extent of that influence remains one of the great questions of Canadian historiography.

II

The movement of the trade west produced the differentiation of *marchand équipeur*, or outfitter, and voyageur. The higher costs resulting from travelling long distances, the longer time period between the advance of goods and the return of furs, and the price of annual trading licences, or *congés*, all tended to the concentration of the trade in the hands of the wealthier participants. Before the collapse of the fur trade and the closing of the West, some twenty-odd Montreal outfitters dominated the trade. The western posts were re-established after Utrecht, inaugurating a period of new beginnings characterized by broader participation and more modest outlays. But from 1720 concentration again reduced the number of significant outfitters to about twenty, most of them Canadian-born. This is in striking contrast to the French predominance among the Quebec importers, a group of similar size.[29]

The outfitter was typically a voyageur who had done well enough financially and possessed the requisite talents to withdraw from arduous travel and live by supplying his former companions. His role, as his designation implies, was to provide the outfit carried west by the voyageur: the French goods that he either imported himself or bought from Quebec importers, provisions, and Montreal-made goods such as clothing sewn of French textiles. He also provided services such as hiring canoe crews and carters and acquiring new canoes. Either the outfitter or the voyageur might hold the *congé* or a commandant's permission or be in partnership with a commandant. But invariably, the outfitter extended the credit necessary for the conduct of the trade.

The files of Montreal and Quebec notaries contain many fur trade obligations and partnership agreements that reveal both consistency and variety in business relationships. Usually a Montreal outfitter supplied a voyageur or two or three voyageurs in partnership. But outfitters also formed occasional partnerships; and a voyageur could be the outfitter of his companions. Some voyageurs were outfitted by Quebec merchants, and – tit for tat – there is one example of a Montreal merchant outfitting a ship in the provisioning trade to Louisbourg.[30]

"Everyone is aware that Canada is very poor," observed La Vérendrye, contemplating his own difficulty arranging financial backing. "Few merchants are in a situation to be able to make advances, especially for an enterprise of that nature, being obliged to make their returns every year."[31] It is a lament that finds many echoes in the correspondence of the period. The fortunes of Montreal outfitters were small by comparison with those of *leading* French merchants. A net worth of 50,000 livres made one a substantial businessman.[32] Given this lack of capital, the outfitter's required annual outlay in five figures would scarcely have been possible without credit. At 6 to 8 per cent, money was not cheap; and the longest term one finds reference to is the eighteen months given by the outfitters themselves to voyageurs leaving Montreal in the spring.

The slowness of transport and the poor articulation of the transatlantic and inland legs of the required journey served the outfitter and everyone else badly. Ships could not easily arrive at Quebec before July, yet most canoes had to leave Montreal for the West in May or June to reach the more distant posts or to make the round trip from nearer ones before freeze-up.[33] A great deal of merchandise must have gathered dust in Quebec or Montreal warehouses for as long as ten months. Most often, two and a half years must have elapsed between the shipment of an item of merchandise from a French port and the return to the same port of the Canadian pelt for which it was exchanged. Thus an outfitter, to begin a commercial correspondence with a supplier, must have first established a credit by providing money or furs, or the latter must have waited two years for a return on goods he supplied. Thereafter, each year the outfitter traded furs acquired with last year's trade goods for next year's trade goods.[34] Business, therefore, was marked by slow turnover, an essential but barely adequate access to credit, and consequently the immobilization of capital and what we would today call a cash-flow problem. Small wonder, then, that it took a consortium of nine to support the first expedition of the explorer La Vérendrye or that Beauharnois brought together groups of twelve and fifteen merchants in 1727 and 1731 to support the trade to the far-distant Dakotas.

We cannot leave the question of traders without inquiring into prices, profits, and Montreal's share in them. As we have seen in Chapter 7, the mark-up taken by Quebec importers was 26 to 36 per cent on most goods. The Montreal outfitter further marked up the same goods by 25 to 33 per cent, and it is generally believed that the voyageur's mark-up was about 100 per cent. Thus an item valued at 100 livres at its point of origin in France might be valued at 315 to 360 livres in the Indian country. The outfitter supplied local goods at cost price. He may have profited by charging interest for the advance of money constituted by these furnishings. As for returning furs, there is little information on their price at point of origin. In the colony, they passed from hand to hand without change in price except for the cost of transportation. On the final sale of furs in France, there was a substantial gross profit, as high as 40 per cent, but it was considerably reduced by costs. Once allowance is made for costs, it is doubtful that the profits earned by any one party to the trade exceeded 10 to 15 per cent on turnover. Converted to an annual rate, profit figures would be even lower.[35]

Before the closing of the West in 1696, participation in the trade had been limited to the lessee of the Traite de Tadoussac, the Northern Company, a few well-connected traders with monopolies at various posts, and the holders of *congés* who traded principally out of the "free" post of Michilimackinac. These licences were given to needy institutions or the indigent well-born, who either engaged in trade themselves or sold the *congés* to those who did. Then followed a long period during which trade was legally confined to Detroit and Frontenac and the decadent Montreal fair, while in fact a clandestine trade operated with the governor's blessing (and participation) at Michilimackinac. In 1715 Vaudreuil was at Versailles and Paris lobbying for a return to the old system of posts and *congés*, and no lobbyist could have been more lucky. First, in 1714 the supply of *castor gras* was unexpectedly exhausted. This made it easier for Pontchartrain to reconcile strategy with economics, and on a trial basis he authorized the issue of fifteen *congés* for 1715 to trade at the existing posts and among the Dakotas in the following year, 1716. Then, with the death of Louis XIV on September 1, 1715, the ministries were swept aside, and Vaudreuil found himself expert adviser to the new Marine Council, not only inexperienced but inclined to be visionary and expansionist in its attitudes. The council re-established the twenty-five *congés* to be distributed by the Governor as one element in an ambitious programme to bolster French authority in the interior.[36] The *congés* were again repressed in 1720 but revived in 1726. In their new guise they were sold at good prices, and the resulting fund was used for various purposes that included the original charitable intention. The trade at Fort Frontenac was always undertaken by the King's storekeepers with the exception of that brief period when the post was operated by the Colony Company. When Fort Niagara was founded in 1720, it too was a Crown trading post. Detroit's trade had always been in the hands of its commandant, as agent of the Colony Company or as a *farmer* who also shouldered all its costs.

Registers of trade licences are still extant for many years of the eighteenth century. In the records for 1718, we see the *congé* system in its classic form. Licences are granted to persons of social standing and sold by them to traders without it, who usually go west themselves to trade. In 1721 there is a totally new pattern. The word *congé* barely appears, but there are plenty of governor's *permis*. Almost all

of them authorize military officers to take canoes west – usually one
or two. The eight allowed Detroit commandant Alphonse de Tonty
are a remarkable exception. This pattern seems to continue through
the Vaudreuil years and is still there in 1726, Beauharnois's first year
as governor. Later, although some military names remain, most appear
to be those of Montreal merchants who do not go west and of voyageurs who do.[37]

The evidence of the registers suggests that the suppression of the
congés threw the trade into the hands of the military. Their subsequent
revival made it easier for private traders to do business at Michilimackinac and, as we shall see, at Detroit after 1727. But the commandants did not relinquish their control of the trade at their posts, where
congé holders must have traded only with their co-operation. It is
most probable that relationships already in place must be understood
to have continued and that the appearance of many merchants' names
must be construed as a surfacing of previously unmentioned participants whose interests in the trade were connected with those of military holders of *permis*.

From 1721 can be dated the evolution of a kind of military-
commercial complex that came to dominate the trade of the interior,
but for the most part its workings remain obscure. Liaisons were
inevitable between, on the one hand, officers who had *de facto* monopolies of trading rights at posts, or were in a position to dominate traders
at the "free" posts of Michilimackinac and, after 1727, Detroit, and,
on the other hand, Montreal merchants with trading know-how,
commercial connections, capital, and credit. Commandants at Detroit
and Michilimackinac demanded fees from private traders. According
to Beauharnois, this was also the case at Fort Ouiatanon, on the Wabash,
and St Joseph River in the early forties. Others formed their own small
partnerships with professional voyageurs or relatives who would go
west with them and signed agreements with Montreal outfitters who
advanced trade goods on credit and held mortgages on their return
cargoes of furs.[38] Both methods of exploiting the trade might co-exist
at a single post.

The tangled skein of arrangements between commandants and the
state has never been completely unravelled. It is not clear whether the
officers invariably "farmed" the posts and therefore paid the expenses
for their maintenance or what these expenses might have included. To
a considerable extent, the trade did underwrite the costs of the French
presence in the West in one way or another. The sale of *congés* netted
the government several thousand livres each year. The requirement
that traders carry a certain quantity of provisions to the posts free of
charge reduced transport charges. The state could pay its officers

abysmal salaries so long as the commandants and their senior subordinates were permitted to trade or to demand fees and perquisites from civilian traders. In certain cases, which may prove to have been the rule, we do know that the state transferred to the commandants the cost of establishing and maintaining posts in return for a monopoly of trade or the right to the *congé* fees. As early as 1722, an officer at Kaministiquia, Jean Viennay-Pachot, suggested that this system offered the best means to proceed to the discovery of the Western Sea. It was, in fact, the method chosen by Beauharnois nine years later to support La Vérendrye's explorations. Louis Denys de La Ronde, commandant at Chagouamigon on Lake Superior, was given a nine-year monopoly of his post in 1733 to underwrite his efforts to develop Lake Superior copper mines. Temiskaming, a "safe" post far from intertribal rivalries and Albany intrigues, was for many years given to Vaudreuil in lieu of back pay. In the case of the post among the Dakotas referred to above, private companies rather than officers were given the monopoly of trade. The commandants were not partners in the 1727 and 1731 companies, but in the latter case, the company paid the commanding officer a salary of 2,400 livres a year.[39]

The extent to which commandants shared the profits of their trade with the governors is difficult to determine. In the case of Vaudreuil, the evidence is strongly against him. For example, from 1717 to 1727 when Detroit was held by his crony Tonty, the required kickback is said to have been 300 livres a year. Beauharnois recalled Tonty, but only because of Huron complaints, and made of that post what Michilimackinac had traditionally been, a major centre for *congé* holders. Beauharnois claimed his own hands were clean. A suspicion lingers that he had replaced Vaudreuil as the beneficiary of Temiskaming and that the trader at that post, Paul Guillet, who had been Vaudreuil's agent, was his as well. If Beauharnois's hands were clean, his successors' demonstrably were not.[40]

Maurepas had never been comfortable with the way the Canadian post system was developing and was confirmed in his views both by Ramezay's grumbling against Vaudreuil and by the reports of the intendants. In 1724 he turned down a request for a post monopoly from the Governor of Montreal on the grounds that it was unbecoming to his rank. The following year, he complained to Vaudreuil: "I know that the French post commandants behave like fur merchants. . . . They do not even attempt to conceal the fact that they seek post commands solely to have the opportunity to do business."[41] Farming out posts to businessmen, reducing or eliminating the military presence in the West, was an alternative favoured by intendants. Bégon farmed out Temiskaming in 1724, a sort of pilot project, but with the restoration of the *congés* in 1726, the farm was cancelled. Claude-Thomas Dupuy, who arrived in Canada in the summer of 1726 in company with Beauharnois and who served as intendant for three stormy years, challenged the whole system of trade dominated by commandants and *congé* holders as costly, inefficient, and harmful to French-Indian relations. In his bustling way, without a moment's consultation with the seething governor, Dupuy detached the post of Toronto from the trade of Niagara and leased it out for a year. Maurepas believed that the commandants' monopolies and the high interest charges borne by their business for want of capital led to exorbitant prices, the embitterment of the Indians, and a consequent transfer of trade to the English. Claiming that the collapse of French trade and the destruction of the colony were at hand, he announced in 1728 his plan to withdraw all officers and soldiers from the western posts, which would then be farmed out to businessmen.[42]

Beauharnois and the Marine commissary, d'Aigremont, were quick to the defence, arguing that merchants were only motivated by pecuniary interest, would leave forts to dilapidation, and would flood the West with brandy. The nub of their argument, however, was that Indians wanted to deal with military men representing the King, that officers alone had the ability to negotiate peace and war among the tribes, and that politics and trade in the West were not separate. For the time being, Maurepas accepted Beauharnois's argument, but he continued to regard Canada much as a stern and dubious bank manager might regard a failing small business. At heart, he was a believer in the compact colony policy. He foresaw the day when the fur trade would disappear and regarded the occupation of the West as a regrettable necessity that diverted colonial energies and royal funds from more promising endeavours. He refused Beauharnois's requests to build more posts or to fortify the province more extensively. He continued to distrust an officer corps that behaved "like fur merchants" and looked to the intendant to produce economies. From 1739 on, Gilles Hocquart, who had evidently been given his orders, was frequently at odds with the Governor over the costs of the western post system.[43] He and the Marine controller, Jean-Victor Varin de La Marre, continued the critique, long identified with the intendancy, of the administration of the western posts.

Finally, the King's Memorandum of 1742 announced a fur-trade, revolution. Maurepas had found a lessee for Niagara and Frontenac. The other posts were to be farmed out to Canadian merchants, excepting the posts west of Kaministiquia known as the Western Sea posts, Chagouamigon, which was to be leased to La Ronde's son, and Michilimackinac and Detroit, which were to be the only posts open to *congé* holders. In spite of his belief that at several posts "officers can be of scarcely any utility," Maurepas did not propose to withdraw the garrisons as he had in 1728. Officers persisting in trade would, however, be dismissed from the service. While he thus restored their dignity, Maurepas also provided that each would be handsomely rewarded by the lessee at his post every year in accord with the profitability of the trade – this to discourage sabotage of the new system. Beauharnois was affronted by a decision that revealed such condescension toward the Canadian military and was sprung on him without warning. His protest was testy, but he obeyed his orders. Hocquart, on the other hand, must have been pleased to see a favour consciously bestowed upon the Canadian trading community by the elimination of military interlopers. And he was no intendant if he did not join Maurepas in anticipating the return of lease fees to the treasury – it was always someone else's exactions that were an incubus on the trade.[44]

A set of two documents governing the exploitation of Fort La Baie (Green Bay) under Maurepas's new system of leases merits closer attention because its arrangements arise out of the experience of the first half of the century and point the way to the greater complexities of the future.[45] In 1747 Alexis Lemoine *dit* Monière and Louis de Clignancourt joined with one Jean Lechelles to lease the post from the King for three years. Subsequently, Monière and Lechelles ceded their share of the lease to a new company got together by Clignancourt. Lechelles and Monière bound themselves to outfit the post for three years, and Clignancourt and Company were equally bound to send their furs to none but them. A number of conditions on both sides were spelled out. One construes that the original triumvirate had been a union of the capital, credit, and first-rate reputation in the marketplace necessary to acquire a lease (Monière and Lechelles) with the skills of an experienced *marchand voyageur* who was willing to organize the trade to the interior (Clignancourt). The latter had then taken partners of a lesser status who would never have been granted the lease themselves. Separate corporate identities mirror a traditional division of roles, give each group some protection from the other's possible failures, and reflect the superior position of the suppliers of credit. If these agreements are not an exact prefiguring of the Montreal partner/wintering partner system that would emerge in the 1780s, nevertheless they exhibit the same solicitude to bring both the Montreal and the western trades under the control of a single, long-term monopoly and yet provide an independence, dear to the eighteenth century, from large, encumbering business structures.

The new leasing system, which pitted metropolitan administration against colonial practice, bourgeois lessees against dispossessed commandants, began in an atmosphere of rancour and was soon caught up in a war that made it impossible to supply the upper country properly and financially ruinous to try. Naturally, the system was the scapegoat. In 1749 a new minister, Rouillé de Jouy, wrote to a new governor and a new intendant that "the arrangements that were made some years ago for the exploitation of the posts of the upper country having been frustrated in some places and upset in others in consequence of the war and the movements of the Indians," new arrangements were to be made.[46] There was a reversion to *congés* at many posts although leases continued at others. The officer corps was once again busy, staking out its territory in the marketplace.

*   *   *

The West, with its imperial purpose, its economic contribution, and its social challenge, was fundamental to Canada. France was of two minds on the West: it was a strategic area, a source of allies and of riches; it was also costly, diverting Canadians from more promising economic endeavours and schooling them in the free ways of Indians. Canadian society was not marked by the doubts that tortured the bureaucrats. Those in its upper levels, whether merchants or soldiers or missionaries, owed to the West their sustenance and their place in society. Many more humble folk shared the bounty of the West. The whole apparatus of importers and exporters, outfitters and voyageurs, commandants and garrisons, existed to divide its spoils. For the Canadian psyche, the West was a counterpoise to all that was traditional and that had behind it the full weight of rural life and of the imperial connection.

CHAPTER 9

The *Pax Gallica* after Utrecht

In the years immediately after Utrecht, the new Regency government was a tonic to a flagging imperialism. But in the 1720s the vision of the West that had taken shape at the turn of the century and that had been associated with the heartland strategy lost ground at Versailles to views that harkened back to Louis de Pontchartrain's idea of the West as militarily indefensible and as a free field for Canadian greed.[1] The governors of Canada in the inter-war period, Vaudreuil and Beauharnois, for their part remained steadfastly loyal to the imperial idea and by advocacy and inertia kept their myopic masters from losing sight of it.

In fact, no one really thought it possible to withdraw from the Great Lakes as had been envisaged in 1696. Thus commissioners who prepared to discuss the boundaries question in 1724 were instructed to make substantial claims in the West as well as in the East. With regard to Hudson Bay and the unfortunate cession of "all lands, seas, sea-coasts, rivers, and places situate in the said bay, and straits, and which belong thereunto," the French fell back upon the verb in the treaty, "to restore," since what the English had not actually possessed could not be given back to them. This denied an application of the height-of-land principle that might have been inferred from Article 10 and that would have stripped Canada of valuable trade and strategic Indian alliances. As was the case with the reference to Acadia's "ancient boundaries," English phraseology was turned against its authors.[2]

With regard to the Iroquois and the Great Lakes, the government accepted a proposal laid down in the Bégon-Aubery memorandum of 1713 that a straight line connecting two points of undisputed sovereignty, the mouth of the St George River and the headwaters of the Hudson, should be projected south and west along the height of land. This would shut up the English east of the Appalachian barrier and would place three of the Five Nations, the Senecas, Cayugas, and Onondagas, on French soil.[3] This, of course, was to ignore Article 15, which conferred sovereignty over the Iroquois on the British Crown.

It was French policy to behave as though that part of the clause had never been written or to argue that it was contingent upon the findings of the boundary commission.[4]

A satisfactory boundary settlement in the interior was an idle dream. The Iroquois accepted neither European sovereignty. For both the French and the English, the stakes in the West were too high to be risked at the bargaining table, and the conflict of interests was too great to be brought to a satisfactory resolution. Both Canadian governors worked to secure Iroquois neutrality and good will and to re-establish the *pax gallica* among the western tribes, secured by garrisoned trading posts. Both explained to the Minister that if the Canadian domino were to fall, there would be a general collapse of France's North American empire and of maritime trade. The domino concept presented so forcefully by Governor La Galissonière in 1748 thus had a long and continuous history.[5]

At the time of Utrecht, there were French garrisons at Frontenac, Detroit, and Michilimackinac. French officers had been sent to the countries of the Miamis and Illinois. They constituted a wholly inadequate presence to cope with the disintegrating alliance system and the ambiguous legacy of the Battle of Detroit – the French had participated in a crushing victory but had made inveterate enemies of the Foxes and had fallen from the lofty position of arbiter above tribal strife. To the south, fledgling Louisiana had no military presence beyond the Bay of Mobile and the post at Biloxi. When Versailles authorized Louisiana to establish inland posts among the Natchez and on the Wabash in 1714 and Canada to regarrison Saint-Louis-des-Illinois at Pimitoui, there were not the means to do so.[6]

The Canadian historian sees the colonization of Louisiana out of the corner of his eye. As a narrative, it begins as an adjunct to Canadian history and it remains full of Canadian characters and references. Soon it diverges to its own distinct and distant focus. But at the level of imperial concerns, the two narratives remain entangled. The history of Louisianan experience and policy on the Indian frontier as well as on those of the English colonies obtrude regularly into the historian's peripheral vision.

In 1712 Governor Robert Hunter of New York had established a fort (named after himself) and a chapel among the Mohawks. Both during and after the war, the agents of Albany's trade circulated in the interior. "You could not see through it at first," Hunter lectured the Five Nations in 1710, "but the only way to strengthen you and us and to weaken the enemy is to have as many brought into the Covenant

Chain as possible.''[7] After some resistance, ''opening the path'' was becoming the ascendant policy among the Iroquois. In 1715 Far Nations from the upper lakes were among the Senecas, explaining that they had travelled a path long overgrown. And in 1717 the Iroquois were lecturing Hunter that better prices would bring in the nations, ''the Indians would desert Canada.''[8] Allowing western Indians to have direct trade relations with Albany was a calculated risk for the Iroquois. It may be that the economic gains and losses cancelled out: lost middleman profits versus wages for portaging and presents received from the western tribes, Canada, and New York. Iroquois diplomacy sought to secure by other means (offering the open path) a dominance formerly maintained by war. Western tribes and New York traders were to be dependent friends; Canada was to be neutralized. The danger for the Iroquois was that they might lose control of the path and fall victim to an alliance between New York and the Far Nations. A Canada too weak or a New York too strong was a peril. Thus it was in their best interests to keep New York traders out of the interior as far as possible, a point seen with perfect clarity by Governor Vaudreuil in 1708.[9]

The Iroquois were fortunate that immediately after Utrecht their manpower was significantly increased. In 1711-13 several towns of Tuscaroras, who were kindred to the Five Nations, rose against North Carolina, were defeated by the intervention of the South Carolina militia, and began a migration northward to the safety of the Iroquois cantons. ''They are no longer a nation with a name, being once dispersed,'' the Onondaga chief and diplomat Teganissorens explained to Governor Hunter, but they would eventually become recognized as the sixth nation of the league.[10]

In the West there remained the question of the Foxes. From their secure home on Green Bay, surrounded by the friendly and kindred Kickapoos, Sauks, and Mascoutens, they raided the French allies, causing them to fear for their lives and ruining their trade and hunting. Vaudreuil was wary of Indian wars, but it was becoming difficult for him to refuse to act without losing face – and the trade of the Lakes as well. Late in the summer of 1714, he received Pontchartrain's permission to make war on the Foxes as a last resort but also his advice to send Louis de Louvigny, a trusted officer and man of great reputation among the western tribes, to negotiate an honourable peace. Pontchartrain and Louvigny had discussed in person the advisability of a Fox war and agreed that victory was problematic and that the engagement of the Foxes' Green Bay allies and even the Iroquois might unleash a long war upon Canada. Vaudreuil authorized an expedition with these alternative objectives, put matters into the hands of his replacement, de Ramezay, and departed for two years' leave in France.

The expedition was prepared by successful diplomacy and gift giving among the allied tribes intended to isolate the Foxes and build up an Indian fighting force. But the 1715 campaign was a complete fiasco. Measles and delays prevented a required rendezvous of southern Indians, while the Michilimackinac Indians were blasted by brandy brought in by a late-arriving contingent of trader-volunteers up from Montreal and coureurs de bois who had been promised an amnesty. The local commandant, Constant de Lignery, who was to have led the army to Green Bay, threw up his hands, while the Canadians paddled home in their fur-laden canoes. The next summer, Louvigny, who had been prevented by illness from taking command in 1715, led an expedition that reached the main Fox stronghold. Seeing themselves surrounded and their fortifications being sapped, the Foxes delivered up hostages and surrendered on terms: a general peace, the return of prisoners, the replacement of killed slaves, and reparations to pay the costs of the expedition. The peace occasioned some adverse comment both at the time and since because it was construed that Louvigny had been bought off by slaves and beaver skins – the reparations. But Louvigny was acting on Pontchartrain's orders. And the policy was successful. The Foxes were for the time restrained, and this was reflected in the increasing volume of furs that descended to Montreal.[11]

While the Fox campaigns were unfolding, Vaudreuil was in France making his successful bid for the re-establishment of the twenty-five annual trading *congés*. The new Marine Council also agreed that the licences should be distributed by the Governor, who was in addition given authority to appoint and dismiss post commanders. It accepted his proposals to establish new posts in the Great Lakes country, to maintain an Indian gift fund of 20,000 livres a year, and to sell brandy at Fort Frontenac. It granted amnesty to the coureurs de bois and pledged to send Canada over a hundred military recruits a year, a promise kept until the return of the ministries in 1723.[12]

The re-establishment of posts in the Great Lakes basin was preceded by Louisiana's first moves to occupy its Mississippi hinterland. In the summer of 1716, Fort Rosalie was built among the Natchez, and the approach to Mobile from South Carolina and the Cherokee country was blocked by building Fort Toulouse on the upper Alabama. Founding this second post was facilitated by a rising of numerous tribes against South Carolina in the so-called Yamasee War. The old Carolina trading system, the foundation of English influence in the south, was broken up, in particular by the defection and migration west of the Chattahoochee of the Creeks, who led the revolt against "barbarous usage . . . from our villainous traders," as a Carolina parson put it.[13]

Vaudreuil increased Canada's western posts from three to eight.[14]

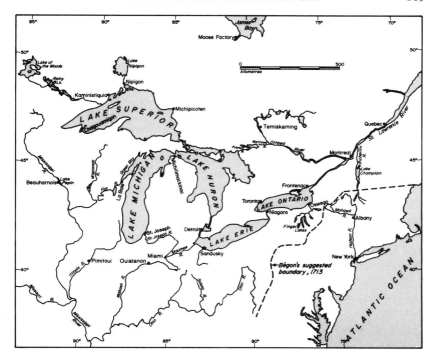

The Great Lakes Heartland

Fort Frontenac remained a listening post and subsidized trading house to bolster French influence among the upper Iroquois. Detroit, which Vaudreuil had once considered abandoning, was now thought of as a useful bulwark against the penetration of the region by New York traders. Still, there were no new posts in the lower lakes, where Iroquois sensibilities had to be respected and indeed depended upon to prevent English post building. The new posts were all in the upper lakes, the traditional area of French influence before 1698. Fort Michilimackinac had already been re-established and, *circa* 1715-17, moved to the south shore of the straits the better to control the entrance to Lake Michigan. Southeast of the lake were the related Miamis and Weas tribes, which had moved during the Fox Wars from the St Joseph River and the Chicago portage respectively to the comparative safety of the Maumee, emptying into Lake Erie, and the upper Wabash. In 1717 Vaudreuil sent detachments to persuade them to return to their old homelands, farther away from English and Iroquois influence. The St Joseph River post was rebuilt some distance inland from the old site of

Saint-Joseph-des-Miamis at the river's mouth but was only partially successful in attracting Indians. The building of Fort Miami on the Maumee in 1721-22 and Fort Ouiatanon on the upper Wabash, perhaps around 1720, indicate French acquiescence in the failure of their policy of westward removal.

While in France, Vaudreuil had found there was much debate over the existence of an inland Western Sea, supposed to lie west of Canada and to be accessible either via the Missouri or via Rainy Lake and Lake of the Woods. Material from a wide array of sources, Indian, Spanish, and French, in which there may have been cryptic references to Lake Winnipeg, were "consolidated into one identifiable inland sea at the hands of the Paris geographers."[15] Two of these, Jean-Baptiste Nolin and Guillaume Delisle, disputed primacy of discovery in a plagiarism trial in 1705-6 before the Conseil d'Etat. The Regent himself, a former pupil of Delisle's father, Claude, had a keen scientific interest in the discovery of the sea. No surprise, therefore, that immediately after Vaudreuil's return to Canada, Vaudreuil and Bégon forwarded to Paris a plan for the discovery of the sea by the northern route and the following summer (July 1717) sent an expedition under Zacharie de La Noue to re-establish Kaministiquia on Lake Superior as the anchor for anticipated voyages westward.

Vaudreuil and Bégon's motive was not science for science's sake. Kaministiquia was the key to the best fur country on the continent. At that time, almost all the furs from the area were carried to Hudson Bay. But since Canada had lost its bay posts at Utrecht, it was important to tap the region through the Great Lakes. The project was approved at Paris. But wars fought by the local Assiniboins and their Cree and Monsonis allies against the Dakota Sioux prevented La Noue's getting beyond Kaministiquia. And the wars, together with the continued competition of the Hudson's Bay Company, prevented the post from becoming a major collection point for furs.

Good relations with the Dakotas seemed the key to further French expansion. They were a wide-ranging and powerful people, not much given to fraternizing with their neighbours. But they were friends of the Ojibwas, old allies of Canada, hunters and traders centred at La Pointe de Chagouamigon on the south shore of Lake Superior, one of three posts occupied by Vaudreuil in 1718. The Ojibwa-Dakota alliance, which dated from Daniel Greysolon Dulhut's diplomatic intervention of 1679, was based upon the Ojibwas' possession of guns, their provision of French goods to the Dakotas in exchange for furs, and a sharing of Dakota hunting grounds at the headwaters of the Mississippi – "nothing but lakes and marshes, full of wild oats [rice]" in the words of Nicolas Perrot.[16] La Pointe was thus a post providing a rich fur trade and a possible avenue to the Dakotas. They might also be reached from Fort La Baie, a new post securing the Fox-Wisconsin route from the bottom of Green Bay and meant to control the defeated Foxes.

South and west of Lake Michigan, Pimitoui, the principal Illinois town, was regarrisoned to maintain the Illinois at peace with the Miamis and Weas. But by a decree of September 27, 1717, the Illinois country had already been attached to Louisiana because of the interest shown by Law's Occident Company in mines supposed to exist there.[17] Thus the Canadian garrison was replaced by one from Louisiana.

While securing the upper lakes, Vaudreuil counted upon Iroquois self-interest to keep New Yorkers pent up in their province. But the energetic Hunter, who had built the fort among the Mohawks and encouraged the Iroquois to let numerous "Far Nations" trade at Albany, had from 1716 also prevailed upon them to let numerous trading expeditions into the interior. When Albany traders appeared among the Senecas and, rumour had it, would build a post at Niagara, Vaudreuil decided to forestall them. In 1720 his agent, Louis de Joncaire, an officer and an adopted son of the Senecas, deceitfully asked an assembly of chiefs if he could build a house among them and upon being granted the request, hastened to build, first, "a kind of cabin of bark where they displayed the King's colors" and subsequently "a trading house or block house . . . made musket proof with port holes for firing small arms." Such was the beginning of Fort Niagara, almost immediately given additional support by small posts at Toronto and Quinte. The Senecas had been tricked, and the more discerning Iroquois such as Teganissorens saw that the fort could be used to close the West to them or prevent western nations visiting Albany. In a characteristic move, an Iroquois assembly that excluded the Senecas offered to help tear down the fort if the English would lead the way. The assembly pointed out, as the Iroquois had done many times, that Albany itself was by its smuggling activities deeply involved in Canadian trade on Lake Ontario. In view of the Anglo-French entente, of course, New York's response was necessarily limited to fulminations.[18]

The occupation of Niagara has been described as "the most brilliant diplomatic and military coup of Vaudreuil's career."[19] It has also been condemned as a thoughtless and arrogant move that opened the way for a direct Canada–New York confrontation on the lower lakes.[20] One must conjecture that Vaudreuil was convinced by the appearance of Hunter's licensed traders that the traditional Iroquois policy of keeping New York out of the West was dangerously weakened and that diplomacy among the Iroquois was therefore inadequate to stop the English penetration of the interior. Certainly, a dozen years earlier Vaudreuil had categorically stated that the Iroquois would never let New York fortify Niagara and that consequently it was unnecessary for Canada to do so.[21]

In September 1720, New York welcomed a new governor, William Burnet, who grasped the full significance of the blockhouse at Niagara, not only the negative aspect of foiling the New York advance, but also the positive one of keeping "the communication between Canada and Mississippi by the River Ohio open."[22] Many English colonists were beginning to understand the need for intercolonial solidarity in the face of French encirclement. As one Colonel Heathcote of Scarsdale had explained to Hunter in 1715, "For as every part of North America is struck at, so all our interests are the same and what number soever is wounded or hurt, the whole ought to reckon themselves aggrieved."[23] But it had never been all for one and one for all in British America. Colonel Peter Schuyler, President of the Council of New York, complained that his province had borne the whole "burden and expense" of the Five Nations and that the other colonies had ignored them even though they were in great measure "the balance of North America."[24]

In the Middle Colonies, but more especially in South Carolina, there was also great consternation at French encirclement. From all over the American colonies, the Board of Trade at London was bombarded with memoranda on frontier policy; and on September 8, 1721, the Board produced its own plan, recommending to deaf ears that England imitate France by building forts beyond the Appalachians and by bringing all the Indians and all the colonies into one vast treaty system. In the same year South Carolina built Fort King George on the Altamaha in a region taken from Spain in the Quadruple Alliance's brief war against her (1718-20).[25] This presaged the founding of the march colony of Georgia, while in the north Burnet was preparing to build the fort at Oswego on Lake Ontario that Lord Bellomont and Robert Livingston had contemplated at the beginning of the century.

As to Indian alliances, in the north, diplomatic overtures in which the Iroquois had long persisted bore some fruit in a conference at Albany in 1722 between themselves, New York, Pennsylvania, and Virginia.[26] In the south, while the Creeks made their position on the French, Spanish, and English frontiers the foundation of neutrality, South Carolina continued to count on the support of the Cherokees and the Chickasaws, alienated from the French by the resurgence of endemic Choctaw-Chickasaw warfare (1720-25). South Carolina also made constant efforts to draw the Choctaws and lesser tribes away from the French. France was a poor market for deerskin, and gifts to the Indians could not pull up the slack left by trade because of the inadequate funds allotted by Louisiana's profit-minded masters – first Crozat, then Law's Occident and Indies companies. The dismissal of diplomats knowledgeable about the Indians, especially the Command-ant-General Le Moyne de Bienville (1725), left the colony in the hands of men more used to balancing account books than dealing with fron-tier politics. It was difficult for Louisiana to hold its own.[27]

From 1721 Burnet had traders at Oswego and Irondequoit.[28] At the annual renewal of the Covenant Chain at Albany in 1724, he extracted permission from the Six Nations to build a blockhouse at Oswego to protect the traders. Vaudreuil, ill and entering the last year of his life, saw Oswego as the ultimate challenge to Canada's western hegemony and acted swiftly. His envoy, Charles de Longueuil *fils*, failed to per-suade the Iroquois to expel the New Yorkers from Oswego, but by suggesting that the English were challenging Iroquois ownership of Oswego he did persuade them to rescind the permission to build a blockhouse and received himself permission to rebuild the French post at Niagara in stone.[29]

It was a diplomatic triumph much like Joncaire's building of the Niagara post in 1720. It included an element of trickery that rankled among the Iroquois headmen – for Longueuil had obtained permission to rebuild Niagara, not from the Senecas, but from an unrepresentative group of Onondagas. And if it may be conjectured that the building of Joncaire's post led to the original Iroquois permission to build at Oswego and more Iroquois permissions for New York traders to visit Lake Ontario, it is clear that the fortified stone house, built by the royal engineer Chaussegros de Léry in 1726-27, made the building of an off-setting New York house at Oswego a certainty. Thus in 1726 Bur-net received from the three upper Iroquois nations bordering Lake Ontario a confirmation of the Five Nations' 1701 trust deed placing their hunting grounds under the King's protection and an extension of it to the lands bordering Lakes Ontario and Erie "to be protected and defended by his said Majesty his heirs and successors for ever to our use."[30] Fort Oswego, a stone house similar to the French building at Niagara, was built in the summer of 1727.

The trust deed of 1701 had been a clever ruse. None of the lands north of the lakes proffered to William III had been the Iroquois' to give. But the document given to Burnet in 1726 included even the Iroquois cantons, and it naturally raises the question of Iroquois notions of deed and title. Neither transaction, it should be noted, was in any sense a transfer of land ownership. Rather, both established a British protectorate over lands held in a kind of Indian mortmain. Such docu-ments could be precious to the English as indications of sovereignty.

As to Iroquois ideas of them, it would be foolish to aver where an angel might fear to interpret.

At the time of Governor Beauharnois's arrival in Canada in August 1726, there still had been every appearance that Longueuil's *coup* of the previous summer had put Canada once again on top in the struggle for the interior. It was only in July 1727 that Beauharnois became aware that the New Yorkers were building their substantial post at Oswego. Communicating a highly creative interpretation of Article 15 to Burnet, he demanded that the building be demolished and threatened force. But in the face of Burnet's firm refusal, there was nothing a governor bound by the Anglo-French entente could do. Nevertheless, the reintroduction of *congés* in 1726 and the trade in brandy in 1727, and the conduct of business at Niagara and Frontenac in the years that followed at a loss chargeable to the King, enabled Canadians to keep a substantial share of the trade and to survive the Oswego crisis of 1725-27.

In the interests of peace and security, the Six Nations had to some certain degree ceased to be "the balance of America." In this they had little choice. With remarkable consistency, especially given the splintered decision-making process in their society, they had worked to break the Canadian grip on the interior without transferring it to New York. The incursions of the one were balanced by concessions to the other. But while they professed friendship with both Canada and New York, the Anglo-French alliance, upon which they depended for peace, was a constant worry to them as it suggested a possible pact on the part of the Europeans to unite and "cut them off."[31]

The Albany traders applauded Burnet's sending of representatives and traders west, had mixed feelings about his post on Lake Ontario, which gave the province a certain security yet also undermined Albany's historic trading monopoly, but were outraged by Burnet's determination to end their smuggling trade with Montreal. Trade between Albany and Montreal on a regular and organized basis dated back to the peace of 1696.[32] The abortive overland expeditions against Canada in 1709 and 1711 had disrupted the trade momentarily, but in 1712 the Caughnawaga Indians, who were the carriers in this trade, were at Albany looking to repair the breach. Thanks to the Albany trade, Montreal merchants were able to weather the collapse of French demand for beaver between the 1690s and the early 1720s. Thereafter the profitable habit of smuggling continued to thrive. Leaving aside the slippery question of whether or not Montreal merchants thereby obtained better or cheaper goods for the Indian trade, for long periods of time they certainly got better prices for their beaver. They also exchanged French manufactured goods as well as furs for English goods for their own use.[33] Even the colonial government benefited from the trade, for Albany merchants sent to Canada the fathoms of wampum that could have no other use than forest diplomacy.[34] Still, mercantilists were used to biting the hand that fed them. Royal edicts, decrees, and declarations forbade the export of beaver, the import or use of foreign merchandise, or visiting the English colonies without the governor's passport. Regulations were devised to enforce the laws; penalties were laid down; but all to no avail.[35] And since the major carriers were Indians rather than Canadian subjects, it was difficult for a government solicitous of these necessary allies to stop them.

Burnet now led the attack from the other side of the border. He was the leader of a growing number in New York who appreciated the imperial dimension of the fur trade and saw no reason why English goods should support French influence among the Indians when they could serve to extend British influence. He had no time for the Albanians' plausible argument that their system had secured the frontier for years and profited British industry to boot. In the 1720s, he had the New York assembly pass laws that prohibited the Canada trade and required, *inter alia*, that challenged traders proclaim their innocence under oath. "Montreal will sink to nothing which now flourishes by its trade with Albany," he confidently wrote home.[36] In fact, it is not clear that the new laws had any appreciable effect other than to increase instances of perjury in the province before the business lobby at Whitehall had them disallowed in 1729. In any case, the trade was moving from Albany, which had lost its monopoly in 1727, to Schenectady and Oswego; and Indian affairs had been taken out of the hands of the Albany aldermen. Clearly, New York's relations with the West were changing.

Fort Saint-Frédéric, commanding the route between Albany and Montreal from the top of Lake Champlain, was founded in August 1731. Although it was built for strategic reasons, Beauharnois and Hocquart expected much from it as a customs post.[37] They were both zealous at first to combat the contraband trade. But through the complicity of officers and civil servants, the fort, as has been written elsewhere, "seems to have functioned as a toll gate rather than as a barrier."[38] That smuggling declined in the 1730s owed something to sporadic vigilance by French officers but more to a depressed market in New York and better prices at Montreal. Oversupply of trade goods caused a complete turnabout by the later thirties; Albany merchants were paying for Canadian pelts half in cash. It would have taken a very committed mercantilist to stop that trade. Certainly Hocquart, who estimated that it accounted for about one third of Canada's beaver exports (down from a probable 50 per cent in its heyday), was by then turning a blind eye to smugglers.

The crisis on Lake Ontario and the conclusion of Dummer's War in Acadia were not the only frontier problems bequeathed to Beauharnois by Vaudreuil. Again there were the Foxes. Late in 1719 a chance encounter between Illinois hunters and a party of Foxes, Mascoutens, and Kickapoos had resulted in a battle and the outbreak of war in the Illinois country. At the same time, an officer sent from Kaministiquia to the Dakotas via La Pointe to encourage trade and bring about a peace with the northern tribes had met with failure. "The Foxes had so predisposed the Sioux against us," he had reported.[39] The Foxes had gone to war against the Ojibwas as well as the Illinois, while the endemic warfare of Dakota against Assiniboin had continued in the north. The entire "Far West" from the Pigeon River–Lake of the Woods chain through the headwaters of the Mississippi and down to the Illinois River had become a war zone to be entered at peril.

As the war progressed, it was the Illinois and the Louisianan outposts in the Illinois country that felt the brunt of it. Pimitoui was soon abandoned. Throughout Vaudreuil temporized, blaming the Illinois and Louisiana and alternating promises of action with cautionary memoranda on the pitfalls of Indian wars. When he finally sent Lignery west to Green Bay, the mission resulted in a Fox-Ojibwa treaty (August, 1724) that reopened the La Pointe corridor to the Dakotas and the Western Sea. Lignery's efforts to bring the Illinois into the treaty seem to have been feeble at best. The next year, 1725, Maurepas received a sheaf of twelve documents from a former commander in Illinois: letters written by Jesuits, Indian chiefs, and the commander himself providing damning evidence that Vaudreuil was content to let the Illinois country suffer at the hands of the Foxes so long as the Canadian fur trade could be saved.[40] It was even charged that the Canadian commandants at Green Bay and St Joseph River were supplying the arms and ammunition. But extenuating circumstances there were. Lignery rehearsed all the risks relating to punitive expeditions that Louvigny had presented years before. He pointed out that the Foxes could inadvertently be driven into the arms of the Dakotas or Iowas, a disaster for New France. Nevertheless, it was only a timely death that saved Vaudreuil from ministerial wrath and probably recall. Subsequently Lignery negotiated a new treaty (June 7, 1726) that included a Fox promise to end the war on the Illinois. Such was the situation upon the arrival of Beauharnois.

Nature had given the new governor a generous nose, a monument of aristocracy and disdain. His penetrating eyes were set in an impenetrable countenance, with no revealing tension and only the hint of a smile. He looked like what he was: unflappable and prudent, tough and tenacious. Gossip of Beauharnois's unpleasant relations with his wife may also have given fair warning of the petty and vindictive strain that ran through his character. Confronted with the problems of the West, Beauharnois's first instinct was to trust in diplomacy. He instructed his western commandants to use their influence to break up the Foxes' alliances, to stop the Iroquois' meddling among the western tribes, and to maintain an Indian barrier between them and the Foxes, to whom they offered asylum in case of need. On June 16, 1727, an expedition left Montreal to establish the long-projected trading post and mission among the Dakotas. Beauharnois saw this post as a means of making the Dakotas independent of the Foxes and isolating the latter as well as fulfilling the long-term aims of bringing about peace between the Dakotas and Crees and Assiniboins, adding Dakota territory to the Canadian fur-trade empire, and furthering the search for the Western Sea. But after a deceptively quiet winter, war already had broken out again (May? June? 1727) with a Fox ambush of eight Frenchmen bound for the Missouri, an outbreak that may have been triggered by the death of the Fox chief Ouachala, a dove and pro-French, and the consequent ascendancy of the war party under the hawkish Kiala.

War was Beauharnois's response to what he characterized as "the menaces of Indians who want to shake off the yoke" – no honeyed illusions about the nature of the *pax gallica* there![41] Canadians had every reason to expect a successful campaign against the Foxes until Lignery, the commander, for whom the expedition seems to have been an occasion for trading, so delayed it that the forewarned Foxes escaped. Lignery burned their towns and crops as well as Fort La Baie and returned home under a cloud. The garrison and priests of the Dakota expedition abandoned their new Fort Beauharnois on Lake Pepin and fled, only to be captured by Kickapoos and Mascoutens. At this critical juncture, Beauharnois's western policy was saved by the Foxes themselves, who ambushed a party of Dakotas and then killed a Mascouten and a Kickapoo because these tribes refused to give up the Lake Pepin refugees. The Foxes were left friendless; and out of anti-Fox hostility Beauharnois built a coalition to support a new war effort.

The year 1730 was one of decisive and grisly encounters. The Foxes were harassed by former friends and ancient enemies. In July they attempted to run the gauntlet of their hostile neighbours to find sanctuary among the Senecas. Surprised en route between the Illinois and the Wabash, they retreated to a stockade by a small river and began a long and punishing wait. Through all of August and into September, a hostile siege force grew to some 1,400 men, including some 150 Frenchmen from Canada and Louisiana. One night, under cover of darkness and rain, the Foxes attempted to slip undetected from their fort, but a child's crying alerted their enemies; the next day, September 9, the French allies caught up with them. Three hundred Fox men, women, and children were killed, another 400 were captured, and only 200 escaped.

Although Beauharnois began peace negotiations with a Fox delegation that descended to Montreal in 1731, he refused to prevent the Indian allies from harassing the Fox remnant, hoping that they would fulfil his policy "that this damnable nation will be totally extinguished."[42] With considerable ease, the Minister, the Governor, and the Western commandants all accepted the idea of a "final solution" to the Fox problem. They were slow in attempting to achieve it only because of their fear that the failure of such a difficult policy would make matters worse.[43] Beauharnois's most merciful alternative for dealing with the Fox remnant was to have them rounded up, the men sent as slaves to the West Indies, and the women and children distributed among the mission Indians. While this was the fate of some, including Kiala, as a general policy it failed completely. A force sent in the winter of 1734-35 to kill or capture the Fox remnant living with the Sauks was as complete a fiasco as any in the long history of the Fox wars. The Indian allies proved unreliable. Indeed, while many of the Foxes' old friends were again being reconciled to them, even their old enemies were releasing their Fox prisoners. "The Indians have their policy as we have ours," Beauharnois wrote to Maurepas, explaining the behaviour of his allies. "They are most ill at ease at seeing a nation destroyed for fear that they will have their turn. . . . The Indians in general greatly fear the French, but they do not love them."[44]

Historians have been more successful in describing the Fox wars than they have been in explaining them. If the Battle of Detroit in 1712 was the result of traditional tribal rivalry animated by a martial spirit and an ethic of revenge, these motives seem also to explain the resurgence of warfare in 1714-16. There is evidence, however, that the fighting beginning in 1719 was a direct response to the French garrisoning of the interior, the supply of arms and ammunition to the Foxes' enemies (as well as to the Foxes themselves), and the challenge to the Foxes' security, or possibly even to their middleman position, by the French attempts to open a direct trade to the Dakotas. Even before 1692, the Foxes and Mascoutens had plundered French traders on the grounds that they carried guns to these long-standing rivals.

Should either an economic explanation or an explanation based upon Fox security be accepted, of course, the outflanking of the Foxes by the building of Fort Beauharnois would have to be considered a most obtuse blunder. A fur-trade explanation, however, makes it difficult to understand why the Foxes' main thrust was against Louisiana and the Illinois. The contrast between Fox belligerence and the steadfastness in the French alliance of the Ojibwas, equally threatened by the expeditions to the Dakotas, underscores the unsatisfactory character of these White-minded explanations. One must look as well to the particular character of the Fox tribe and its leaders. The diplomatic machinations of New Yorkers and Iroquois must also be taken into account, although direct evidence is hard to come by. Nor must arguments favourable to the Foxes be discounted, especially the points made by Vaudreuil, Louvigny, and Lignery that inept Louisianan Indian policy and the warlike behaviour of the Foxes' enemies must be accounted in the balance. Finally, we must disabuse ourselves of the notion that the Foxes' refusal to be caught in the net of the *pax gallica* implies a wrongheaded, even savage, disposition on their part.[45]

It was in 1720, when the renewal of Fox hostility had made penetration of the "Far West" impossible, that Father Charlevoix had arrived at Quebec with instructions from the Regent to investigate the most probable routes to the conjectured Western Sea. Charlevoix had garnered little but vague and cryptic references during a year-long epic journey that had taken him from Montreal (March 1721) through Lakes Ontario, Erie, Huron, and Michigan, down the Illinois (where he had seen the devastations of war) to the Mississippi, and thence to New Orleans and Biloxi (March 1722). "All my research has had no great success," he noted in his report, dated January 20, 1723, and complained that the Canadians to whom he looked for information, "travel without bothering much to investigate the country through which they pass."[46] But Charlevoix had come away with a notion of the Western Sea that we can recognize as based upon evidence for the existence of Lake Winnipeg. Since warfare made the direct route from Lake Superior impracticable, he had recommended that the sea be sought by tracing the Missouri to its source or that missionaries be placed among the Dakotas and ordered to collect further information. Paris had approved the second expedient. It had been in response to this decision that Beauharnois had overseen the formation of the private company that had built Fort Beauharnois four years after Charlevoix had tendered his report. Abandoned at the height of the war, the post had been re-established by a new company in 1731. But that was not the only initiative that had been taken in the "Search for the Western Sea."

The intended chain of posts leading west beyond Kaministiquia to the Western Sea had not yet materialized in the 1720s. New posts had, however, been established to the north at Nipigon (1716?) and Michipicoten (1726?) to block Indian routes to Hudson Bay. In 1728 Pierre Gaultier de La Vérendrye succeeded his brother as commandant of these three posts, known collectively as the Postes du Nord. La Vérendrye discussed with Indian informants the country that lay beyond the posts and became convinced that he could find the Western Sea.[47] In 1730 he recounted to Beauharnois Indian tales of travel west and showed him maps drawn on birchbark by Indians illustrating how Rainy Lake and Lake of the Woods could be reached from Lake Superior and how a river would lead on to Lake Winnipeg, given its familiar two-celled profile. The maps were abstractions, lakes appearing as enlargements in a straight-line river system, but they recorded with great care the numbers of lakes and portages. For the man in the canoe, they were invaluable. In particular, the sketch by one Auchagah showed the route via Grand Portage as superior to that from Kaministiquia, and this would dictate La Vérendrye's choice. According to the information given him, Lake Winnipeg was not to be confused with the Western Sea. Of the number of rivers shown to connect with the lake, the identity of the Red, the Nelson, and the Saskatchewan can be inferred. The latter was described by several Crees as flowing *out* of the lake, as leading past a "shining mountain" and as exhibiting ebb and flow that La Vérendrye surmised to be tidal. There was also report of a house-dwelling horticultural tribe living south of the river. These were the Mandans of the upper Missouri of whom La Vérendrye would soon hear marvellous tales. Although eyewitness accounts and folk legend were mingled, directions were hazy, distances telescoped, and difficult phenomena misunderstood by both informants and listener, La Vérendrye learned that any Western Sea must lie beyond Lake Winnipeg. The Saskatchewan appeared to be Delisle's long-sought River of the West that emptied into that sea. From the first, however, La Vérendrye did not confine his attention to this one possibility. As several rivers descended to Lake Winnipeg from a watershed to the southwest, he believed that it was "probable that from this height of land there are also those that fall to the Western Sea."[48] If La Vérendrye's surmise was wrong, it nonetheless led him one giant step beyond that of Charlevoix.

In undertaking exploration, La Vérendrye hoped to win a name for himself. There is nothing in his actions or his writings to cast doubt upon his statement that money was a secondary consideration for him because of the hope he had "of succeeding and of obtaining some consideration from His Majesty," in particular a captaincy and the Croix de Saint-Louis.[49] "I left Montreal on the 8th of June 1731," he wrote many years later, "intending to mark my perfect attachment to the service to which I confine all my ambition."[50] La Vérendrye's deep involvement in the fur trade has led some, then and since, to regard him primarily as a trader. But for him, exploration was consolidating new lands into the King's dominions. He wanted to claim these territories, extend Canada's trade to them, and thereby cut off that of the rival English on Hudson Bay. His discoveries, his attention to Indian relations, his founding of posts and trading in furs and slaves were various aspects of a single unified programme. Tempering the quest for *la gloire* with phlegm and practicality, he much resembles Champlain, the two of them quintessential French explorers.

In sending La Vérendrye west beyond Lake Superior in 1731, Beauharnois gave him a three-year monopoly of the trade and presents for the Indians to underwrite the venture. That fall, he authorized the re-establishment of the "Sioux post" and Fort La Baie, both to keep the Dakotas friendly "so as to enable us to carry on a trade with the Assiniboins and Crees."[51] For the Governor, La Vérendrye's mission was the extension of the *pax gallica*, with its political and economic dividends, ever farther westward. The discovery of the Western Sea was just one more dividend. For him, La Vérendrye was essentially a frontier diplomat like Joncaire, Louvigny, or Paul Marin de La Malgue.

Unfortunately, this was not a line of argument to satisfy the Minister. Maurepas gave a guarded approval to this expansionist scheme because, like the Regent before him, he was passionately interested in science. But he was also the standard-bearer of the compact colony policy that was never long forgotten in the offices of the Marine. "All these distant posts dissipate the colony's strength and retard its growth too much," he wrote in 1729, forbidding wilderness ventures at the very time that La Vérendrye was planning his.[52] Maurepas was also concerned that too aggressive a stance in the interior might antagonize Great Britain and endanger the Franco-British alliance. It should be no surprise that neither La Vérendrye nor Beauharnois was completely candid with him. They tended to downplay the herculean nature of the task of western discovery so as not to alarm him. They both knew that without considerable financial support, discovery could only be a by-product of the fur trade – which is not the same thing as what they permitted themselves to write, that the explorer would finance his advance by trading. Maurepas, for his part, had to view La Vérendrye in terms of past experience, which told him Canadian explorers were all too often just fur traders covering their activities by promises of discovery. Persons willing to bolster this interpretation were not wanting. It was also hard for Maurepas to understand realistically the extent of the western wilderness and the difficulty of coping with it and its inhabitants. Just as the Pontchartrains thought they could close the West by decree, Maurepas seems to have thought it could be opened by a mere matter of paddling. Almost from the beginning, he was suspicious of and unsympathetic to La Vérendrye. When the discovery of the Western Sea was not forthcoming after a number of years, he was in no mood to receive excuses.

The necessity for cultivating good Indian relations and the urgency for La Vérendrye's Montreal partners to make a profit governed the speed of the westward advance.[53] In 1731, his nephew and second-in-command, Christophe La Jemerais, together with Jean-Baptiste, La Vérendrye's eldest son, founded Fort Saint-Pierre on Rainy Lake, bringing them as far west as the voyageur Jacques de Noyon had been in 1688. Fort Saint-Charles was founded on the southwestern shore of Lake of the Woods in 1732, and in 1734 Fort Maurepas was built on the lower Red River. It had taken the La Vérendrye group three years to reach Lake Winnipeg. A map attributed to La Jemerais and dated 1733 tells us much about the development of the group's ideas to that point. La Jemerais had not yet descended the Winnipeg River to the lake, but the lake and the river system surrounding it are shown in considerable detail, all from the reports of Indians. The Red, Assiniboine, and Souris rivers are evident, as is Lake Manitoba. A height of land, the Pembina escarpment and more northerly continuations, separates these rivers from a great stream shown as an arc just below the Assiniboine, coming from and returning to the western edge of the map. Here, labelled River of the West, is the upper Missouri, with its most northerly Mandan Indian villages marked. La Vérendrye had come to believe that these people, transfigured in Indian report by confused echoes of the distant Spanish missions and fruitful imagination, were a "race of men white in colour and civilized" who would give signal help in the discovery of the Western Sea.[54] This new identification of their river, instead of the Saskatchewan, as the route to the sea appeared as a vindication of La Vérendrye's earlier guess that the presumed direction of discovery lay to the south and west, thus diverging from what in fur-trade terms was the profitable direction. It also placed the path of discovery where it was most difficult to avoid the native warfare that was breaking out beyond Lake Superior.

"These nations are almost all at war with one another," said La Jemerais.[55] It is a phenomenon known only piecemeal and to which historians have yet to give serious attention. To simplify greatly the numbers and geographical arrangement of tribes in the Canadian sphere of interest west of the Great Lakes by way of explanation, the Dakotas, situated on the Mississippi headwaters, the rice lake country to the north, and the prairies to the west, may be regarded as a hub around which other tribes were disposed. North of them were enemies of long standing, the Assiniboins, Crees, and Monsonis in whose lands La Vérendrye was building his posts and opening a trade. To the east were the Ojibwas (Dakota allies), the Winnibagos, and both the "subdued" and the "renegade" Foxes. To the west were the Mandans, traditional enemies of the Dakotas, Assiniboins, and Crees, and the Pawnees, the Mandans' traditional allies. Within this group, the 1730s witnessed diplomatic shifts and escalated warfare. About 1732, the Mandans allied themselves with the Assiniboins and Crees, and two years later they broke with the Pawnees. Dakota hostility toward the Mandans, Assiniboins, Crees, and Monsonis as well as the French reached a peak in 1736, when they killed two Frenchmen on the Missouri and perpetrated the well-known massacre of La Vérendrye's eldest son and a party of Canadians at Lake of the Woods. In the same year, they harried the Ojibwas and Winnibagos and made life for traders at Lake Pepin so dangerous that the post was abandoned for the second time in May 1737. By then the "renegade" Foxes had thrown in their lot with the Dakotas, and the long-standing Dakota alliance with the Ojibwas had dissolved. The latter subsequently became allied with the Assiniboins, Crees, and Monsonis and began decades of warfare by which they eventually drove the Dakotas from the forest and the rice lakes. It is hard to believe that these various acts were not related to each other and that the whole warlike effervescence was not connected to the Canadian advance beyond the lakes. But war was no part of the Canadian plan, and officers in the West worked hard to prevent it or to divert military actions in the least harmful directions – a prime motive for the encouragement of slave raids on distant or politically unimportant tribes.

The insufficient capital of La Vérendrye's Montreal backers, an inadequate organization of supply, and the unprofitable character of exploration as such stultified the explorer's continuing efforts. Yet the more time elapsed without the discovery of the Western Sea, the more did Maurepas suspect him and the harder was it for Beauharnois to defend and support him. La Vérendrye kept a promise to the Governor that he would reach the Mandans in 1738, but his map of 1737 shows that he had already set aside any notion that the upper Missouri, known to him only as the River of the Mandans, was the River of the West. It is shown going south to a sea (the Pacific?). To the northwest of it is a lake on a height of land; a relocated River of the West flows from it to an "unknown sea," while another river flowing east from it is the

Saskatchewan. Thus the Saskatchewan was brought back into the reckoning; but if the map were correct, then a direct overland approach would be a considerable shortcut to the sea. With Beauharnois on his back, La Vérendrye had every reason to want a shortcut, not to mention the éclat that the discovery of the fabled Mandans might bring. Thus when he built Fort La Reine (1738) on the site of Portage la Prairie, a convenient spot to intercept Assiniboins bound for Hudson Bay, and set out from there on foot to the Mandans, he anticipated finding information about the River of the West rather than the river itself. That the Mandans turned out to be Indians of characteristics well within the range of previous experience may have disappointed the explorer, but of their river he had had no illusions.

The brief voyage of La Vérendrye's son Pierre in 1741 and the anabasis of his other sons, Louis-Joseph and François, with the *engagés* La Londette and Amiotte in 1742-43 were, and were intended to be, voyages beyond the Mandans in search of other nations that it was hoped would be able to lead them to the sought-after river and sea. If Louis-Joseph and his party traversed only badlands and prairies, their journey was far from a failure. They saw the Big Horn Mountains and thus gained a realistic impression of the continental divide and discovered that the River of the Mandans and the Missouri were one and the same – unless Pierre had already established that. They walked and rode right across Guillaume Delisle's Western Sea without getting their feet wet. If the La Vérendryes lacked the stamp of genius, it is shown in their failure to make the leap in imagination from their dry moccasins to the entirely mythical nature of the Western Sea. But in extenuation, there remained an unexplored quadrant of North America ample enough to contain it.

In 1739 Louis-Joseph had been sent north to reconnoitre the country between Lake Winnipegosis and Lake Winnipeg and to visit the mouth of the Saskatchewan – a smallpox epidemic had prevented his reaching it in 1737. A fort, Bourbon, was built there in 1741 as was another, Fort Dauphin, at the bottom of Winnipegosis. Fort Paskoya was built in 1743 near the discharge of the Saskatchewan into Cedar Lake, where the French could forestall the trade to Hudson Bay or launch voyages into the interior. It was thus a northern equivalent of Fort La Reine. All the while that the reconnaissance beyond the Mandan villages was being undertaken, La Vérendrye was also opening this route to the north, superior for trade and, given the 1737 map, also a possible route to the sea. Unfortunately, time had run out for La Vérendrye and his remarkable family. After temporizing for a year, Beauharnois was forced to write to La Vérendrye that, following the Minister's orders, he was to be required to train and pay a salary to an officer chosen to replace him. Rather than accept such humiliation, La

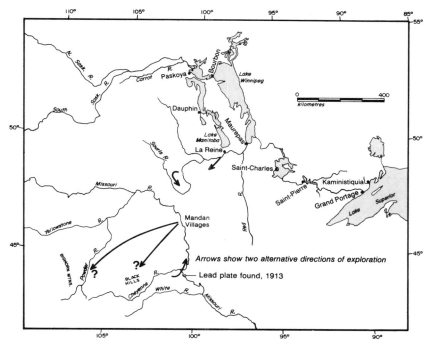

La Vérendrye and the Western Sea

Vérendrye resigned for reasons of ill health. Beauharnois made him the captain of his guard, which may have done something to dilute the bitterness he felt.

The fruit of La Vérendrye's explorations was only partly assimilated by French geographers. In this they were certainly blameable, but the fault was partly La Vérendrye's. He was no Verrazano who could draw inspired scientific conclusions from his explorations. But after him there was no one at all. The Canadian presence in the West after 1744 was a fur-trade presence only. In 1750 Father Bonnécamps, Professor of Hydrography and Mathematics at the Jesuit College in Quebec, in replying to a letter from a Parisian colleague, wrote that there was no one around who wanted to undertake exploration. He cast his barbs at the academic geographers who would buckle under the strain of a canoe trip if they could even be brought to attempt one. As to the Western Sea and all the scientific conjectures his excited colleague presented in its favour, Bonnécamps was the complete sceptic. "A system, however well conceived and well concocted it is, is not always in accord with the operations of Nature," he lectured. "From among an infinity of combinations, she will often choose capriciously those least direct and the least conformable to our ideas."[56]

While the Canadian frontier of trade and Indian alliances extended far to the west, the Anglo-American frontier of settlement followed at a distance, advancing at the slow speed of the plough. The advance of New England settlement into the Abenaki territories of mainland Acadia has been considered in a previous chapter. In New York settlement was gradually moving up the Mohawk Valley. Much of the valley was in the hands of speculators, if not settlers, by the end of the 1730s. The speculator was also opening the back country of Pennsylvania and Virginia in the 1720s and 1730s and selling it to the settler, most often a German or Scotch-Irish immigrant. In the 1730s Virginian settlement was crossing the Blue Ridge Mountains into the valley of the Shenandoah. Nine new townships were created in the interior of South Carolina in the same decades; and in February 1733, James Oglethorpe arrived from England with the first settlers of Georgia.[57]

Settlement constituted a relentless pressure on the Indians of the frontier zones and a challenge to French influence in the interior from the borders of Canada to Louisiana. Yet except for the building of Fort King George in 1721 and the creation of Georgia twelve years later, Great Britain exhibited no frontier policy whatever. In many colonies, tidewater indifference to frontier problems was Olympian. There is little evidence of concerted, intercolonial efforts to deal with the Indian question before 1739, when the War of Jenkins's Ear, which pitted Britain against Spain, suggested to the least clairvoyant that the peace between Britain and France could not last much longer.

George Clarke, Governor of New York from 1737 to 1746, pursued the frontier question with a vigour not seen since the departure of Burnet in 1728. It was crystal clear to Clarke that the winning of the West was not to be a mere matter of ploughing. One of his first objectives had been to establish a post at Irondequoit, on the south shore of Lake Ontario between Fort Niagara and Fort Oswego. This the Iroquois had steadfastly refused to permit, "the great ruling principle of the modern Indian politics" being, as the New Yorker Peter Wraxall observed, "to preserve the balance between us and the French."[58] Notwithstanding this long-held position, in 1741 Clarke secured a Seneca deed to the site and permission to settle – but willing settlers were nowhere in evidence.[59]

From the first Clarke had grasped that the safety of the Thirteen Colonies in a conflict with the French depended upon the Indian barrier, primarily the Six Nations in the north and the Cherokees in the south, but these two groups were themselves traditional enemies. At an Albany conference in 1740, the Six Nations gave in to his forceful insistence that the Covenant Chain be extended to the southern tribes. "All the Indians which were formerly our enemies are now entered into the Covenant with us," the Iroquois spokesman proclaimed, "almost as far as the river Mississippi."[60] From South Carolina, Lieutenant-Governor Bull wrote that he had held a conference with the Cherokees and Catawbas to explain the Albany talks and he descanted on "our dependence on the Cherokee Indians as a barrier against the designs and encroachments of the French."[61] Oglethorpe reported from Georgia that through his good offices the Creeks and Cherokees had made peace and both would send deputies to meet the Six Nations, "surely the best measure that can be taken to guard against the French in case of a war."[62]

Although Clarke reported to the Six Nations in 1742 that the southern tribes had accepted the Covenant Chain, these tribes sent no delegates north, perhaps because of their involvement in the war with Spain. As the Iroquois had not had long-standing and friendly relations with all the colonial governments southward, it was helpful on that occasion that Clarke was able to present them with gifts bought by Virginia and Georgia. One interesting relationship they had developed was with Pennsylvania. From the 1730s that province recognized Iroquois suzerainty over the Indians within its own borders, peoples whom white settlement displaced into the valleys of the Allegheny and the upper Ohio, a hunting ground won by the Iroquois in their seventeenth-century wars and over which they claimed dominion.[63] Thus during the War of Jenkins's Ear, the British colonial governors did what they could to bind the tribes of their western periphery into a fragile alliance against the French.

Louisiana was maintaining its grip on the southern interior only with difficulty.[64] Fears for their lands and their cultural integrity led the Natchez, an important tribe on the Mississippi west of the Choctaws, to revolt against the French. While their nation was crushed and their ruler, the Great Sun, sent into slavery in Saint-Domingue, many refugees fled to the Chickasaws, to whom the Louisianans carried the war. Choctaws were visiting Charleston and receiving Georgia traders. The anxious colony thus greeted with high hopes the reversion to royal rule in 1731 and the return of Bienville as governor two years later. There would be no peace for Louisiana, Bienville and his officials agreed, unless the Chickasaws were destroyed as utterly as had been the Natchez and the Foxes before them. A Chickasaw war would also occupy the Choctaws and inhibit the consolidation of a Carolinan trade alliance encompassing all the frontier tribes.

Canada was necessarily involved. The old jealousies remained between Canadian and Louisianan, in particular over the Illinois country to which Beauharnois persistently sent Canadian traders and over which he repeatedly argued, to no avail, for jurisdiction. Bienville complained that Beauharnois sent insufficient help against the Chickasaws, an echo of old complaints against Vaudreuil in the First Fox War. From 1729 Beauharnois had been encouraging northern Indians to attack the Chickasaws, adding them to the "Flatheads" (Cherokees and Catawbas), against whom French allies and Senecas had long been encouraged to direct their raids, giving them an outlet for their martial ambitions and preventing inconvenient alliances. Now in 1736 and 1739 Beauharnois was persuaded to send Canadian expeditionary forces to participate in the Chickasaw War. The problems of mounting ambitious military expeditions in the North American wilderness within the financial constraints imposed upon the colonies and using undisciplined forces composed largely of colonists and Indians were such that in describing them, *fiasco* can become a much overworked noun. But like the Beaucours expedition against New England settlements in 1704, Walker and Nicholson's land-and-sea pincers campaign against Canada in 1711, or Lignery's march against the Foxes in 1715, that is what the Chickasaw campaigns were. That of 1739 was the more ambitious of the two. Bienville intended by a liberal use of horses and oxen to build roads and drag cannon and mountains of supplies to the Chickasaw stockades. The Canadian force of some five hundred Frenchmen, Canadians, and Indians did rendezvous with Bienville's army of over a thousand, but the combined force never managed to confront the enemy in strength. In the years that followed, there was a return to more traditional guerrilla tactics, including the burning of cornfields, to harass an enemy that could not be destroyed. As to the problem of combating the English superiority in the skin trade, nothing, it seemed, could be done.

As the long peace was drawing to a close, Beauharnois believed that Canada had little to fear on the New York frontier.[65] He had the Lake Champlain route to Montreal blocked. Six Nations neutrality protected the long frontier from Fort Saint-Frédéric to Fort Niagara. He was sufficiently confident that he refused to commit himself to neutrality with New York itself. The valleys of the Alleghany and upper Ohio were another matter. Before the 1730s they had been an Iroquois hunting ground, a buffer of space between English Indians and the nearest French allies on the Maumee and the Wabash. They then had rapidly filled with displaced Delawares and Shawnees from Pennsylvania and Iroquois from several tribes who became known as Mingos. By 1743 these Mingos had migrated farther west to the Scioto. With all these tribesmen came English traders, whose rum reached the Weas and Miamis.

In 1738 the French alliance experienced a stunning upset. The Detroit Hurons announced that they had made peace with the Flatheads and even joined them in ambushing a raiding party of Ottawas, Potawatomis and Ojibwas. "It is a very delicate affair that demands the most careful handling," Beauharnois remarked, "the Hurons being allied with the Five Nations, and the Ottawas with all those of the upper country."[66] The result was the migration of the Hurons to Sandusky on the south shore of Lake Erie, a possible prelude to neutrality or even defection.

If Canada had lost the cordon sanitaire that had so long separated its western allies from the influence of English traders, and Louisiana was struggling to maintain its trade influence with the Choctaws, the English colonies, which had long lagged behind in Indian politics, were having trouble bringing their grand alliance of frontier tribes into being. From March 1743, the official English colonial documents suddenly come alive with news and comments on "the affair at the back of Virginia."[67] A group of Iroquois young men, presumably gone to raid the Flatheads in spite of the entreaties of the sachems, became involved in an exchange of gunfire with a group of white frontiersmen. A number were dead on each side. It was hoped that the Covenant Chain would not be broken.

*　　*　　*

Vaudreuil had succeeded in regarrisoning the West. The revival of the fur trade from the mid-1720s once again served to provide economic underpining to the alliance system. Beauharnois found, as had his predecessor in his last years, that it was hard to keep Versailles alive to the necessity for a strong presence in the interior. Some progress was made in strengthening the frontiers of the colony proper and in consolidating the position of Louisiana. But French ministers were as reluctant to spend money in the West as were their British counterparts across the Channel, unmoved by the anxieties of the Board of Trade. Nevertheless, Beauharnois managed a considerable war against the Foxes and was long able to protect La Vérendrye from the full force of ministerial distrust. British colonial governors, increasingly aware of the stakes in the West, did what they could with inadequate funds to establish a joint diplomacy in the interior to counter the extension of the *pax gallica*. In the spring of 1744, all America was bracing itself for the first shots of the war that was upon it. The threads of alliance spun out by the frontier diplomatists in hope of binding the interior to their interests were fragile indeed.

CHAPTER 10

The "One Continued Village"

On August 2, 1749, the Swedish botanist and traveller Peter Kalm was lodged in a farmhouse near Trois-Rivières, having descended the St Lawrence in a bateau from Montreal. He confided his impressions to his diary:

> It could really be called a village, beginning at Montreal and ending at Quebec, which is a distance of more than one hundred and eighty miles [289 kilometres]; for the farm-houses are never above five *arpens* [293 metres], and sometimes but three, asunder, a few places excepted. The prospect is exceedingly beautiful when the river goes on for some miles together in a straight line, because it then shortens the distances between the houses, and makes them form exactly one continued village.[1]

The description might well include the towns as well as the countryside, for although more densely populated and with the depth of several streets, they were essentially a part of the parade of houses along the north shore that was mirrored by the farms across the river. At the beginning of the century, Kalm's metaphor of spectacular linearity would not yet have been appropriate. It would not have accommodated the green interludes of forest and marsh still prominent in the landscape when the surveyor and cartographer Gédéon de Catalogne made his survey of Canada in 1712.[2] The making of Kalm's "one continued village" within the narrow parallelogram of usable soil along the St Lawrence is a central theme in the history of Canada in the first half of the eighteenth century. In its straggling rows of farms and in the houses of its few town streets, the vast majority of Canadians lived their lives of daily routines, "countless inherited acts, accumulated pell-mell and repeated time after time."[3] Sometimes, here and there, merchants, intendants, and even governors invaded the village, attempting to bend its patterns to the needs of trade or policy, to save it from crop failures, or to marshal it for war.

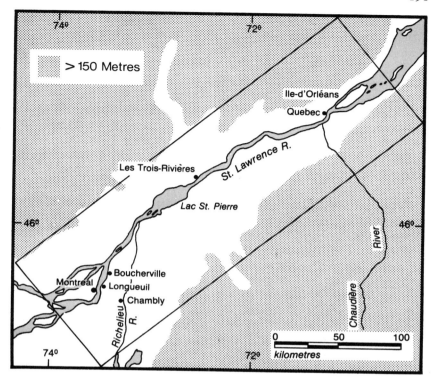

The Canadian Parallelogram

I

By the turn of the century, the French population of Canada, some fifteen thousand strong, was spreading along the banks of the St Lawrence from initial nodes of settlement at Quebec, Trois-Rivières, and Montreal, the administrative centres of the three districts into which Canada was divided.[4] A sixty-four-kilometre stretch of the north shore with Quebec, a town of fifteen hundred, at its middle, was already beginning to approximate Kalm's village. The circumference of the Ile d'Orléans was inhabited. A few farms were dotted along the south shore in an attenuated line that extended all the way to Rivière Ouelle. From Trois-Rivières, settlement was reaching down almost to the boundary of the Quebec district, beyond which was a long break in the chain of farm houses. Trois-Rivières was a small village and therefore a small market without the magnetic attraction that Quebec and Montreal exercised on pioneer farmers. Opposite it, the south shore was almost uninhabited, and the flooded and inhospitable shores of Lac Saint-Pierre were silent and empty. Beyond the lake in the Montreal district, few settlers were found, especially along the north shore, until the island was reached. Montreal town itself sheltered around a thousand souls, although the population of the island had grown to over two thousand; and on the opposite shore the seigneuries from La Prairie de la Madeleine to Boucherville vied with Beauport near Quebec as the most densely populated countryside in Canada.

By the eve of the War of the Austrian Succession, the French population had more than trebled to around 45,000. The population of Quebec had increased proportionately to 4,600 and that of Montreal to 3,500. Along the north shore, new farms had filled in a line of settlement of which the terminal points, opposite Ile Jésus and some fifty kilometres below Quebec, had remained almost the same since the end of the seventeenth century. The Lac Saint-Pierre region had received some settlers in the late thirties, after being opened by a thoroughfare, but was still sparsely populated. Settlement along the south shore from opposite Montreal Island to the end of the lake had increased considerably, although farms were thinly scattered from there to a point well within the Quebec district. A road was built from La Prairie to a settlement at Chambly. Several farms were established on the lower Richelieu and at the mouths of the Yamaska and Saint-François, rivers that empty into Lac Saint-Pierre. Even more than in the upper districts, tributary rivers were opened to settlement in the district of Quebec. The best example was the thickly settled Rivière-du-Sud, but it was also true of the Boyer and the Chaudière. The older communities along the south shore had increased in density and had been extended to Rivière-du-Loup, fulfilling the promise of the few farmsteads that had been staked out in the region by 1712.

The "one continued village" had become a reality well before 1749 or even 1744, especially along the north shore, but the valley from Montreal to Fort Frontenac on Lake Ontario remained empty. To enforce the policy of the compact colony and prevent a westward rush of colonists more interested in fur trading than in farming, settlement there was forbidden. Still, had there been sufficient settlers, the prohibition would not have lasted. De Catalogne tells us (1712) that rapids in the St Lawrence and a scarcity of manpower were the reasons that these lands, "the finest in the country," remained virgin forest.[5]

As people spread out and became rooted in the St Lawrence Valley, they knitted together the landscape with roads. Trails passable by simple carts came into being with the first grist mills, and others, perpendicular to the St Lawrence, with the first inland, or second-range, settlements. Roads were an early necessity around Quebec and on Montreal Island, where settlement was less decidedly riparian. In the later seventeenth century, trails already connected the numerous stockade forts that protected Montreal Island and the adjacent south shore. Public through-roads, built by the authority of the state, were longer in coming.[6] Considerable density of settlement and a degree of wealth were necessary to make them realizable alternatives to the river. The road that has received the most attention from historians is the *chemin du roi* along the north shore from Quebec to Montreal, built primarily between 1731 and 1737 under the direction of the *grand voyer*, Jean-Eustache Lanoullier de Boisclerc: a dirt road up to seven metres wide, ploughed and harrowed like a field, with occasional corduroy, ditched and supplied with culverts, wooden bridges and ferries – or, in some cases, leading to fords.[7] Before the end of the Old Regime, there were also roads from Montreal to Fort Chambly and Fort Saint-Jean, along the Richelieu and Chaudière, and connecting most of the settled south shore. This realization of a network of connecting roads was related to the increased keeping of horses. Together they made transportation increasingly rapid and less burdensome and did much to overcome the isolation of the early Canadian settlers.

The "continued village" took its form not only from the domination of a narrow plain by the two shores of the St Lawrence River but also from the Canadians' rejection of real villages and their perpetuation instead of the settlement pattern of "the medieval zones of street-type land clearing" in Western France.[8] From a common access road (or in Canada, originally from the St Lawrence shore), each settler established the beachhead of his own farmhouse and began his years-long assault on the forest. In Canada, where the shores of the river were marshy or were confronted by high embankments, strip farms were fronted on tributaries or on inland roads, as was the case at Lac Saint-Pierre in the 1730s. The Canadian farm was thus a long ribbon of land with a house and buildings at one end that fronted a river, a road, or both. Over the years, the ratio of width to length tended to stabilize at about one to ten. While there were some farms of forty arpents and others of two hundred, the average seems to have been eighty (about twenty-seven hectares). The Chevalier de La Pause described them as being two to four arpents (117 to 234 metres) wide by forty to fifty arpents (2,340 to 2,926 metres) deep. A holding that was large by French standards was made possible in Canada by the availability of land and necessary by the considerable need for firewood. Cleared land, divided between ploughed fields and hay meadows, accounted for only a quarter to a half of the farm's surface. The average Canadian size of this "arable," thirty-four arpents or about eleven hectares, approximates the minimum figure beyond which a minority of French peasants – the *laboureurs* or *ménagers* of which *habitants* is an obvious analogue – owned their equipment and livestock and lived in respectable comfort.[9] Farms much larger would not have been practical. The limitations of manpower aided by draught animals inadequate in number and quality and by only the most elementary tools imposed a low ceiling on the amount of land that could be sown to crops or harvested at one time.[10] The Canadian settlement pattern gave as many persons as possible access to fishing and transportation. As in the French street village, farm families lived in community without the social suffocation of the true village. Straggling lines of farmsteads were broken naturally by tributaries, marshes, outcroppings, or forest into discrete units known as *côtes*. These became the rural communities of New France, corresponding to the *terroirs* of the mother country.[11] And the *côte*, like the French *terroir*, took no account of seigneurial frontiers. Although a few villages and hamlets did develop, these were usually service centres and not communities of farmers as were villages typically in Europe or in the earlier years of New England settlement.

Much has been written about the seigneurial system, but the topic is far from exhausted. Historians for many years described the seigneur as a kind of benign colonization agent, basing their portrait on the well-documented royal intention that the seigneur ought to build up the population of his seigneury in return for his grant and in anticipation of future rental income. Demonstration that the settlement pattern was governed by markets and geography and that there seems to have been no strong relation between seigneurial boundaries and settlement patterns points to the conclusion that, with a few important exceptions, the colonizing seigneur is a myth to be relegated to the sidelines of historical explanation.[12] Whereas the neglectful seigneur and the lone seigneur-farmer make numerous appearances in de Catalogne's 1712 report, the improving landlord is rare. In part this reflects the impoverished period in which de Catalogne made his survey. The two examples he does provide are instructive. The seigneur of Ile Perrot lived alone on his seigneury although his land was good and he had built a mill and a small fortification. The nearby seigneury of Longueuil, in contrast, was well populated by habitants "very well off, even rich" although the land was either stony or swampy. The seigneur at considerable expense had drained wet fields and had cleared the stones from others, using them to build a fort and houses. He had begun a road. It was the efforts of the seigneur possessed of the poorer land with better access to rivers and markets, being directly opposite Montreal, that were rewarded. Ile Perrot remained unpopulated because it was far from town and isolated by the Lachine rapids. Thus the examples underscore the primacy of location but also are evidence of the existence of improving landlords, if not colonizers, who may have been more numerous in the prosperous decades that followed.[13] As the seigneurs of both estates were fur traders, the examples also raise the almost unexamined question of the transfer of wealth from trade to the land. Unfortunately for historical analysis, seigneuries held by the religious orders, some of the most improving landlords in the colony, were also among the best placed in relation to transport and markets. The role of seigneurial management is in their case difficult to isolate.

Seigneuries had been granted with a too lavish hand. One hundred and eighty rural seigneuries have been counted for the year 1715, although de Catalogne's survey lists only ninety-eight, many of them uninhabited or nearly so. It was clear to Pontchartrain by 1711 that although many seigneuries had been granted, land clearing was not proceeding rapidly and much of the seigneurial land remained in forest. He had received alarmist reports from the Intendant, Jacques Raudot, claiming that seigneurs hindered settlement by holding uncleared land for higher prices or demanding exorbitant rents. These allegations were added to the time-honoured complaint that "libertine" habitants neglected their farms to become coureurs de bois. Raudot, who was not a product of the Marine bureaucracy, stands out among the eighteenth-century intendants as genuinely interested in rural life for its own sake. He lamented what he took to be the invasion of the colony by "the business spirit," full of "subtlety and chicanery" as well as the loss of that perennially rediscovered and largely imaginary "simplicity in which people used to live." He also feared for the people's title to their land as there was, according to him, "almost nothing in their commerce together done according to rule." He proposed a whole battery of reforms for the seigneurial system. Largely as a result of Raudot's investigations, the King issued the Decrees of Marly (July 6, 1711). In the first of these, seigneurs were instructed to grant land on the traditional terms of *cens et rente* only. Seigneurs were warned that if they had not cleared *domaines* within a year and had placed no habitants on the land, they would face confiscation. The second warned habitants that undeveloped farms would similarly be reunited with the seigneurial *domaines*.[14] Although these draconian pronouncements were not followed by much real action, the King's Memorandum of 1714 did announce an end to seigneurial grants. Until 1732 almost none were made. Under ministerial pressure, the Governor and Intendant withdrew sixteen grants along the Richelieu and Lake Champlain in 1741, but a few years later many of these undeveloped lands were reconceded to their original owners. It is hard to escape the impression that these occasional outbursts of official activity had little real effect on the settlement process. By the end of the Old Regime there were 250 seigneuries. They were of every size, reflecting changes in official policy over the years, those granted in the eighteenth century averaging about 104 square kilometres.

By a tenure of feudal origin, the King granted the seigneury to the seigneur for fealty and homage; and the seigneur in turn granted the habitant a piece of land, the *roture*, with a title encumbered by the requirement to pay the *cens et rente*, the former a quitrent, the latter a more substantial revenue for the seigneur cunningly confounded with it. A farm consisted of one or often two (the maximum) *rotures*. The habitant by virtue of paying the *cens* was a *censitaire*.[15] The seigneurial system was a law of real property based on the hereditary tenancy of the *censitaires*, the seigneurs' immediate ownership of the land, and the King's shadowy and ultimate possession, which made possible the revocation of seigneurial grants. Free disposition of land was hedged about with restrictions, particularly for the *censitaire*, who was required to pay the *cens et rente*, the *lods et ventes* (transfer fees payable when *rotures* were sold), fees for the use of the common, fees paid at the seigneur's mill, where the *censitaire* was required to have all flour for his own consumption ground. In some cases he submitted to the seigneur's harvesting of valuable wood from his land, paid a little for the right to fish and a fee for the use of the common, and, where the seigneur had driven a hard and quite illegal bargain, was held by the sanctity of contract to owe him labour service (*corvée*). If he lived in the neighbourhood of Montreal, his land was subjected to the customary usage of *vaine pâture*, the turning loose of the community's stock on the fields from fall until spring.[16] It is stretching a point to describe the habitant as the proprietor of the soil,[17] but it is a little misleading to the modern reader to describe him as a tenant.

In economic terms the kernel of the system was the transfer of rents and fees from the producer to the seigneur. The well-established habitant family must have paid (or owed!) the seigneur between thirty-nine and forty-three livres each year. If we were to deduct from this the milling cost of twenty livres, which was a fee for a monopolized service much like a modern public utility, the resulting levy would be in our eyes rather modest.[18] Nevertheless, such payments would have been a burden to producers of only marginal surpluses. Unless the seigneur had undertaken considerable improvements for the benefit of the habitants, his was a parasitic role. His seigneury was essentially a big farm (the *domaine*) plus a rent roll. The use of seigneurial mills and roads, the seigneurial ownership of the common, and the concentration of rents in a common manor gave the developed seigneury an economic identity.[19]

Probably a third to a half of Canadian seigneurs laboured on their own *domaines* and lived much like habitants. Most of the other half to two thirds would have passed for substantial farmers, employing hired men and doing much less, perhaps none, of the manual work.[20] There would be no contradiction in the habitant's seeing many of these as real gentry and a few even as plausible lords. But we have very little information on *domaine* management. It is not clear that the *domaine* ever became of great economic importance, even when export markets were developed for Canadian flour. We know of very few impressive *domaines*. That of the Séminaire de Québec at Beaupré is one. Another is the *domaine* of the seigneury of Terrebonne. This was built by the unparalleled industry of the Abbé Louis Lepage, who sold the seigneury to Louis La Corne *l'aîné* in 1745 for the unprecedented sum of 60,000 livres. In 1752 the royal engineer, Louis Franquet, had dinner with La Corne, discussed the seigneury, and visited its grist mill and sawmills. He observed that the improvements had been costly, but that annual revenue, which presumably contained both *domaine* income and feudal revenues from the *rotures*, averaged 12,000 livres a year.[21]

If large-scale rural enterprise was as rare as it seems to have been, then most *domaine* agriculture must have been little different from habitant agriculture. The point is an important one, for large-scale farming is more apt to produce a surplus for the market because of the smaller share of the harvest required for the producer's own consumption. In any case, *domaine* farms and farms owned by religious communities, merchants, or government functionaries occupied only a small portion of the land. Canada was a country of peasant agriculture. The presumed insignificance of *domaine* agriculture also means that in terms of the nature and probably the size of his income the seigneur as such was only to be distinguished from the habitant by the feudal revenues he received from the *rotures*.[22] In this the Canadian rural economy was strikingly different from that of France, where feudal revenues had become ancillary to those from the *domaine* and the *domaine* farmer (in the etymological sense of the word) was such an important figure in the social landscape.[23]

Of the various feudal rights accepted in Canadian law, only four produced important revenues: the *cens et rente*, the *lods et ventes*, fees for the common, and milling fees. In an undeveloped seigneury, the capital and running costs of a new mill were a dead loss to the seigneur, and the revenues from feudal dues were derisory. However, theoretical calculations indicate that once a seigneury was populated by about fifty well-established families farming two *rotures* each, the dues could produce a good income of some 1,500 livres annually. Much depended upon the profitability of the mill.[24]

Canadian seigneurialism was something that grew. By the beginning of our period, its minutiae were well established in law. And as more seigneuries were settled and more settled seigneuries grew old and established, more people came under the sway of a fully developed system supported by the courts – in some cases, the seigneur's own court of *bas justice*. Thus while the primacy of *domaine* agriculture in the mother country gave at least a superficial modernity to the rural economy, the Canadian rural economy, as it developed, enmeshed the population more and more in peasant agriculture and the leftovers of feudalism. That the Canadian habitant enjoyed greater prosperity than did the French peasant was not the result of release from the cage of seigneurialism. Seigneurial exactions in Canada may well have been fewer and lighter than for peasants in many regions of France, although the landlord is never popular and the habitants emulated their French cousins in forgetting and disputing payments and obligations.[25] But more important, *the land was theirs* and had not been swallowed up by the *domaine*. For that reason, habitants avoided sharecropping and debt. And while the most crushing burdens were heaped upon the French peasant by the state and in some regions by the Church, the Canadian habitants paid a reasonable tithe, an obligation that was also subject to some chicanery, and very few taxes.

The Canadian countryside was much praised for its beauty and its bounty. The Intendant de Meulles in 1685 credited winter cold with producing in the soil "a kind of salt that makes for the rapid germination of seeds" so that manure was not needed.[26] Decades later, Nicolas Boucault was repeating a version of the same explanation, that "the snow that falls there abundantly during the winter enriches the earth and gives it a kind of nitre that renders it fertile."[27] Upon this land, apparently blessed in mysterious ways, the habitants grew field peas, oats, and barley for animal feed, a very great proportion of wheat, and almost no rye, the "food of the poor" that still dominated French fields in the early part of the century.[28] Canadian wheat was a northern spring variety, one story being that it was brought from Scandinavia. It matured in ninety days and was reported to be as good as French spring wheat, although of smaller grain. French winter wheat, which was agreed to be superior, was grown only experimentally as it was usually killed by heavy frosts in early spring or in fall before it was safely blanketed with snow.[29] Even Kalm's matter-of-fact description of these Canadian fields conveys a certain lyricism: "well-cultivated, and nothing but fine houses of stone, large grain-fields, meadows, pastures, woods of deciduous trees, and some churches built of stone";

"large fields, which look quite white with grain"; "excellent grain fields, charming meadows and delightful woods."[30]

Much controversy has centred on the Canadian "yield ratio," the ratio of seed planted to seed harvested. There has been a tendency to find the ratio unacceptably low and to attribute this to incompetent farming methods. But it is most probable that Canadian yields were better than those of France and normal for North American agriculture. De Catalogne reported that of Canadian lands, "the worst although badly cultivated render ordinarily six, seven and eight for one unless accidents occur."[31] According to Hocquart, "ordinary land" produced from eight to fifteen from one and new land more.[32] Kalm reported yields of nine or ten from one on land "reckoned pretty fertile" as well as yields "generally ten or twelve fold."[33] Franquet in 1752 reported a ratio of one to eight on "very bad" land, adding, "that's worth the trouble of cultivating the land."[34] And, of course, there was always new land under cultivation with wheat yields of fifteen, twenty, twenty-four, or even twenty-six from one. Such figures represent what farmers in their conversations expected from good years without "accidents" – rust, frost, insects, and so forth. By way of comparison, Pennsylvania farmers obtained yield ratios between one to five and one to twelve with one to six considered normal. In France one to five or six was a normal ratio with much less being common in many areas.[35] A recent attempt to calculate Canadian yields from older fields has resulted in more conservative ratios between 1 to 4.5 and 1 to 7.5.[36] But these low figures, which incorporate "accidents," only confirm that Canadian yields seem to have been at least normal for the time. The eighteenth-century norm, of course, was low by modern standards. The percentage of the crop needed for the next year's seed and for the producer's own consumption was high. A drop in yield of one or two grains in a head of wheat could turn a passable crop into a crop failure, just as an increase of the same amount could be a considerable boon. Thus the agriculture of the time was remarkably susceptible to "accidents," and poor crops were frequent.[37] Canadian agriculture must have owed much to its high-yield new land.

Historians, considering yield ratios to be the touchstone of agricultural performance in times past, have criticized the habitant farmer unjustly on that account. But they have also pointed the shaming finger, sometimes in common with the habitant's upper-class contemporaries, at his poor tools, his superficial ploughing, his weedy fields, his imputed ignorance of rotation, his scrawny livestock, and his self-indulgence in raising an uneconomical number of horses. Some of these observations are just, but perhaps they are better understood as criticisms of the eighteenth-century farmer in general than as criticisms of the Canadian habitant in particular.

There is not an abundance of detailed first-hand criticism of Canadian farming. Kalm's few precious remarks are indispensable, but he really tells us little; and the criticisms in his amiable pages are mild. He does not like the design of plough, harrow, and hay rake; he believes that drainage could be better tended to.[38] De Catalogne argues that land would produce more if cultivated as carefully as in France, but the yields he reports are greater than contemporary French yields. And his references to good yields from indifferent land resulting from "the great care of the habitants," "the habitants' application and care" suggest that care was proportional to need. It is remarkable that de Catalogne focuses much of his criticism on what we would consider the structural problems of the rural sector: the labour shortage, the inadequate roads and bridges, the paucity of mills, the plethora of religious holidays (a shortcoming corrected in 1744 when several were shifted to Sunday), the absence of public granaries, even the need for more river pilots – matters that fell within the purview of the administration.[39]

Canadian farmers ploughed their fields in the fall and the best of them again in the spring, using the costly and cumbersome wheeled plough with fixed mouldboard that produced the ridged field – a rise of one foot in a width of about nine – providing an element of drainage. Sometime between mid-April and mid-May, seed was broadcast by hand and harrowed in. Although oxen were often, perhaps most often, used for ploughing, drawing the triangular harrow was a job for horses, as their greater speed was necessary to break up the clods before they had dried and hardened. The grain was harvested sometime after the middle of August with a serrated sickle, the scythe being confined to haying as it knocked too much ripe grain from the head. When the sheaves had ripened, they were carried to the barn and stored. Grain was threshed with a flail as needed, usually beginning the following January. The grain was then winnowed in baskets made of thin wooden strips.[40]

Newly broken land was planted to grain for some years without resting. Even Kalm observed, "There is no occasion for leaving it fallow."[41] On older land, some kind of rotation was observed. The evidence of ridges in hay meadows indicates that the grain fields were shifted to new locations from time to time.[42] Within this long-term rotation, the fields in use appear to have been divided into two equal portions, one in crop and the other fallow, that is, left in weeds for the cattle to graze. But it is unclear whether land was cropped every other year or whether this was the classical biennial rotation in which the fallow was left for two years, and the wheat was sown the first year on one half of the cropped land and the second on the other half. One might well ask whether the rotation practised on older lands was as systematic as either of these alternatives and whether it was practised uniformly throughout the period. Whether the large crop of peas was included in a rotation cycle the year before wheat so that its nitrogen fixing could be turned to good account is not known.[43]

"The habitants are not accustomed to manuring their lands," wrote Jacques and Antoine-Denis Raudot in 1708. "The manure is carried upon the fallow grounds in spring," Kalm wrote in his diary in 1749. In between are any number of documents supporting the one assertion or the other.[44] A certain amount of manure landed in the right place as a result of the customs of using fallow for pasture and of *vaine pâture*. But where cattle and horses were turned into the forest to shift for themselves, much of the stuff was lost. If a certain amount was employed for the more intensive land use of gardening, there was nevertheless considerable nonchalance in the reported abandoning of stable manure (that is, winter manure) by depositing it on the river ice. It reveals an attitude shared with other communities of extensive land farmers. Habitants may have agreed with the many Pennsylvania farmers who believed that fertilizer was bad for the land, giving good crops today but leaving a ruined soil for posterity.[45] In any case, no Canadian farm could have produced sufficient manure to fertilize its fields adequately.[46] Thus the debate on manuring becomes a discussion of the habitants' good intentions more than a consideration of practical results. De Catalogne's report and the ordinances of the intendants indicate considerable ditching of fields. But on the evidence of Kalm, practice was not what it could have been.[47]

Every farm had its cultivated hay meadows, covering something less than 10 per cent of its area. These seem to have received special attention – even manure. Haying took place in July around Montreal, in early August near Quebec. Men mowed with scythes while the women raked. The mown hay was carried off by carts for stacking. Meadows appear rarely to have been fenced, the cattle being kept out of the fields by cowherds. For pasture, habitants depended upon common lands, often along the river or even on islands, and on their fallow land. Kalm has described the contrasting sown and fallow fields in autumn. "The sown ones looked yellow," he writes, "and the fallow ones green. The weeds are left on the latter all summer, for the cattle to feed upon." Thus weeds, perhaps inadvertently, were left to serve as soil builders, although they must at the same time have been harmful to adjacent wheat fields.[48]

The habitant maintained a considerable menagerie of fowl and, as shown in Table V, of cattle, pigs, sheep, and horses. In the later seventeenth and early eighteenth centuries, two yoke of oxen and two to

Table V
Livestock: Percentage Increases, 1706-1739

Total for Year:	Sheep	Horses	Pigs	Cattle
1706	1,820	1,872	7,408	14,191
1739	26,260	9,718	27,258	38,821
%Increase 1706-1739	1,342	419	267	173

Source: Annual statistics for most years in A.J.E. Lunn, "Economic Development in New France, 1713-1760," Ph.D. dissertation, McGill University, 1942.

three milk cows were kept on the average farm on Montreal Island. For
Canada as a whole in the eighteenth century the estimate is five to six
cows and one to two head of oxen. Both pigs and sheep were fewer in
numbers than were cattle.[49]

The horse became prominent in the Canadian farmyard at the very
end of the seventeenth century. Administrators inveighed against keeping the animals, as horses require more food than oxen and threatened
to upset the delicate economic balance of the farm. Jacques Raudot
issued an ordinance in 1709 prohibiting each habitant from keeping
more than two horses and a foal. The bogy plague of horses was much
overdrawn if the administration's own census figures can be given any
credence. In 1706 there were not quite enough horses in the colony to
average one to a family, and in 1739 the average had risen to not quite
two. (It was sheep that had increased most dramatically in numbers –
by more than 1,000 per cent.) The horse indeed proved indispensable.
Quicker and more agile than the ox, it was used for harrowing, logging,
hauling, and ploughing. Although horses never fully replaced the yoke
of oxen at the plough, their presence must have been responsible for
the reversed balance between oxen and milk cows that appears to have
taken place. Moreover, the horse may not have strained fodder supplies as much as feared. Being a tough animal with long legs that
enabled it to move over a snowy terrain, the horse was turned out in
the woods for the winter, as Kalm observed: "The horses are left out
of doors during the winter, and find their food in the woods, living
upon nothing but dry plants, which are very abundant; however, they
do not lose weight by this food, but look very fine and plump in
spring." This use of wild woodland, which also received cattle and
swine in summer, is a signal difference between the land-rich, extensive agriculture of North America and the land-conserving agriculture
of Europe, where horses could not be fed without the intensive land
use of the triennial rotation.[50]

Administrators also expressed concern that the habitants were riding horses, arguing that this weakened them and made them useless for guerrilla raids on snowshoes. It is hard to escape the conclusion that they were simply scandalized at seeing common people on horseback. It was the horse as a symbol of upward mobility and liberty that caught the eye of the administrator and caused such consternation. Thus the horse was a doubly important acquisition for the habitant.

If Canadian horses seemed robust, the other stock was indeed malnourished and degenerate. To eke out their supply of fodder, habitants slaughtered all supernumeraries at the end of December and fed their animals little in winter. They left the carcasses outdoors overnight to quick-freeze them. The family's supply of meat was stored in a loft, and surplus beef by the quarter, whole sheep with their wool, and poultry in feather were disposed of in the town markets.[51]

De Catalogne, in his 1712 survey, mentions textile making only twice, at Beaupré and Ile d'Orléans, where cloth was even made for the market. The marked increase in the numbers of sheep starting in the early years of the century is evidence of the increasing importance of spinning and weaving. The same period also saw growth in the raising of flax and the making of linen. "Every countryman sows as much flax as he wants for his own use," wrote Kalm on September 4, 1749. "They have already taken it up some time ago, and spread it on the fields, meadows, and pastures, in order to bleach it."[52]

To complete the agricultural landscape, it is necessary to add only the sugar maple in the habitant's woodlot, an apple tree near the farmhouse, the tobacco patch, and the kitchen garden. Cabbages and onions seem to have been the most important European importations to which were added the North American watermelons in more southern regions and squash and pumpkins, the latter seeming to Kalm to dominate the gardens – as anyone who has grown pumpkins will understand. Red currant shrubs bore profusely. And if in 1749 Kalm found French grapes being grown by Montreal townsmen and prudently reserved only for eating, de Catalogne in 1712 found native grapes growing wild in the woods and used by optimists to produce the first Canadian wine: "a strong acrid wine and black as ink."[53]

The worst that can be said of habitant farming in the first half of the eighteenth century is that it did not measure up to the standards of intensive land use and care in the most advanced parts of Europe. Most of the mother country itself was not a part of that world of progressive technique. While gardens within the confines of the French farmstead were lovingly cared for, the fields often received and gave back little. If Canadian fields were given less care than French fields, and this has yet to receive convincing historical demonstration, one obvious cause lay in the invitation of a land-rich country to a type of farming that was extensive and land-using rather than intensive and labour-using. This Canada had in common with the English colonies to the south.[54]

Eighteenth-century farmers, whether in Canada, the English colonies, or Europe, also thought differently than we do about life and work. Pierre Goubert has described the economic viewpoint of the French peasant that, *mutatis mutandis*, might describe the outlook of any of these farming communities. "The vast majority," he writes, "still see the perfect state of affairs as a kind of localized autarky relieved by a little 'commerce' . . . the ideal being to produce everything on one's own land, supplementing it where necessary with shrewd deals." The world was still one of small, independent producers and subsistence "relieved by a little 'commerce' " the norm of expectations. Yet it cannot necessarily be assumed that everyone's expectations were satisfied or that even the most well-off expected to subsist without the "shrewd deals."[55] The grain trade was primarily local, an exchange between farmers and a nearby town or even between farmers themselves. Only a fraction of the grain consumed had been the object of ocean carriage.[56] The linking of Canadian agriculture to an export market in this period really placed it on an economic frontier quite out of phase with a traditional outlook.

These ordinary people expected remarkably few of the things of this world. History gave them no reason to think otherwise. They exerted themselves for their necessities and for the few luxuries they were accustomed to, but their consumer demands, and consequently their willingness to produce, were not open-ended. This explains the behaviour of coureurs de bois and Indians who "wasted" on high living any unaccustomed accumulations of wealth. It also helps us to understand why habitant farmers produced less than the intendants wanted and were not zealous in their efforts to develop new cash crops. And it reflects the fact that during the whole of the Old Regime the market was not grand enough in size or duration to encourage their efforts and to refashion their thinking at the profound level of structure.[57]

Overproduction and falling prices characterized Canadian agriculture before the mid-twenties. This has been seen as only one phase in the depression lasting three quarters of a century, from 1650 to 1725.[58] Any considerable export of flour beyond supplying the garrison at Placentia was unusual in the early years of the century. The towns of Quebec and Montreal were the principal markets – not negligible ones in an economy of marginal surpluses, but insufficient to complement a growing rural population. But during the 1720s there was a significant reversal of this major tendency. Export markets became an important factor for the agricultural sector, and there was a healthy, sustained rise in the prices of agricultural commodities. An increase in production was attained by means of clearing new land, although this fact does not exclude the possibility that either improved techniques or soil mining contributed to larger surpluses.[59]

Census figures show a large increase in the area of land under cultivation in 1723. Although this change might not have occurred so suddenly as these rough and relative Old Regime statistics report, 1723 may be taken at least symbolically as the point beyond which it was possible to produce crops in excess of those required to feed the people and support "a little commerce." (The statistical summary in Table VI leaves little doubt as to the long-term trend.) Up until 1723, the good, *subsistence plus* crops had provided a small surplus for the soldiers and fishermen of Placentia and, in the second decade, for the founders of Louisbourg. But export was fitful because surpluses were small and uncertain and the colony was not yet in a position to secure faithful markets at a distance. Small yields and isolation produced the violent price swings typical of the Old Regime. Prices collapsed at the advent of even small surpluses. They were driven up by unaccustomed demand, such as occurred in 1710 when a famine in France caused shippers to buy up Canadian flour for the West Indies. When adverse weather reduced yields to dangerous levels, prices soared and then, with good harvests, plummeted to rock bottom. This was the pattern between 1712 and 1721, although a monstrous grain price bubble between those years also owed much to inflation.

Table VI
Population, Land, and Crops: Decade Averages

Decade	Population	Arpents in cultivation per head	Arpents in meadow per head	Minots of wheat harvested per head	Minots of peas harvested per head
1711-20	21,400	2.76	0.37	11.01	2.05
1721-30	29,400	3.00	0.45	12.30	2.64
1731-40	39,300	4.10	0.54	14.50	1.90

Sources: Annual statistics for most years in A.J.E. Lunn, "Economic Development in New France, 1713-1760," Ph.D. dissertation, McGill University, 1942, pp. 443-44; J. Henripin and Y. Peron, "The Demographic Transition of the Province of Quebec," in D.V. Glass and R. Revelle, eds., *Population and Social Change* (London, 1972), p. 217, for population.

Harvests were not always better after 1722, but the area under cultivation was so much greater and the surplus of a good year was so much larger in the decade from the mid-1720s to the mid-1730s that the people were fed and a dependable and substantial surplus was exported. Swings in prices were also much more contained. As we have seen in Chapter 7, 1727 was the year of a take-off in grain export. The trade to Louisbourg and the West Indies reached an unprecedented level. More and more land was being put under the plough, especially between 1732, the year of a bad crop, and 1734, truly a year of abundance. But just as the volume of the crop, the surplus over local needs, and the importance of wheat in the colony's trade reached hoped-for proportions, disastrous crop failures staggered the economy. There were crop failures in 1736 and 1737, and the poor crop of 1741 was followed by failures in 1742 and 1743. These were the most spectacular reversals since the crop failure of 1700. The failure that dominates the period from the mid-thirties to the mid-forties is directly proportional to the success achieved in the previous decade.

Crop failures were bitter experiences. Of the famine of 1700, an eyewitness reported: "The country folk were reduced to living on wild roots and everywhere one saw only wan and wasted faces. The townsmen suffered even more."[60] Although the colony could withstand one crop failure, it was hard hit by two in succession or by a series of poor harvests. When the bread supply failed, economic life simply ground to a halt. The export trade in flour and biscuit, of course, collapsed. Ships could not easily be provisioned and put to sea. Operations dependent upon hired labour such as lumbering and shipbuilding were suspended because workers could not be fed. Eventually, the import trade collapsed along with the credit of workers without wages and both employers and traders without profits. (It is not clear that crop failures had any effect upon the fur trade unless it was an increase in the number of hired hands, fleeing the disarray of the agricultural sector.[61]) On occasion, people relieved their anxieties by demonstrating or even taking up arms in riot, as they did at Montreal in 1717. Preventing panic and starvation taxed the skills of the administrators.

The mercantilist – or more generally interventionist – administrator kept a watching brief over the fortunes of agriculture. He knew little about farming and had done nothing to improve farming on his own *domaine* lands in France.[62] The English passion for turnips and rotation was to have little impact on Canada's mother country; the enchantments of physiocracy were yet to come. There was really no such thing as agricultural policy in Canada under the Old Regime; rather, intendants subsumed agriculture under the headings of trade, subsistence, and military supply. Keenly desirous of lessening Canada's economic dependence upon the export of furs, they encouraged the production of exportable agricultural produce that would improve Canada's balance of trade, its economic stability, and its usefulness within the empire. When Canadian flour had eventually begun to penetrate the West Indian market, the government took effective measures to improve the product. The Regulations of Compiègne (May 18, 1732) controlled the quality and identification of exported flour. The provision at cost of up-to-date cylinder sieves to ten good-sized flour mills in 1732-33 ensured that the exported product was as clean as possible.[63] Finally, under the heading of military supply, the Marine put a high priority on the feeding of garrisons. For many years and to little avail, it encouraged the growing of hemp, which was used for rope and sailcloth.[64] It was an agricultural counterpart to the encouragement of production of the forest-based naval stores, tar and turpentine.

While free trade within some system of mercantilist regulation was always an article of faith at the Marine, there was one exception to this rule. A poor crop and rising prices brought price controls or export curbs or both plus charity from the king, the bishop, and the local administrators as individuals. For if a mechanical mercantilism was one side of the interventionist coin, a genuine paternalism was the other. It was the responsibility of an intendant to ensure that the people were fed when the food supply failed. In a 1709 dispatch the two Raudots explained succinctly the administrator's problem of balancing freedom, trade, and subsistence: "This country being without any resource in time of scarcity, it is necessary to watch the flour trade continually. In this business one must accommodate the interests of the habitant, of the merchant, who in buying flour exports it and procures a trade to the country, and of those who, harvesting no wheat, are obliged to buy it."[65] Demonstrating that preference for the rural that marked them off from most Marine administrators, they underscored that it was the habitant "who will be the strength of this colony." The townsman would sacrifice him for low grain prices, but they saw that without a good return, the farmer had no encouragement to produce. To these usual precautions, Hocquart in 1743 added a job-creation programme – improvements on the shipyards, docks, and the fortifications of both Quebec and Montreal, "to provide a living for the greater part of the craftsmen and day-labourers of this town who would be dead of hunger and poverty, they and their families, without these special projects."[66] Here was innovation.

Although some observers complained about Canadian farming techniques, the intendants demonstrated no interest in dealing with the question. The closest they came to addressing the matter of productivity was their effort in conformity with the Decrees of Marly to ensure that good land did not remain out of production. The inten-

dants were, perhaps, most successful in the encouragement they gave
to the export of agricultural products. The shortcomings of agriculture,
exacerbated by the small area devoted to farming and the uniformly
difficult climate, remained the Achilles's heel of both trade and subsistence. But it is pointless to assume that administrators should have
dealt with technique and productivity head-on. If the habitants were
imprisoned by their own tradition-bound and fatalistic outlook, higher
up the social scale, in what was in many ways a different and distinct
society, the governing elite inhabited their own prison of ideas and
expectations – more spacious, better lighted, but a prison all the same.
While thousands of years before Pharaoh had known that lean years
followed fat ones and made provision accordingly, in New France the
establishment of public granaries never got beyond the talking stage.[67]
Crop failures were always emergencies to be dealt with by the application of legislative band-aids. Subsistence policy therefore was a failure
and constituted an unacceptable sacrifice of safety to the demands of
export.

Because administrators and others in the "service" tended to see the
state as a national economic enterprise, they saw the common people
primarily as workers and producers who were to be kept working and
productive, much like collectivized peasants within the framework of
a five-year plan. De Catalogne, for example, advised that habitants
ought not to be *allowed* to go off on fur-trading expeditions even if
they could earn thirty to forty *écus*, that they ought to be *obliged* to
raise more flax and hemp, more cattle and fewer horses. Franquet, in
presenting an elaborate plan for a Canadian agricultural council,
described as laziness the habitant practice of planting less grain when
the price was low than when it was high, dismissing the market mechanism with the back of his hand. Habitants should be *obliged* to plant
more, he advised, and vagabonds and small merchants should be *put*
to the land, "because it is necessary in a well-administered State that
everyone keep usefully busy and work." The number of horses in the
country *must absolutely* be reduced to encourage walking and paddling, Jérôme de Pontchartrain ordered. "It is in the interest of those
who are at the head of the colony that the inhabitants be strong and
robust."[68] There is a more modern touch, one more in keeping with an
age of encouragement and exhortation rather than regulation, in
Maurepas's 1733 suggestion that the habitants ought to be driven to
greater productivity by the goad of taxation. In this way, he suggested,
the resources of the country would be developed and the habitants
would enjoy a higher standard of living that, apparently, they would
not achieve of their own volition.[69] This rough high-handedness was
the common quality of both absolutism and the cog-and-wheel mentality
of mercantilism. That the state really interfered very little in the lives

of ordinary people says much for the tempering effect of much-maligned paternalism and even more for the recalcitrant inertia of the people themselves.

II

The urban counterpart of the life of the *côtes* was the world of craftsmen and workers. Just how numerous these urban common folk were is impossible to say with much precision. Quebec and Montreal accounted for about a fifth of the population of Canada, less than 400 households in 1700, around 1,100 to 1,200 in 1744. Taking into consideration the whole of New France, thus including Louisbourg, boosts the urban component of the population slightly and the number of urban households by over 200 for the late thirties and early forties. Including Trois-Rivières would add a few more. The blacksmiths, carpenters, and masons of the four villages would have to be included along with many habitant-artisans if one focused on the practice of the craftsman's skills rather than on the development of an urban social stratum. Arriving at an estimate of numbers in that case would be even more difficult.

Apprenticeship indentures have become for historians a window on the eighteenth-century craftsman's world.[70] From them we learn of the practice at Quebec of the wide array of crafts grouped in Table VII into the food, building, marine, clothing, leather, and metal trades in addition to surgery and barbering. They also reveal the system within which trades were recruited and practised as well as conditions of work. There were no guilds to monopolize trades and no guild-masters with power of certification. Craftsmen who had completed their apprenticeship were free to set up their own shops as masters rather than to labour as journeymen in the shops of others. This was the principle of *métier libre*, "the free exercise of manual trades without requiring a certificate of mastery . . . for all but the surgeons."[71] Whereas in France apprentices paid for their training, free apprenticeship became the rule in Canada. After 1725 payment was confined to only a few trades that combined prestige with superior incomes, for example silversmithing and jewellery making. Indeed, from 1685 an opposite trend had been developing; masters were paying their apprentices wages equivalent to those of household servants or farm labourers. The apprentice had replaced the journeyman as a paid worker in the master's shop.

The favourable conditions of apprenticeship indicate that there was no mob of aspiring and unemployed young men to depress the value of labour – nor should such be expected in a colony with an expanding

Table VII
Numbers of Craftsmen at Quebec in the Eighteenth Century

	1716	1744
Food Trades		
Miller	2	1
Baker	7	16
Butcher	4	18
Other	2	–
Building Trades		
Mason-stonecutter	11	32
Carpenter	12	84
Joiner/sculptor/turner	17	42
Roofer	3	1
Chimney sweep	–	4
Glazier	1	1
Marine Trades		
Shipwright	11	2
Cooper	6	26
Other	–	17
Clothing Trades		
Tailor/couturière	7	20
Other	2	7
Leather Trades		
Tanner/currier	1	6
Shoemaker	18	26
Saddler	–	3
Metalworking		
Blacksmith/farrier/toolmaker	12	30
Locksmith	3	3
Armourer/gunsmith	2	3
Silversmith	1	6
Other	3	5
Miscellaneous		
Surgeon	7	6
Wigmaker/Barber-wigmaker	2	11
Other	1	5
TOTAL	135	375

Source: P.N. Moogk, "The Craftsmen of New France," Ph.D. dissertation, University of Toronto, 1973, facing p. 262.

agricultural frontier and the further advantage of the fur trade. But they are not a very convincing demonstration of the opposite condition, a severe shortage of labour. By paying his apprentice, the master was recognizing the value of the apprentice's labour, which was at his disposal for three years or even more, although it was reckoned that a craft was learned in two. The disappearance of payments by apprentices to masters first in one trade, then in another, would seem to indicate that short-run scarcities of personnel that rendered these various trades highly desirable were being overcome. And the failure of the age of first indenture to drop below the French norm would seem to indicate further that there was a sufficient number of candidates for apprenticeship. The increase of this age in the eighteenth century from sixteen years to seventeen and a half and a decrease in the wages of apprentices after 1720 are proof that population growth and the apprenticeship system were creating an adequate pool of skilled labour.

Apprenticeship developed free from monopolistic regulation, and the indentures mirror with minimal distortion the history of the labour market and hence the history of the growing body of craftsmen. A history of wages and prices would probably confirm that for the eighteenth century at least the legendary high wages in New France reflect labour scarcity much less than they reflect the high cost of living. The frequent complaints of administrators about the shortage of skilled labour probably reflect the short-run needs that the indentures reveal as well as the demand for new skills required by plans for economic diversification, needs that could not be met by the conservative institutions of apprenticeship.

The craftsman with the economic means to marry and establish his own shop soon left his master's household. For that reason, the craft shop was small. There was the master and one or two apprentices. The exceptions were a few master builders, who employed modest retinues of journeymen masons on the French model. As the years of the apprentice's indenture went by, he earned a larger and larger salary, recognition that he was becoming less a trainee and more the equivalent of the journeyman. Nevertheless, he continued to be the one to rise at five and light the morning fire and to sweep out the shop and put away the tools before his supper at eight or nine in the evening. The master's concession to his own rank was to rise with the sun and to find his shop already open, but he too worked until called to the late supper that preceded an early bedtime.

The need for lumber and provisions at Louisbourg and the acceptability of these same Canadian exports at Martinique and Saint-Domingue once cargoes were "assorted" with a sufficient component of Louisbourg cod, made possible the development of the lumbering and ship-building industries. It will be recalled that shipbuilding had ceased at the beginning of the Nine Years' War (1688) but that the industry was reborn with Louis Prat's building of the *Joybert* in 1704.[72] The real take-off of the industry came in 1724 when seven ships described as "considerable vessels" were constructed. In 1732 the King instituted a system of bounties amounting to about 2.5 per cent of construction costs on all Canadian-built ships. The abolition of the bounty system after 1739 had only a marginal effect, if any, on construction. The real incentive for builders was the increasing trade in lumber, Canadian provisions, and cod. Of the ninety ships of known tonnage constructed by private interests in Canada between 1704 and 1745, fifty-one were between 14 and 78 tons, suitable for use only on the St Lawrence or for voyages to Louisbourg. The remainder, twelve between 80 and 96 tons, twenty between 100 and 192 tons, and nine in the 200- to 350-ton range, were considered suitable for Atlantic crossings.

A number of ships were built at Quebec by French merchants. Between 1736 and 1746 the agents Havy and Lefebvre launched six ships valued at 300,000 livres for their principals, Dugard and Company of Rouen. An explanation of why French merchants would build at Quebec, where costs were higher than in France – the Marine estimated by 15 per cent – must reconcile Havy's statement that "the vessels that we have built in this country come at a high price" with Hocquart's observation that Havy's continued programme of shipbuilding was "certain proof that he found profit in the first."[73] The bounties were, of course, one explanation. A second was that merchants paid their shipbuilders and lumber contractors partly in kind and thus earned the same profit on these goods that they would have had by selling them. Thirdly, even that part of the costs paid in cash represented profits made at Quebec on goods exported from France. A fourth explanation is that investing in a ship was one way a French exporter could "patriate" profits earned in Canada, where the only alternative export was often bills of exchange that constituted no profit in themselves and were often paid only after long delays. Finally, it is possible that the cost of shipbuilding declined with the establishment of shipyards and a skilled labour force. The first Dugard ship built at Quebec cost 277 livres a ton, the second 209, the third 195, and the fourth and fifth 178.[74]

There were ten sawmills in Canada in 1710 and seventy in 1739.[75] Shipbuilding provided an obvious impetus to lumbering, but much more Canadian timber went into the holds of the new ships than into their hulls. The extant statistics describe a trade primarily in shingles and pine planks for Louisbourg and the West Indies that burgeoned almost out of nowhere in 1727, that familiar date marking the take-off of shipping to those two markets. The export of pine planks, which may be taken as an index of this trade, increased from 42,000 feet in 1727 to 147,000 in 1732, 162,000 in 1736, and 252,000 in 1752.[76]

Exports in the public sector did not always fare as well. The state was always interested in the export of naval timber. The intendants Bégon and Dupuy had masts cut at Baie St Paul. The Abbé Lepage, the Ramezay family, and Bégon himself all supplied oak and pine to the naval dockyard at Rochefort. There was grumbling at the cost and quality of the Canadian product, and the navy was never in a position to provide adequate transport for the timber. This was particularly true in the case of masts, most of which rotted where they were cut. In 1726 Dupuy gave it as his opinion that the king would never enjoy the full benefit of Canada's woodland resources until he built his own ships at Quebec.

Canadian intendants viewed the economy primarily as a trading system.[77] They were acutely aware of the need to exploit all the colony's resources to provide the mother country with rare raw materials and to produce a greater variety of export items to balance the colony's imports. Gilles Hocquart pursued this goal of diversification with considerable energy and with the advantages of a long tenure and a favourable economic climate. The hallmark of Hocquart's policy was his patronage of a select group of Canadian businessmen in whom he hoped to fan the flame of entrepreneurship. By the mid-thirties, he had become convinced that his fledgling industrial barons were inadequate to the tasks at hand and that the state must intervene to establish major industries. In this regard, the history of the Forges du Saint-Maurice, an ironworks near Trois-Rivières, a progression from private to mixed to state enterprise, illustrates both the education of an intendant and the imperatives of the Canadian economy.

The iron deposits near the St Maurice River had been discovered in 1687, but in spite of the repeated requests of local officials, the Marine had not seen fit to initiate their development.[78] In 1730 a Montreal merchant, François Poulin de Francheville, who owned the seigneury of Saint Maurice in which the principal mine was located, received a royal brevet conferring a monopoly over the exploitation of mines and the manufacture of iron in a wide region centred on the St Maurice. In 1733 he accepted a royal loan of 10,000 livres and formed a partnership to exploit his privilege.

Francheville's modest plan was to duplicate in Canada the primitive bloomery forge technology used in New England and New York, a method in which iron ore was heated to a pasty consistency and then had the impurities beaten out of it.[79] After two visits to English colonial forges, the smiths at Saint-Maurice had by 1733 duplicated the bloomery process only imperfectly. The iron produced was not of the highest quality, and, as was characteristic of the bloomery process, the quantity of charcoal used was enormous. At this time of uncertain beginnings, Francheville suddenly died. Maurepas subsequently sent an ironmaster, Pierre-François Olivier de Vézin, to investigate affairs at Saint-Maurice. Vézin was critical of the plant built by Francheville and of the wasteful bloomery method but lyrical on the possibilities offered by the water power, the endless supply of timber for charcoal, and the high-grade bog iron ore. In response to Beauharnois and Hocquart's honeyed solicitations, Maurepas agreed to lend a further 100,000 livres to the enterprise. The Bureau de Commerce had advised him that in addition to lessening France's dependence upon Sweden and Spain, the impetus an ironworks would give to shipbuilding in Canada was alone sufficient cause for supporting the enterprise. Reflecting the gradual infusion of liberal ideas into mercantilist thinking, they added that the competition would be good for French ironmasters.[80]

On October 16, 1736, a new company was formed. The director was François-Etienne Cugnet, first councillor of the Conseil supérieur and director of the Domaine d'Occident in Canada, an official with a flair for business. He and a Montreal merchant, Ignace Gamelin, remained from Francheville's original company. They were joined by Thomas-Jacques Taschereau, the man who as local representative of the Marine treasurers would be paying the subsidy, by Vézin, and by a second ironmaster recruited by Maurepas, Jacques Simonet. On the site of Francheville's inadequate forge there now rose the shapes of a blast furnace and first one and then another forge where the pig-iron of the furnace was heated again and hammered into wrought-iron bars. Water wheels powered bellows and hydraulic hammers. An untidy industrial village sprang up. Vast quantities of money were consumed. It was a heady experience for the five partners, who had not invested a sou of their own.

The blast furnace was finally lighted on August 20, 1738, after several failed attempts in the course of the previous year. The building of the plant at Saint-Maurice had been beset by technical difficulties that betrayed the shortcomings of the ironmasters. Vézin, who was rashly optimistic, had seriously underestimated costs. He also overestimated the availability of water power, erecting a forge to accommodate six water wheels where the use of only two was practicable. There may be as much to criticize in the management of the ironworks as there is in the ironmasters' technical work.[81] The real problem, however, was that the costs of establishing and running the ironworks were unavoidably high. Saint-Maurice was a remote location. Specialized workers brought there from France had to be housed and paid on a year-round basis whether or not the state of the plant or the weather at any given moment permitted them to exercise their crafts. Even Canadian labourers were far enough from their homes that they had to be housed. Roads had to be built from the mines to the smelter. Horses and carts had to be maintained. The blast furnace and forges themselves were in their time massive and costly structures. The undertaking was beyond the financial capacities of any group of Canadian businessmen and was underfinanced by Maurepas, who was unrealistic (along with everyone else) in his expectation of costs and of a reasonable period for the repayment.

By the end of 1738, a second government loan of over 80,000 livres had been spent, one forge had still to be built, and the company's credit had collapsed. Cugnet was transacting all the company's purchases and loans in his own name. In this way the company continued in operation until October 1741, when one by one the five partners gave up and resigned. At the same time, Cugnet was being hounded by his creditors. He was driven into bankruptcy by December. Although his partners could not escape their joint and several liability for the company's debts, they did refuse responsibility for such of Cugnet's life-saving transactions that did not bear the company's stamp and on which his signature did not include the designation "and Company." While the former partners deluged each other with recriminations, Hocquart took over the management of the ironworks in the interests of their principal creditor, the King. On May 1, 1743, following Maurepas's decision, they became a state enterprise in settlement of the company's debt to the Crown. For the period 1741 to 1745, Hocquart reported a profit in excess of 40,000 livres. The lesson learned was that undertakings of the size of the Forges du Saint-Maurice could only succeed if the King provided generous and long-term credit or invested directly. Hoquart had every reason to believe that if the latter course were followed, the King's funds would be in better hands.

The principal product of the Forges du Saint-Maurice was forged iron bars. Much of this bar iron was exported to France, but it also found a market in the West Indies, at Louisbourg, and in Canada. Between 1737 and 1741, the ironworks produced about a million pounds of iron, less than half of what Vézin had predicted. In the years that followed, an annual output of 400,000 pounds was achieved. Hollowware casting began in 1741, and in 1744 the first Trois-Rivières stoves were produced, modelled on those that had for years been imported from Holland.

The smiths that Francheville had relied on were men recruited in France. Simonet and Vézin between them brought seventy-seven skilled workers from the iron-mining regions of Franche Comté, Burgundy, and Champagne. Most of these men appear to have come as bachelors; but they quickly married, and they and their families formed the nucleus of the village at Saint-Maurice. Day labourers and skilled workers such as bakers or carpenters were recruited from the region. By all accounts the work force were a turbulent lot, given to drinking and brawling. In accordance with custom, wine or brandy was given to them to mark a variety of occasions from a very hot day to a feast day. The ironworkers were also a colourful lot. Those recruited by Simonet were described as expensively dressed, wearing hats fringed with silver that as a term of their indentures were replaced each year by the company.[82]

The ironworkers of Saint Maurice lived in what we would now call a company town. Everyone who lived there worked for the company. They bought from a company store. They heard mass in a company chapel. They were forbidden to leave the village without the iron-master's permission, a curb on their freedom of movement sanctioned by their legal status as indentured servants. In 1745 this servitude was given additional support by Hocquart's ordinance prescribing the penalties of fines and corporal punishment for offenders. The ordinance also enjoined punishment for "scandals and public debauches."[83] Most workers lived in houses belonging to the company. Rudimentary shacks constructed of poles, plastered with mud, and provided with clay chimneys sheltered carters, charcoal burners, and temporary day labourers. The skilled workers lived in solid houses with stone fireplaces, glass windows, and locked doors. Many of them lived in buildings containing three or four separate apartments or shared houses with other families. The typical craftsman's house with shop attached was also present. Indeed, one foundryman's house was built onto the hall of the blast furnace and another's onto the hall housing the great bellows. An inventory of the ironworks in 1741 lists fourteen dwellings belonging to the company. There may have been others, privately owned, each with an *arpent* of land. The ironworkers tended their gardens and kept their own cows and steers, chickens and pigs. Theirs was a rural life, their community a special byway of the one continued village, forbidding to outsiders for the hellish connotations of its constant, roaring fires and pillars of smoke.

Hocquart may have had his fill of state-assisted private enterprise by the time he came to establish the second large-scale industrial undertaking for which he is remembered.[84] This was the creation of the royal shipyard that Dupuy had proposed, as had many others, including Bégon before him and the industrious Abbé Lepage, whose 1730 memorandum on the subject is impressive in its vision, its good sense, and its detail. In that year Hocquart was fostering private shipbuilding by developing a shipyard near the palace. By 1738 conditions had changed. The Anglo-French *entente* was wearing thin, war was in the air, and a vigorous shipbuilding programme was taxing the resources of the Marine's metropolitan shipyards. Maurepas not only agreed to a request by Beauharnois and Hocquart that they be allowed to construct a *flûte*, he also announced that he was sending all the fittings for the vessel and an experienced builder.

The shipbuilding programme, which began in 1739 and ended only with the Conquest, was from start to finish under the direction of René-Nicolas Levasseur, who arrived in the colony young at thirty-three but already experienced and competent. Hocquart allocated the palace shipyard to Levasseur's use and by 1746 had secured permission to

Table VIII
Ships Built in New France, 1700-1760

Year	Private Shipping		Government Shipping	
	No. of Ships	Tonnage Range	No. of Ships	Size and Type
1704	1	50		
1706	1	unknown		
1709	1	130		
1711	1	90		
1713	1	300-400		
1714	1	150		
1715 to 1717	8	100-250		
1716	1	25		
1718	1	unknown		
1723	1	unknown		
1724	7	unknown		
1729	7	20-100		
1730	5	150-200		
1731	2 *or* 3	unknown		
1732	10	40-100		
1733	10	14-90		
1734	9	18-192		
1735	11	10-140		
1736	10	up to 300		

	Private Shipping		Government Shipping	
Year	No. of Ships	Tonnage Range	No. of Ships	Size and Type
1737	2	78-96		
1738	4	61-300		
1739	10	40-250		
1740	6	68-300		
1741	9	30-177		
1742	12	unknown	1	500-ton flûte
1744			1	700-ton flûte
1745	1	300?	1	70- to 80-ton corvette
			1	26-gun frigate
			3	local-use vessels
1746			1	22-gun frigate
1748			1	60-gun vaisseau
1750			1	60-gun vaisseau
1753			1	72-gun vaisseau
1758			1	30-gun frigate
1759			2	10-gun corvettes
TOTALS	132 *or* 133		14	

Sources: A.J.E. Lunn, "Economic Development in New France," Ph.D. disser-tation, McGill University, 1942, pp. 473-76; J. Mathieu, *La Construction navale royale à Québec, 1739-1759* (Quebec, 1971); D. Miquelon, *Dugard of Rouen* (Montreal, 1978), pp. 167-70.

begin a second yard. By the end of 1744, Levasseur had launched three ships into the waters of the St Charles. Of three smaller vessels built in 1745 for government use in Canada, one was a sixty-ton schooner destined to carry iron from Saint-Maurice to the shipyard.

Over the years the shipyards employed nearly two hundred persons in a setting totally alien to Canadian workmen. The yards were fenced, and workmen were locked within during the workday, which was regulated by the clock. Although a number of carpenters were brought from France, in particular specialists such as the master pulley maker, the majority of workmen were Canadian. Their workmanship met with official approval. Not so the quality of the wood. Officials were much puzzled by the persistence of rot until it was determined that the largest trees of the Canadian virgin forest were frequently unsound at the heart by reason of their antiquity and that consequently great care was required in selecting and cutting timber. Hocquart obtained about half of the lumber from contractors, which was in accordance with his desire to favour local businessmen, but he all too often had recourse to cutting timber as a public work. Perhaps many would-be contractors preferred the less exacting assignment of providing lumber for ships' cargoes.

Neither the Saint-Maurice ironworks nor the royal shipyards were failures. Although Cugnet and Company failed to maintain control of what they had built and the forge building was marked by much technical bungling, the ironworks did become a reality. They were a technical triumph for colonial America and a considerable benefit to Canada for over a century. In the end the King took upon himself an enterprise well beyond the capacities of the private sector that had been expected to push it to a successful completion. The question of the royal shipyards is more complicated. The rule was for the Marine to build its own ships. And although there was a successful private-sector shipbuilding industry at Quebec, only the state had the capacity to undertake work so demanding technically, administratively, and financially. To judge Hocquart's policy of establishing the royal shipyards, historians ask whether their presence strengthened or weakened Canadian industry. For many, this means the private sector.

It was certainly Hocquart's intention to stimulate private enterprise.[85] State contracts were expected to nurse related supply industries into being and develop entrepreneurship. The construction of large and sophisticated naval vessels under expert supervision was expected to train more and better workers. The Intendant anticipated more private construction, more and cheaper Canadian ships, and hence an improved link with external markets for Canadian produce. Precious experience was gained and skills were honed; but the more tangible goals proved elusive. The extinction of private shipbuilding after 1744 has been blamed on this smothering state enterprise, but at worst it was only one cause among many. The agricultural crisis and the crisis of war that followed disrupted economic development. Thereafter there was no thought of releasing shipwrights from military projects to oblige private contractors. For years at a time, maritime trade was throttled by war on the seas. Distant markets drifted away. Militia duty disrupted Canadian agriculture, which, in any case, retained all its old structural weaknesses and experienced a number of bad harvests. The question of the royal shipyards thus becomes entangled with many others.

Far from being mainly a stimulus to private industry, the building of naval ships at Quebec became part of a trend discernible since Utrecht of shifting the economic foundations of New France from trade and agriculture to preparations for war and war itself. The building of Louisbourg, the extension of the system of fortifications within Canada itself, building naval vessels, and maintaining troops all represented an enormous state investment in the colonies. It is simply another aspect of the rapid entanglement of Canada in militarism and imperialism. In 1746, when the long era of peace was over and Canada was plunged again into war, the merchants Havy and Lefebvre reflected with misgiving on these developments. "The court has approved all Monsieur the Intendant's expenditures for this colony," they wrote to a Montreal friend, "and the fortifications for this town are also approved as well as a quay that is to be built in the Cul de Sac for the building of ships for the King. All that will pour a lot of money into the colony, but we need a good peace in order to be able to work solidly at increasing the trade of this country."[86]

III

The increase of population, doubling every twenty-five to thirty years, was the determining factor in the growth of the economy in town and countryside. Compared to the increase in numbers of productive people, growth of productivity per head was less important. Immigration played a secondary part in this increase.[87] Although Canada received more immigrants in the eighteenth century than in the seventeenth, they were additions to a much larger population and so, demographically considered, were less important. Most of the new settlers arrived after 1744. Less than two thousand, presumably almost all male, came in the century's first four decades.

Among these newcomers were the inevitable troops. The Canadian garrisons of *compagnies franches de la Marine* were not particular about the quality of their recruits. Still, many soldiers had craft skills useful to the colony. Others availed themselves of an ordinance of May 21, 1698, providing that if given the governor's permission, soldiers intending to marry and settle on the land were to receive a year's pay and their equipment. Although duty in Canada seems in retrospect to have been a real opportunity, the garrison remained understrength and plagued by desertion.[88] From time to time we find descriptions of such as were guilty of desertion or other crimes, for example Etienne Pagy, thirty years old, four feet eleven, marked by smallpox and with a scar over his right eye, and Jean-Baptiste Marot, twenty-five years old, five feet one, tattooed in red and black, the Holy Spirit on his right arm, a serpent on his left leg, and his name "Marot" on his left hand, men not to be quarrelled with in a Montreal tavern or in the unlit streets.[89]

The Marine Council's experiment of sending criminals to Canada in the early twenties withered in the face of colonial protests, although the category of salt smugglers and poachers was an exception. The misdemeanours of these could not have raised an eyebrow among the independent habitants, unless in admiration. About 850 of these men were sent to Canada and a few hundred more to Ile Royale. Most were of rural background and succeeded as indentured farm labourers. But by 1743 officials claimed that they could no longer find places for them.[90] Occasionally, prisoners were rejected by the local authorities. In 1734 Beauharnois and Hocquart returned two men to France, one being a cripple and the other "so badly formed that he could pass for an hermaphrodite." "These two men can be of no use to this colony," they sniffed.[91]

Sons of good family exiled to the colony at their families' request, the precursors of the "remittance men," were more troublesome than statistically important. The picaresque *Avantures du s. C. Le Beau* (1738), in which the author upgrades his social station and improves upon his experiences, provides a very indulgent portrait of the type.[92] In the long history of the French colonies, the *engagé*, or indentured worker, had played an important role in emigration.[93] Well-to-do colonists hired workers in France, either in person or through the agency of French shippers, under thirty-six-month contracts. In other instances, the state had at various times in the seventeenth century required shippers to send flour, guns, animals, or *engagés* to the colonies. The indentures of these *engagés* were then sold to the colonists. In Canada, by an analogy with the training of craftsmen, their service was seen as a kind of apprenticeship. The attorney general explained in 1715 that "during the time of their service, these servants will learn the work of the country, will begin the farms where at the end of their terms they will settle and marry."[94] Immediately after Utrecht, Canadians needing farm labourers requested that their La Rochelle agents send them *engagés*. Up until 1720 these personal contracts were the most common. A new ordinance of March 20, 1714, reiterated the rule that vessels going to Canada as well as those going to the West Indies must carry *engagés* on a speculative basis. Although further regulations were passed in 1716, 1721, and 1724 to tighten up the system, shippers tricked and bribed their way out of this onerous obligation.[95] Nevertheless, in the years between 1720 and 1740 speculative indenture did become the principal mode of supplying *engagés* to Canada. Immigrant workers fulfilled the need for farm workers, day labourers, and servants. After 1740 more and more *engagés* were skilled craftsmen especially recruited for the new industries. Some hundreds of *engagés* came to Canada in the three decades after Utrecht, not men driven by wretchedness but usually not tradesmen of the highest qualifications.

The growth of the Canadian population after 1700 was mainly the result of "natural" increase, really as much a cultural as a natural response to the opportunities and limitations presented by the environment as well as by other elements of the culture itself. Location, climate, soil, and resources, the strength and variety of diseases abounding, ultimately the qualities of the human organism itself, are the natural determinants to which must be added the level of technology, the development of economic and governmental institutions, and the shared ideas, or *mentalité*, of the people.

The fundamental characteristic of the social organization of western Europe had become the economically independent nuclear family.[96] Other modes of living might have saved resources, but the nuclear family was a cultural choice that had become an unquestioned social reflex. This is the basis of what English historical demographers call the "new pattern." Within the confines of this choice, European populations lived with their shoulders jammed against the ceiling of economic possibilities. From this predicament followed the two further alternative choices of celibacy and late marriage. Among women, lifetime celibacy may have been of the order of 15 to 20 per cent. The delayed age of first marriage reduced the number of children born to those who were not celibate and made it easier for them to succeed to the estates of their parents, who very often died before their children's marriages. Long nursing of children resulting in a high percentage of cases of lactation sterility may also have been a cultural choice, but it can as easily be placed among the biological factors, a blend of the cultural and the natural, that limited population growth: the onset of female sterility at an earlier age, famine amenorrhoea, spontaneous abortion related to malnutrition and over-exertion, the early death of marriage partners, and the devastating rates of mortality among persons of all ages but particularly among infants and children under ten. Discussion of the choices limiting family formation and growth must seem ironic when they are associated with an age so overshadowed by death, but they were economic rather than demographic ones. As we have seen in the Canadian case, the technical limitations on agricultural production were considerable. In addition, in European states a scandalous share of production was appropriated by a small and largely parasitic class.

The Canadian demographic pattern was only a variant of the French, but the variations (see Table IX) are significant.[97] Although Canada remained an obdurately difficult country from which to extract riches, through its abundance of land it offered all comers a subsistence of which they were not despoiled by others. It was therefore more hospitable than the mother country to the formation of new families. Nevertheless, the creation and equipping of new farmsteads were so

Table IX
Demographic Comparisons: France and Canada in the Eighteenth Century

	Age of Wife at First Marriage (average)	Number of Children per Family (average)	Infant Mortality (1st year of life)	Birth Rate/ 1,000 of Population/ Year	Mortality Rate/ 1,000 of Population/ Year
FRANCE	24.6	5-6	25%	39-40	33
CANADA	22.4	7+	25%	51-56.8	30-35?

Sources: For France, figures are from M.W. Flinn, *The European Demographic System, 1500-1820* (Brighton, 1981), p. 28; P. Chaunu, *Histoire, science sociale* (Paris, 1974), pp. 338-40, 343-47; P. Goubert, *The Ancien Régime* (New York, 1969), p. 36; and J. Henripin, *La Population canadienne au début du XVIIIe siècle* (Paris, 1954), pp. 39-41, 103. For Canada, figures are from the last, pp. 95-99, 106, and J. Henripin and Y. Peron, "The Demographic Transition of the Province of Quebec," in D.V. Glass and Roger Revelle, eds., *Population and Social Change* (London, 1972), pp. 30-35.

difficult and expensive that pubertal marriage remained impossible as long as the independent, nuclear family continued to be the norm. Yet the Canadianization of demographic choices did result in the lowering of the age of first marriage by two or three years, almost certainly in a greater participation rate in marriage, and in the social acceptance of larger families in an age when French parents sent children by the thousands to die in foundling hospitals.

A better standard of clothing, nutrition, and housing in Canada may have resulted in greater fertility, more conceptions carried to term, and better-fed babies. The common people in Canada should have had sufficient income to clothe themselves against the weather; that they survived the winters suggests that they did. But although items of dress have been catalogued with exactness, the quantity and condition of the people's clothing remains unknown. Information on the habitant's diet is also exceedingly sketchy. Bread was the foundation of the diet both in France and in Canada, but the Canadian habitant's wheaten bread was marginally more nutritious than the French peasant's bread of rye or *méteil* (rye and wheat ground together). Farm meat, fish, and game also played a considerable role in the habitant's diet, while in many regions French peasants were nearly vegetarian. Both habitant and peasant consumed pulse and vegetables. The fundamental difference between these two consumers was that the average habitant had more to eat than the average peasant and much more protein. Both experienced bad harvests with harrowing regularity, but the Canadian had greater access to alternative food sources from hunting and fishing. Being less burdened with levies, he could keep a greater share of his own farm's produce. Common people living in towns may often have done without the luxuries of many vegetables and fruits, being content with bread, pulse, butcher's meat, and water to drink.[98]

Most Canadians, except perhaps in the town of Quebec, lived in small, one-storey houses of squared logs laid horizontally and mortised into upright posts. Roofs were of plank, and the few windows, although they might be of glass, were often of oiled or waxed paper. Such houses offered from twenty-three to eighty-four square metres of living space on the ground floor, most having forty-five square metres or less. A loft provided additional storage and seasonal sleeping room. While such houses might contain one or two "cabinets," small rooms for storage, one of them perhaps with a bed, almost all activities – sleeping, eating, visiting, working – took place in the "chambre," the all-purpose room of which the fireplace was the inevitable focus. One rarely slept alone, and the only privacy was that sometimes afforded by the curtains of the conjugal four-poster. Furniture was simple, and in the confines of that single room, there was space for little of it. Inventories of the estates of Saint-Maurice ironworkers reveal large quantities of tablecloths and napkins, curtains and covers. Perhaps textiles, the pre-eminent and costly product of pre-industrial manufacture, will prove to have been the one luxury widespread in Old Regime Canada.[99]

Seigneurs and farmers in easy circumstances were building much larger stone houses. Some might have had 170 square metres, occasionally more, on two floors and an attic, but such homes were still as uncommon as they were impressive. The majority of houses provided cramped quarters for the large families of the time. After 1744 Canadians experienced a kind of liberation when the Saint-Maurice ironworks began the manufacture of iron stoves. The Canadian house could at last be warm – and larger. Stoves of brick or stone covered with an iron plate, a type observed by Kalm, may have penetrated the countryside at an even earlier date.[100]

Canadian existence had its less rosy side. Accident, disease, and death remained the inevitable counterpoint to a swelling theme of life and abundance. Society had barely begun to attack mortality. Government management of food supplies once a famine was unleashed upon the country was one assault. But personal and domestic filthiness and the rudimentary character of public health measures stood in the way of curbing disease. The Canadian house, if warm, was crowded and unsanitary; its inhabitants fatalistically shared their accommodation with a host of vermin. Here Kalm is our best source. He comments on the houseflies and mosquitoes and on the crickets, "abundant and disagreeable everywhere." Bedbugs "abound in Canada," he writes. "I met with them in every place where I lodged, both in the towns and country, and the people know of no other remedy for them than patience." He reports the frequency of tapeworm: "Some of these worms, which have been evacuated by a person, have been several yards long." Everywhere he was confronted by dirty floors, "sometimes . . . hardly cleaned once in six months."[101] Frequently ignored legislation requiring the construction of privies in Quebec provides us with a glimpse of a very cavalier attitude toward the disposal of urine and feces. There is malodorous historial reality behind the hackneyed cliché of the servant dumping a chamber pot from a second-storey window. Guilty parties were motivated, according to the Prévôté court of Quebec, "very often out of malice and to do harm to their neighbour." The court recognized not only the disagreeable possibility of passers-by being splashed, but that "the smell of this refuse" could result in sickness.[102] There is, however, little evidence to persuade us that the connection between filth and disease was taken very seriously.

Certainly, diseases abounded in Canada. Pleurisy and venereal disease were endemic, according to Kalm.[103] Epidemics were frequent.[104] Some of the diseases are familiar to us. Influenza struck in 1700-1701, and smallpox in 1702-3, 1716, 1731 to 1733, and 1738. But the colony was also swept by "pestilential" or "malignant" fevers, often brought by ships. Such was the case in 1710-11, 1718, 1720-21, 1734, 1740, and 1743 to 1746. Contemporaries tell us little of the day-in, day-out toll of endemic communicable diseases or of chronic ailments, but the spectacular epidemics often made a great impression on them. The annalist of the Hôtel-Dieu of Quebec describes the smallpox epidemic that ran its course from December 1702 to February 1703 as responsible for the deaths of 2,000 of Quebec's population. Four hundred is the correct number, a sufficiently frightening one without exaggeration.[105] Suffice it to add that medicine had no cures whatever for diseases.

For France and Canada alike, we know much more about birth than about death. Famine starvation had been largely conquered in France and seems not to have been an important cause of death in Canada. But diseases continued to strike down the well-fed and healthy along with the hungry and weak; otherwise it would be difficult to explain the high rates of mortality suggested by historical demographers as probable for Canada.[106] In both countries, a quarter of all persons died before the first anniversary of their births. Children and the aged provided many more victims. Mothers frequently died in childbirth. The high colonial rate of population growth appears attributable to a high birth rate, an unmeditated response to abundance, rather than to any conscious effort to challenge the causes of death.

*   *   *

In 1744 Canada was quite a different "village" from what it had been in 1701. It was so much more populous, so much more continuous. Its oldest and best-located areas were shedding their rusticity. Horses and roads had transformed the country. Abundant sheep meant wool and homespun textiles. The opening of overseas markets for Canadian grain had a dramatic impact on the farm. Land was cleared, and grain prices increased and were stabilized, pulling the "village" out of an economic morass from which the only escape hitherto had been the fur trade. There were more and different trades, even real industries. There were Canadian ships, Canadian stoves and pots and nails. Yet it was left to misty-eyed historians looking back from a century and more later to proclaim the first half of the eighteenth century a Canadian golden age. Too many problems ran too deep, in particular in agriculture and in economic and political organization. Canadian demographic history remained an image of mankind still the plaything of nature. Hunger and uncertainty were not banished.

Only in the upper ranks of society was there any sense that the conditions of life could be significantly refashioned by human agency. Even among the enlightened administrators of the colony, it was a limited notion. The common people must have had some sense of improving conditions, but they continued to see their crops destroyed by frost, insects, or rust, to witness the inexplicable swings in demand for the products of their labour, to be struck with fear when mysterious sicknesses spread among them, to watch their infants sicken and die. The average man and the average woman, tending their farm in a time-honoured way or practising traditional crafts, retained a fatalistic attitude, accepting life much as it came.

CHAPTER 11

The Old Regime: Linkages

The Marquis de Crisafy, King's Lieutenant at Quebec and the town's highest ranking military officer after the governor, was a vain and quarrelsome man. He had certainly managed to rattle Champigny, if one can judge from the letter the Intendant wrote to the King himself on October 15, 1700. It tells a typical Old Regime story. The people of the colony, suffering from poor harvests and disease, were assembling in the churches daily to adore the Blessed Sacrament and soften God's anger. Twice Champigny had attended the Récollet church, standing near the altar rail on the epistle side with only his kneeling cushion. Crisafy and his wife stood before their *prie-Dieu*, or prayer desks, about three feet from the railing on the gospel side. Governor Callière being absent from Quebec, Crisafy could not resist the temptation to exalt his own station at the expense of the Intendant. After writing Champigny what the Intendant regarded as an insulting letter on the question of precedence in church, at the next service, Crisafy placed the *prie-Dieu* at which he and his wife prayed in the centre of the church against the altar rail, placed armchairs behind them, and appeared at the next service with a retinue of three lackeys instead of his usual two, and two armed guards, who had been told to ensure that their firearms were in good order. His pretensions extended the whole length of the railing. It is not clear whether Champigny was present on this occasion, but when the services were transferred to the Jesuit church, Champigny was ready. To avoid all scandal, for the remaining services he worshipped out of sight in the vestry. Champigny hoped that in future Callière would send Vaudreuil down to Quebec during his absences. An intendant could decently play second fiddle to a commander of the troops but not to a local commandant.

There is more to the story than meets the twentieth-century eye. Champigny asked the King to consider the possible consequences of Crisafy's pretensions:

> Permit me only to beseech you . . . to consider that if an intendant, who has the honour of being the second person [in dignity], was rendered

inferior to local governors and king's lieutenants in matters not pertaining to the command of arms – that being none of his concern – his character would be so besmirched that it would be impossible for him to protect the liberty of the people against the oppression of those who are capable of abusing their authority.[1]

This connection between hierarchy and liberty is the very essence of Old Regime political and social thought.

I

"Social structures, types and attitudes are coins that do not readily melt," remarks J.A. Schumpeter: "Once they are formed they persist, possibly for centuries, and since different structures and types display different degrees of this ability to survive, we almost always find that actual group and national behaviour more or less departs from the dominant forms of the productive process. Though this applies quite generally, it is most clearly seen when a highly durable structure transfers itself bodily from one country to another."[2] This transfer, although by no means intact, of a "highly durable structure," is fundamental to the social history of New France. How does one begin to define this society of Old Regime type? With *linkages*: the connections of persons to persons that incarnate and perpetuate notions of dignity and social worth and of the proper channels for the exercise of authority, that dispose society's members in relation to a system of production and consumption, and that by the place assigned to a body of clerics, links this temporal construct to the spiritual.[3]

Fundamental to the whole design was the inequality of condition in a hierarchical society of ranks or *orders*. In principle, each order found its place in a vertical chain on the basis, not of its wealth or its role in the productive system, but of the perceived dignity and worth of its social functions. Priests were at the top of the social pyramid, followed by a noble order of military origin, by the jurists and administrators of the state, and by merchants, the last group to be described as "honourable men" or "decent persons" according to the seventeenth-century jurist Charles Loyseau. The broad base of the pyramid was comprised of craftsmen, peasants, labourers, and vagabonds – all classified as "vile persons."[4]

The place of merchants in this hierarchical arrangement, which extends from spirit-and-mind to body-and-hand, is not so clear-cut and for that reason is very telling. On the one hand, merchants did work, and they worked for lucre, which is material, related to the body, and base. On the other hand, their work had a considerable intellectual content – they read and wrote (sometimes in many languages) and ciphered and kept accounts. Loyseau also tells us that they gained respect because they gave work to artisans and labourers – that is, they commanded them. The nobility and the crowd of jurists and functionaries who surrounded the throne shared in much greater measure this quality of command. It was a second hierarchical justification: the division of society between those who commanded and those who obeyed. The identification of command with spirit or mind and of obedience with body or hand is obvious.

An essential aspect of the hierarchy of orders was its complexity. Orders were minutely subdivided. Today, we know that in the Church hierarchy there are cardinals, bishops, and priests. But can the most hierarchically minded remember the entire gradation of holy orders: cardinals, primates, patriarchs, archbishops, bishops, priests, deacons, subdeacons, acolytes, exorcists, readers, porters, those who bear the tonsure? Subdivisions such as these continued down through all the *ranks* of society so that any crowd of Old Regime persons could have sorted themselves out into a procession from the greatest and most honoured to the least. The sorting would not have been without difficulty. A principle of overlap would have been accepted such that the highest persons of some orders might have found themselves accorded smaller dignity than lesser members of higher orders, but it was not an easy principle to apply. And many who bore the long robe of the law believed that they were closer to the source of authority and the fount of justice than those who bore the sword, who in enforcing obedience themselves merely obeyed. Rank meant argument without end.

Dignity depended upon leading what was called the noble life, and this was demonstrated by liberality, hospitality, service to the King or the Church, and keeping clear of all remunerated work. This brings us to where Marxists would have wanted us to begin: to production. Since the first two orders or estates, the clergy and nobility, devoted themselves to specialized functions for the commonweal and since work for purposes of production was base and not allowed them, they received a living from *rents*. These were primarily the *cens et rente* paid to seigneurs and, in the case of the clergy, the tithe. But other rents such as the earnings of annuities or royalties from mines or monopolies might also enter into this category. The *cens et rente* and the tithe were fundamental to any society to be identified as "Old Regime." The remuneration of jurists, high functionaries of state, and army officers, of course, was not base, and a rich French vocabulary distinguished between honourable, less honourable, and base payments for service.

From the materialist perspective, the dividing line of the rent is the fundamental one, since it separates a mass of rent payers and wage slaves from a privileged class – the owners of the means of production with remarkably homogeneous interests. The hierarchy of orders becomes, by comparison, a mask designed to justify and confuse. There is, of course, no reason why class and order cannot co-exist if class is thought of as an underlying economic uniformity and order as an overt identification of rank and dignity. The argument against a thorough-going Marxist interpretation is that in the Old Regime world, wealth accrued to dignity rather than dignity to wealth; rank came first. Where wealth in fact came first, it had to be deodorized by a couple of generations of noble living and royal service. Doubtless, reality was not quite so tidy. If we glance for a last time at Loyseau's description of businessmen, we find that, within limits, money talked:

> Both in Rome and in France, the principal jurists are followed by the merchants, as much because of the utility, even the public necessity, of trade . . . *as because of the usual opulence of merchants, which brings them credit and respect, and the means they have of employing artisans and labourers, which gives them considerable power in the towns.* Thus the merchants are the last of those people who have the quality of honour, being described as honourable men, decent persons and bourgeois of the towns: qualities that are not attributed to ploughmen, sergeants, artisans and even less to labourers, who are all reputed vile persons [italics added].[5]

Old Regime people often stand out as remarkably individualistic and assertive, but their shared notions of rank circumscribed their actions. Each individual is a mere member of the body of society, Jean Domat, another French jurist, tells us:

> That every man, being a member of the body of society, each ought to fulfil for society his duties and functions, as is determined by the rank he occupies and by his other engagements. . . . That each individual being bound to this social body of which he is a member, he ought not to undertake anything to injure its organization, which includes the obligation of submission and obedience to the power that God has established to maintain this order.[6]

To the notion of orders was attached that of family. Society was thought of as composed not of individuals but of families, which provided the connective tissue binding the orders together. Family conceived of as a house or lineage also united past, present, and future. French legal codes, including the Coutume de Paris that was the foundation of Canadian law, encouraged this by protecting the property of families and not just that of individuals. By means of the civil disabilities encumbering married women and persons under twenty-five, they encouraged the family to act under one head, the father.

Orders and families; relationships governed by the *coutume*, by *rente* and seigneury, by tithe and parish; authority and obedience (and perhaps a dialectically related individualism); old-fashioned notions of the virtues of clergy, military, and judiciary: these are the linkages of the Old Regime. The extent to which they were indeed transferred "bodily from one country to another" defines the extent to which Canada was indeed an Old Regime society.

Those at the apex of Canadian society were status conscious to a degree. Quarrels over precedence, such as the confrontation of Crisafy and Champigny, remained standard behaviour for officials, French and Canadian. In particular, that constant procession that was Old Regime society was sorted out and fought over in the church, the one place where the entire community assembled. There were always arguments over the right to have *prie-Dieu* and to place them in prominent locations. In 1710 the churchwardens of Notre Dame de Montréal demanded that a *prie-Dieu* used by the local commander and by the king's attorney be removed from their church, and they took their case to the Superior Council. In another instance, in 1719, the Marine Council, no less, ruled that Governor Vaudreuil was not to permit his son to use his *prie-Dieu* in the Montreal church in his absence, "something that besmirches the character of the local Governor of Montreal," and he was himself no longer to worship, as he was accustomed to, with an entire retenue of soldiers. In the same year, the Marine Council also doused the pretensions of Louvigny to receive the palms and ashes within the chancel of the church in the same manner as the Governor General.[7]

Many questions of precedence had been settled by an omnibus regulation of the King in Council in 1716.[8] The most arcane matters were considered, including who should have torches to light bonfires on festive occasions and who should receive incense at mass, but in particular it dealt with rights to *prie-Dieu* and precedence in processions. It is a testimony to the power of rank that human ingenuity kept on devising ever more ingenious manifestations of dignity requiring the subtle adjudications of a royal council. One of the questions settled in 1716 was that which had so exercised Champigny a decade and a half earlier: could an officer like Crisafy claim precedence over an intendant? When a governor general was absent, the council determined, the local governor or the local commander was to have precedence, not the intendant. But when a governor general was not in attendance but yet was not absent from the city, then the intendant was to have precedence. Could Solomon have done better?

To what extent were people of all walks of life – out of range of the example of imported officials – imbued with a sense of rank and hierarchy? In a famous dispatch of 1707, Jacques Raudot wrote of the Canadian people that, "never having any education because of the laxity that results from a foolish tenderness that their fathers and mothers have for them in their childhood, imitating in that the Indians," they grew up without discipline and developed a "hard and ferocious character."[9] They lacked respect for their parents and their superiors, including their *curés*. For this reason, there was "no decency in their conduct towards one another." Raudot claimed that he tried hard to draw them from this barbarism by fining their acts of violence and ferocity but felt himself engaged in a losing battle. The bonds of society unravelling and the pernicious Indian example: Raudot provides a contemporary and negative anticipation of Turner's frontier thesis as it has been reworked in the hands of a modern Canadian historian.[10] For all his decrying of colonial mores, however, Raudot did not despair of Canadians. He pinned his hopes on the efficacy of education. He supported François Charon's school at Montreal. In every parish he hoped someday to see schoolmasters who in addition to the instruction they would give Canadian children "will teach them early to be submissive." At the same time, Raudot did not give up on their parents. By exalting the position of the local captains of militia – giving them subaltern rank in the regular troops and honoraria – the habitants, he argued, would be brought into a greater dependence. Over thirty years later, his argument still held sway. The King approved Beauharnois's act of sending an officer among the parishes to ensure that the militiamen were learning their drills, "as nothing is more appropriate to maintain discipline and subordination among them."[11]

Raudot's proposals for honoraria and anomalous rank came to nothing. In 1710 he therefore ordained a more economical and orthodox system of reward and recognition. Captains of militia followed by lesser militia officers would take their place in processions directly behind the churchwardens, and the captain would receive the *pain bénit*, or blessed bread, before the ordinary habitants. Although Bishop Saint-Vallier opposed this measure on his return to the colony in 1713, the King accepted the arguments of Vaudreuil and Bégon in favour of Raudot's distinctions and in addition their own assignment of a "fixed place" to the captain right behind the seigneur and the churchwardens.[12] This appears to be the origin of the captain's right to rent a pew in that location.

Our pursuit of the question of rank thus takes us, hot on the intendant's heels, right into the nave of the parish church. The distribution of the *pain bénit* was a ceremony in which bread brought to the church by parishoners was blessed by the priest and eaten reverently by the faithful. In an age and place where believers communicated rarely, the ceremony fulfilled a quasi-sacramental role, affirming the communion of the faithful with the Church and with each other. But as the bread was distributed by the beadle to those present according to rank, it was also one of many ceremonies in which the children of the Canadian farmsteads and forests found themselves within the confines of a European affirmation of rank and precedence. Processions were also the order of the day. The provision that captains take their place behind seigneurs and churchwardens was only a variation on a theme that can be found in Saint-Vallier's *Rituel* of 1703: ". . . each will come according to his rank with order and modesty . . . the clergy first; the seigneur next; then the men and boys, the women and girls."[13] To the extent that Canadians had access to the teaching, preaching, and sacraments of the Church, they affirmed both rank and community while they affirmed faith. Access to the church becomes a fundamental question for the interpretation of Laurentian social history.

Townsmen were well integrated into the liturgical cycle of the church year and enjoyed ample access to confession and the sacraments. In the earlier eighteenth century, 80 per cent of the clergy lived in the towns, although only a quarter of the population was urban. Because of the presence of many religious orders, there were chapels in addition to the parish churches. The obvious counterpart of this was that the three quarters of Canadians who lived in the countryside were served by only 20 per cent of the clergy. Not only were the clergy in short supply but many of them were also loath to live in the countryside where they were often poorly housed and received little from the tithe. After Saint-Vallier toured the parishes in 1685 (he was to become bishop three years later), he wrote that aside from the town churches, "all the others were either threatening to collapse or were so destitute of the most necessary things, that I was sorely afflicted by the poverty in which I found them."[14]

The establishment of the parishes became a principal aim of Saint-Vallier's episcopate. Bishop Laval had established a system whereby the priests of the Seminary of Quebec were sent out as missionaries to the country districts, much like the Upper Canadian circuit riders of the nineteenth century. A king's regulation of 1692 broke the hold of the seminary over the secular clergy, but while Saint-Vallier in this way gained control over his pastors, their small number and the scarcity of resources in the countryside obliged him to use the seminarians as missionaries as had been done in the past. The people developed a measure of religious self-reliance. They frequently baptized their own children and showed no haste to have births registered by the priest. In 1699 the Bishop obtained a decree from the French Council of State giving himself rather than the seigneurs, who had been inactive, the authority to locate and build churches. His vicar general, one Abbé Geoffroy, was soon touring the parishes, building churches in stone. It was a beginning.[15]

In 1721, in the cold of winter and the floods of springtime, Attorney General Collet and a clerk, Nicolas-Gaspard Boucault, journeyed across the Canadian farmlands, interviewing the habitants of every *côte*, gathering information to determine the location of parish boundaries. As a result, eighty-two parish districts were confirmed, adjusted, or created. Ten years later there were a hundred. Even then most of these were still extensive mission districts comprising several communities. Only about a fifth had resident *curés*.[16]

Thus while the influence of the Church upon the urban communities seems to have been considerable from the colony's earliest days, its influence in the country parishes remains problematical. The historian must balance rural society's long period of social incubation during which the Church was a fugitive influence against the growth of an ecclesiastical presence as the countryside became more settled and more affluent. He must also consider the equally uncertain influence of the town and urban leadership upon society as a whole.

The religious orders were an element of urban leadership and urban society that merits attention. The ideas of social linkage shown to have animated the communities of nuns, for example, were decidedly hierarchical and can only have been a reflection of secular society. It would be difficult to argue that they reflected a metropolitan influence that flew in the face of a colonial egalitarianism. A mother superior governed her community armed with the power of a kind of temporary excommunication, excluding impenitent sisters from the communion rail. The main body of nuns were the choir nuns, who sang the holy office and who were equal within the community yet observed an order of seniority determined by years since profession. But beneath them were the *soeurs converses*, the Cinderellas of the convents, country girls who were to be *robuste* and *docile*. It was they who shouldered the heavy work of the stables, gardens, kitchens, and laundries. They were the perpetual tail end of the conventual procession. They might not sing in church, might read only with the approval of the mother superior, and if they were unable to read were not to be taught. And if they were poor, they were not to seek equality of riches in a convent, the principle being that "those who had nothing in the world may not seek in the convent what they never had outside it."[17] The different religious orders were themselves ranked in the esteem of the community. Jesuits were admired more than liked. Récollets were liked more than admired. To oversimplify somewhat a complex analysis of the populations of the Quebec convents, the Hôpital-Général attracted a disproportionate number of aristocratic women; the Ursulines, of the daughters of the bourgeoisie; and the Hôtel-Dieu, of the daughters of artisans.[18]

The Church saw as one of its major functions keeping fast the bonds of society, both horizontal and vertical. In Saint-Vallier's catechism, for example, the idea of subordination varies from implicit assumption to explicit lesson as one follows the chain of questions and answers designed for those who were ignorant of the faith, according to his preamble, the usual condition of children, artisans, and servants.

It is, of course, at the fourth commandment, "Honour thy Father and thy Mother," that the doctrine of obedience is most fully addressed. Everything follows from an initial explanation: "Not only does God wish that we honour them, but He also orders us to be submissive towards and to have respect for those who represent Him and who are clothed with His authority; for those who resist the order He established in the world, become worthy of eternal damnation."[19] From this it was clear that servants were to serve masters with respect and fear, that all persons were to be submissive to kings, princes, and governors, to bishops and pastors. "Be submissive, says Saint Peter." "Saint Paul says obey your pastors." What lesson can be drawn from this commandment? the catechist asks. "That we are obliged to become well informed of what we owe to our superiors."[20]

The fifth commandment provides another opportunity to reinforce the lesson. After explaining that a person attacked can defend himself with means proportionate to the need, the equivalent of the common law's doctrine of reasonable defence, the catechist is to continue with a second, and at first sight redundant, question:

> If we are mistreated with blows, can we not return them and avenge ourselves?
> No, vengeance is forbidden us, and God has reserved it to Himself.[21]

One can only assume this is a qualification inserted for the benefit of wives, children, and servants.

The Church's support of authority, of state authority, and of the cult of kingship was a repeating pattern in the fabric of daily life. And at times of crisis, there was always an episcopal *mandement* to support the government. For example, when in 1742 the Superior Council ordained that habitants surrender their hidden grain for urban consumption, Bishop Pontbriand reminded the flock that "those who contravene the Council's regulations will render themselves grievously guilty before God and before men . . . it is not permitted to pass the limits prescribed by a legitimate authority," and, to clinch the argument, "he who resists the authorities resists God's order, and those who resist it render themselves worthy of eternal damnation." The only recourse of good Christians was to remain "amenable [*docile*] to the instructions of your pastors."[22] A book could be written on the use of the words *subordination* and *docile* in early Canadian documents, English as well as French, after 1760 as well as before. They enshrine a social idea according to which all members of society have their place, know their place, and take their place in a stable, hierarchical arrangement. But they are easy words to misunderstand. *Docile*, a favourite description of a well-loved son or nephew or of an orderly population, implied not lack of spirit but spirited obedience to an authority that of its nature ought to be obeyed.

Styles of description and address also mirrored a system of ranking simplified by the simplicity of colonial society and by the tendency to claim the status of *bourgeois* and the title of *sieur* or even *monsieur* on the part of many who would have been denied them in France: retired habitants living in town, innkeepers, voyageurs, and artisans employing men. At Montreal, the Sulpicians could be relied on to point a finger at social climbers and ration out the titles.[23]

Quantifiable data provide another avenue to the solution of the problem of rank and social solidarities in New France. A researcher in the notarial archives tells us the answer is to be found in marriage contracts. The key is the value of the *douaire préfix*, an amount of money that was to be taken from the estate of a deceased husband by his widow to permit her to live, to quote an eighteenth-century jurist, "according to the condition of her husband."[24] It was a value arrived at by both families in concert and subject to the censorship of the large number of relatives and sometimes friends who always signed marriage contracts – one did not want to look ridiculous. It was a direct reflection of rank and a sense of rank, a good measure in a society in which rank was manifested more by expenditure than by income.

The result of tabulating *douaires* is a table of rank remarkably in accord with metropolitan ideas but simplified, compressed, and highlighting the stratification of trades not much noticed by the jurists Loyseau and Domat. Individuals are classified in groups: an elite of military, judicial, and administrative officers, followed by honourable employments, good trades, modest occupations, and base occupations. The plain habitant farmers placed themselves at the very bottom of the list, which may not have been at all in accord with their wealth.

The lamentations of Raudot over the presumed Indianization of Canadian upbringing and character are hard to interpret. Those in the upper ranks of society, who embraced the fur trade, the wilderness, and the guerrilla, also embraced the notion of hierarchy. Hierarchy

Table X
Rank: French Views and Canadian Realities

Loyseau (1610)	Domat (1697)	Moogk (*douaires*)	Moogk (estimated)
HONOURABLE AND DECENT PERSONS			
Upper Stratum			
The Clergy	The Clergy		Senior clergy, Nuns
The Nobility	Profession of arms Ministers of state Magistracy, Admin.	Military officers Judicial and admin. officers	
Middle Stratum			
Learned men Advocates Financiers (King's revenue)	Officials (revenue, public works)	Architects Master builder in stone	
The Long Robe: Court clerks Notaries Attorneys *The Short Robe:* Bailiffs Trumpeters etc.	Learned men Ordinary gentlemen	Rustic seigneur	Royal notaries Minor clergy
Lower Stratum			
Merchants Those reputed merchants: Apothecaries, Goldsmiths, Jewellers, etc.	Merchants	Silversmiths Non- commissioned officers	Wholesale merchants
VILE PERSONS			
Peasants	Craftsmen	*Good Trades:* Hatmakers Surgeons Shoemakers *Modest Occupations:* Metalworkers Woodworkers Private soldiers	Land surveyors Huissiers

Loyseau (1610)	Domat (1697)	Moogk (*douaires*)	Moogk (estimated)
Craftsmen	Peasants	*Base Occupations:* Stonemasons Habitants (peasants) Tailors	Food retailers
Labourers			Carters Servants
Vagabonds			

Sources: C. Loyseau, *Oeuvres* (Lyons, 1701); J. Domat, *Les Lois civiles* (Paris, 1697); P. Moogk, "Rank in New France," *HS/SH* 8 (1975): 34-53.

was enjoined upon the people, built into their institutional life, and, as the evidence of the *douaire préfix* demonstrates, found acceptance among them. Quarrels of precedence occurred at the parish level as well as among high officials and captured the interest of rustic seigneurs and captains of militia. Lording it over others, if not subordination, had a distinct appeal. This was certainly Hocquart's conclusion. "They love distinctions and attentions," he wrote, "pique themselves on their bravery, are extremely sensitive to slights and the least punishments." These special qualities of Canadian individualism were reflected in the comments of a host of contemporary French officers and officials. The common denominator of their disapproving social analysis was that, to continue quoting Hocquart, Canadians were "naturally ungovernable [*indocile*]."[25] The testimonial avalanche is irresistible. Canada was, in Pontchartrain's phrase, "a land of another spirit, other manners, other sentiments."[26] It is as though one half of the social testament of the Old Regime were cherished and the other utterly forgotten.

Both Indian society, with its essential equality of persons, and White society, with its history of hierarchical structure, made room for slavery. Isolated instances of slavery can be found in Canadian society from early in the seventeenth century. Toward the end of the seventeenth century, the argument was made that Black slavery would solve Canada's perennial labour shortage. Although the King agreed to this in 1689 and 1701, nothing came of it. Bégon was repeating the arguments in favour of Black servitude in 1716 and 1719, and in 1721 the Regent actually invited the Indies Company to send a cargo of Blacks to Quebec.

There was, in fact, no great influx of Black slaves. But Indians taken in war by Canadian allies and sold to Canadians made their appearance in the central colony. Large numbers of these were of the Pawnee tribe situated in what is now the state of Nebraska, and their name in French, *Panis*, became a synonym for Indian slave. That they served mainly as domestics, were often indistinguishable from free servants, and were often Christianized and well integrated into Canadian households can lead us, erroneously, to discount the foundation of their condition: unfree and subject to sale and purchase.

The legal foundation of slavery in Canada was Raudot's 1709 ordinance proclaiming the legality of the slavery of "Panis et Negres." That not everyone was at ease with the concept of slavery is evident from Raudot's specific denial that France's constitutional freedom from slavery could apply to a colony and also from a curious challenge to slavery that occurred in 1733. A fur trader whose slave had been confiscated to satisfy a debt and subsequently sold to a third party challenged the whole proceeding on the grounds that a Christian could not be sold. The council referred the matter to Hocquart, who ruled that both confiscation and sale were legitimate. Following the advice of the King's memorandum of 1735, he further ordained that slaves could only be freed by a written act before a notary.[27]

Slaves were never a large group in New France. Only from 1710 do the annual additions to the Indian slave population in the White colony reach double digits, the average annual additions for the period 1710 to 1744 being slightly more than twenty-six. From 1700 to 1742, annual additions to the Black slave population averaged slightly in excess of two. In 1742, the increase was fifteen, and from that date double digits prevail for Blacks as well.[28] The condition of slavery as understood by Canadians must have been an amalgam made up of the Indian notion of slavery resulting from capture in war, traditional class notions of the servant, and the idea of the human chattel, the classic conception of slavery associated with the development of Black slavery in the Americas.

The half-Indianized *indocilité* of the documents that has influenced the modern environmental interpretation of Canadian society, the "boundless license" that in Francis Parkman's view battled "a stiff handed authority,"[29] was startlingly congruent with the ethos of the nobility itself, a set of values at the core of Old Regime society. It is this congruence of noble values percolating down and Indian values seeping in that explains the underlying unity of Canada and the Old Regime.

Country gentlemen of straitened circumstances, most of them serving as officers in the regular troops, were a small but important segment of the migration to Canada. Encouraged by the King to stay in Canada, they were the progenitors of a Canadian nobility. Some of these families, such as the D'Aillebousts or Ruette d'Auteuils, were present in the earliest period in the colony's history. Others, such as the Lanaudières, Saint-Ours, and Contrecoeurs, were descended from officers in the Carignan-Salières regiment sent to Canada in 1665. Many more such families arrived in the decades that followed. From its inception, Canada had its *noblesse*, marked by all the traditionalism of the impoverished backwaters of French rural life from which they had sprung, saturated with the values of army life and service to the King.[30]

Frenchmen could not have conceived of a society without nobility, but too many nobles were too much of a good thing. Although about a dozen Canadian families, among them the Le Moynes and Le Bers, were ennobled to fill out the ranks of the superior order, the practice of ennoblement ceased in the earlier eighteenth century. Refusing letters of nobility and concessions *en fief et seigneurie* seem to have gone hand in hand, measures intended to keep within bounds families of rank, needed but as specialized as drones.[31]

In the eighteenth century, this *noblesse* dominated the officer corps of the twenty-eight Free Companies of the Marine, the regular troops that served in Canada: thirty-five of its eighty-seven officers were Canadian at the beginning of the century, 100 per cent by 1750. As sons followed fathers into the officer corps, a sure sign of an Old Regime ethos, it assumed the character of a hereditary caste. Youngsters of only eight or ten years were being enrolled as common soldiers pending the opening of more exalted positions. As it was repugnant that young gentlemen should serve in such a base capacity, by an edict of May 8, 1731, Maurepas provided that each company should make room for two officer cadets. As promotion in peacetime was by seniority, an occasional cadet languished in the ranks into his fifth decade.[32]

Opening the officer corps to aspiring Canadian nobles left most ranks in the militia to aspiring bourgeois and habitants, although the highest ones remained attractive to nobles. In the towns, notable merchants had always held rank and they became increasingly important in the eighteenth century as the nobles dropped out. In the *côtes*, the original seigneur had often been a soldier, for example a Carignan-Salières officer, and so had become the first captain. But after him, the local captain was an habitant.[33]

A *noblesse* was a problem as well as a necessity, indeed a necessitous problem. "Knowing no trade, not being born to plough the land and not having the credit that would enable them to enter business, they occupy themselves mainly with hunting and fishing," so a late seventeenth-century observer described them.[34] In 1737 Bishop Dosquet wrote of them, "The gentlemen . . . have much multiplied . . . and have no profession."[35] Thank God for the army. Young seigneurs sought entry into the officer corps, Hocquart wrote in 1737, "to find a modest resource in the King's pay rather than from other motives."[36] We even find in Canada a recrudescence of noble violence, young nobles taking advantage of the near immunity of their station to terrorize and rob lesser persons, something that Louis XIV had been at pains to root out in France's own backwoods nobility in the celebrated Grands Jours d'Auvergne.[37] No wonder Vaudreuil recommended that youngsters be employed on privateers, "not finding a more glorious or a more suitable way to occupy youth,"[38] a sentence which must seem puzzling or shocking when encountered without reference to a social order and an age so prone to violence.

Military appointments in the Marine companies were one means at the King's disposal to provide for the *noblesse*, and the possibilities went beyond salaries, which although low compared to those of the regular army in France were still substantial, to include what officers could make by acting as paymasters and storekeepers to their men or, above all, what they could skim from the fur trade by being posted as western commandants. Many monopolies were granted to men of rank – sealing and fishing stations, mines, and within the framework of the army, trading posts. As they collected only fees or shares of profits, their remuneration was in the nature of a rent and perfectly suited to their rank and values.[39]

Nobles infiltrated the civil establishment as well, but, as should be expected, without the same overwhelming success. For example, a rough count turns up blue blood in about a third of appointments to the Superior Council between 1700 and 1744. There was no common denominator to the council. Unalloyed men of business sat side by side with colonial nobles of military and seigneurial background, French lawyers, and newcomers with modest experience in the Marine administration or in finance. A count of the lesser law courts and the administrative offices might well show a smaller proportion of nobles in the civil establishment as a whole.[40]

"It is unsuitable for an ordinary habitant to hold fiefs," observed Hocquart.[41] Seigneuries were for the elite. If a *noblesse* was to be encouraged to sink its roots in Canadian soil, it had to be seigneurial soil. As the preamble to an early title deed expressed it, officers in the troops sent to Canada conformed to the King's own desire "to unite themselves to the country by developing lands and seigneuries of an extent proportional to their capacity."[42] Although seigneuries were on occasion granted to persons Hocquart would have found unsuitable, generally they were for persons of some standing, impoverished nobles of the kind attracted to Canada or bourgeois who had and inspired high hopes. The relation of tenure to rank can readily be seen in secondary grants made by the seigneurs themselves. Grants to ranking persons or religious orders were sub-fiefs, those to habitants, even examples of gifts for loyal service, were *en censive*.[43]

Many seigneuries were indeed granted in the first instance by the King to commoners, but it is remarkable that fully 66 per cent of seigneurial grants made between 1670 and 1760 were in favour of the *noblesse*. And although seigneuries might be alienated to bourgeois by purchase, over half were in the hands of nobles in 1760 and another quarter belonged to the First Estate, leaving just a quarter for commoners.[44]

Beneath the upper echelon of officers-seigneurs-nobles was the body of merchants. Success in trade was seen by many as the surest avenue to social promotion. "All their great ambition is to do business," La Pause wrote of the common people, "seeing that that brings them esteem."[45] Franquet made the same observation, and his notorious and ill-founded diatribe against the education of country girls was motivated by his fear that the educated girl "wants an establishment in town, that only a merchant is good enough for her and that she regards as beneath her the estate to which she was born."[46] The formula for business success was a group way of life and an ethos as venerable as *la vie noble*: early rising and long hours, financial prudence and shrewd dealing, the use of bookkeeping, a blameless and sober life free of superfluous expense, a very visible support of the Church – all characteristics that inspired confidence and respect and for which there seems to be genuine evidence in the lives of early Canadian merchants. Needless to say, many were called but few were chosen. There was not much room at the top of the business pyramid among the Quebec importers or the fully Canadianized Montreal outfitters. Dozens of names surface in the documents to claim our attention and then disappear without trace.

The merchant was himself by no means impervious to the siren call of official status and seigneury. But in New France as in Old, only the very successful merchant with capital and prestige could negotiate this social mutation so difficult and full of risks. One could not be without livelihood. The route via the castelike officer corps was virtually closed. Civil officialdom provided only a very few promising openings. That left the seigneury and, *faute de mieux*, the militia.

Being a militia officer was like being a churchwarden – another target of socially conscious merchants. It had a certain aura, it was in line with traditional bourgeois concepts of civic virtue, and it cost nothing.[47]

The question of the seigneury is more complex. A historian of the seventeenth century has argued that fiefs produced little or were even a financial liability, were a drug on the market, and were not seen as instruments of social mobility. A historian of the eighteenth century has seen them as *par excellence* the social escalator.[48] An undeveloped seigneury in an agrarian economy without external markets could only have been a drain on a merchant's resources; trying to develop it could only have been ruinous; and leaving it undeveloped might have rendered ridiculous the *bourgeois gentilhomme* who had purchased it. Once prospects for profits had improved, seigneuries became desirable investments, but, unfortunately, it is quite impossible for the historian to prove whether they were purchased as economic or as social investments. There is only circumstantial evidence: when a merchant buys seigneurial land in a French colony where even the trade is dominated by landed military officers and where some feeling for rank is manifest, it is hard to believe that social prestige is not in the bargain. In any case, the King was becoming increasingly parsimonious in his concession of seigneuries to the Third Estate. If 44 per cent of the concessions prior to 1663 had been to the bourgeoisie, they had received only 35 per cent in the period 1670-99. Bourgeois were recipients of 29 per cent of the new concessions in the first thirty years of the century and only 25 per cent in the three decades that followed. The decline was a trend evident even in the second half of the seventeenth century, one that seems to indicate that social stratification was hardening from gristle to bone and that the King was lukewarm to social mobility. It could also indicate declining bourgeois interest. An analysis of recipients in the last three decades muddies the waters. Many of them were not merchants but highly placed officials.[49] Does this indicate that officials were being favoured over merchants or does it confirm that merchants in general were becoming less interested and that the kind of person attracted to seigneuries was the official? Social history is full of such quandaries.

The upper orders of society received some encouragement to act in concert and maintain a kind of corporate identity. This is evident, for example, in the assemblies of "the better part of the people" that established the Colony Company in the presence of governor, intendant, bishop, and prominent clergy, or in the assemblies of notables called to give advice on policy questions. The assembly was an institution that declined dramatically after about 1720, but this coincides with the authorization to elect merchant syndics in Quebec and Montreal in

1717. Petitions were signed by these officials, elected by the business community, but soon styling themselves syndics "of the bourgeois, merchants and inhabitants" of their respective towns.[50]

This tolerance of collective deliberation and representation was not extended to the lower orders. Local officials tended to dismiss any petitions from craft groups except those from the food trades protesting government regulations that might threaten their livelihood. Nor, as we have seen in the previous chapter, did the government permit the establishment of trade guilds and the "closed shop" of guilds controlled by an elite of masters. It was thought that there would be time enough for monopolization and restraint once a pool of skilled labour had been built up. The only organization of workers tolerated was the *confrérie*, the functions of which amounted to little more than an annual mass and dinner. It may be that in all this official policy moved in the same direction as the tradesmen's own inclinations. In the experience of those who had immigrated from France, the guilds may have been a repressive apparatus rather than institutions of group solidarity. Canadian craftsmen over the generations demonstrated little family loyalty to crafts, allowed journeymanship, which associated junior with senior craftsmen, to fall into decay, resolutely avoided partnerships, and made the individual family shop the Canadian norm. Old Regime corporate structures dissolved in the face of absolutist policy and, it would appear, the individualist bent of the people.[51]

As to the countryside, the rejection of the village left the habitants with only the most attenuated institutions of community. In the oldest, most densely populated areas, well-defined *côtes* and established churches with resident *curés* provided some social cohesion. The pageant of hierarchy was played out, and the weekly sharing of the *pain bénit* became a kind of sacrament of community. Of the efficacy of the militia as an instrument of subordination and solidarity no firm pronouncements can be made.

The fading of many social patterns leaves in stark relief the one institution that lost none of its potency: the family, both nuclear and extended. Various social solidarities tended to be transformed into family networks. For example, families that produced one militia officer tended to make it a family tradition by producing more and by marrying into other militia families, producing a coherent social stratum of related persons. Family was irresistible. When Vaudreuil reported to Pontchartrain that he had named a certain habitant a captain of militia, he explained that he had followed the custom and that not only was his choice the best man for the job but his father-in-law had been captain for twenty or thirty years. "I would have believed I was doing an injustice not to give it to his son-in-law," he explained and added that the co-seigneurs of the place had requested it. Even without a common social function such as militia service to draw them together, families tended to marry into the same families over and over again, eschewing strangers, surrounding themselves with extensive networks of kin that were the foundation of social life. In the marriage contracts of craftsmen, it has been found that family accounted for most of the signatures. Only among the elite do marriage contracts show evidence of a social solidarity of rank distinguishable from family.[52]

Colonial social structure bore very much the same relation to metropolitan social structure as did Canadian architecture to French architecture. It was smaller in size and much less grand. It lacked the variation and fine detailing of the original. Nevertheless the relationship was unmistakable. Canadian society was a ranked society of the Old Regime type, but it was compressed, simplified, and oddly skewed to emphasize prickly dignity and autonomy at the expense of due subordination. The lower orders of society, in particular, lost much of the institutional embodiment that existed in France. But family, the principal institution of Old Regime linkage, lost none of its vigour and gained in importance from the absence of other linking institutions. In the bosom of the family, the individual flourished.

II

In his political testament, Louis XIV explained his choice of ministers of middling rank. "I could undoubtedly have cast my eyes on persons of higher standing," he admitted. "But . . . it was not in my interest to select individuals of greater eminence. It was . . . necessary . . . to make the public realize, by the very rank of those whom I selected, that it was not my intention to share my authority with them."[53] We are apt to forget how intrinsic to the individual was the possession of rank and the exercise of authority. It was the King's intention to be served by men faithful to himself alone and not by men who were themselves great patrons. His royal "coup d'état" of 1661 put in place a new pyramid of vertically linked individuals and lineages dependent upon himself, but the political style remained the same. One man was a master, protector, or patron; another was his "faithful," his "creature," or, more prosaically, his client. The word *fidélité* describes this personal, heartfelt, and reciprocal link between master and faithful. So could we describe the feelings of an old soldier, Duplessis Faber, who spent the last years of his life in Montreal, writing regularly to his distant patron, the Maréchal de Vauban, of whom he cherished a portrait.[54] These relations in the political sphere can be described as *clientage*, a term that allows for a little less of the heart and a little more of the head and of calculation. The extent to which *fidélité* might have been draining out of clientage as the eighteenth century wore on and the extent to which such styles of social linkage may have penetrated to the lowest levels of society are equally unknown.

Fidélité and clientage are evidence of a very personal style of politics congruent with a society of orders, a society that could not, for example, have conceived of the offices of the Marine in terms of an abstract model of bureaucracy, but rather saw them as vertical linkages of great men to lesser men. It was only to be expected in a system in which thousands of men did in fact own their offices, and could sell them or pass them on to descendants, that the attitudes of those who did not own the positions they filled would nevertheless be imbued with the same values. Each man tended to exercise authority as though it were his possession, using it to advance his personal interests, those of his family, and those of his clients. The king's interest, while it was indeed *la chose publique*, still had about it something of an overarching private interest, that of the king as a person, not so different, perhaps, from the many private interests the advancement of which was part and parcel of the process by which policy was effected.

The Old Regime administrator or officer was constantly in situations that we would see as involving conflict of interest and was constantly committing acts that we would define as corruption. Knuckles were rapped and individuals were removed from the scene of action (rarely dismissed) when the advancing of private interest interfered with high policy. So once again we have the opportunity to affirm the extreme individualism and personal style of the Old Regime.[55]

Behind the history of *policy* that has earlier claimed our attention lay a *politics* of patronage, the personal style in action, that we can now explore. The theory of royal government did not easily accommodate the expression of community interests, their clash and reconciliation, geared as it was to the notion that policy originated with the king and was handed down from above. The institutional provision for the reception of advice from the community, as we have seen, was minimal. Colonials of rank influenced policy mainly through their membership in *clientage clusters*, the same way in which they shared in the state's largess. Undignified by formal structures and lacking the sanction of theories of popular expression or legitimate opposition, this advocacy of interests always appears sordid and fractious.[56]

At the heart of this system of quasi-institutionalized squabbling was the division of power between two patrons, the governor and the intendant. To read Pontchartrain, one would think there was nothing simpler and more straightforward than the joint administration of these two officials. Writing to Michel Bégon, he professed what must be assumed to have been a feigned surprise that the Intendant was not maintaining the "union and good understanding" with Governor Vaudreuil so necessary to the "Service":

> As regards war or what pertains to it, there is no doubt that the view of the governor general must prevail over those of the intendant, and when the latter cannot do as he is bidden for want of funds for an enterprise that is not pressing and unavoidable, he must explain this to the governor with decency, politeness, and good reasoning without any spirit of haughtiness, caprice or bad humour. The same tone must prevail with regard to matters they determine jointly, which they must always consider decently and with decorum.[57]

Why, then, was it necessary for Pontchartrain, like Colbert before him and Maurepas at a later date, to wag a finger? The fault was fourfold. First, governors and intendants were men of a different stamp. Governors, whether at Quebec, Port Royal, or Louisbourg, were military officers – after Vaudreuil specifically naval officers, "old men nearing the ends of their careers." A governor under fifty was a rarity as was an intendant over fifty. The intendants were career civil servants in the Marine bureaucracy, men still on their way up for whom colonial service was a necessary stage. "One can hope for no intendancy in the ports of France if one has not served in the colonies," Maurepas admonished François Bigot.[58] Age and career outlook, military and civilian background, thus separated the two parties destined for "union and good understanding."

Second, it is also true that the *esprit de hauteur* was in generous supply. People stood on their rank, which was essentially a dignity and thus easily sullied. To write a detailed political history of New France would be to retail a long list of petty incidents, slights real and imagined, minor jurisdictional raids and incursions. To represent many of these occurrences as significant *events* would be to court ridicule, but they are nevertheless significant *facts*, since they reveal the nature of the society of orders and demonstrate how perfectly co-ordinated was the nature of politics with the nature of society.

Third, there was much overlapping of jurisdictions, for example, the planning and executing of a military undertaking by the governor and the organization of the *matériel* and the authorization of payments by the intendant. Fourth, it has long been recognized that the conflicts that focused in the persons of the governor and intendant were "struggles of influence" that sometimes took on the "aspect, rather confused in truth, of party struggles, that is, conflicts of interest and of ideas."[59] And this brings us back to the clientage cluster. It is possible to conceive of those Canadians surrounding the governor and intendant as politicians, as a governing elite narrowly based in a political class.

It was the governor who recommended to the king all decorations and all promotions. He had in his gift places in his guard, commissions in the militia, the positions of blacksmith and interpreter at the western posts and, the presumed Open Sesame to riches, the commands of these posts. Before the abolition of the *congés* in 1720, their sale for very little to persons of rank undergoing financial difficulties or to religious communities was itself a form of patronage. Later, when Beauharnois was selling them for high prices, influence remained an important factor, and a large part of the receipts was doled out to the perennial group of ranking indigents.

The governor and intendant jointly granted seigneuries and fishing and sealing monopolies. The intendant recommended candidates for the Superior Council and appointed many judicial and civil officers. As some of these offices involved handling the king's money, they could be quite profitable. The intendant also let contracts and made purchases and argued the case with the minister for monopolies and grants.

Intendants commonly carried on a more or less legitimate trade in partnership with Quebec or French businessmen, using whatever advantages their position afforded to do so with profit. Merchant partners fronted for officials supplying the government at inflated prices. Intendants benefited from regulations of their own devising. Card money and other fiduciary paper were manipulated. Champigny, François Beauharnois, Jacques Raudot, and Bégon were all accused of questionable practices.[60]

Dispensing patronage had its own peculiar Old Regime character; it was not a straightforward rewarding of friends. For example, when Governor Brouillan of Acadia solicited a commission for the son of a respected officer, he was careful to point out that "the services that his father has rendered to the King and renders still speak sufficiently to garner him this place." We have already seen an example of how a Canadian militia appointment could tend to remain in the possession of a family as if by right. When Beauharnois and Hocquart solicited a subsidy for the King's Lieutenant at Quebec in 1734, they drew attention not only to his past services but to those of his sons who served as officers and to the fact that he was "a man of rank, related by marriage to Duke Tallard." But they also reported how difficult it was for a man in his position to live on his salary and seigneurial income and mentioned his substantial losses in a fire. Similarly, when Vaudreuil was Governor of Montreal, Champigny had solicited a bounty for him because he was poor, because he had many children, and because he had had to build a large house suitable to his rank. Authorities were sensitive to disparities of rank and income, an attitude that also lies behind the annual distributions of subsidies to "decent families."[61]

One of the most skilled writers of begging letters was the Marquise de Vaudreuil, always alert to the needs of her husband and a wide family connection. Here she is, imploring favours from Maurepas:

> As the Marquise de Vaudreuil had heard that you are taking away the command of Detroit from M. Tonti, she takes the liberty, Monseigneur, to ask you for it for M. Ademars de l'Antagniac, grandnephew of her late husband, whose birth is known to you, and who has a gentle and obliging disposition, suitable to fill that post well. By granting him this post, Monseigneur, you will enable him to rear a large family with which he is burdened. The Marquise de Vaudreuil knows that you like to do good to people of rank; she and her children will be infinitely grateful, Monseigneur, for what you may be good enough to do for M. de l'Antagniac.[62]

The higher orders of Canadian society, as of French society, always got a hearing. For these, the king really did have a kindly and paternal regard; he liked "to do good to people of rank."

The French governing class from which Canadian governors and intendants were chosen was itself an intricate network of family alliances. Within it, great men advanced relations who became their clients but also clients who sometimes became relations. The Marine, and hence Canadian, appointments were dominated in the eighteenth century by the great family of Phélypeaux de Pontchartrain and its lesser connections, the Beauharnois and the Bégons, the latter a family that owed its rise to prominence to an earlier liaison with the Colberts. The Pontchartrains had both ancestors and marriage partners among the Beauharnois. The brothers François, the Intendant of Canada and later of Rochefort, and Charles, the Governor, were cousins to Jérôme de Pontchartrain and to his son, Maurepas. Their sister, Jeanne-Elisabeth, was the wife of the intendant Michel Bégon. Upon her marriage, Jeanne-Elisabeth found herself the daughter-in-law of the brother-in-law of Jacques de Meulles, a Canadian intendant of the later seventeenth century, and sister-in-law of the grandmother of La Galissonière, the governor who would succeed her brother Charles. These examples among many that could be cited show what an intimate and reassuring milieu the governing class was for its members and what a labyrinth of joy it must remain for the genealogical enthusiast.[63]

Governor and intendant, each with his own connections in the Marine bureaucracy and at the court, were the clients of great men. We should not be surprised to find that in the miniature elite of New France they were the great men and that each became the focus of a local connection in which family played its part. The archives of eighteenth-century Canada bulge with accusations that officials trans-gressed policy and sullied dignity to enrich themselves and their friends. Much of this defies verification. Nevertheless, it is clear that Callière, Vaudreuil, and their officers were deeply involved in the fur trade even during the period when the West was closed. The mass of evi-dence supports the bitter accusations Attorney General Ruette d'Auteuil pressed from his sour grapes, that Vaudreuil and his officers built posts in the West "under pretext of suppressing the coureurs de bois, but in reality to secure their own shipments and to themselves undertake a trade made more extensive and more advantageous by the agency of the commanders of these posts."[64] And evidence from the other side of the Atlantic provides us with the report of powerless customs offi-cials surprising Vaudreuil and a band of smugglers, including soldiers and sailors with fixed bayonets, landing bales of furs from a naval vessel onto the shore at Fort Vergerou near Rochefort.[65]

The quarrels that split the Canadian elite in the first years of the century are particularly instructive of political style. Vaudreuil had married into the family of Joybert, which in turn was connected to the Lotbinières. This connection constituted a fur-trade interest opposed to another, the Ruette d'Auteuil–Aubert clan to which the Governor of Montreal, Claude de Ramezay, was related by his marriage to a Denys de la Ronde. To this group Cadillac gravitated as well. (There must have been an extra degree of tension between Vaudreuil and Cadillac as poor southerners sequentially protégés of Jérôme de Pontchartrain.) These two factions divided the Colony Company and divided the elite. Vaudreuil attacked Cadillac's stewardship at Detroit and revealed his covert deals with Ramezay and Ruette d'Auteuil. They, for their part, attacked Vaudreuil for his weakness in handling riots in 1704 and 1705 and criticized his military decisions in the war. Ruette d'Auteuil and Cadillac thought they had found their way to the Minister's Gallican heart by attacking the Jesuits, who, along with the Sulpicians, were among Vaudreuil's loyal supporters. The Governor, hard pressed and losing Pontchartrain's confidence, found allies in the Raudots.

Taking in hand the reform of the Colony Company, Jacques Raudot abolished its board of directors, on which Ruette d'Auteuil was a power, and replaced it with a committee of two men, one of them Vaudreuil's uncle, René-Louis Chartier de Lotbinière, chief councillor. Ruette d'Auteuil, being the Attorney General, attacked the Intendant over his policy of judging legal cases himself rather than leaving them to the courts. Their acrimonious disputes ended with Raudot's triumph. Ruette d'Auteuil, a brilliant but rash, bitter, and unstable man, squandered his career to prevent his sister-in-law, Charlotte-Françoise Juchereau, Madame de la Forest, from losing her County of St Laurent (the Ile d'Orléans), which she had bought with her worthless promissory notes. Ruette d'Auteuil wrote documents for her and gave her others in his keeping. The result was scandal and the Attorney General's dismissal in 1707.

By destroying the Attorney General, Jacques Raudot confirmed his supremacy in the legal and civil administration and brought unity to those who were a part of it. Vaudreuil too had gained from Raudot's victory. Soon, however, the two patrons fell out. There is no great conflict of principle to be found in it, but it is fascinating to observe how predictably it divided the elite into factions, civil versus military.[66]

Raudot's successor, Michel Bégon, provides a clear and good example of an intendant involved in business. He carried on a considerable import-export trade in partnership with two brothers-in-law, one of them Beauharnois, by that time Intendant of Rochefort. Although he forbade the export of flour to prevent famine, he bought up supplies in the name of the King that he subsequently exported for his own profit. His accounts were in general disarray when in 1723 Cousin Maurepas dealt with the situation by promoting him to the intendancy of Le Havre. A councillor complained that Bégon spent all his time on private business. Bégon argued that everything he did benefited the colony. One of an intendant's main tasks, after all, was to promote trade.[67]

With Vaudreuil dead and Bégon departed, old clientage clusters broke up and new patterns formed.[68] Charles de Beauharnois's appointment was in part the result of a decision not to confer the governorship upon another officer burdened with the expectations of a Canadian family. It was also the manifestation of a new policy of appointing Marine careerists that was earlier evident in the appointment of his brother, François, as intendant in 1702. This "reform" also had the effect of serving the interests of family connections within the Marine, for example the Phélypeaux-Bégon-Beauharnois group, something that must have been weighed in the balance alongside more professional considerations. And if Beauharnois did not have Canadian relatives, his metropolitan connections had already spilled over into Canada. François Foucault, keeper of the royal stores at Quebec, was a relative who had come to Canada in 1716 and managed lands in the colony belonging to Bégon, who was Beauharnois's brother-in-law. Foucault's Montreal counterpart, Etienne Rocbert, was the father-in-law of Bégon's brother, Chevalier Claude-Michel Bégon. While Beauharnois was at pains to mollify the Vaudreuils and bestowed favours on a wide array of individuals, it is true that the "outs" under Vaudreuil, the Ramezays, Boishéberts, La Rondes, and the engineer Chaussegros de Léry, came in with the new governor.

The civil establishment of which Foucault and Rocbert were a part tended to gravitate toward the intendant, who was their obvious patron. Many found it difficult to maintain this loyalty in the face of the antics of Bégon's successor, Claude-Thomas Dupuy. Men such as the *commissaire*, François Clairambault d'Aigremont, the Marine controller, Jean-Eustache Lanoullier de Boisclerc, and the councillors Mathieu-François Martin de Lino and Mathieu-Benôit Collet were drawn instead into the governor's circle.

The appointment to the Canadian intendancy of an outsider is explained by the prior deaths on the Atlantic crossing of two successive appointees drawn from the Marine bureaucracy. The money of a rising and ambitious family had bought Dupuy the office of *maître des requêtes*, which talent and education enabled him to fill. He appears to have had no patron himself. He was a "new man" with energy, intelligence, and ideas. But his learned legal judgements and analyses of colonial conditions are crowded offstage by the theatrical outbursts that marked his Canadian performance. His meddling in the administration of the Western Posts described in Chapter 8 is only one example among many of his characteristic intrusions into the jurisdictional concerns of others. "As for prudence," his biographer remarks, "he seems to have been devoid of it."[69]

Anxious to get on well with Dupuy, Beauharnois conceded him irregular honours of the Intendant's own devising: sentries and a bodyguard and the right to receive incense at mass. But when Beauharnois refused to authorize the appointment of a drummer to accompany the posting of ordinances and Dupuy appointed one himself, all pretence to *bonhomie* was cast aside. In March 1727, Quebeckers were treated to a theatrical "happening" the like of which they had not seen since Intendant Duchesneau barricaded his house against Governor Frontenac's soldiers in 1681. The Governor had got hold of Dupuy's ordinance appointing the drummer and refused to give it up. When subsequently he summoned the Intendant to the château to discuss another matter, Dupuy assumed the ordinance was to be discussed and refused to comply. The Governor's emissary, Captain François-Antoine Contrecoeur, having returned from palace to château without an intendant in tow, the dean of the Superior Council, Mathieu-François Martin de Lino, and a Sulpician father made the same journey to reason with Dupuy, only to hear his impassioned denunciation of the Governor as a feudal despot. They returned to Beauharnois with Dupuy's demands for the return of the ordinance, for the Governor's word of honour sworn "between the hands of Monsieur the Bishop of Quebec" that Dupuy would not be mistreated, and for the prior communication in writing of the subjects of future meetings. Dupuy's stand challenged a fundamental tenet of the absolutist system, the right of a legitimate superior to demand obedience without question. It was an impertinence as typical of the Old Regime as absolutism itself. Next, no less a personage than Bishop Saint-Vallier was parading from Governor to Intendant and back. At the last moment, with Dupuy claiming that he would not be taken from the palace without a struggle, Beauharnois gave in to a toned-down list of demands – no oaths between the bishop's hands, no written agendas. For his part, Dupuy had subsequently to be content with the posting of ordinances by a loud-voiced bailiff. All this for a drummer: the Old Regime had its priorities.

The drummer affair was a mere curtain raiser to the main act that followed, which led to Dupuy's recall. On December 26, 1727, the Bishop, an aged cleric much alienated from his clergy, died at his retreat at the Hôpital-Général outside Quebec. Aside from the hospital nuns, who adored him, Saint-Vallier had two particular friends: Dupuy, his executor, and Eustache Chartier de Lotbinière, who was both a member of the Superior Council and Dean of the Cathedral Chapter. When the canons elected one Etienne Boullard as capitular vicar and decided that he rather than Lotbinière should preside at Saint-Vallier's funeral, Lotbinière complained to Dupuy. The Intendant hastened to gird up his loins and join battle with the priests. Crediting a wild rumour that the canons planned to carry off Saint-Vallier's body for burial in the cathedral, Dupuy ordered an impromptu funeral, Lotbinière presiding, in the hospital chapel, where the Bishop had asked to be interred. Boullard thereupon deposed the mother superior and placed the nuns under the interdict. Dupuy next claimed that as a coadjutor bishop resided at Paris, the see was not vacant and ecclesiastical authority ought to be exercised by Lotbinière as Saint-Vallier's grand vicar. Boullard insisted – correctly – that the see was vacant until claimed. Dupuy ordered the canons to appear before the Superior Council, claiming it held jurisdiction in the matter. Boullard and the canons – correctly – refused.

Beauharnois, biding his time with much greater self-control than in the drummer affair, did not intervene until March 8, when he appeared in council to suspend proceedings against the canons. The council refused to heed the Governor's ordinance. To the issue of civil jurisdiction over the Church was thus added that of the proper spheres of governor and intendant. Now innocent bystanders enjoyed the spectacle of

Dupuy's ordinances being torn down by priests and by Beauharnois's soldiers and these same soldiers posting the Governor's ordinances to shouts of "Vive le roi et Beauharnois," the bailiff having refused to publish them. Two officials who refused to publish Dupuy's ordinances were jailed by the Intendant and liberated by force of arms on the Governor's order. Beauharnois jailed two military officers who had sided with Dupuy and exiled two councillors to their country estates. Most councillors kept their mouths shut at meetings, and two of them, Dr. Sarrazin, the King's Physician, and Martin de Lino, stopped attending. Nicolas Lanoullier, clerk of the Marine treasurers, Dupuy's client and business associate, discovered he was needed at Montreal. Beneath the councillors was the even more discomfited group of lesser judicial officials who later explained in tortured petitions that they had only been following orders.

Dupuy was the model of the silly savant without practical sense; he was, in Beauharnois's words, "a man absolutely out of his element."[70] He failed to see that the Superior Council was not the place to carry on the Gallican good fight that seemed appropriate in the Paris *parlement* and that the superiority of the robe to the sword was anything but a self-evident proposition outside the salons of Paris magistrates. The normal clientage cluster could not long coalesce around so preposterous and inappropriate a master. In September 1728, the King's ship *Eléphant* arrived with the dispatches announcing Dupuy's recall. The former intendant was found to owe considerable sums in Canada, in particular a debt to the King's storekeeper, Foucault, probably in his private capacity but construed as a debt to the King. On that ground, Dupuy's replacement, Clairambault d'Aigremont, ordered Dupuy's goods seized. While Beauharnois looked the other way, Dupuy was left to say his last goodbyes, demoted, shamed, and pillaged.

Gilles Hocquart, the new intendant, avoided Dupuy's old supporters, offering places to Frenchmen who had come out with him or to men in Beauharnois's entourage. Rivalry between the Governor and Intendant and their circles was for many years insignificant, possibly nonexistent. In making appointments, Hocquart preferred metropolitans with proficiency and experience in law or civil administration to colonials, who appear to have lacked the qualities he sought and, in any case, to have been uninterested in jobs with scant remuneration. "In general, in a country as poor as this one, an honourable place counts for little if there is no profit in it," the joint letter of 1732 informs us.[71] Clearly, the army and the fur trade rather than the civil establishment were still the major supports of the Canadian elite.

As we have seen in considering trade and the development of industries, Hocquart soon threw himself into the task of developing a

Quebec-based entrepreneurial group that he hoped would be the salvation of the Canadian economy. The pursuit of this policy was inseparable from a politics of patronage, the doling out of monopolies, subsidies, contracts, and jobs. Hocquart came to support many resident merchants, both French-born and Canadian.

To search for the names of Hocquart's clients is to enter a thicket only here and there brushed out: Foucault, Estèbe, Taschereau, the names of aggressive and capable men of affairs in their own right protected and advanced by Hocquart, all three made councillors as part of the Intendant's policy of changing the complexion of the council from law to business; Varin, Michel de Villebois, Bricault de Valmur, trusted career administrators who had come to Canada with Hocquart or shortly after him; and, of course, François-Etienne Cugnet, a veritable *alter ego* with the nerve and business flair to give concrete realization to Hocquart's policy directions.

The names of Jacques de Lafontaine de Belcour and Charles-René Gaudron de Chevremont, both Beauharnois's secretaries, demand special comment. Hocquart had arrived in Canada in the wake of the Saint-Vallier affair. Until 1731, his title was only that of *ordonnateur*, which meant he was on probation. In such circumstances, it is not surprising that he took under his wing with little enthusiasm but much policy the Governor's own chicks – ugly ducklings to Hocquart. He made Belcour a councillor and a clerk in his offices and granted him a sealing concession; Chevremont he made first a scrivener, then a notary and a clerk. Hocquart dismissed the first in 1735 for spending all his time on his own business and the second in 1741 for his dilatory conduct. With regard to Chevremont, Beauharnois played out to perfection the role of protector. First he was affronted, then he was solicitous. To provide for his man, he sent him to France as his own attorney to oversee family business.[72]

Chevremont's dismissal was a signal: the long administrative truce between Beauharnois and Hocquart was at an end. It was clear that this would be so as early as 1737, when Maurepas insisted that Hocquart realize significant economies.[73] The Intendant sought to divert attention from his own bottomless pits of industrial investment to profligate military spending. In 1739 cuts were made in the military budget; officers' accounts were subjected to unwonted scrutiny. Clients were not left untouched by this conflict between their masters' policies and projects. That spring's dispatches brought to Hocquart Maurepas's request that some financial support be found for Nicolas Lanoullier the unlucky, still floundering in debts nearly a decade old. For years Hocquart had promised Lanoullier the farm of the Tadoussac trade should it ever cease to be operated as a government enterprise. But in

1737 he had leased it to Cugnet, the driving force of the newly formed Forges du Saint-Maurice. Hocquart suggested that Lanoullier be given the monopoly of supplying the trader at Temiskaming. This was to thrust an unwelcome nose into the Governor's sphere, a very audacious nose if Beauharnois had an interest in the post as Vaudreuil had had before him.

Beauharnois must have got wind of this, for three weeks later, in an apparent parry to Hocquart's thrust, he wrote to Maurepas suggesting that the Abbé Louis Lepage, another entrepreneurial casualty, ought to receive an ironworks concession, which would, the Governor claimed, in no way inconvenience Cugnet's establishment on the St Maurice. When Maurepas officially informed him of the Temiskaming plan the following year, carefully shielding its author, a knowing Beauharnois countered that Tadoussac was the more appropriate support for Lanoullier and that it appeared to have been given to Cugnet "as a favour or with much facility . . . without observing the formalities of the public call for bids."[74] This could not help but awaken suspicion at Versailles that Hocquart was profiting from Tadoussac and so balance any suspicions about Beauharnois's involvement in Temiskaming.

As we have seen in previous chapters, if Maurepas did not find Hocquart blameless for the Canadian financial morass, he did determine that Beauharnois, the army, and the post system would bear the brunt of retrenchment. The revolutionary plan of leasing the western posts that was announced in 1742 had been in the back of Maurepas's mind before Hocquart ever arrived in Canada and in the mind of Bégon before Maurepas had taken office. It would therefore be incorrect to suggest that Hocquart originated the leasing option to further his interests and those of his clients at the expense of Beauharnois and his followers. But he and the Marine controller, Varin, did recommend the lease of Frontenac and Niagara and contributed mightily to the rich critique of the military that decided Maurepas finally to embrace the hoary lease-for-economy doctrine.[75]

The decision was a body blow that winded and floored Beauharnois's patronage system, focused in the officer corps. Hocquart was given greater scope to favour his own. It must have helped François Chalet, recipient of the pilot-project lease of Frontenac and Niagara, that he was a crony of Hocquart's, that the Intendant had "for a long time" been acquainted with "his activity and his intelligence,"[76] although Chalet, who came home from France in 1742 as inspector general for the Indies Company and with a lease in his pocket, must have moved beyond the point of being merely the Intendant's client. As for Cugnet, who must have been a man of winning ways, he was granted the lease not only of Kaministiquia and Michipicoten but even of much-quarrelled-over Temiskaming.

All this was not accomplished without a considerable correspondence very illuminating to us: Beauharnois receives the news of the lease system with icy correctness. He will do his duty and set aside the plan he has been about to announce to increase competition at the posts and will institute instead the Minister's monopoly system. In Varin's pages, although Hocquart is never criticized, he yet emerges as an administrator who has failed to deal with the unsatisfactory situation he has inherited and to whom Varin has for quite some time been suggesting the appropriate solutions. Hocquart, for his part, excuses his own excessive spending and suggests that he is at last getting everything under control. In a cloying display of concern for Beauharnois, he manages to convey the impression that the old fellow is beyond coping with an importuning horde of uniformed beggars. Thank heaven he has an intendant at his side.[77] Behind the phrases of allusive and courtly supplication, it is every man for himself.

At Ile Royale, a similar politics of patronage prevailed. In the words of François Bigot, it was a colony with "a great penchant for cabals."[78] Governor and *ordonnateur* set the example in a system in which scarcely an officer, civil or military, disdained to roll up his sleeves and, literally, get down to business. Lesser officers at outports had the same free hand to trade that officers in Canada had at the western fur posts. The foundation of their business was usually the employment of a number of fishermen. Trading and smuggling were further developments of vertically integrated systems. Selling goods and services to the King, selling the King's goods to others, and using his troops as labourers were further sources of profits for soldiers and civilians alike. *Ordonnateurs* and their cronies, the storekeepers, were especially well placed to defraud the King by bookkeeping obfuscations. Favouritism in letting contracts and unfair trade legislation or judicial hearings were common complaints. By 1715 government officials were firmly entrenched in the colony's business.

The use of front men by offenders and the absence of inside documentation make it difficult and in many cases impossible to verify the existence of the official skulduggery decried by losers and outsiders. The origins of François Bigot's considerable fortune, for example, remain shrouded in a thick Louisbourg fog. Governor Saint-Ovide and Ordonnateur Le Normant de Mézy were both removed from Ile Royale in April 1739, in the face of mounting evidence of their corrupt practices. The use of office to favour their own smuggling activities, fiddling the storekeeper's accounts in the case of Le Normant, profiteering in the building of Louisbourg's fortifications in the case of Saint-Ovide, were the principal causes of dissatisfaction. Saint-Ovide was retired, but Le Normant was simply transferred to Saint-Domingue. The ministry's tolerance of theft was fatalistic; one can imagine the

Gallic shrug. The result of removal, or any such action, was thus to appease public opinion and to break up an extant clientage cluster. At least some of the players would change, but the game would continue.

*   *   *

In Canada, the sense of personal dignity and honour that was the very marrow of Old Regime behaviour and a pillar of the French notion of rank found serendipitous support in Indian individualism. Subordination, the second pillar of rank, found no such happy echo in the new environment. Its support was in the untidy mountain of cultural baggage unloaded at Quebec, a stock added to by every ship that docked, every immigrant that disembarked, and every pouch of government dispatches. Its message was hammered home in sermon and pastoral letter. At the edge of the European world, the old lesson was necessarily weaker, but everyone who believed he ranked above someone else had a vested interest in maintaining it. Without question – and without surprise – rank, supported on its twin pillars, animated the courtly system of Canadian politics. Tremors of outraged dignity and insubordination regularly disturbed its serenity without threatening its solidity. Canada was a country of the Old Regime, *mais pas comme les autres*.

Subordination and individualism were the two faces of a single Old Regime coin. At every toss of the coin, one or the other appeared uppermost, but the relation between the two was deep and enduring. The aggregate of a thousand tosses was the multitude of compromises between the need for social and political organization and the need for freedom and independence.

CHAPTER 12

Conclusion

In January 1744, the Marine circularized the French Atlantic ports, encouraging outfitters to send provisions to Canada in the greatest variety and greatest quantity possible. The Canadian harvest had failed yet again in 1743. Two months later, the Minister was writing to all his distant officials to inform them officially of a declaration of war. "The King finds himself forced to declare war on England," he explained, "after having done all that fell to His Majesty to do to avoid it."[1]

The European war had been begun in 1740 by Frederick the Great of Prussia to despoil twenty-four-year-old Maria Theresa of Austria of her dominions. In France, a war party of idle nobility, trussed up for years by the prudent Cardinal Fleury, broke their bonds and stampeded the court into war. Although it was clear by 1742 that Austria was not to be destroyed, France continued to move its pawns and knights about the European chessboard without any clear aim. For a country such as France, on the threshold of modernity and commercial greatness, the whole purposeless business was a kind of social throwback. In 1739 war had broken out between Spain and Great Britain, a war for the wealth and trade of Spanish America. Nevertheless, on the seas, where a ruthless *realpolitik* might have dictated military participation, France had held aloof. It was the spectre of English armies in Germany that stirred it to a declaration of war in 1744. "One ought not to be astonished that princes declare war on each other for almost nothing" was the cynical conclusion of two French merchants at Quebec.[2]

The provision ships reached Canada in the summer of 1744, and in the fall a good crop was harvested. That was the extent of Fortune's gifts. Transatlantic trade was at a standstill, and fur dealers were setting their bales aside for a better day. Indian hunters would soon be transformed into warriors. Of course, there were wartime profits to be made on defence works and provisioning. "Poor King, how you are robbed!" became Hocquart's constant refrain.[3]

Bishop Pontbriand revealed to his flock in August that he had for a

259

long time been contemplating the calamities besetting the colony. God's controversy with New France had seemed to be ending. But if bakers' shops were full of bread and barns full of grain, the colony still faced the spectre of war. "Remember, weak and fragile man," Pontbriand warned, "that the author of blessings is the same who afflicts and punishes." The Church, of course, stood shoulder to shoulder with the State. Pontbriand reminded the faithful that the King was exposing his own person in battle and that it was just to pray for the safety of "a monarch who is the delight of his people, the strength and joy of his armies, the admiration of the great, the honour of France" – all this of Louis XV![4] France was portrayed as a disinterested party coming to the defence of a beleaguered emperor, meaning the Elector of Bavaria, a puppet whose election the French and Prussians had engineered. Pontbriand ordained that High Mass would be celebrated in the Quebec cathedral on Sunday, August 30, after which the Te Deum would be sung to give thanks for the arrival of the ships, the abundant harvest, and the recent successes of French arms in Europe.

From the eve of the War of the Spanish Succession in 1701 to 1744, when the Americas became involved in yet another war between great powers, there are forty-three years of Canadian history dominated by the imperial rivalries of France and Great Britain, including, ironically, thirty years of peace and growth guaranteed by the great rivals' alliance of convenience. A number of themes have served as guides through the complexities of these years, and it seems appropriate, not to restate them, but to reflect on them in the light of the previous pages.

Imperialism was the first of these. The new-style imperialism from political and strategic motives that appeared in 1701 and was prominent especially after 1715 did not eclipse the older mercantilist imperialism with its economic preoccupations. And Canada's western expansion cannot be cleanly divided into a fur trade (or economic) phase before 1696 and an imperial (or political) phase in the eighteenth century. While the French government placed officers at posts for political purposes, the officers were enthusiastic to go for an economic reason: to reap the profits of the trade. If the *pax gallica* was thought to provide for Canada's military security, it also secured its economic foundations. If the reoccupation of the West was partly conceived to keep the English out of it, the policy was successful only because of a reviving fur trade. As for the expansion of Louisiana, that was as much a result of the Indies Company's dreams of wealth as of military strategy. The thematic strands of trade and empire, of private interest and public policy, are found to be inseparable. France always had a clearer sense of its imperial mission in the Atlantic region and backed it up with money. The bulk of its North American defence spending went into Louisbourg, which clearly protected the fishery and, arguably (such was the power of auto-suggestion), the continent. There, at least, imperialism was not just a dog-in-the-manger policy.

Imperialism was a frame of reference within which it was desirable and morally acceptable to expand into geographical areas politically weak or of doubtful sovereignty – Indian country. Within that frame of reference, many motives came into play. On the Canadian periphery, from La Pointe de Chagouamigon north and east through Kaministiquia, Nipigon, Michipicoten, Temiskaming, and on to the King's Posts, the economic motive was paramount. At La Baie it vied in importance with the political necessity of dominating the Foxes. At St Joseph River and throughout the Weas-Miamis country, the political aspect was increasingly important. To the south, only imperative political reasons induced France to maintain the posts of the lower lakes and their subsidized trade or the Canadians to occupy the Ohio country after 1748. The French presence did not have an identical purpose in all areas and it meant different things to different people. In a remarkable passage, Father Charlevoix, for example, discerns in the search for the Western Sea scientific, economic, political, and religious benefits. After pointing out the commercial advantage of finding new routes to China and Japan, he adds, "It is not to be doubted that in extending the frontiers of the Kingdom of Jesus Christ, one will acquire new provinces for the King."[5]

If the French presence was imperial, it did not constitute an empire. Events at the French stronghold of Detroit are ample reminder that a French commandant with a token garrison was not in a position to give the law to large and warlike tribes. The commandant resembled less an imperial administrator in a frontier province than a consul with a few armed retainers, promoting the interests of his country and protecting its merchants in an alien territory.

The second and third themes in the preceding chapters have been the development of the Canadian economy and the importance for it of the growth of the French economy and of the French empire of trade. The view developed in these pages is that the wider context was of overriding importance. It is of enormous significance that almost the entire history of the colony unfolded in what French economic historians, following François Simiand, a pioneer of price curves, call a "phase B" movement, a century-long recession marked by falling prices and difficulty in mobilizing capital. Canada, like Colbertism and French mysticism, was born in a tough and Spartan time. The expansion of its economy in the twenties and thirties was only the first flickering smile of what French historians, again, call the "smiling eighteenth century," a "phase A" movement of rising prices and plentiful money. These are developments that, like the changes in material life, a fourth theme, are difficult to capture in a history of four decades. To come to grips with economic change, including changes in the social capital of cleared land, buildings, and industrial and commercial facilities of all kinds as well as changes in the food, clothing, and amenities of the people, we have to accept the challenge of working in Fernand Braudel's *longue durée*, taking the whole history of New France, or all of the eighteenth century, as our period.[6] In price, demographic, and other quantitative series, patterns and developments now seen in a fragmentary way will reveal themselves more completely.

The fifth theme has been social development. Canadian society has been described as a society of orders, and this may give a slightly artificial clarity to a somewhat less clear-cut reality. The question of class has only been touched on. As we have seen, with the passage of time and the development of markets, more and more seigneuries were becoming profitable to their owners. From the 1720s, the improvement of seigneurial revenues, the militarization of the fur trade, the granting of fishing and fur-trading monopolies in the Gulf of St Lawrence and of sealing concessions on the coast of Labrador were together bringing about the consolidation of a *rentier* class whose great days still lay in the future, an economic class containing within it clerics, military and rustic nobles, officials, and a good part of the bourgeoisie, all retaining their prejudices as members of separate orders but for whom the rent, and to a large extent the seigneury, were becoming common denominators. But to surrender completely to class terminology is to gloss over the divisions and complications that made the Old Regime what it was.

The influence of France upon Canada has been overwhelming. Canada also had an influence upon the mother country, on the fortunes of its imperial policy and of its economy. In the great port cities, business people and Marine officials knew much about Canada, and it often entered into their calculations. But beyond the few ports that dominated its trade and the inner circles of officials who directed its destinies, the image of Canada impinged very little upon the French imagination. A modest stream of travel books continued to tease Frenchmen with notions of the exotic, although for exoticism Canada could not compete with South America, which seems to have constituted the French notion of the New World, an unknown jungle onto which one could project the wildest fantasy.[7] The Canadian Indian, however, did not lose his fascination, and the Baron de Lahontan's *Mémoires de l'Amérique septentrionale*, published in 1703, transmuted him into the Noble Savage and secured him a place in the world of French letters.

The chanting of the Te Deum Laudamus in Quebec's cathedral on that last Sunday of August, 1744, before a congregation that included Pontbriand, Beauharnois, Hocquart, many other officials whom we might recognize, a goodly representation of the trading community, and so many ordinary Canadian men, women, and children, is the last historical scene that we behold. For the participants, of course, life went on. It brought them more than their share of pain and of adventure. Some of them, perhaps, lived happily ever after.

Finding the Path: A Note on Sources and Bibliography

The great French administrative series of dispatches and enclosures that passed between the King and his ministers and the governors and intendants in Canada, Acadia, Ile Royale, and the other French colonies remains the documentary backbone of the written history of New France. These have always been complemented by the archives of the Church and the religious orders. New historiographical preoccupations have brought hitherto neglected sources to the historian's desk. Principal among these are business papers, the files of notaries, and the records of law courts. Here is the documentation of private lives and of commerce, material sometimes amenable to statistical treatment.

The reader who wishes to begin at the beginning may consult Erwin K. Welsch (ed.), *Libraries and Archives in France: A Handbook* (Pittsburgh, 1973). An overview of relevant French administrative archives is provided in Didier Neuville, *Etat sommaire des Archives de la Marine antérieures à la Révolution* (Paris, 1898) and in Pierre Boyer et al., *Marine et Outremer*, Vol. III of *Les Archives nationales: état général des fonds* (Paris, 1980), each volume with its own virtues. The Public Archives of Canada (PAC) has published a *Guide des sources de l'histoire du Canada conservées en France* (Ottawa, 1982). The vast number of French documents as well as British documents of the colonial period that are duplicated in Canada as transcriptions or microfilms together with many colonial documents both public and private are catalogued in the PAC's *General Inventory Manuscripts*, Vols. 1 to 3 (Ottawa, 1971-76). The Province of Quebec has developed a comprehensive system of regional archival depositories. In addition to local documents public and private and copies of French documents, these archives now house the notarial archives of the colonial period that for so many years were hidden away in provincial court houses. *Archives du Québec: état général des archives publiques et privées* (Quebec, 1968) catalogues documents that at the time of publication were housed in the Quebec City depository. Some of these have now been transferred to other centres. The great religious houses in the Province of Quebec all possess archives. Of these none is richer in documentation and more welcoming to the researcher than the Archives du Séminaire de Québec in Quebec City. This archive does not publish a catalogue but has a comprehensive card index of its holdings.

The quantity of published documents relevant to the history of New France is considerable. The bibliographies in the *Dictionary of Canadian Biography*, Vols. I to IV (Toronto, 1966-79) are the best guide to these. (They also provide an excellent bibliography of the secondary literature and, together with the *Index, Vols. I to IV* [Toronto, 1981], are the indispensable companion to every researcher on New France from tyro to professional.) The usefulness of published documents will be evident from the endnotes to the present work. It is nevertheless worth underscoring the importance for the historian of New France of the *Calendar of State Papers. Colonial Series: America and the West Indies* (London, 1860-   ; reprint, Vaduz, 1964-   ; editor varies) as an outsider's entrée to the British colonial documentation.

It is the peculiar fate of bibliographies never to become useless but to be always out of date. The only exception is the continuing bibliography, and the best of these is the "Bibliographie d'histoire de l'Amérique française (Publications récentes)" edited by Paul Aubin and Paul-André Linteau that has appeared regularly since 1967 in the *Revue d'histoire de l'Amérique française*. Less daunting productions and good starting points for the non-specialist are D.A. Muise et al., *A Reader's Guide to Canadian History*, Vol. I, *Beginnings to Confederation* (Toronto, 1982) and Jean-Jacques Messier, *Bibliographie relative à la Nouvelle-France* (Montreal, 1979).

Some of the most important writing on New France has never reached print but remains in the typescript of unpublished theses and dissertations. The present work is particularly indebted to this literature. The indispensable guide to these hidden treasures is the *Register of Post-Graduate Dissertations in Progress in History and Related Subjects* that is published annually by the Canadian Historical Association.

Journal articles on the history of New France appear in many surprising and unexpected places, including Italian journals hospitable to Canadian studies and French regional periodicals. The most important journals for the field are the aforementioned *Revue d'histoire de l'Amérique française* (Montreal), the *Canadian Historical Review* (Toronto), and *Histoire sociale/Social History* (Ottawa). Important articles from time to time appear in the *Revue française d'histoire d'outre-mer* (Paris), and the *William and Mary Quarterly* (Williamsburg, Va.), the latter being also the essential journal to inform the New

France specialist on the sayings and doings of his colleagues in the cognate American colonial field.

The journal *Ethnohistory* (Lubbock, Texas) has become increasingly useful as historians have become more interested in the role of the Indian in New France. Two volumes of the Smithsonian Institution's new *Handbook of North American Indians*, ed. W.C. Sturtevant, will be particularly useful for the study of New France: Vol. VI, June Helm, ed., *Subarctic* (Washington, 1981) and Vol. XV, Bruce Trigger, ed., *Northeast* (Washington, 1978).

It is difficult to find one's way about New France without good maps, and these have always been in short supply. Marcel Trudel, *Atlas de la Nouvelle France/An Atlas of New France* (Quebec, 1973) is a cut above the standard school atlas and includes both original period maps and maps drawn by Dr. Trudel himself. Volume I, ed. R. Cole Harris, of the *Historical Atlas of Canada/Atlas historique du Canada*, William G. Dean, Director (Toronto, forthcoming) will do much to orient errant historians – and to standardize troublesome spellings!

Of general histories of New France, there are few that can be recommended to the non-specialist, who stands most in need of such. The present volume constitutes part of an extended general history with its companions in the Canadian Centenary Series: Marcel Trudel, *The Beginnings of New France, 1524-1663* (Toronto, 1973); W.J. Eccles, *Canada Under Louis XIV, 1663-1701* (Toronto, 1964); and G.F.G. Stanley, *New France: The Last Phase, 1744-1760* (Toronto, 1968). W.J. Eccles's two one-volume histories, *The Canadian Frontier, 1534-1760* (New York, 1969) and *France in America* (New York, 1972), have not been superseded and include excellent bibliographical essays.

The history of New France cannot be written without reference to the history of France itself. For narrative history in the grand manner, the reader will still have recourse to the magisterial Ernest Lavisse et al., *Histoire de France depuis les origines jusqu'à la Révolution* (Paris, 1901-10) and the great works of the last century. The French remain masters of the discipline and continue to pose inspired questions and answer them by means of the most advanced theory and techniques. New approaches associated (although by no means exclusively) with the journal *Annales: économies, sociétés, civilisations* (Paris) received the cachet of mainstream acceptance by being admitted into the pages of *L'Histoire et ses méthodes*, Charles Samaran, ed., "Encyclopédie de la Pleiade" (Paris, 1961). The proceedings of a 1965 colloquium at the Ecole normale supérieure de Saint-Cloud were published as a book that became widely influential: *L'Histoire sociale: sources et méthodes* (Paris, 1967). The continuing development of this rich historiography can be followed in Jacques Le Goff, ed., *La Nouvelle Histoire*, "Les Encyclopédies du savoir moderne" (Paris, 1978).

The journal articles, the monographs, and the documents upon which the present volume has drawn are all fully cited (and in many cases discussed) in the endnotes. They reveal both the perennial need to consider and reconsider the primary sources and the great debt that the modern historian necessarily must owe to others.

Notes

ICS	*Inventaire des insinuations du Conseil souverain,* ed. P.G. Roy (Beauceville, 1921)
MVHR	*Mississippi Valley Historical Review*
NYCD	*Documents Relative to the Colonial History of the State of New York Procured in Holland, England and France,* ed. John R. Brodhead and Edward B. O'Callaghan, Vols. IV-VI, IX, X (Albany, 1853-61)
PAC Report	Annual report of the PAC (title style varies)
RAPQ	*Rapport de l'archiviste de la Province de Québec,* later *RAQ*
RAQ	*Rapport des archives du Québec* continuing *RAPQ*
RHAF	*Revue d'histoire de l'Amérique française*
WMQ	*William and Mary Quarterly*

NOTES TO CHAPTER ONE

1. Guillaume Delisle in AM, Hydrographie, 2 JJ 57 (ex. 115^{xi}) 12 E, "Des descouvertes qui ont été faites dans l'Amérique" (1702).

NOTES TO CHAPTER TWO

1. Viner's article "Power versus Plenty as Objectives of Foreign Policy in the Seventeenth and Eighteenth Centuries" is reprinted in D.C. Coleman, ed., *Revisions in Mercantilism: Debates in Economic History* (London, 1969) together with seven other well-chosen articles. This collection with its excellent bibliography gives a good idea of the dispute, highly tinged by ideology, over the meaning of the term "mercantilism." As with most "isms," getting a grip on this chameleon is not easy. Charles Wilson's pamphlet, *Mercantilism* (London, 1958; reprinted 1963) will also be of considerable assistance. Beginning with Adam Smith's caricature published in 1776 in *The Wealth of Nations,* Book IV, the mercantilists' reputation has suffered at the hands of economists. In 1936 John Maynard Keynes came to their defence in the appendix to his *General Theory of Employment, Interest and Money*; since that time, they have received more sympathetic study. The classic exposition, Eli F. Heckscher's *Mercantilism* (2nd ed., ed. E.F. Soderland, London, 1965, 2 vols.), remains essential for its factual information, although its argument is now regarded by historians as wrongheaded. Net gain from Jacob Viner's *Studies in the Theory of International Trade* (New York, 1965) and the brilliant and sympathetic treatment in Joseph A. Schumpeter's *History of Economic Analysis* (New York, 1954) varies directly with the reader's grasp of economic theory. The present treatment of mercantilism depends heavily upon the magisterial volumes by Charles W. Cole, *Colbert and a*

Century of French Mercantilism (New York, 1939), 2 vols., and *French Mercantilism 1683-1700* (New York, 1943) as well as J.J. Spengler, "Mercantilist and Physiocratic Growth Theory," in B.F. Hoselitz *et al.*, *Theories of Economic Growth* (Glencoe, Ill., 1960), pp. 3-64, and Lionel Rothkrug, *Opposition to Louis XIV* (Princeton, 1965), in which, however, the definition of mercantilism, which includes royal absolutism and mechanistic theory, is far too broad. Pierre Vilar, *Or et monnaie dans l'histoire*, Collection Science Flammarion (Paris, 1974) has some very sensible things to say about bullionism. See also nn. 2 and 4 below.

2. "Peasant Society and the Image of Limited Good," *American Anthropologist* 67 (1965): 293-315 (quotation, p. 296).

3. Cole, *Colbert*, I: 334.

4. The model provided in Robert B. Ekelund Jr. and Robert D. Tollison, *Mercantilism As a Rent-Seeking Society: Economic Regulation in Historical Perspective* (College Station, Tex., 1981) is limited in its capacity to explain the historical facts.

5. Charles de La Roncière, *Le Crépuscule du grand règne: l'apogée de la guerre de course*, Vol. VI of *Histoire de la Marine française* (Paris, 1932), anglophobic, militant, and an embarrassment to read, gives a histrionic account of the decline of the navy and is content to quote whatever gossip is at hand – the quotation is from p. 311. Georges Lacour-Gayet, *La Marine militaire de la France sous le règne de Louis XV* (Paris, 1910) cuts the acid with Pontchartrain's defence of himself, pp. 27-29, but takes no sides. It is entirely likely that Pontchartrain's physical defects had an adverse effect upon his character, producing an inferiority complex, anger, and aggression. They may also be related to the humane attitude he showed toward suffering inferiors, which was in marked contrast to his gruffness toward everyone else.

6. Marcel Giraud, "Tendances humanitaires à la fin du règne de Louis XIV," *Revue historique* 209 (1953): 217-37, and "Crise de conscience et d'autorité à la fin du règne de Louis XIV," *Annales: ESC* 7 (1952): 172-90; Louise Dechêne, ed., *La Correspondance de Vauban relative au Canada* (Quebec, 1968), pp. 6-7.

7. Dechêne, *Correspondance de Vauban*, p. 23, Vauban à Pontchartrain, Lille, 7 jan. 1699.

8. Ibid., pp. 23-30, Vauban à Pontchartrain, Lille, 7 jan. 1699, with the Minister's marginalia; Minister's reply, Versailles, 21 jan. 1699, pp. 30-36; Vauban's response, n.d., pp. 37-43; Vauban, "Moyen de rétablir nos colonies de l'Amérique et de les accroître en peu de temps (28 av. 1699)," in Albert de Rochas d'Aiglun, ed., *Vauban: sa famille, et ses écrits, ses oisivetés, et sa correspondance* (Paris, 1910), II:413-40.

9. Compare "Moyen de rétablir," p. 426, with Cole, *Colbert*, II: 78.

10. Dechêne, *Correspondance de Vauban*, pp. 26-27, marginalia to Vauban à Pontchartrain, Lille, 7 jan. 1699.

11. Ibid.

12. AC, B 34 pt. 1: 15, Mémoire du Roi aux Vaudreuil et Bégon, Marly, 15 juin 1712; 27 pt. 3: 231r, Ministre à Raudot, Versailles, 9 juin 1706; 34 pt. 1: 78, Ministre à Bégon, Marly, 27 juin 1712.

13. Dechêne, *Correspondance de Vauban*, p. 31, Pontchartrain à Vauban, Versailles, 21 jan. 1699.

14. AC, B 24: 20, "Mémoire pour servir d'instruction au Comte Denos choisis par le roy pour commander dans les Isles françoises," Marly, 9 fév. 1701. See also ibid., fol. 236, Pontchartrain à Galiffet, Versailles, 7 déc. 1701, and 20: 22, Pontchartrain à Villebon, Versailles, 26 mars 1698.

15. Dechêne, *Correspondance de Vauban*, p. 32, Pontchartrain à Vauban, Versailles, 21 jan. 1699.

16. Cole, *French Mercantilism*, pp. 229 (quotation), 267-69, and Warren C. Scoville, "The French Economy in 1700-1701: An Appraisal of the Deputies of Trade," *Journal of Economic History* 22 (1962): 231-52, are revised in Thomas J. Schaeper, *The French Council of Commerce, 1700-1715: A Study of Mercantilism after Colbert* (Columbus, 1983).

17. Dale Miquelon, *Dugard of Rouen: French Trade to Canada and the West Indies, 1729-1770* (Montreal, 1978), p. 134.

18. Rothkrug, *Opposition to Louis XIV*, finds earlier roots for opposition to mercantilism and absolutism, usually identified with the Enlightenment, while John F. Bosher, *The Single Duty Project: A Study of the Movement for a French Customs Union in the Eighteenth Century* (London, 1964) projects forward the reforming spirit of Colbertism, showing that reforms usually credited to physiocracy were the work of Colbertist administrators.

19. AC, B 34 pt. 1: 78, Pontchartrain à Bégon, Marly, 27 juin 1712.

20. Quoted in Henri Legoherel, *Les Trésoriers généraux de la Marine, 1517-1788* (Paris, 1965), pp. 211-12.

21. Quoted in Alfred T. Mahan, *The Influence of Sea Power upon History, 1660-1783* (1890; reprinted Boston, 1918), p. 213 n. 1.

22. Geoffrey Symcox, *The Crisis of French Sea Power, 1688-1697: From the Guerre d'Escadre to the Guerre de Course* (The Hague, 1974); Cole, *French Mercantilism*, p. 108; Rothkrug, *Opposition to Louis XIV*, pp. 384-85, n. 12.

23. John S. Bromley, "The French Privateering War, 1702-1713," in Henry E. Bell and Richard L. Ollard, eds., *Historical Essays, 1600-1750, Presented to David Ogg* (London, 1963), p. 207 (quotation); "Mémoire sur la Caprérie" in Rochas d'Aiglun, *Vauban*, I: 454-61; Symcox, *Crisis of French Sea Power*, pp. 177-87.

24. Bromley, "The Privateering War," pp. 208-10; Symcox, *Crisis of French Sea Power*, p. 150; Arthur M. Wilson, *French Foreign Policy during the Administration of Cardinal Fleury, 1726-1743* (Cambridge, Mass., 1936), pp. 83–86.

25. For general background, David B. Horn, *Great Britain and Europe in the Eighteenth Century* (Oxford, 1967), and

John B. Wolf, *Louis XIV* (New York, 1968). On the partition treaties, see Frances G. Davenport, *European Treaties Bearing on the History of the United States and Its Dependencies* III (Washington, 1934), and Henri Vast, *La Succession d'Espagne, traités d'Utrecht, de Rastadt, et de Bade (1713-1714)*, Vol. III of *Les Grands Traités du règne de Louis XIV* (Paris, 1899).

26. Marcel Giraud, *Histoire de la Louisiane française*, 4 vols. (Paris, 1953-74), I: pt. 1.

27. *PAC Report, 1899, Supplement*, p. 334, Memorial to serve as instructions to D'Iberville, 23 July 1698.

28. Ibid., p. 342, Memorial to serve as instructions to D'Iberville, n.d.

29. Verner W. Crane, *The Southern Frontier, 1670-1732* (Durham, N.C., 1928), Chaps. 2, 3 and 5.

30. *PAC Report, 1899, Supplement*, p. 103, Minister to Callière and Champigny, 31 May 1701.

31. W.J. Eccles, *Canada under Louis XIV*, Canadian Centenary Series No. 3 (Toronto, 1964), p. 249.

32. W.J. Eccles, *Frontenac: The Courtier Governor* (Toronto, 1959), pp. 285-95, and in brief in Eccles, *Canada under Louis XIV*, pp. 202-4, in which volume the phrase "compact colony policy" was coined. See also Yves F. Zoltvany, *Philippe de Rigaud de Vaudreuil, Governor of New France, 1703-1725*, Carleton Library (Toronto, 1974), pp. 37-38. The key documents are calendared in *PAC Report, 1899, Sup-*

plement, pp. 94-106, 316-32. For direct evidence that the Pontchartrains knew what they were giving up and of their unrealistic appraisal of the importance of Indian alliances to Canada, see AC, B19 pt. 1: 72, "Mémoire du Roy pour les Srs de Frontenac et de Champigny," Versailles, 26 mai 1696; pt. 3: 223, "Mémoire du Roy . . ." 27 av. 1697.

33. AC, C11A 19: 3, Callière et Champigny au Ministre, 5 oct. 1701.

34. Vast, *La Succession d'Espagne*, pp. 207-8.

35. PAC, MG 5 A-1 16: 39-80 (A.E. vol. 208), "Mémoire pour servir d'Instruction au Sr. Comte de Tallard . . ." 7 juil. 1698.

36. Ibid., 15: 53 (A.E. vol. 180), Tallard au Ministre, Londres, 10 mars 1699; 16: 101 (A.E. vol. 208), Pontchartrain à Tallard, Versailles, 24 fév. 1699.

37. Ibid., 15: 51 (A.E. vol. 180), Tallard à Pontchartrain, Londres, 3 mars 1699.

38. Ibid., 15: 58 (A.E. vol. 180), "Projet de lettre de Mr de Pontchartrain à Monsr le Comte de frontenac tel quil avoit esté proposé par les commissaires de france; projet de lettre de Monsr de Pontchartrain à Mr le Comte de frontenac qu'on en est convenu." AC, B 20: 135, Louis XIV à Frontenac, 25 mars 1699.

39. *PAC Report, 1899, Supplement*, pp. 325-26, Royal Memorial to MM. de Frontenac and de Champigny, 27 Ap. 1697.

40. PAC, MG 5 A-1 15: 51 (A.E. vol. 180), Tallard à Pontchartrain, Londres, 3 mars 1699.

41. Peter Wraxall, *An Abridgement of the Indian Affairs Con-*

tained in Four Folio Volumes, Transacted in the Colony of New York, from the Year 1678 to the Year 1751, ed. C.H. McIlwain (Cambridge, Mass., 1915; reprinted New York, 1968), p. 33; *CSPCS* 18: item 167, Bellomont to Lords of Trade, 28 Feb. 1700.

42. PAC, MG 5 A-1 15: 51 (A.E. vol. 180), Tallard à Pontchartrain, Londres, 3 mars 1699.

43. H. Têtu and Charles-O. Gagnon, eds., *Mandements, lettres pastorales et circulaires des éveques de Québec*, 2 vols. (Quebec, 1887, 1888), I: 206-7.

44. *CSPCS* 18: item 167, Bellomont to Lords of Trade, Boston, 28 Feb. 1700; item 845, same to same, New York, 17 Oct. 1700; Wraxall, *Abridgement*, pp. 34-35; *CSPCS* 18: item 466 iii, "Observations of Robert Livingston, Secretary for the Indian Affairs, in his voyage to the Onnondage in April 1700"; 19: item 436, Livingston to Lords of Trade, New York, 13 May 1701.

45. *CSPCS* 18: item 167, Bellomont to Lords of Trade, Boston, 28 Feb. 1700.

46. Ibid., 19: item 436, Livingston to Lords of Trade, New York, 13 May 1701.

47. Ibid. Our understanding of the peace of 1700-1701 is materially altered if we take account of the aims, victories, and gains of Canada's western allies. See, *inter alia*, Donald B. Smith, "Who Are the Mississauga?" *Ontario History* 67 (1975): 211-22; Leroy V. Eid, "The Ojibwa-Iroquois War: The War the Five Nations Did Not Win," *Ethnohistory* 26 (1979): 297-324; Victor Konrad, "An Iroquois Frontier: The North Shore of Lake Ontario in the Late Seventeenth Century," *Journal of Historical Geography* 7 (1981): 129-44.

48. T.E. Norton, *The Fur Trade in Colonial New York, 1686-1776* (Madison, Wis., 1974), pp. 19-20.

49. *CSPCS* 18: item 666 vi, "Propositions of the Five Nations to Commissioners, Albany, 30 April 1700." See also enclosure iv, "Memorial of Johannes Groenendyk and Abraham Provoost, lately come from Onondage, 16 June 1700."

50. Ibid., 18: item 845, Bellomont to Lords of Trade, New York, 17 Oct. 1700; Wraxall, *Abridgement*, p. 37.

51. *CSPCS* 18: item 666 vi, "Propositions of the Five Nations to Commissioners, Albany, 30 April 1700."

52. AC, C11A 18: 79, "Réponse de Monsieur le Chevalier de Callières," 27 juin 1700.

53. Ibid., fol. 139, "Du 3 septembre 1700" (treaty).

54. Ibid., 19: 114, Callière au Ministre, Québec, 4 oct. 1701.

55. *CSPCS* 19: item 758 vii, "Journal of Capt. Johannes Bleeker junr. and David Schuyler, Journey to Onnondage," Albany, 2 June 1701.

56. AC, C11A 19: 41-44, "Ratification de la paix." Frequently the treaty of 8 Sept. 1700 is wrongly regarded as preliminaries and the ratification as the treaty. See facsimile signatures in *NYCD* IX: 722, and the version of treaty, ratification, and relevant negotiations in Claude Bacqueville de la Potherie, *Histoire de l'Amérique septentrionale* (Paris, 1722), Vol. II.

57. AC, C11A 19: 112, Callière

au Ministre, Québec, 6 août 1701.

58. *PAC Report, 1899, Supplement*, p. 103, Meetings of M. de Callière with the Iroquois chiefs, 1 (7?) August 1701; AC, C11A 19: 114, Callière au Ministre, 4 oct. 1701.

59. AC, C11A 19: 123, Callière au Ministre, Québec, 31 oct. 1701. Most accounts say this occurred a few days later; however, this letter says "yesterday." Some Mohawks, who perhaps were not present, came to ratify on 4 July 1702 (*PAC Report, 1899, Supplement*, p. 104, from Moreau St. Méry Collection 6: 308).

60. *CSPCS* 19: item 758 viii, "Conference of Lt. Gov. Nanfan with the Indians, 10 July 1701." See also Norton, *Fur Trade in New York*, pp. 25-26; Allan W. Trelease, *Indian Affairs in Colonial New York: The Seventeenth Century* (Ithaca, N.Y., 1960), p. 362; and William T. Morgan, "The Five Nations and Queen Anne," *MVHR* 13 (1926-27): 169-89, see p. 176 and n. 29.

61. *CSPCS* 19: item 758 viii, "Conference of Lt. Gov. Nanfan with the Indians, 10 July 1701."

62. AC, C11A 19: 3, Callière et Champigny au Ministre, Québec, 5 oct. 1701.

63. Ibid., fol. 232, "Projets sur la Nouvelle Angleterre, Canada, 1701."

64. David A. Armour, "The Merchants of Albany, New York, 1686-1760," Ph.D. dissertation, Northwestern University, Evanston, Ill., 1965, pp. 88-90. Unfortunately there is no corroboration in C11A dispatches for the curious story of the meeting of Callière and Schuyler.

65. *CSPCS* 20: item 1009 (ii) e, "His Excellency to the Five Nations, Albany, 15 July 1702."

66. Ibid., enclosure b, "Proposals of the Twightwighs and Tionondadees from Detroit, Albany, 10 July 1702." Note the similarity to the seventh belt of four of the Iroquois nations to Callière in C11A, 18: 81, 18 July 1700.

67. Ibid., 19: item 38, Bellomont to Lords of Trade, New York, 16 Jan. 1701; doc. 758 viii, "Conference between Lt.-Gov. Nanfan and the Five Nations of Indians," Albany, 19 July 1701; Armour, "Merchants of Albany," pp. 74-76.

68. *CSPCS* 20: item 1009 (ii) (i), "Conference held at Albany between governor Lord Cornbury and the Indians, July 9-20, 1702," Cornbury's reply, Albany, 20 July 1702.

69. Ibid., enclosure d, "Answer to Twightwighs and Tionondadees, Albany, 14 July 1702."

70. Yves F. Zoltvany, "New France and the West, 1701-1713," *CHR* 46 (1965): 301-22, p. 308.

71. Kenneth M. Morrison, "The People of the Dawn: The Abnakis and Their Relations with New England and New France, 1602-1727," Ph.D. dissertation, University of Maine, Orono, 1965, and Pierre-André Sévigny, *Les Abénaquis: habitat et migrations (17e et 18e siècles)*, Collection Cahiers d'histoire des Jésuites (Montreal, 1976), supplant earlier studies. On tribal taxonomy, see Chap. 1 of each. The notion of an Abenaki Confederacy has resulted from the ignoring of chronological and other obscurities in Frank G.

Speck, "The Eastern Algonkian Wabanaki Confederacy," *American Anthropologist*, new ser., 17 (1915): 492-508. See Morrison, pp. 40-41.

72. On the Abbadies de Saint-Castin, see *DCB* II: 3-7; III: 3.

73. Morrison, "People of the Dawn," p. 273.

74. AC, B 20: 22v, Ministre à Villebon, Versailles, 26 mars 1698.

75. Ibid., 22: 144, Mémoire du roi à De Brouillan, Versailles, 23 mars 1701.

76. J.B. Brebner, *New England's Outpost: Acadia before the Conquest of Canada* (New York, 1927), p. 45.

77. AC, C11D 1: 150-51, Concession à Bergier, 6 jan. 1682; fols. 198-98v, Mémoire de l'ambassadeur de France sur l'Acadie, 1685; ibid., C11G 8: 68, Arrêt contre les héritiers du Marquis de Chevry, 10 sept. 1714; *ICS*, p. 107, arrêt, 20 mars 1703; "Bergier," "Charles Duret de Chevry de la Boulaye," *DCB* I: 89-90, 298-99.

78. AC, C11D 4: 55-82, "6 8bre 1701 . . . Mémoire de ce qui regarde les intérests du Roy touchant Lestablissement que Sa Majesté a dessein de faire dans Sa province de Lacadie."

79. Morrison, "People of the Dawn," p. 278.

80. PAC, MG 5 A-1 16: 39-80 (A.E. vol. 208), "Mémoire pour servir d'Instruction au Sr. Comte de Tallard . . ." 7 juil. 1698; fol. 119 (A.E. vol. 209), Tallard au Ministre, 17 juin 1699; fol. 120 (A.E. vol. 185), "Copie, Tallard au Ministre, 19 fév. 1700"; AC, B 22: 122, Ministre à Tallard, Versailles, 2 juin 1700. The original French demand for the Kennebec as frontier was thought to be supported by the Temple-Grandfontaine Treaty of 1670, but on the face of it, the document will not support such a construction. See PAC, MG 5 B-1 7: 2.

81. PAC, MG 5 A-1 16: 39-80 (A.E. vol. 208), "Mémoire pour servir d'Instruction au Sr. Comte de Tallard . . ." 7 juil. 1698; Davenport, *European Treaties*, II: 309, 324, Treaty of Neutrality, 1686, Agreement 1687.

82. PAC, MG 5 A-1 15: 120-23, (A.E. vol. 185), "Copie de la lettre escritte à monsieur le comte de Pontchartrain par Monsieur le Comte de Tallard le 19 févier 1700."

83. Ibid., fols. 140-41 (A.E. vol. 189), "Estrait de la lettre de Monsieur le Comte de Tallard escritte à Monsieur le Comte de Pontchartrain le 14 juillet 1700."

NOTES TO CHAPTER THREE

1. Philippe Sagnac and Alexandre de Saint-Leger, *Louis XIV (1661-1715): la prépondérance française*, Peuple et Civilisations (Paris, 1949), p. 461, but see Mark A. Thomson, "Louis XIV and the Origins of the War of the Spanish Succession," in Ragnild Hatton and John S. Bromley, eds., *William III and Louis XIV: Essays 1680-1720 by and for Mark A. Thomson* (Toronto, 1968), pp. 140-61.

2. The story of Cadillac is drawn from the following articles by Jean Delanglez, all published in *Mid-*

America: "Cadillac's Early Years in America," 26 (1944): 3-39; "Antoine Laumet, alias Cadillac, Commandant at Michilimackinac," 27 (1945): 108-32, 188-216, 232-56; "The Genesis and Building of Detroit," 30 (1948): 75-104; "Cadillac at Detroit," 30 (1948): 152-76; "Cadillac, Proprietor of Detroit," 32 (1950): 155-88, 226-58; "Cadillac's Last Years," 33 (1951): 3-42.

3. Reuben G. Thwaites, ed., *The French Regime in Wisconsin*, in *Collections of the State Historical Society*, Vols. 16-18 (Madison, Wis., 1902-8), 16: 126. Note that the memoir attributed to Dulhut c. 1686 is really Cadillac's of 1701, unless Cadillac had access to such a document as that posited by the editor, which seems highly unlikely.

4. Ibid., p. 87 (altered).

5. Yves F. Zoltvany, *Philippe de Rigaud de Vaudreuil, Governor of New France, 1703-1725*, Carleton Library (Toronto, 1974), pp. 55-56.

6. AC, C11A 20: 26-77, d'Aigremont à Pontchartrain, 14 nov. 1708.

7. Zoltvany, *Vaudreuil*, pp. 82-84.

8. Delanglez, "Cadillac at Detroit," 30 (1948): 153-62.

9. Ibid., "Proprietor of Detroit," 32 (1950): 240.

10. Ibid., p. 254.

11. Ibid., "Last Years," 33 (1951): 24.

12. AC, B 22: 226, Ministre à Vaudreuil, 20 juin 1703; Zoltvany, *Vaudreuil*, p. 216.

13. Thomas E. Norton, *The Fur Trade in Colonial New York, 1686-1776* (Madison, 1974), p. 129.

14. The present treatment of Vaudreuil's Indian policy is largely based upon Zoltvany, *Vaudreuil*. Footnotes have been kept to a minimum.

15. *PAC Report, 1899, Supplement*, pp. 354 (31 May 1701), 360 (6 May 1702), 367-68 (20 June 1703 and n.d., royal memorial to Callière and Beauharnois [1703]).

16. The idea was perhaps not "unthinkable." It certainly crossed Vaudreuil's mind, and he put it to paper in the excerpt described by Zoltvany as the "Vaudreuil doctrine" (*Vaudreuil*, pp. 51, 82).

17. Delanglez, "Proprietor of Detroit," 32 (1950): 229-30.

18. Ibid., p. 250.

19. AC, F3 2: 277-79, Callière aux Abénakis, 1 oct. 1702; Zoltvany, *Vaudreuil*, pp. 41-42; Kenneth M. Morrison, "The People of the Dawn: The Abnakis and Their Relations with New England and New France, 1602-1727," Ph.D. dissertation, University of Maine, Orono, 1975, pp. 277, 286 (second quotation), where the mistaken impression is given that Callière enjoined neutrality even after the declaration of war.

20. Morrison, "People of the Dawn," p. 287; Zoltvany, *Vaudreuil*, pp. 45-49.

21. *PAC Report, 1899, Supplement*, pp. 369 (18 July 1703), 370 (6 June 1703), 375 (14 June 1704), to Vaudreuil and royal memorial to Vaudreuil and Beauharnois.

22. "Benjamin Church," "Jacques-François de Monbeton de Brouillan," *DCB* II: 145-46, 478-81.

23. George M. Waller, *Samuel Vetch, Colonial Enterpriser* (Chapel Hill, N.C., 1960), p. 82, downplays the idea of trade, but

Zoltvany, *Vaudreuil*, based on Canadian sources, disagrees.

24. AC, B 27: 47, Pontchartrain à Vaudreuil, 17 juin 1705.

25. Morrison, "People of the Dawn," pp. 287-92.

26. Ibid., pp. 295-98.

27. Zoltvany, *Vaudreuil*, pp. 77-78; "Daniel d'Auger de Subercase," *DCB* II: 35-39.

28. Zoltvany, *Vaudreuil*, pp. 74-79.

29. Ibid., pp. 79-80.

30. Quoted in Waller, *Vetch*, p. 75.

31. Norton, *Fur Trade in New York*, p. 130.

32. Material on Vetch and the attempts to conquer Canada is taken from Waller, *Vetch*.

33. Bruce T. McCully, ed., "Catastrophe in the Wilderness: New Light on the Canadian Expedition of 1709," *WMQ* 11 (1954): 442.

34. Zoltvany, *Vaudreuil*, p. 103.

35. Waller, *Vetch*, pp. 152-63.

36. Ibid., p. 166.

37. Ibid., p. 171.

38. *CSPCS* 25: item 194, "The Four Indian Kings ('Sachems'). Speech to the Queen, London, April 20, 1710"; W.T. Morgan, "The Five Nations and Queen Anne," *MVHR* 13 (1926-27): 182.

39. Zoltvany, *Vaudreuil*, pp. 104-5.

40. *CSPCS* 25: item 412, "Articles of Capitulation," 2 Oct. 1710; "Subercase," *DCB* II: 35-39.

41. *CSPCS* 25: item 673, "A Journal of ye Travails of Major John Livingstone," Annapolis Royal, 23 Feb. 1711.

42. G.M. Trevelyan, *England under the Stuarts* (Harmondsworth, Middlesex, 1960), p. 484; Maurice Ashley, *England in the Seventeenth Century, 1603-1714*

(Harmondsworth, Middlesex, 1961), p. 210; Waller, *Vetch*, pp. 208-10.

43. A.T. Mahan, *The Influence of Sea Power upon History, 1660-1783* (1890; reprinted Boston, 1918), p. 216.

44. *CSPCS* 25: item 859, George Clarke to Lords of Trade, May 28, 1711, New York.

45. Norton, *Fur Trade in New York*, pp. 132-33.

46. Waller, *Vetch*, pp. 210-16; Gerald S. Graham, ed., *The Walker Expedition to Quebec, 1711* (Toronto, 1953), pp. 30-38. In the absence of any scholarly monograph, Graham's collection of documents remains the major study. "John Hill," "Sir Hovenden Walker," *DCB* II: 286-87, 658-62. Providential history and both lurid and amusing description are found in Jeanne-Françoise Juchereau de St Ignace and Marie-Andrée Duplessis de Ste Hélène, *Les Annales de l'Hôtel-Dieu de Québec, 1636-1716*, ed. Dom Albert Jamet (Quebec, 1939), pp. 359-72.

47. Zoltvany, *Vaudreuil*, pp. 108-9; Graham, *Walker Expedition*, p. 43.

48. Rev. John Buckingham, "A Diary of the Land Expedition against Crown Point in 1711," in *The Journals of Madame Knight and Mr. Rev. Buckingham from the Original Manuscripts Written in 1704 and 1710* (New York, 1825).

49. Juchereau de St Ignace, *Annales de l'Hôtel-Dieu*, p. 368.

50. The relevant documentation is in AC, C11A, vol. 33, some of it translated with errors and omissions in Thwaites, *French Regime*

in Wisconsin, 16: 267-95. The Battle of Detroit is narrated in François-Emile Audet, *Les Premiers Établissements français au pays des Illinois: la guerre des Renards* (Paris, 1938), in which the Fox-Iroquois-English connection is inflated into a conspiracy, and in Louise P. Kellogg, *The French Régime in Wisconsin and the Northwest* (Madison, 1925) and Zoltvany, *Vaudreuil*, both of which ignore Dubuisson's testimony and see the battle only as a tribal quarrel. See also Louise P. Kellogg, "The Fox Indians during the French Regime," *Wisconsin Historical Society Proceedings, 1907*, pp. 142-88.

51. Dubuisson's report, Detroit, 15 June 1712, in Thwaites, *French Regime in Wisconsin*, 16: 275.

52. Morrison, "People of the Dawn," pp. 298-313. See Treaty of Portsmouth, 13 July 1713, in the following: James P. Baxter, *Documentary History of the State of Maine Containing the Baxter Manuscripts*, 23 (Portland, Me., 1916), 37-50; Samuel Penhallow, *A History of the Wars of New-England with the Eastern Indians* (Boston, 1726), pp. 77-80, and Peter A. Cumming and N.H. Mickenberg, *Native Rights in Canada*, 2nd. ed. (Toronto, 1972), pp. 296-99.

53. Marcel Giraud, *Histoire de la Louisiane française*, 4 vols. (Paris, 1953-74), I: 195.

54. Charles de La Morandière, *Histoire de la pêche française de la morue dans l'Amérique septentrionale (Des origines à 1789)*, 2 vols (Paris, 1962), I: 493-95.

55. John S. Bromley, "The French Privateering War, 1702-1713," in Henry E. Bell and Richard L. Ollard, eds., *Historical Essays, 1600-1750, Presented to David Ogg* (London, 1963), pp. 216-17, 222; James S. Pritchard, "Ships, Men and Commerce: A Study of Maritime Activity in New France," Ph.D. dissertation, University of Toronto, 1971), pp. 268-75.

56. Mahan, *Sea Power*, pp. 208-9.

57. Trevelyan, *The Stuarts*, pp. 486, 492.

58. PAC, MG 5 A-1, vol. 17 (A.E. vol. 232), "Remis par M. Hooke au Marquis de Torcy, février, 1711."

59. J.B. Colbert, Marquis de Torcy, "Mémoires du Marquis de Torcy, pour servir à l'histoire des négociations depuis le traité de Riswick jusqu'à la paix d'Utrecht," *Nouvelle collection des mémoires relatifs à l'histoire de France depuis le XIIIe siècle* 32 (Paris, 1854): 666-67. On Gaultier, see MG 5 B-2, vol. 17, "Fait en 1724 Decembre 31 par M le Dran, Chef du Dépôt des Affres. Etrangères."

60. Henri Vast, *La Succession d'Espagne, traités d'Utrecht, de Rastadt, et de Bade (1713-1714)*, Vol. III of *Les Grands Traités du règne de Louis XIV* (Paris, 1899): 39; Frances G. Davenport, *European Treaties Bearing on the History of the United States and Its Dependencies*, Vol. III (*1688-1715*) (Washington, 1934): 141.

61. "Réflexions générales," quoted in Vast, *La Succession d'Espagne*, 40.

62. PAC, MG 5 A-1, vol. 20 (A.E. vol. 237), untitled memorandum, 1712.

63. PAC, MG 5 A-1, vol. 18 (A.E. vol. 233): 88, "Délivré à Londres le 29 aoust/9 septembre 1711 avant Midy"; Davenport, *European Treaties* III: 147-49.

64. PAC, MG 5 A-1, vol. 18 (A.E. vol. 233): 111, Mesnager à Torcy, Londres, 25 sept./6 oct., 1711.

65. Ibid., fol. 95, Mesnager à Torcy, Londres, 21 sept./2 oct., 1711.

66. Ibid., A-3, vol. 1: 77-82 (A.E. vol. 232), "Règlement pour l'ouverture & la méthode des Conférences à Utrecht, & ce qui en dépend."

67. Willem Buys quoted in J. Drummond to Oxford, Aug. 28/ Sept. 8, 1711, in Davenport, *European Treaties* III: 154.

68. PAC, MG 5 A-3, vol. 1 (A.E. vol. 235), Plenipotentiaires au roi, Utrecht, 20 juin 1712.

69. PAC, MG 40 D (PRO, S.P. 103, vol. 98), Louis aux plenipotentiaires, 20 mars 1712.

70. Davenport, *European Treaties* III: 828-29 (A.E. vol. 250), Plenipotentiaires au roi, 12 av. 1713.

71. The French text of the Treaty of Utrecht is in ibid., III: 208-14. The English text quoted here is from C. Jenkinson, *A Collection of Treaties*, 3 vols. (London, 1785), II: 5-40.

72. E.E. Rich, "The Hudson's Bay Company and the Treaty of Utrecht," *Cambridge Historical Journal* 11 (1954): 183-203.

73. PAC, MG 5 A-3, vol. 3 (A.E. vol. 240), "Plenipres le 23 xbre 1712, Propositions"; "Addition à Mrs Les Plenipres, A Versailles le 23e xbre 1712."

74. PAC, MG 40 D (PRO, S.P. 103, vol. 98), "Réponses aux demandes faites par les Srs. Plenipotres d'Angleterre," 20 mars 1712 (Louis XIV and Torcy).

75. PAC, MG 5 A-3, vol. 3 (A.E. vol. 242), Chevry à ?, St Germain-en-Laye, 11 juil. 1712; "Copie de la lettre écrite à M. l'abbé de Polignac le 13e juillet 1712." The author was the son of Charles-François Duret de Chevry, Marquis de Villeneuve, a founder of the company. He appears to have believed he retained claims in the area.

76. See n. 74 above.

77. PAC, MG 40 D (PRO, S.P. 103, vol. 100), "Mémoire pour Mrs les Plenipotentres du Roy . . . 17 août 1712."

78. See n. 74 above.

NOTES TO CHAPTER FOUR

1. Nicholas Denys, *The Description and Natural History of the Coasts of North America*, ed. and trans. W.E. Ganong (Toronto, 1908), pp. 363, 365. Denys's beaver reach Moll's map via the De Fer map (Paris, 1698).

2. J.F. Crean, "Hats and the Fur Trade," *Canadian Journal of Economics and Political Science* 28 (1962): 373-86, at 375. This article and that by E.E. Rich (n. 8 below) form the start for work that must be done on the little-known histories of the hat industry and the marketing of beaver in Europe.

3. Carl J. Friedrich, *The Age of the Baroque, 1610-1660*, Rise of Modern Europe series (New York, 1952), p. 45.

4. Millia Davenport, *The Book of*

Costume (New York, 1948), I: 506, 508, plates on pp. 513, 531, 538; Maurice Leloir, *Dictionnaire du costume et de ses accessoires des armes et des étoffes des origines à nos jours* (Paris, 1951), pp. 85-87; Blanche Peyne, *History of Costume: From the Ancient Egyptians to the Twentieth Century* (New York, 1965) – compare Louis XIV's hat in the 1680s, fig. 371, with that of 1660, fig. 366.

5. Crean, "Hats and the Fur Trade," p. 380.

6. Charles W. Cole, *French Mercantilism, 1683-1700* (New York, 1943), pp. 68, 151.

7. Ibid., pp. 69-70.

8. E.E. Rich, "Russia and the Colonial Fur Trade," *Economic History Review*, 2nd ser., 7 (1955): 307-28.

9. Jacques Savary des Bruslons, ed., *Dictionnaire universal de commerce: contenant tout ce qui concerne le commerce qui se fait dans les quatre coins du monde*, 3 vols. (Amsterdam, 1726), I: 648.

10. Crean, "Hats and the Fur Trade," p. 384; Warren C. Scoville, *The Persecution of the Huguenots and French Economic Development, 1580-1720* (Berkeley and Los Angeles, 1960), pp. 228-30, 329; H.A. Innis, *The Fur Trade in Canada: An Introduction to Canadian Economic History*, rev. ed. (Toronto, 1970), p. 76, n. 133.

11. Cole, *French Mercantilism*, p. 68.

12. Innis, *Fur Trade*, pp. 64, 407 (quotation).

13. On the ancient practice of tax farming, see George T. Matthews, *The Royal General Farms in Eighteenth-Century France* (New York, 1958), Chap. 1. The colonial farm (*Domaine d'Occident*) had belonged to Colbert's West India Company and reverted to the King in 1674. Most of its rights were taxes. Those in Canada were a 10% ad valorum duty on wines, spirits, and tobacco entering the colony, a 25% tax in kind on beaver exported (the *quart*), a similar 10% tax on moose hides, and a 2% tax by weight on exported beaver intended to indemnify the farmer for deficiencies in weight or quality in the beaver received. There were also the fur-trade monopoly, known as the Traite de Tadoussac (lower St Lawrence posts), domainal dues and fines owed the King, and the beaver export privilege. See Mary A. Johnston, "The King's Domain: The Domain of the West in New France, 1675-1733," M.A. thesis, University of Western Ontario, 1961. The *Domaine* farmer paid at Quebec an *état des charges* or *état du domaine*, salaries and fixed charges of government in Canada. This was deducted from the lease price, the balance – the *parti du roi* – being paid into the coffers of the Controller General. The farmer's other principal obligation was to accept at a fixed price all beaver brought to his Quebec office. The profitability of the farm in all its aspects depended mainly upon the fortunes of the beaver trade, in other words, upon the ability of Canadians to pay.

14. Johnston, "King's Domain," p. 35; AN, G7, vol. 1312, item 235, "Cautions du bail du domaine d'occidt sous le nom de Louis Guigues . . . ."

15. Johnston, "King's Domain." See Chap. 2, n. 4 above.

16. Cole, *French Mercantilism*, pp. 72-73.

17. Savary des Bruslons, *Dictionnaire* I: 575-76. This is corroborated by AN, G7 vol. 1312, item 177, Arrêt du Conseil, 25 fév. 1702.

18. "Beaver Trade Agreement," *PAC Report*, 1928, p. 38.

19. AC, B 20: 141v-43v, "Arrest qui règle le prix des castors en Canada, A Versailles le 24 février 1699." On Canadian opinion, see Edward Borins, "La Compagnie du Nord, 1682-1700," M.A. thesis, McGill University, 1969, p. 176.

20. AC, B 20: 140v-41v, Ministre à Champigny, Versailles, 1 av. 1699. Cf. Chap. 2, n. 3 above. Daubenton de Villebois's mission is outlined in AN, G7 vol. 1312, item 181, Arrêt du Conseil d'Etat du roi, 9 fév. 1700, and Joseph Dufresne de Francheville, *Histoire de la Compagnie des Indes*, Vol. III, *Histoire générale et particulière des finances, où l'on voit l'origine, l'établissement, la perception, et la régie de toutes les impositions* . . . (Paris, 1738): 101, 407.

21. AC, C 11 A 17: 62, Champigny au Ministre, Québec, 20 oct. 1699.

22. Guy Frégault, "La Compagnie de la Colonie," in *Le XVIIIe siècle canadien: études*, Collection Constantes, 16 (Montreal, 1968): 242-88, provides a detailed narrative, mostly reliable. See also item 181, n. 20 above; *PAC Report, 1899, Supplement*, p. 99; Cole, *French Mercantilism*, pp. 75-76.

23. "Beaver Trade Agreement." The translation is not always good. This is really four documents, later clauses in some cases annulling earlier ones: original agreement, May 15, supplement, June 3, deposition with notary, June 9, Canadian ratification, Oct. 10, all 1700. The brief outlines of terms in Frégault, "La Compagnie de la Colonie," p. 247, and Johnston, "King's Domain," p. 77, are in error.

24. "Beaver Trade Agreement," p. 39.

25. Canada, Assembly of the Province of, *Edits et ordonnances: revus et corrigés d'après les pièces originales déposées aux archives provinciales* (Quebec, 1854), p. 280, "Règlement."

26. Ibid., p. 285, Arrêt du Conseil d'Etat, 31 mai 1701; Mandement du Roi, 31 mai 1701. These documents are also in AC, B22: 268-70 & 270v, where the *mandement* is entitled "lettres patentes."

27. Henri Lévy-Bruhl, *Histoire juridique des sociétés de commerce* (Paris, 1938), pp. 9-14, 42-63, 181, 225, 227. See also Savary des Bruslons, *Dictionnaire* I: 20, 1335.

28. Borins, "Compagnie du Nord," pp. 178-79, 52-53.

29. AC, C11A 18: 40, Champigny au Ministre, 17 oct. 1700.

30. *PAC Report, 1899, Supplement*, p. 104.

31. "Beaver Trade Agreement," p. 37, clause 4; AN, G7 vol. 1312, item 177, arrêt du Conseil d'Etat, 25 fév. 1702, and Déclaration du roi, 20 sept. 1701.

32. "François de Beauharnois de la Chaussaye," *DCB* III: 53.

33. AC, B23: 62, Instructions à Beauharnois, 6 mai 1702; 24: 102, Pontchartrain à Le Haguouis, Versailles, 6 av. 1701; 27: pt. 3: 203, Pontchartrain à Daguesseau, Versailles, 2 juin 1706; fol. 204, Mémoire du roi, Versailles, 9 juin 1701; AN, F12, vol. 799A, "Etat des Recettes et dépenses habituelles de la ferme de la colonie du Canada," Paris, 22 mai 1705; *PAC Report, 1899, Supplement*, p. 105.

34. AC, C11A 23: 4-13, "Raisons du mauvais état des affairs de la colonie de Canada," 1705 (Riverin).

35. Michel H. St. Amant, "The Public Life of Denis Riverin, 1675-1717," M.A. thesis, University of Western Ontario, 1976, pp. 143-47, 127.

36. Riverin, "Raisons du mauvais état." He presents a mass of figures of which one of the first is incorrect – the price of the farmer's inventory is given as 470,000 livres rather than 350,000. The figures cannot be consolidated into a single balance sheet, at least not without considerable elucidation from other sources – if such exist. In this regard, the presentation in Frégault, "La Compagnie de la Colonie," pp. 259-61, may give a false impression.

37. James S. Pritchard, "Ships, Men and Commerce: A Study of Maritime Activity in New France," Ph.D. dissertation, University of Toronto, 1971, pp. 263-67.

38. "Beauharnois," *DCB* III: 52.

39. "Antoine-Denis Raudot," "Jacques Raudot," *DCB* II: 549-61.

40. AC, C11A 23: 29, "Mémoire sur les affairs de la colonie de Canada," Paris, 10 mars 1705.

41. Jeanne-Françoise Juchereau de St Ignace and Marie-Andrée Duplessis de Ste Hélène, *Les Annales de l'Hôtel-Dieu de Québec, 1636-1716*, ed. Dom Albert Jamet (Quebec, 1939), p. 352.

42. St. Amant, "Denis Riverin," pp. 166-67; Johnston, "King's Domain," pp. 81-84; AC, B 29 pt. 1: 24, Arrêt, Versailles, 26 juin 1707. Jean-Baptiste Gayot is not to be confused with Nicolas Goy of Pasquier, Bourlet, and Goy and Goy, Dumoulin, Mercier as Adam Shortt appears to do. See index, *Documents Relating to Canadian Currency, Exchange and Finance during the French Period*, 2 vols. (Ottawa, 1925), Vol. II.

43. St. Amant, "Denis Riverin," p. 192; Johnston, "King's Domain," p. 99; AC, C11A 35: 282, "Deleberation fait au bureau du Corps des Maistres chapeliers de Paris, janvier 1715."

44. AC, C11A 17: 30, Callière et Champigny à Pontchartrain, Québec, 20 oct. 1699; 18: 40, Champigny à Pontchartrain, Québec, 17 oct. 1700.

45. AC, B 32, pt. 2: 107v, Pontchartrain à Raudot, Versailles, 23 mai 1710; fol. 112, Pontchartrain à Amelot, Versailles, 25 mai 1710; 35, pt. 3: 275v, Mémoire du Roi, Versailles, 25 jan. 1713; pt. 1: 19v, Pontchartrain à Amelot, Versailles, 31 jan. 1713; fol. 88v, "Pontchartrain aux interessés en la compagnie de castor," Versailles, 18 av. 1713.

46. Riverin, "Raisons du mauvais état."

47. BN, Nouvelles acquisitions françaises, 885, "Mémoire de l'état présent du commerce de France, 1707," p. 117. Typescript in PAC.

48. Guy Frégault, "Essai sur les finances canadiennes," in *Le XVIIIe siècle canadien: études*, Collection Constantes, 16 (Montreal, 1968): 289-363 at p. 295.

49. Pritchard, "Ships, Men and Commerce," pp. 255-56, 293-95.

50. Frégault, "Finances canadiennes," pp. 311-12.

51. AC, 33: 32, Pontchartrain à Beauharnois, Versailles, 16 mars 1711.

52. Shortt, *Canadian Currency*, I: 255, d'Aigremont to the Minister, Quebec, 15 Nov. 1713.

53. Henri Legoherel, *Les Trésoriers généraux de la Marine, 1517-1788* (Paris, 1965), pp. 197-99.

54. Ibid., pp. 203-4.

55. Ibid., pp. 264-66.

56. Ibid., pp. 187-90.

57. Ibid., pp. 102-3, 145-48.

58. Frégault, "Finances canadiennes," p. 304.

59. Legoherel, *Trésoriers*, pp. 94-95.

60. Frégault, "Finances canadiennes," p. 304.

61. "Nicolas Lanoullier de Boisclerc," *DCB* III: 352.

62. Shortt, *Canadian Currency*, I: 79, "Extract from the replies to the letters received from Canada during the present year 1686," 20 May 1686, and n. 2. Frégault, "Finances canadiennes," asserts incorrectly that the first use of bills was in 1691.

63. Shortt, *Canadian Currency*, II: 141, Ramezay to Minister, Quebec, 12 Oct. 1705.

64. Ibid., p. 145, "Ordinance ratifying cards," Quebec, 24 Oct. 1705.

65. Ibid., p. 207, "Memorandum of new card money prepared in the year 1710," at p. 209, is an example of cards and bills being thought of as alternatives. Frégault overemphasizes the settled and systematic character of the relations between the two in "Finances canadiennes," p. 310.

66. Ibid., p. 171, Messrs. Raudot to Minister, Quebec, 11 Nov. 1707.

67. Ibid., p. 179, Minister to Messrs. Raudot, Versailles, 6 June 1708.

68. Ibid., p. 205. To Minister, unsigned, Quebec, 22 Oct. 1710, and p. 209, "Memorandum of new card money prepared in the year 1710" (quotation); Frégault, "Finances canadiennes," p. 311.

69. Shortt, *Canadian Currency*, II: 219-23, Minister to Vaudreuil and Bégon, Marly, 26 June (1712).

70. "Michel Bégon de La Picardière," *DCB* III: 57-63; Kathryn Young, "Michel Bégon and the Direction of Economic Policy in French Canada from 1712 to 1726," M.A. thesis, University of Manitoba, 1984.

71. Shortt, *Canadian Currency*, II: 229-31, Bégon to Minister, Quebec, 12 Nov. 1712.

72. Ibid., pp. 238-47, various documents, 1713; p. 259, Minister to Vaudreuil and Bégon, Versailles, 19 Mar. 1714; pp. 261-63, Minister to Bégon, Versailles, 22 Mar. 1714; pp. 263-65, Minister to Vaudreuil and Bégon, Ver-

sailles, 22 Mar. 1714; pp. 267-71, Minister to Vaudreuil and Bégon, Versailles, 23 May 1714.

73. Ibid., p. 271, Minister to Bégon, Versailles, 23 May 1714.

74. Ibid., pp. 275-79, Vaudreuil and Bégon to Minister, n.p., n.d.

75. Ibid., pp. 299-303, Minister to Bégon, Marly, 10 July 1715; pp. 317-21, Bégon to Minister, Quebec, 7 Nov. 1715.

76. Ibid., pp. 275-79, Vaudreuil and Bégon to Minister, n.p. n.d.; Frégault, "Finances canadiennes," p. 317.

77. Shortt, *Canadian Currency*, I: 30, Minister to Desmarets, Marly, 17 July [1715].

78. John S. Bromley, "Le Commerce de la France de l'ouest et la guerre maritime (1702-1712)," *Annales du Midi* 65 (1953): 49-66.

79. Pritchard, "Ships, Men and Commerce," tables 2 and 4, pp. 488-89, 491.

80. Charles de La Morandière, *Histoire de la pêche française de la morue dans l'Amérique septentrionale (Des origines à 1789)*, 2 vols. (Paris, 1962), I: 505.

81. Marcel Delafosse, "Annexe – liste des navires partant de la Rochelle," in "Le trafic maritime franco-canadien, 1695-1715," paper presented at the International Colloquium on Colonial History, University of Ottawa, 1969.

82. Jean Hamelin, *Economie et société en Nouvelle-France* (Quebec, 1960), p. 61.

83. Pritchard, "Ships, Men and Commerce," p. 270, quoting C11A 21: 54v, Vaudreuil à Pontchartrain, 4 nov. 1703.

84. "Louis Prat," *DCB* II: 531.

85. Pritchard, "Ships, Men and Commerce," pp. 282-85.

86. Ibid., p. 275.

87. Ibid., p. 286.

88. Ibid., pp. 286-92.

89. Allana G. Reid, "The Development and Importance of the Town of Quebec, 1608-1760," Ph.D. dissertation, McGill University, 1950, p. 176.

90. AC, B23: 62, Mémoire du roi à Beauharnois, Versailles, 6 mai 1702; pt. 3, fol. 180v, Mémoire du Roi aux Callière et Beauharnois, n.d., n.p.; 27, pt. 3: 231, Ministre à Raudot, Versailles, 9 juin 1706; 29, pt. 1: 66, same to same, Versailles, 30 juin 1707.

91. Ibid., 23, pt. 3: 198, Ministre à Beauharnois, Versailles, 20 juin 1703; 27, pt. 3: 231, Ministre à Raudot, Versailles, 9 juin 1706 at fol. 236; 29, pt. 1: 66, same to same, Versailles, 30 juin 1707 at fol. 69.

92. Ibid., 27, pt. 3: 231, Ministre à Raudot, Versailles, 9 juin 1706 at fol. 235.

93. Ibid., 25: 101, Mémoire du Roy aux Vaudreuil et Beauharnois, Versailles, 14 juin 1704; 29, pt. 1: 66, Ministre à Raudot, Versailles, 30 juin 1707 at fol. 73.

94. Ibid., 27, pt. 3: 231, Ministre à Raudot, Versailles, 9 juin 1706 at fol. 235, quote; 29, pt. 1: 66, same to same, Versailles, 30 juin 1707 at fol. 68v, wording.

95. Ibid., 18: 147, "Instruction que le Roy à ordonné estre ez mains du Sr. Robert," Fontainebleau, 12 oct. 1695 at fol. 157; 23: 62, Memoire du roi à Beauharnois, Versailles, 6 mai 1702. Francis H. Hammang's contention in *The Marquis de Vau-*

dreuil: New France at the Beginning of the Eighteenth Century, Part 1 (Bruges, 1938), p. 85, n. 6, that Canada was forbidden to trade directly with the West Indies is without foundation. Nor do the instructions to Beauharnois support the claim of J.S. Pritchard in "Ships, Men and Commerce," pp. 152, 349-51, that this trade was to be confined to metropolitan bottoms.

96. Clarence P. Gould, "Trade between the Windward Islands and the Continental Colonies of the French Empire, 1683-1763," *MVHR* 25 (1939): 473-90, p. 477.

97. AC, B 31: 110, Ministre à Vaucresson, Fontainebleau, 25 juil. 1708; 318, Ministre aux Juges consuls de la Rochelle, Marly, 7 nov. 1708 (also sent to Nantes and Bordeaux); 319, Ministre à Bégon (Rochefort), Marly, 7 nov. 1708; 332, same to same, Versailles, 5 déc. 1708; ibid., fol. 331, Ministre à d'Aguesseau, Versailles, 5 déc. 1708.

98. Ibid., fol. 515, Ministre à d'Aguesseau, 27 sept. 1709.

99. Ibid., 30, pt. 2: 146, Mémoire du roi aux Vaudreuil et Raudot, Versailles, 6 juil. 1709; on diversification: 29, pt 1: 66, Ministre à Raudot, Versailles, 30 juin 1707 at fol. 68.

100. Ibid., 29, pt. 3: 198, Ministre à Goutins, Versailles, 30 juin 1707.

101. Ibid., 35, pt. 3: 274v, Mémoire du roi aux Vaudreuil et Beauharnois, Versailles, 27 jan. 1713.

102. Juchereau de St Ignace, *Annales de l'Hôtel-Dieu*, p. 383.

NOTES TO CHAPTER FIVE

1. Jeanne-Françoise Juchereau de St Ignace and Marie-Andrée Duplessis de Ste Hélène, *Les Annales de l'Hôtel-Dieu de Québec, 1636-1716,* ed. Dom Albert Jamet (Quebec, 1939), p. 385.

2. On Orléans, see Warren H. Lewis, *The Scandalous Regent: A Life of Philippe, Duc d'Orléans, 1674-1723, and of His Family* (London, 1961). The breaking of Louis XIV's testament is in François-André Isambert et al., eds., *Recueil général des anciennes lois françaises depuis l'an 420 jusqu'à la Révolution de 1789,* 21 *(1715–1737)* (Paris, n.d.): 20.

3. Marcel Marion, *Histoire financière de la France depuis 1715,* I *(1715-1789)* (Paris, 1927): 1.

4. Ibid., p. 47; Henri Carré, *Le Règne de Louis XV (1715-1774),* Vol. VIII, pt. 2 of Ernest Lavisse, ed., *Histoire de France depuis les origines jusqu'à la Révolution* (Paris, 1908): 11-14; Pierre Vilar, *Or et monnaie dans l'histoire,* Collection Science Flammarion (Paris, 1974), p. 299.

5. Marion, *Histoire financière,* p. 92; Carl Becker, *The Heavenly City of the Eighteenth-Century Philosophers* (New Haven and London, 1932; reprinted, New Haven, 1964), pp. 30-40.

6. Charles W. Cole, *French Mercantilism, 1683-1700* (New York, 1943), p. 232.

7. Ernest Labrousse et al., *Des Derniers Temps de l'âge seigneurial aux préludes de l'âge in-*

dustriel (1660-1789), Vol. II of Fernand Braudel and Ernest Labrousse, eds., *Histoire économique et sociale de la France,* (Paris, 1970): 280 (first quotation); Marion, *Histoire financière,* p. 91 (second quotation).

8. The present treatment of the Law episode, except where otherwise indicated, is based on Carré, *Louis xv,* pp. 21-44, Labrousse, *L'Age seigneurial,* pp. 276-99, Marion, *Histoire financière,* pp. 90-112, Vilar, *Or et monnaie,* pp. 309-11, and the indispensable Michel Sallon, "L'Echec de Law," *Revue d'histoire économique et sociale* 48 (1970): 145-95.

9. Marcel Giraud, "La Compagnie d'Occident (1717-18)," *Revue historique* 226 (1961): 23-56; Henry Weber, *La Compagnie française des Indes, 1604-1875* (Paris, 1904).

10. George T. Matthews, *The Royal General Farms in Eighteenth-Century France* (New York, 1958), p. 13.

11. AN, F 12, 799A, Extrait. Ve Pascaud à Moreau, La Rochelle, 21 juin 1721; Mémoire concernant la colonie de Canada et le commerce des castors (filed 3 July 1721).

12. Carré, *Louis xv,* pp. 35-36; Labrousse, *L'Age seigneurial,* p. 295.

13. Ibid., pp. 298-99.

14. AN, F 12, 799A, a series of fourteen letters and memoranda dated 12 July 1720 to 10 Jan. 1722; AC, C11A, *inter alia,* 42: 136, Vaudreuil et Bégon, Mémoire sur la liberté du castor, Québec, 6 nov. 1720; 44: 175, Vaudreuil au Conseil, Québec, 10 nov. 1721; ibid., fol. 400, Bégon au Conseil, Québec, 26 oct. 1722; Joseph Dufresne de Francheville, *Histoire de la Compagnie des Indes,* Vol. III, *Histoire générale et particulière des finances, où l'on voit l'origine, l'établissement, la perception, et la régie de toutes les impositions . . .* (Paris, 1738): 122-24, 421-27. The rationale remains obscure. Francheville says the Indies Company desired a short-term release from the burdens of monopoly and got it. One among many manoeuvres used by Law to stave off catastrophe? Such toying with public opinion would have been cynical and imprudent but in keeping with events in that memorable year. Vaudreuil executed a *volte-face* in 1721 and supported monopoly, lending credence to gossip that the *marquise* was behind it. Pontchartrain's intention to free the trade was not likely an influence in this affair.

15. Ibid., Extrait, Ve Pascaud à Moreau, La Rochelle, 21 juin 1721. The company did not acquire the other rights of the *Domaine.* The import taxes, the moose tenth, the domainal dues, and the Tadoussac trade had previously been amalgamated with the General Farms. When the Indies Company took over the farms, these were jettisoned, finding a new lessee in 1721. In 1726 they were re-amalgamated with the restored General Farms. See Mary A. Johnston, "The King's Domain: The Domain of the West in New France, 1675-1733," M.A. thesis, University of Western Ontario, 1961, pp. 113-21.

16. "Origin and Development of

the Card Money, etc.," in Adam Shortt, *Documents Relating to Canadian Currency, Exchange, and Finance during the French Period*, 2 vols. (Ottawa, 1925), I: 376-93; quotation, p. 379.

17. Ibid., "Declaration of the King," pp. 399-403.

18. Ibid., p. 387, and "Draft of the King's Memorandum to Messrs the Marquis de Vaudreuil . . . and Bégon," 5 July 1717, p. 395.

19. Ibid., "To Messrs de Vaudreuil and Bégon, Paris, 13th July 1718," "Messrs de Vaudreuil and Bégon, Quebec, 24 Oct. 1718," pp. 441-43, 449-51. Provision was made to retire existing cards with bills payable one third in March, 1718, one third in March, 1719, and one third in March, 1720, or for latecomers, half in March, 1719, and half in March, 1720, terms not very appealing to Canadian merchants.

20. Ibid., "To Messrs de Vaudreuil and Bégon, 3rd June, 1719," "Messrs de Vaudreuil and Bégon, Quebec, 26th Oct. 1719," pp. 463-65.

21. Carré, *Louis XV*, pp. 42-44; Marion, *Histoire financière*, pp. 110-12.

22. Vilar, *Or et monnaie*, p. 255.

23. In 1716 a mark of gold had been equivalent to 663 livres; by 1720 its equivalent was said to be 1,800 livres. Marion, *Histoire financière*, pp. 125-39.

24. Ibid., pp. 136-50.

25. [Antoine J.B.R.A. Montyon], *Particularités et observations sur les ministres de finances de France les plus célèbres depuis 1660 jusqu'en 1791* (London, 1812), p. 115n. See also

Marion, *Histoire financière,* pp. 151-69.

26. Ibid., p. 161.

27. The present treatment of the "renversement de la conjoncture" of the European economy is based upon Vilar, *Or et monnaie*, Labrousse, *L'Age seigneurial*, and Robert Mandrou, *La France aux XVIIe et XVIIIe siècles* (Paris, 1967).

28. Alexandre de Saint-Leger et al., *Louis XIV: la fin du règne (1685-1715)*, Vol. VIII, pt. 1 of Ernest Lavisse, ed., *Histoire de France depuis les origines jusqu'à la Révolution* (Paris, 1908), p. 163.

29. P. Goubert, *Louis XIV et vingt millions de français* (Paris, 1967), pp. 217-22.

30. Vilar, *Or et monnaie*, p. 312, favours the 1720s over Labrousse's classic date of 1733 as the turning point.

31. Henri See, *La France économique et sociale au XVIIIe siècle*, 7th ed. (Paris, n.d.).

32. Both Vilar, *Or et monnaie*, and Labrousse, *L'Age seigneurial*, underscore the role of bullion but do not state what they consider to have been the relative weight of different causal factors. Mandrou, *La France*, has the merit of clarity: the "moteurs du développement" are described as the improved transportation infrastructure, bullion, the new taste for exotic products, and the capitalist spirit (pp. 76-79).

33. David B. Horn, *Great Britain and Europe in the Eighteenth Century* (Oxford, 1967), p. 31. The present treatment is based upon, in addition to Horn, Sir

Richard Lodge, "The Anglo-French Alliance, 1716-1731," in Alfred Coville and Harold Temperley, eds., *Studies in Anglo-French History during the Eighteenth, Nineteenth and Twentieth Centuries* (Cambridge, 1935), pp. 3-18; Arthur M. Wilson, *French Foreign Policy during the Administration of Cardinal Fleury, 1726-43* (Cambridge, Mass., 1936); and Lewis, *Scandalous Regent.*

34. Lodge, "Anglo-French Alliance," p. 17.

35. See Wilson, *French Foreign Policy*, Chap. 2. The traditional castigation of Fleury and the French government for its neglect of trade, which marks Paul W. Bamford, *Forests and French Sea Power 1660–1789* (Toronto, 1956), p. 160, Richard Pares, *Colonial Blockade and Neutral Rights, 1739-1763* (Oxford, 1938), p. 226, and Maurice Filion, *La Pensée et l'action coloniales de Maurepas vis-à-vis du Canada, 1723-1749: l'âge d'or de la colonie* (Montreal, 1972) demands this corrective.

36. On the Bureau du Commerce, see Bernard Wybo, *Le Conseil de Commerce et le commerce intérieur de la France au XVIIIe siècle* (Paris, 1936), Louis-Jean-Pierre-Marie Bonnassieux and Eugène Lelong, *Conseil de Commerce et Bureau du Commerce, 1700-1791: inventaire analytique des procès-verbaux, introduction et table* (Paris, 1900), and the most recent study, Thomas J. Schaeper, *The French Council of Commerce, 1700-1715: A Study of Mercantilism after Colbert* (Columbus, O.,

1983). On chambers of commerce, see AN, F 12, 908-9, "Epoques de l'Etablissement de chambres de commerces dans diverses villes de France, 1726."

37. AN, AD vii 2A, "Lettres patentes du Roy, portant règlement pour le commerce des colonies françoises du mois d'avril 1717" (Paris, 1717); ibid., 2B, "Arrêt du Conseil d'Estat du Roy qui ordonne que les Lettres Patentes du mois d'avril dernier seront communes pour le commerce du Canada, du 11 décembre 1717"; Canada, Assembly of the Province of, *Edits et ordonnances: revus et corrigés d'après des pièces originales déposées aux archives provinciales* (Quebec, 1854), pp. 358-64.

38. "Arrêt qui permet aux Négocians des Villes de Québec et de Montréal de s'assembler tous les jours dans un endroit convenable pour y traiter de leurs affairs de commerce, 11 mai 1717," in *Edits et ordonnances*, p. 369.

39. AN, AD vii 2A, "Lettres Patentes du Roy de France en Forme d'Edit concernant le commerce estranger aux Isles & Colonies de l'Amérique données à Fontainebleau au mois d'octobre 1727" (Paris, 1727); Wilson, *French Foreign Policy*, p. 79.

40. Quoted in Wilson, *French Foreign Policy*, p. 65.

41. Cole, *French Mercantilism*, pp. 110-11; Filion, *Pensée et l'action de Maurepas*, p. 97.

42. Vilar, *Or et monnaie*, pp. 322-24. The classic source, Ambroise-Marie Arnould, *De la balance du commerce et des relations commerciales extérieures de la France*, 3 vols., (Paris,

1791), from which the estimate of a fivefold increase between 1715 and 1789 is so often quoted, gives figures of 196 million and 305 million for 1720-21 and the 1740s. Maurepas gives 300 million for the 1740s. Necker estimated 80 and 308 million. Bruyard gives 131 and 274 million for 1716-20 and the 1740s. See Filion, *Pensée et l'action de Maurepas*, pp. 59-62, 96.

43. Filion, *Pensée et l'action de Maurepas*, p. 60, n. 55; "Mémoire de Maurepas sur la Marine et le commerce" [1745], in R. Lamontagne, *Aperçu structural du Canada au XVIIIe siècle* (Montreal, 1964), p. 64.

44. "Mémoire de Maurepas," [1745], p. 64.

45. Filion, *Pensée et l'action de Maurepas*, pp. 98-99, based on the work of P. Mantoux; Wilson, *French Foreign Policy*, p. 291.

46. Wilson, *French Foreign Policy*, p. 293. English fears may have been groundless. French merchants certainly worked at a disadvantage from the point of view of business costs (higher interest, larger crews, higher freight rates, etc.). See also Bamford, *Forests and French Sea Power*, pp. 163-67. English trade, on its much larger base, tripled between 1702 and 1773 and doubled again between 1765 and 1800 (Vilar, *Or et monnaie*, pp. 323-34). But, of course, how much of this was due to the military action Decker counselled and to the unforeseen Revolution?

47. The present treatment of the structure of the Marine Department is based upon Louise Dechêne, ed., *La Correspondance de Vauban relative au Canada* (Quebec, 1968); Robert La Roque de Roquebrunne, "La Direction de la Nouvelle France par le Ministère de la Marine," *RHAF* 4 (1953): 470-88; Michel Antoine, "Les Arrêts du Conseil rendus au XVIIIe siècle pour le Département de la Marine (1723-1791)," *Revue française d'histoire d'outre-mer* 55 (1968): 316-34; Albert Duchêne, *La Politique coloniale de la France: le ministère des colonies depuis Richelieu* (Paris, 1928); and D. Neuville, *Etat sommaire des Archives de la Marine antérieures à la Révolution* (Paris, 1898).

48. Roquebrunne (p. 478) and Dechêne (Chap. 3) play down the role of ministers. Filion, *Pensée et l'action de Maurepas*, assumes the minister's signal role, the names of the *premiers commis* not even appearing in the index!

49. Henri Legoherel, *Les Trésoriers généraux de la Marine, 1517-1788* (Paris, 1965), pp. 179-87, 190, 236-61; "Mémoire de Maurepas" [1745]. pp. 179-84.

50. Quoted in Wilson, *French Foreign Policy*, p. 79. Wilson argues a judicious case for Fleury's providing as good a navy as the times were thought to require (pp. 71-90). Filion, *Pensée et l'action de Maurepas*, portrays Maurepas as working for the Marine against Fleury and Orry. There is considerable *partipris* in discussions of this topic. G. Lacour-Gayet, *La Marine militaire de la France sous le règne de Louis XV* (Paris, 1910), borders on hysteria. The size of

the French navy during the period is estimated in Roland Lamontagne, Jacques Bertin, and Françoise Vergneault, "Traitement graphique d'une information: les marines royales de France et de Grande-Bretagne (1697-1747)," *Annales: ESC* 22 (1967): 991-1004. The source (1746? 1747?) takes no account of vessels decommissioned or sunk or those captured by a power other than England or France, or captured by England or France and not recommissioned. The result is of dubious value.

51. Marcel Giraud, *Histoire de la Louisiane française*, 4 vols. (Paris, 1953-74), II: 1-51.

52. Lacour-Gayet, *Marine militaire sous Louis XV*, p. 86, quoting Valincour.

53. For an extended "Portrait de Maurepas," see Filion, *Pensée et l'action de Maurepas*, Chap. 1.

54. The earlier legislation summarized in the Letters Patent of 1727 is in AN, AD vii 2A. The sum required for bonuses was set at 80,000 livres per year. This was to be paid from a fund raised through the 1/2% tax and an additional 1/2% from the *Domaine d'Occident* tax of 3%. When the Marine absorbed the *Domaine d'Occident* in the colonies (1 January 1733), it continued to pay the 80,000 livres. The fund was used for many purposes relative to French trade and industry but seldom to aid colonial trade (the surplus was originally intended for this purpose) and never for bonuses. In 1745 Maurepas attempted to suppress the tax. However, he capitulated

to Orry and the Director of commerce (Antoine-Louis Rouillé) when it was agreed that 50,000 livres of the money would be turned over to the Marine treasurers each year. From 1733 to 1745 the tax collected averaged 122,454 livres per year. See AN, F 12, 799A, various memoranda and letters, Marine B 3 508, fol. 123, Machault au ministre, 13 nov. 1751.

55. AC, B 50, fol. 160, 5 août 1727; Maurepas à Dupuy, 24 mai 1728, quoted in Filion, *Pensée et l'action de Maurepas*, p. 78.

56. Filion, *Pensée et l'action de Maurepas*, pp. 74-76.

57. "Mémoire de Maurepas" [1745], p. 64.

58. Donald J. Horton, "Gilles Hocquart, Intendant of New France, 1729-1748," Ph.D. dissertation, McGill University, 1974, the best treatment of Hocquart, but too dismissive of his imagination and too quick to judge him colourless.

59. Johnston, "King's Domain," pp. 128-29.

60. Shortt, *Canadian Currency*, II: "Ordinance of the King on the subject of Card Money, of March the second, one thousand seven hundred and twenty-nine," 589-95; "Another Ordinance by the King on the Subject of Card Money, dated 12th May, 1733," 641-45; "Ordinance of the King for the new issue of 120,000 livres of card money in Canada, 27th February 1742," 707-11; Guy Frégault, "Essai sur les finances canadiennes," in *Le XVIIIe Siècle canadien: études*, Collection Constantes, 16 (Montreal, 1968): 327.

61. Frégault, "Finances canadiennes," p. 323.

62. Shortt, *Canadian Currency*, II: "Messrs de Beauharnois and Hocquart, October 25, 1729," 601-11 and 605 n.; "Messrs de Beauharnois and Hocquart, October 23, 1730," 615-17.

63. Ibid., "Messrs de Beauharnois and Hocquart, 25 October, 1731," 623-25; "To Messrs de Beauharnois and Hocquart, Compiègne, 6th May, 1732," 627-29; "Ordinance making orders notes and receipts legal tender" (quotation), 635-39.

64. Ibid., "M. Hocquart, October 10, 1734," 655-57.

65. Ibid., "M. Hocquart, 30 October 1741," 701.

66. Ibid., "To M. Hocquart, Versailles, 27th February, 1742," 711.

67. Ibid., Beauharnois and Hocquart to Minister, Quebec, 20 October 1742, 713.

68. Ibid., same to same, Quebec, 30 October 1742, 713.

69. "Mémoire de Maurepas" [1745], pp. 74-75.

70. Weber, *Compagnie des Indes*, pp. 423-71, 513-18, 525-31.

NOTES TO CHAPTER SIX

1. AC, B 35: 67, Ministre à Vaudreuil et Bégon, Rambouillet, 28 juin 1713; C11E 2: 16-29, "Mémoire pour servir à régler les limites entre la Nouvelle France et la Nouvelle Angleterre et l'Acadie, autrement Nouvelle Ecosse, 8 novembre 1713, collationné le 8 novembre 1718, Signé Bégon." It is unclear whether the memorandum was written by Aubery, by Bégon on the basis of information supplied by Aubery, or by both men together. AC, C11A 34: 8-9 implies joint endeavour; Aubery in 1720 referred to the paper as his (n. 28 below).

2. Re Canada, *The Memorials of the English and French Commissaries Concerning the Limits of Nova Scotia or Acadia* (London, 1755), I: 715-16, "Prolongation de la Commission de Gouverneur & Lieutenant-Général à Québec, au sieur Huault de Montmagny, 6 juin 1645"; p. 717, "Provisions en faveur de Sieur de Lauson de la charge de Gouverneur & Lieutenant général du Roi Canada," Paris, 17 jan. 1651; pp. 732-33, "Lettres patents du Gouverneur de la Nouvelle-France en faveur du Vicomte d'Argenson," 26 jan. 1675; re Acadia: ibid., pp. 571-76, "Lettres patentes du Roi, qui confirment le Sieur d'Aulnay Charnisay dans le gouvernement & la possession de l'Acadie, du mois de février 1647"; pp. 576-79, "Lettres patentes du Roi qui confirment Charles de Saint-Etienne, Sieur de La Tour, dans le gouvernement & la possession de l'Acadie," fév. 1651; pp. 614-15, "Mémoire de l'Ambassadeur de France, présenté au Roi d'Angleterre," 16 jan. 1685; AC, C11D 1: 181, "Mémoire sur l'estat present de la Coste de l'Acadie" (1684); 2: 78-84v, "Instruction que Le Roy a ordonné etre ramise au Sr. de Menneval" 5 av. 1687; AC, C11E 1: 164-89v, "Mémoire sur la domination des françois en Canada, juillet 1687, envoyé a M.

De Bonrepaus à Londres'';
CollMSS 2: 283, "Mémoire sur la
riviere de St. George" (1687);
pp. 294-98, "Ministre à De Villebon," Versailles, 26 mars 1698.
3. *CollMSS* 2: 509, "Mémoire sur
les limites" (1709); *Mémoires
des commissaires du roi et de
ceux de Sa Majesté britannique,
sur les possessions & les droits
respectifs des deux Couronnes en
Amérique: avec les Actes publics
& pièces justificatives*, 4 vols.
(Paris, 1755-57), I: 581-87, "Acte
de la cession de l'Acadie au Roi
de France," 17 fév. 1667; IV: 32-
39, "Traité de Paix entre La
France et L'Angleterre Fait à
Breda le 21/31 juillet 1667";
Memorials, I: 604-10, "Ordre du
Chevalier Temple au Capitaine
Walker," 7 juil. 1670; "Acte de
reddition . . . de Pentagouet," 5
août 1670; PAC, MG 5 B1 7: 2-7,
"Traitté Entre Les Srs Granfon-
taine pour la France Et Temple
pour L'angleterre," 14 août
1670."
4. AC, C11E 1: 75v, Tallard au
Ministre, Londres, 19 fév. 1700;
2: 16-29, Aubery-Bégon memorandum (note 1 above).
5. AC, B 41: 56-7, Conseil de Marine à Dubois, Paris, 22 mars 1719;
PAC, MG 5 B-2, vol. 4 (A.E. vol.
17), "Mémoire historique sur ce
qui a esté stipulé par la paix conclue à Utrecht le 11e Avril 1713
. . . Fait en 1724 Decemb 31 par
M. le Dran, chef du Depôt des
Affres. etrangeres" (Le Dran's
memorandum), fols. 222-36. The
most recent treatment of the
Canso affair is Donald F. Chard,
"The Impact of Ile Royale on
New England, 1713-1763,"
Ph.D. dissertation, University of
Ottawa, 1976, Chap. 1.

6. Le Dran's memorandum, fols.
238-40v. Most of the memoranda
on Acadia and Hudson Bay date
from Jan. 1720 and are in AC,
C11E vol. 2, including document
quoted at fol. 185v, "Mémoire
concernant les limites des Colonies presenté in 1720 par le S.
Bobé prêtre de la Congrégation
de la Mission." Charlevoix's memorandum is printed in *CollMSS*
3: 49-54; see also his recollection
in AC, C11E 3: 14, à Rouillé, 23
août 1749.
7. PAC, MG 5 A-1, 24: 33-52 (A.E.
vol. 334), "Janvier 1720: Mémoire general sur les limites de
l'Acadie." There seems no reason
to doubt the later English explanation that the defining phrase was
intended to ensure that the Acadia ceded in 1713 was identical
with that ceded by Temple in
1670: *Memorials*, I: 49, "Memorandum of the English commissioners, 1751."
8. Le Dran's memorandum, fols.
242-58, for diplomatic history to
1723. See also PAC, MG 5 A-1,
vol. 23 (A.E. vols. 284-328) for
correspondence relative to the
commission of 1719-20, in particular, fols. 258-60 (A.E. vol.
328), Mémoire . . . 22 mars 1719.
9. AC, B 44: 120v-21, Conseil de
Marine à Dubois, 28 déc. 1721,
also printed *CollMSS* 3: 67-68.
10. PAC, MG 5 A-1, vol. 23 (A.E.
vol. 327), Chammorel à Monseigneur, Londres, 23 nov. 1719;
see also ibid. (A.E. vol. 326),
anon., Londres, 10/21 sept. 1719.
11. Ibid., 252-54 (A.E. vol. 327),
Destouches à Monseigneur,
Londres, 18 déc. 1719.
12. Ibid., 24: 12-13, Chammorel
à Monseigneur, Londres, 11 juil.
1720.

13. Ibid., 25: 59-110, "Mémoire pour servir d'Instruction au Sr. Comte de Broglio, Versailles, 28 mai 1724," at fols. 65-70.

14. Ibid., 111-18, "Mémoire sur les point qui doivent etre examinez et decidez par des Comm^res du Roy et du Roy de la G^de Bret^e – joint a l'instruction remise au Comte de Broglio le 28e May 1724."

15. Pierre-André Sévigny, *Les Abénaquis: habitat et migrations (17e et 18e siècles)*, Collection Cahiers d'histoire des Jésuites (Montreal, 1976), pp. 117-67.

16. Kenneth M. Morrison, "The People of the Dawn: The Abnaki and Their Relations with New England and New France, 1602-1727," Ph.D. dissertation, University of Maine, Orono, 1975. The present account of Abenaki history is based largely upon Morrison, pp. 298-428, to which footnote references have been kept to a minimum.

17. AC, B 38: 220v, Mémoire du Roi, s.l., 15 juin 1716 (first quotation); 39: 223v, Ministre à Vaudreuil, Paris, 26 juin 1717.

18. Yves F. Zoltvany, *Philippe de Rigaud de Vaudreuil, Governor of New France, 1703-1725*, Carleton Library (Toronto, 1974), pp. 146-48; Sévigny, *Abénaquis*, pp. 175-77.

19. *CollMSS* 3: 5-6, "Lettre de Monsieur de Vaudreuil au Ministre, Québec, le 16 septembre 1714"; pp. 10-12, "Memoire du Roy aux Sieurs de Ramesay et Bégon, à Marly, le 10 juillet 1715." On churches and the gift fund: ibid., 2: 291-92, "Presents des Sauvages de l'Acadie" (1698);

3: 18, "Mémoire du Roi aux sieurs de Vaudreuil et Bégon, Paris, le 15 juin 1716"; pp. 21-23, "Mémoire de Messieurs Vaudreuil et Bégon au Ministre, Québec, 14 octobre 1716"; p. 28, "Mémoire du Roy aux sieurs Marquis de Vaudreuil et Bégon, le 15 juillet, 1718"; pp. 123-24, "Mémoire du Roi aux sieurs Marquis de Vaudreuil et Chazel, A Versailles, le 15 mai 1725"; p. 146, "1728, Dépenses pour les sauvages de l'Acadie."

20. Ibid., pp. 19-21, "Rapport de Monsieur de Vaudreuil au Ministre, Québec, septembre 6, 1716."

21. Ibid., pp. 31-32, "Rapport de Monsieur de Vaudreuil au Conseil, Québec, le 31 octobre, 1718."

22. Ibid., pp. 57-61, Vaudreuil et Bégon au Conseil, Québec, 8 oct. 1721, at p. 60.

23. AC, B 41 pt. 4, Mémoire du Roi, Paris, 23 mai 1719, at fol. 523.

24. *CollMSS* 3: 41-42, "Rapport de MM. De Vaudreuil et Bégon, Québec, le 26 octobre, 1719."

25. Douglas E. Leach, *The Northern Colonial Frontier, 1607-1763*, Histories of the American Frontier (New York, 1966), pp. 125-34; Herman R. Friis, "A Series of Population Maps of the Colonies and the United States, 1625-1790," *Geographical Review* 30 (1940): 463-70; Morrison, "People of the Dawn," p. 322 (quotation).

26. Thomas Hutchinson, *The History of the Province of Massachusetts-Bay from the Charter of King William and Queen Mary, in 1691, until the Year 1750*, 1st

ed. of Vol. II (Boston, 1767): 288-89.

27. See biographies in *DCB*. Micheline Dumont-Johnson, *Apôtres ou agitateurs. La France missionnaire en Acadie* (Trois-Rivières, 1970) is a provocative study that, for this period at least, overemphasizes the authority of missionaries in the tribes and the identification of their policy with that of the governor at Quebec. Kenneth Morrison, "Sebastien Racle and Norridgewock, 1724: The Eckstrom Controversy Thesis Reconsidered," *Maine Historical Society Quarterly* 14 (1974): 76-97 is an excellent study of a missionary and an entrée to a famous controversy. See above, Chap. 2 at nn. 73 and 76 on Jesuit policy pre-war; during war, Morrison, "People of the Dawn," p. 312; post-war, ibid., p. 419.

28. Aubery-Bégon memorandum (note 1 above); AC, C11E 2: 90-93, "Memoire du P. Aubry Jesuite Missionnaire de Canada sur les limites de la Nouvelle France et de la Nouvelle Angleterre Janr 1720"; Aubery to Governor, 1726, quoted, Camille de Rochemonteix, *Les Jésuites et la Nouvelle-France au XVIIIe siècle d'après des documents inédits*, 2 vols. (Paris, 1906), II: 15, note 1; Reuben G. Thwaites, ed., *The Jesuit Relations and Allied Documents*, Vol. LXVII (Cleveland, 1900): 120-25, "Memorial of Father Loyard upon the present condition of the Abnaquis, 1722"; pp. 84-119, "Letter from Sébastien Rasles, Missionary of the Society of Jesus in New France, to Monsieur his nephew, Nanrantsouak, October 15, 1722";

same to his brother, Nanrantsouak, October 12, 1723."

29. Ibid., Rasles to Nanrantsouak, October 15, 1722, p. 93.

30. Morrison, "People of the Dawn," pp. 344-48, 401-2, 421-28 (quotations, pp. 402, 422, 428). Roderick Nash, *Wilderness and the American Mind* (New Haven, 1967), introduces this complex topic.

31. Samuel Penhallow, *History of the Wars of New-England with the Eastern Indians* (Boston, 1726), p. 86. "Wowurna," *DCB* II: 668-69.

32. Thwaites, *Jesuit Relations*, LXVII: 115.

33. Penhallow, *Wars*, pp. 89–90.

34. *CollMSS* 3: 57-61, "Rapport de Messieurs de Vaudreuil et Bégon au Ministre, Québec, le 8 octobre 1721."

35. AC, B 45: 804v, "A Vaudreuil, Paris, 5 juin 1722." This appears to be the only reference to the Abenaki question in 1722 and makes no mention of the diplomatic note. The specific order from 9 June 1723 onward to encourage other tribes to espouse the Abenaki cause is a natural response to the outbreak of war in July 1722. For other years, see *CollMSS* 3: 40, "Mémoire du Roy a Messieurs le Marquis de Vaudreuil et Bégon, A Paris, le 23 mai 1719"; pp. 44-45, "Mémoire du Roy aux sieurs de Vaudreuil et Bégon, A Paris, le 2 juin 1720"; p. 54, "Mémoire du Roy aux sieurs de Vaudreuil et Bégon, Versailles, le 8 juin 1721"; pp. 101-2, "Decision des Ministres sur le rapport du Canada du 14 octobre, 1723, Versailles, le 18 janvier, 1724"; pp. 102-3, "Mémoire

du Roi aux sieurs Marquis de Vau-dreuil et Bégon, A Versailles, le 30 mai 1724"; pp. 123-24, "Mé-moire du Roi aux sieurs Marquis de Vaudreuil et Chazel, A Ver-sailles, le 15 mai, 1725"; pp. 126-27, "Note du ministre sur les dépeches de l'année dernière, Versailles, le 2 mai 1725"; S. Dale Standen, "Charles, Marquis de Beauharnais de la Boische, Gov-ernor General of New France, 1726-1747," Ph.D. dissertation, University of Toronto, 1975, p. 115.

36. Hutchinson, *Massachusetts*, II: 312; Morrison discusses the controversy in "People of the Dawn," p. 380, and article, n. 27 above.

37. Zoltvany, *Vaudreuil*, pp. 200-201; *CollMSS* 3: 117-23, "Lettre de Monsieur de Bégon au Mi-nistre, Québec, le 21 avril, 1725."

38. The Boston treaties have been a source of confusion. The rele-vant documentation is calen-dared in *CSPCS* 35, items 5, 232, 268, 276 and 673, the treaties in these series being *copies* of ori-ginals in colonial collections. The Boston treaty proper as well as treaties with New Hampshire and Nova Scotia are exchanges of do-cuments, one signed by Indians, the other by a colonial official; both parts must be consulted. The following is a list of documents in the particular versions con-sulted: C.O. 5 898: 126-51 (pagi-nation, PAC transcript), "At a Conference with the Delegates of the Indian Tribes . . ." 16 Nov.–7 Dec. 1725; *CSPCS* 35, item 673, Dummer to Lords of Trade, Bos-ton, 15 Aug. 1727; "The Submis-sion and Agreement of the Dele-gates of the Eastern Indians," Boston, 15 Dec. 1725, in Peter A. Cumming and Neil H. Micken-berg, *Native Rights in Canada*, 2nd ed. (Toronto, 1972), pp. 300-302, where "rights of land" er-roneously appears as "rights of God"; but see Penhallow, *Wars*, pp. 119-23 or C.O. 5 898: 122 (pagination, PAC transcript); "By the Honourable William Dum-mer . . ." (Massachusetts's pro-mises to the Indians, Boston, 15 Dec. 1725), reprinted in "The Conference with the Eastern In-dians . . . 1727," pp. 422-24 (see below); *CSPCS* 35, item 95ii, "Articles of Peace concluded with the Eastern Indians by Lieuten-ant Governor Wentworth, Bos-ton, 15 Dec. 1725"; "The Con-ference with the Eastern Indians . . ." (ratification at Falmouth, 30 July–11 August 1726), *Maine His-torical Society Collections*, 1st ser., III (1853): 377-405; "The Conference with the Eastern Indi-ans . . ." (further ratification at Falmouth, 17 July–27 July 1727), ibid., pp. 407-47. The document described as the Treaty of Fal-mouth, 1727, in *CollMSS* 3: 134-35 is a French commentary on the treaty's clauses. The participa-tion of the Maliseets is uncertain. See William D. Williamson, *The History of the State of Maine from Its First Discovery, A.D. 1602, to the Separation, A.D. 1820, Inclusive* (Boston, 1832), II: 147 n., 155. For treaty with Nova Scotia and ratification, see note 79 below.

39. *CSPCS* 34, item 718, Arm-strong to (Newcastle?), Canso, 5 Sept. 1725.

40. C.O. 5, 898, p. 140 (PAC tran-

script), "At a conference with the Delegates of the Indian tribes . . . 16th of November 1725."

41. Rochemonteix, *Eighteenth-Century*, II: 16, n 3.

42. Standen, "Beauharnais," pp. 106-7, 115-19.

43. *CollMSS* 3: 152-53, "Resumé d'une lettre de Messieurs de Beauharnois et Hocquart au Ministre, A Québec, le 6 nov. 1730."

44. Roland O. Macfarlane, "The Massachusetts Bay Truck-Houses in Diplomacy with the Indians," *New England Quarterly* 11 (1938): 48-65. Leach, *Frontier*, 172-76.

45. *CollMSS* 3: 101-2, "Décision des Ministres sur le rapport de Canada du 14 octobre, 1723," Versailles, le 18 jan. 1724.

46. Chap. 3, n. 74 above.

47. AC, B 34: 68v, Ministre à Vaudreuil et Bégon, Marly, 26 juin 1712; ibid., 35: 230v, Ministre à Bégon, Marly, 24 fév. 1713; ibid., fol. 91, Ministre à M. Desmaretz, Versailles, 21 av. 1713. See also Terence A. Crowley, "France, Canada and the Beginnings of Louisbourg: In Search of the Great Fortress Myth," in *Papers and Abstracts for a Symposium on Ile Royale During the French Régime* (Ottawa, 1972), pp. 51-54; Robert Le Blant, *Un Colonial sous Louis XIV: Philippe de Pastour de Costebelle, gouverneur de Terre-Neuve puis de l'Ile Royale, 1661-1717* (Dax, 1935), p. 168.

48. AC, B 35: 53, Ministre à Beauharnois (Rochefort), Versailles, 5 mars 1713; ibid., 36: 338, Ministre à Vaudreuil et Bégon, Versailles, 19 mars 1714; Le Blant, *Un Colonial*, pp. 169-70; C. de La Morandière, *Histoire de la pêche française de la morue dans l'Amérique septentrionale (Des origines à 1789)* (Paris, 1962), I: 506; II: 646-50. On property rights of Placentians, see PAC, MG 5 A-1, vol. 23 (A.E. vol. 284), "Mémoire sur les habitans de Plaisance," n.d.

49. Frederick J. Thorpe, "Fish, Forts, and Finance: The Politics of French Construction at Placentia, 1699-1710," *HP*, 1971, pp. 55-64.

50. AC, C11C 8: 10-39, "Mémoire pour l'établissement d'un colonie à l'Ile du Cap Breton, Paris, 30 Novembre 1706" (attributed to Riverin); also in John S. McLennan, *Louisbourg from Its Foundation to Its Fall* (London, 1918), pp. 22-31. On authorship, see Crowley, "Beginnings of Louisbourg," note 13, and Le Blant, *Un Colonial*, pp. 166-67; AC, C11C 8: 40-51v, A.-D. Raudot, "Mémoire sur les affaires présentes du Canada et l'établissement du Cap Breton, Québec, 7 août 1706"; on Pontchartrain's views, AC, B 35: 111v, à Desmaretz, Versailles, 1 juin 1713; fol. 257, à Bégon, Versailles, 29 mars 1713; fol. 467, Mémoire du roi, Versailles, 25 juin 1713.

51. Ibid., 37: 27, à Desmaretz, Versailles, 10 fév. 1715.

52. Crowley, "Beginnings of Louisbourg," pp. 55-64.

53. Frederick J. Thorpe, *Remparts lointains: la politique française des travaux publics à Terre-Neuve et à l'Ile Royale, 1695-1758* (Ottawa, 1980). For an English text see the original, "The Politics of French Public Construction in the Islands of the

Gulf of St. Lawrence, 1695-1758," Ph.D. dissertation, University of Ottawa, 1973. McLennan, *Louisbourg*, is largely superseded, although there is no synthesis of new research. La Morandière, *La Pêche française*, II: 643-89, contains a good history. Papers on Louisbourg, many technical, are published by the National Historic Parks and Sites Branch in *Canadian Historic Sites* and *History and Archaeology*, among which are B. Adams, "The Construction and Occupation of the Barracks of the King's Bastion at Louisbourg," *CHS* 18 (1978): 59-147, and A. Greer, "The Soldiers of Isle Royale, 1720-1745," *H&A* No. 28.

54. Thorpe, *Remparts lointains*, "En somme."

55. Crowley, "Beginnings of Louisbourg."

56. The London and Utrecht talks (see Chap. 3 above), Pontchartrain's comments in this chapter, and the Raudot and Riverin memoranda support the view that Ile Royale was considered a key strategic location for both Canada and the fishery. The argument that Louisbourg was never intended to defend the route to Canada (Thorpe, *Remparts lointains*, p. 127) is unconvincing.

57. Beauharnois à Maurepas, Québec, 13 oct. 1727, quoted in Standen, "Beauharnais," p. 144; Maurepas à Beauharnois, Versailles, 14 mai 1728, quoted in Crowley, "Beginnings of Louisbourg," p. 69.

58. Bernard Pothier, "Acadian Emigration to Ile Royale after the Conquest of Acadia," *HS/SH* 6

(1970): 116-31, p. 120; Terence A. Crowley, "Privileged Entrepreneurs: The Louisbourg Officer Corps and Commerce," *HP*, 1978, and "Government and Interests: French Colonial Administration at Louisbourg, 1713-1758," Ph.D. dissertation, Duke University, Durham, N.C., 1975.

59. La Morandière, *La Pêche française* (the fundamental work on the fisheries) II: 635-730, and Jean-François Brière, "Le Trafic terre-neuvier malouin dans la première moitié du XVIIIe siècle, 1713-1755," *HS/SH* 11 (1978): 356-74 are the basis for the present treatment.

60. David Lee, "The French in Gaspé, 1534 to 1760," *CHS* 3 (1970): 25-64.

61. Christopher Moore, "The Other Louisbourg: Trade and Merchant Enterprise in Ile Royale, 1713-58," *HS/SH* 12 (1979); 79-96.

62. La Morandière, *La Pêche française* II: 669-73; Guy Frégault, *François Bigot: administrateur français*, 2 vols. (Montreal, 1948), I: 159-60; Andrew H. Clark, *Acadia: The Geography of Early Nova Scotia to 1760* (Madison, Wis., 1968), p. 313.

63. Jean-François Brière, "Le Reflux des terre-neuviers malouins sur les côtes du Canada dans la première moitié du XVIIIe siècle: réponse à un changement de climat?" *HS/SH* 12 (1979): 166-69. On Canso, see Chard, "Impact of Ile Royale," table 3, p. 33A.

64. La Morandière, *La Pêche française* II: 635-36; Brière, "Trafic terre-neuvier malouin," pp. 356-61.

65. Moore, "Other Louisbourg";

DCB II for merchants mentioned in text plus Jean Claparède, J.B. Lannelongue, François Milly, Nicolas Deslongrais, and Léon Fautoux, whom Crowley names a secretary to Saint-Ovide in "Government and Interests," p. 90.

66. Chard, "Impact of Ile Royale," pp. 11-61; on Acadian trade see also Clark, *Acadia*, Chap. 6 and pp. 318-23.

67. Frégault, *François Bigot* I: 167, 185.

68. "Mémoire du roi," Paris, 12 mai 1722, quoted in Chard, "Impact of Ile Royale," p. 43; see also pp. 43-48 and, on English, pp. 35-38; Moore, "Other Louisbourg," p. 89 on merchant influence.

69. Daniel C. Harvey, *The French Régime in Prince Edward Island* (New Haven, 1926).

70. Nicole Durand, "Etude de la population de Louisbourg, 1713-1745," mimeo. report (Louisbourg, 1970); Clark, *Acadia*, pp. 276, 293-96.

71. Cf. James S. Pritchard, "Ships, Men and Commerce: A Study of Maritime Activity in New France," Ph.D. dissertation, University of Toronto, 1971, tables 10, 12 and 13 (pp. 496-99) with Chard, "Impact of Ile Royale," table 1 (p. 43A).

72. Moore, "Other Louisbourg," pp. 93-96.

73. Clark, *Acadia*, pp. 275-82 (p. 276, population figure), and his "New England's Role in the Underdevelopment of Cape Breton Island During the French Régime, 1713-1758," *Canadian Geographer* 9 (1965): 1-12.

74. AC, F 3 50: 4v, Pontchartrain à Saint Ovide, 10 av. 1713, quoted in Olive P. Dickason, "Louisbourg and the Indians: A Study in Imperial Race Relations, 1713-1760," *H&A* 6 (1976): 1-206, p. 66. Except as otherwise noted, the present treatment is based upon the Dickason article and Leslie F.S. Upton, *Micmacs and Colonists: Indian-White Relations in the Maritimes, 1713-1867* (Vancouver, 1979).

75. AC, C11C 7: 227, Félix Pain à Costebelle, Aux Mines, 23 Sept. 1713, quoted in Dickason, "Louisbourg and the Indians," p. 68.

76. Upton, *Micmacs and Colonists*, p. 35 (quotation). The role of French missionaries in the Anglo-French confrontation is controversial. Gerard Finn, "La Carrière de l'Abbé Jean-Louis Leloutre et les dernières années de l'affrontement anglo-français en Acadie," thèse de doctorat de troisième cycle, Université de Paris, 1974, is successful in showing Le Loutre's essentially religious viewpoint but also the overwhelming wartime "ideological" context. The memoirs of P. Maillard, "Lettre sur les missions de l'Acadie et particulièrement sur les missions Micmaques," in *Soirées canadiennes* 3 (1863): 289-426, are used by Dumont-Johnson (see n. 27) and L.F.S. Upton to show culpable partisanship. NB, the offending anglophobic remarks are in a sermon rebuking the Micmacs for torturing an English prisoner and reminding them the English are men like themselves. Maillard's description of English attitudes toward Micmacs

is mistaken for his view of the English themselves in Upton, p. 35, with startling results.

77. Dickason, "Louisbourg and the Indians," p. 90.

78. Ronald O. Macfarlane, "British Indian Policy in Nova Scotia to 1760," *CHR* 19 (1938): 154-67 supplements Upton.

79. The relevant documentation on the Nova Scotia treaty and ratifications is as follows: C.O. 5 898: 149-50 (PAC pagination, transcript), "At a Conference with the Delegates of the Indian Tribes . . ." 16 Nov.–7 Dec. 1725; C.O. 217 4: 349, "Articles of Submission and Agreement" (Re Nova Scotia, Boston, 15 Dec. 1725), first quotation; fol. 348, "By Paul Mascarene . . ." (Nova Scotia's promises, Boston, 15 Dec. 1725), second quotation; fols. 316-18, Doucett to Lords of Trade, Annapolis Royal, 16 Aug. 1726, third quotation; fol. 620, "Whereas by Articles of Peace . . ." (ratification of Indian submission, Annapolis Royal, 4/15 June 1726), with Doucett's dispatch bearing 64 signatures without affiliations; fols. 351-52, second copy with Armstrong's dispatch bearing 16 signatures identified by band; fols. 350-51, "Whereas Major Paul Mascarene . . ." (Doucett's ratification of Mascarene's promises, Annapolis Royal, 4/15 June 1726), a fragmentary copy with Armstrong's dispatch. The tribes ratifying the treaty on 4/15 June are described as Micmacs and two Abenaki groups, the Penobscots and Passamaquoddies. The omission of the Maliseets is probably correct since they alone signed a later ratification: "Treaty No. 239"

(ratification re Nova Scotia, Annapolis Royal, 13/24 May 1728), Cumming and Mickenberg, *Native Rights*, pp. 302-4.

80. Clark, *Acadia*, pp. 161-62. Economic and social description is based on Clark. Political history is based on J.B. Brebner, *New England's Outpost: Acadia before the Conquest of Canada* (New York, 1927). See also N.E.S. Griffiths, "The Acadians," in *DCB* IV: xvii-xxxi with its useful bibliography.

81. *CSPCS* 27, item 370, "H.M. Warrant to Col. Nicholson, Governor of Nova Scotia," Kensington, 23 June 1713. The once standard work by F.E. Rameau de Saint-Père, *Une Colonie féodale en Amérique: l'Acadie (1604-1881)*, 2 vols. (Paris and Montreal, 1889), presents a singular argument for the political history of the period 1713-44 that turns on the notion that Queen Anne's bounty (*infra*, note 80) was without time limit and gave the Acadians a kind of French subject status in reserve, a legal foundation for neutrality until the option had been freely rejected or freely exercised, which was never permitted, making exaction of an unqualified oath of allegiance unjust – ingenious but wishful thinking. The English officers in Nova Scotia lack only horns and tail, which is unjust to some of them. Like Rameau, most nineteenth-century writers on Acadia are mainly of historiographical interest.

82. "Extract of a letter from Sam Vetch to Board of Trade, Feb. 21, 1715-16, London," in *Collection de documents inédits sur le Canada et l'Amérique publiés*

par Le Canada-Français 1 (Quebec, 1888): 116.

83. PAC, MG 5 A-1 23: 1145-49, "Mémoire sur les habitans de Plaisance et de l'Acadie," n.d.

84. Pothier, "Acadian Emigration to Ile Royale," pp. 116-31.

NOTES TO CHAPTER SEVEN

1. Dale Miquelon, *Dugard of Rouen: French Trade to Canada and the West Indies, 1729-1770* (Montreal, 1978), p. 69. Much of the material on Quebec trade footnoted to this source is also available in Miquelon, "Havy and Lefebvre of Quebec: A Case Study of Metropolitan Participation in Canadian Trade, 1730-60," *CHR* 56 (1975): 1-24.

2. Miquelon, *Dugard of Rouen*, pp. 171-89; James S. Pritchard, "Ships, Men and Commerce: A Study of Maritime Activity in New France," Ph.D. dissertation, University of Toronto, 1971, pp. 28-39; examples of voyage literature: Benjamin Sulte, ed., "Un voyage à la Nouvelle-France en 1734 (Joseph Navrières)," *Revue canadienne* 22 (1866): 15-35; "Lettres du Père Aulneau," *RAPQ, 1926-27*, pp. 261-330 (letters of Aulneau and Nau); Pierre-François-Xavier de Charlevoix, *Journal d'un voyage fait par ordre du roi dans l'Amérique septentrionale adressé à Madame la duchesse de L'esdiguières*, Vol. III, *Histoire de la Nouvelle France* (Paris, 1744); Louis-Armand de Lom d'Arce, Baron de Lahontan, *New Voyages to North America*, ed. Reuben G. Thwaites from the English ed. of 1703, 2 vols. (Chicago, 1905).

3. To descriptions by Aulneau, Nau, Charlevoix, and Lahontan above, add Peter Kalm, *Travels into North America*, trans. J.R. Forster (1772; reprinted Barre, Mass., 1972), 6 Aug. 1749; Jacques Dargent, "Relation d'un voyage de Paris à Montreal en Canada en 1737," *RAPQ, 1947-48*, pp. 5-17, and Allana G. Reid, "The Development and Importance of the Town of Quebec, 1608-1760," Ph.D. dissertation, McGill University, 1950, pp. 61-144.

4. André Charbonneau, Yvon Desloges, and Marc Lafrance, *Québec, the Fortified City: From the 17th to the 19th Century* (Ottawa, 1982).

5. Louis Beaudet, ed., *Recensement de la ville de Québec pour 1716* (Quebec, 1887); "Le recensement de Québec en 1744," *RAPQ, 1939-40*, pp. 1-154.

6. Charlevoix, *Journal of a Voyage to North-America* (Ann Arbor, Mich., 1966, facsimile ed. of 1761, 2 vols.), I: 112.

7. Louise Dechêne, *Habitants et marchands de Montréal au XVIIe siècle* (Montreal and Paris, 1974), pp. 212-14, describes the France-Canada link as "horizontal," marked by reciprocity of debt, whereas it is argued here that, on balance, horizontal reciprocity was exceptional and fugitive. On the role of the colony for young French traders, see Miquelon, "Havy and Lefebvre"; John F. Bosher, "Writing Early Canadian History: The Case for French Merchants in the Canada Trade," *The Written Word/*

Prestige de l'écrit, proceedings of the 22nd Symposium, ed. A.G. McKay (Ottawa, 1980), pp. 24-36.

8. Marcel Delafosse, "La Rochelle et le Canada au XVIIIe siècle," *RHAF* 4 (1950-51): 483-84.

9. Pritchard, "Ships, Men and Commerce," pp. 159-60; John F. Bosher, "French Protestant Families in Canadian Trade, 1740-1760," *HS/SH* 7 (1974): 179-201, and, "A Quebec Merchant's Trading Circles in France and Canada: Jean-André Lamaletie before 1763," *HS/SH* 10 (1977): 24-44.

10. Pritchard, "Ships, Men and Commerce," pp. 72-87, 160-61, 248.

11. Ibid., pp. 299-300; "Antoine Pascaud," *DCB* II: 508–9.

12. AC, F2B I, fol. 268, "Messieurs les directeurs et sindics de la chambre de commerce de la Rochelle, 22 jan. 1734" (memorandum).

13. Pritchard, "Ships, Men and Commerce," p. 327.

14. Helen Nolan, "The Port of La Rochelle, 1715-1745," M. A. thesis, University of Ottawa, 1969, p. 24.

15. Pritchard, "Ships, Men and Commerce," pp. 163-64. Tables and graphs, pp. 487-506, an important source for the present chapter, are also in James S. Pritchard, "The Pattern of French Colonial Shipping to Canada before 1760," *Revue française d'histoire d'outre-mer* 63 (1976): 189-210.

16. Pritchard, "Ships, Men and Commerce," p. 321; John F. Bosher, "Une famille de Fleurance dans le commerce du Canada à Bordeaux (1683-1753): les Jung,"

Annales du Midi 95 (1983): 159-84.

17. For example, see the letters of Jean Jung to Antoine Paris of Louisbourg in AC, G2, carton 181.

18. Pritchard, "Ships, Men and Commerce," pp. 314-16.

19. Miquelon, *Dugard of Rouen*, p. 85.

20. Pritchard, "Ships, Men and Commerce," p. 326.

21. A. Jean E. Lunn, "Economic Development in New France, 1713-1760," Ph.D. dissertation, McGill University, 1942, p. 351, now published as *Développement économique de la Nouvelle-France, 1713-1760*, trans. B. Morel-Nish (Montreal, 1986).

22. AC, B 59: 401v, Maurepas à Hocquart, 17 mars 1733.

23. The meanings of words become blurred. The tag *forain* was a convenient slur applied to newcomers by metropolitans longer resident or by natives. Hocquart writes (AC, C11A, 60: 263, à Maurepas, Québec, 25 oct. 1733), "Les forains ont effectivement embrassé cette année tous le commerce encore avec plus d'estendue que les années précédentes." But how many real *forains* were present in a year that saw the arrival of four ships from La Rochelle, four from Bordeaux, one from Le Havre, and only one from a port without established connections in Canada, Marseilles? On Hocquart's attempt to create a Canadian bourgeoisie, see Donald J. Horton, "Gilles Hocquart, Intendant of New France, 1729-1748," Ph.D. dissertation, McGill University, 1974.

24. AC, C11A 59: 116, Hocquart au Ministre, Québec, 27 oct. 1732.

25. "Approbation d'une Assemblee des marchands . . ." 6 oct. 1740, Canada, Assembly of the Province of, *Arrêts et règlements du Conseil supérieur de Québec et ordonnances et jugements des intendants du Canada* (Quebec, 1855), pp. 554-55.

26. Lunn, "Economic Development," p. 354.

27. For a more extended treatment, see Miquelon, *Dugard of Rouen*, pp. 73-82.

28. E.g., see "François Havy," *DCB* III: 280-83; "Denis Goguet," ibid., IV: 306-7.

29. AN, 62AQ40, receipt, 18 July 1734; Dugard à Havy, Rouen, 14 juil. 1760; AQ, AJQ, Etude J-C Panet, 4 nov. 1751, "dépot d'un acte de société entre le sieur Lapointe et le sieur Lamaletie"; AC, F2B 1: 268, "La chambre de commerce de La Rochelle, 22 jan. 1734."

30. Miquelon, *Dugard of Rouen*, pp. 73-76.

31. PAC, Collection Baby, pp. 569-71, Havy et Lefebvre à Guy, Québec, 23 mars 1745.

32. AC, C11A 77: 143, Beauharnois à Maurepas, Québec, 1 nov. 1742.

33. AC, F2B 1: 268, "La chambre de commerce de la Rochelle, 22 jan. 1734."

34. AQ, AJQ, Etude Dulaurant, obligation Monfort, 23 oct. 1742.

35. PAC, Collection Baby, pp. 543-44, à Pierre Guy, Québec, 1 jan. 1745. See also Miquelon, *Dugard of Rouen*, pp. 79-80.

36. Lunn, "Economic Development," p. 477, table.

37. AC, C11A 67: 295, Hocquart à Maurepas, Québec, 2 oct. 1737.

38. Miquelon, *Dugard of Rouen*, p. 79.

39. AC, C11A 59: 121, Hocquart à Maurepas, Québec, 30 oct. 1732.

40. Lunn, "Economic Development," pp. 190-91, p. 466, table. The only new post after 1733 seems to have been Manicouagan, 1749.

41. Mary A. Johnston, "The King's Domain: The Domain of the West in New France, 1675-1733," M. A. thesis, University of Western Ontario, 1961, pp. 74, 85, 100-111, 119, 130.

42. Lunn, "Economic Development," pp. 195-97.

43. Marcel Trudel, *The Beginnings of New France, 1524-1663*, Canadian Centenary Series No. 2 (Toronto, 1973), p. 13.

44. P.G. Roy, *Inventaire des pièces sur la côte de Labrador*, 2 vols. (Quebec, 1940-42), I: 10, 13.

45. Ibid., I: 16.

46. "Augustin Le Gardeur de Courtemanche," *DCB* II: 383-84 (quotation); "François Martel de Brouague," ibid., III: 433-34; Lunn, "Economic Development," p. 198; William G. Gosling, *Labrador: Its Discovery, Exploration and Development* (London, 1910), p. 131.

47. Roy, *Côte de Labrador*, I: 24.

48. Canada, Department of Justice, *Canadian Case: Labrador Boundary: Atlas of Maps* (Ottawa, n.d.), p. 7.

49. Henry Youle Hind, *Explorations in the Interior of the Lab-*

rador Peninsula, the Country of the Montagnais and Nasquapee Indians (London, 1863), pp. 183-85.

50. "Le Gardeur de Courtemanche"; "Louis Fornel," *DCB* III: 224-25.

51. Gosling, *Labrador*, pp. 133-69; George Cartwright, *Captain Cartwright and His Labrador Journal*, ed. Charles W. Townsend (London, 1911), pp. 13-14.

52. Lunn, "Economic Development," p. 467, list of posts. Posts and concessions, of course, are not the same thing. A sign of continued activity was often further subletting and subdividing of concessions. See also Roy, *Côte de Labrador*, I and II.

53. Lunn, "Economic Development," p. 204.

54. David W. Zimmerly, *Cain's Land Revisited: Culture Change in Central Labrador, 1775-1972* (St. John's, 1975), p. 45.

55. Roy, *Côte de Labrador*, II: 181, Beauharnois et Hocquart au Ministre, Québec, 14 sept. 1739.

56. Ibid., II: 249, "Mémoire de MM Cugnet et Estèbe, 28 oct. 1744."

57. Lunn, "Economic Development," pp. 206-15.

58. Pritchard, "Ships, Men and Commerce," pp. 357, 364, H.A. Innis notwithstanding.

59. Ibid., pp. 359-61; Reid, "Town of Quebec," p. 181.

60. Reid, "Town of Quebec," pp. 181-82.

61. Pritchard, "Ships, Men and Commerce," table 13, p. 499.

62. Ibid., p. 364.

63. AC, C11A 62: 77, Hocquart au ministre, Québec, 11 oct. 1734; ibid., 63: 73, "Réponse au mémoire du roy, Québec, 13 oct. 1735"; ibid., 65: 28, "Réponse au mémoire du roy, 1736" (quotation).

64. Pritchard, "Ships, Men and Commerce," table 12, p. 498. A trade of similar volume between the West Indies and Louisiana based upon an exchange of mainland produce for French manufactures became established ten years later and lasted until 1763. See Clarence P. Gould, "Trade between the Windward Islands and the Continental Colonies of the French Empire, 1683-1763," *MVHR* 25 (1939): 473-90, p. 474.

65. AC, C8A 39: 337-72, "Mémoire sur le service des Isles du vent de l'Amérique, 6 xbre 1728," Versailles.

66. Ibid., 56: 110, "Eclaircisments données à M. De Ranchés par M. de la Croix."

67. Ibid., 42: 245, d'Orgeville au Ministre, Fort-Royal, 2 sept. 1731.

68. Ibid., 79: 319, Hocquart au Ministre, Québec, 8 oct. 1743. For a similar exposition of the problem (but not the solution), see C8B 3, "Mémoire de Vaucresson, 25 jan. 1713." Gould, "Windward Islands and Continental Colonies," claims cod made up 70% of Canadian cargoes by value.

69. AC, C11A 69: 243, Hocquart au Ministre, Québec, 2 oct. 1738.

70. Ibid., 61: 65, "Réponse au mémoire du Roy, Québec, 7 oct. 1734"; ibid., 76: 187, "Mémoire sur le commerce de Canada, 1741," also in Adam Shortt, *Documents Relating to Canadian Currency, Exchange and Finance during the French Period*, 2 vols.

(Ottawa, 1925), II: 691; AC, C8A 53: 411, De La Croix au Ministre, 28 déc. 1741.

71. AC, C11A 59: 171, Beauharnois et Hocquart au Ministre, Québec, 1 oct. 1733.

72. Ibid., 57: 156, Beauharnois et Hocquart au Ministre, Québec, 15 oct. 1732.

73. Calculated from tables 2 and 3, Pritchard, "Ships, Men and Commerce," pp. 488-90.

74. Calculated from Appendix C, Miquelon, *Dugard of Rouen*, pp. 191-95.

75. AC, C8A 40: 426, La Neuville au Ministre, Saint-Pierre, 6 sept. 1729.

76. AC, B 65: 118v-119r, Ministre à Dugard, 30 déc. 1737; ibid., 67: 145, same to same, 28 déc. 1738; ibid., 76: 228, Ministre à De Larnage et Maillart, 12 juin 1743 (quotation).

77. AC, C11A 60: 280, Hocquart au Ministre, Québec, 3 nov. 1733.

78. Pritchard, "Ships, Men and Commerce, p. 384, agrees.

79. Jacques Mathieu, *Le Commerce entre la Nouvelle-France et les Antilles au XVIIIe siècle* (Montreal, 1981), pp. 152-62 and the by no means self-explanatory tables, pp. 224-27.

80. AC, C11A 54: 57-60, Beauharnois et Hocquart au Ministre, Québec, 4 oct. 1731; ibid., 57: 156-59r, same to same, Québec, 15 oct. 1732; ASQ, Polygraphie 24, nos. 10 B, 10C, 36K.

81. AC, C8A 55: 340, Havy et Lefebvre à De La Croix, Québec, 30 mai 1743 (copy).

82. Calculated from tables 2-10, Pritchard, "Ships, Men and Commerce," pp. 488-96.

83. Ibid., pp. 337-39.

NOTES TO CHAPTER EIGHT

1. Pierre-François-Xavier de Charlevoix, *Journal d'un voyage fait par ordre du roi dans l'Amérique septentrionale ...* (Paris, 1744), pp. 137-38.

2. Edward R. Adair, "The Evolution of Montreal under the French Regime," *CHAAR*, 1942, pp. 20-41; Louise Dechêne, "La Croissance de Montréal au XVIIIe siècle," *RHAF* 27 (1973): 163-80; Jean-Claude Marsan, *Montreal in Evolution* (Montreal, 1981), pp. 3-18.

3. AC, C11A 20: 26-77, d'Aigremont à Pontchartrain, Québec, 14 nov. 1708. As to quantities and varieties of furs, some impression can be gained from A. Jean E. Lunn, "Economic Development in New France, 1713-1760," Ph.D. dissertation, McGill University, 1942, pp. 456-65, a subject much in need of revision.

4. Arthur J. Ray and Donald Freeman, *"Give Us Good Measure": An Economic Analysis of Relations Between the Indians and the Hudson's Bay Company before 1763* (Toronto, 1978), pp. 41-42.

5. Antoine Champagne, *Les La Vérendrye et le poste de l'Ouest*, Cahiers de l'Institut d'Histoire no. 12 (Quebec, 1969), pp. 117-18.

6. Louis-Edmond Hamelin, "La population totale du Canada depuis 1600," *Cahiers de Geographie de Québec* 9 (1965): 159-67.

See also William M. Denevan, ed., *The Native Population of the Americas in 1492* (Madison, Wis., 1976).

7. Lawrence J. Burpee, ed., *Journals and Letters of Pierre Gaultier de Varennes et de La Vérendrye and His Sons* (Toronto, 1927), p. 285, quoting Beauharnois to Maurepas, Quebec, 1 Oct. 1738, in AC, C11E 16: 372-82. For an introduction to an enormous literature see Bruce G. Trigger, *The Indians and the Heroic Age of New France*, CHA Historical Booklet No. 30 (Ottawa, 1978), the best short introduction to Indian ways in New France; see also Marshall D. Sahlins, *Tribesmen*, Foundations of Modern Anthropology Series (Englewood Cliffs, N.J., 1968), Wilcomb E. Washburn, *The Indian in America*, New American Nation Series (New York, 1975), and Marcel Giraud, *Le Métis canadien: son rôle dans l'histoire des provinces de l'ouest* (Paris, 1945). The bizarre thesis of Calvin Martin, *Keepers of the Game* (Berkeley and Los Angeles, 1978), is not supported by the evidence presented, but his "Subarctic Indians and Wildlife," in C.M. Judd and A.J. Ray, eds., *Old Trails and New Directions: Papers of the Third North American Fur Trade Conference* (Toronto, 1978), pp. 73-81, is excellent.

8. Ivy A. Dickson, trans., *Letters from North America by Father Antoine Silvy, S.J.* (Belleville, Ont., 1980), p. 111, a translation of Camille de Rochemonteix, ed., *Relations par lettres* (Paris, 1904), still unaccountably attributed to Father Antoine Silvy, S.J.; Cornelius J. Jaenen, *Friend and Foe: Aspects of French-Amerindian Cultural Contact in the Sixteenth and Seventeenth Centuries* (Toronto, 1976) introduces the topic to which James Axtell, *The European and the Indian: Essays in the Ethnohistory of Colonial North America* (New York, 1981) provides breadth and penetration.

9. Burpee, *Journals of La Vérendrye*, pp. 175-76, quoting La Vérendrye's report, 1733-34, from A.E., Mémoires et documents, 8:46.

10. Chap. 2 at n. 66. On Indian trade practices, Ray and Freeman, *Good Measure*, supersedes all previous work. See also Sahlins, *Tribesmen*, for gift exchange. With the exception of Bruce Trigger's work on the Hurons in the seventeenth century, research in this field has not dealt directly with the French-Indian trade, and conclusions on it are therefore provisional in this context.

11. AC, C11G 8: 183v, "Requeste des marchands negocians et habitans du Canada," s.d.

12. AC, C11A 67: 104, Mémoire de [Hocquart], Québec, 1737.

13. AQ-Québec, Etude Dulaurent, 23 oct. 1742, Facture, Havy & Lefebvre à Mme Ve Monfort, Québec 13 oct. 1742. Cf. graph in Louise Dechêne, *Habitants et marchands de Montréal au XVIIe siècle* (Montreal and Paris, 1974), p. 507. Dechêne discusses trade goods, pp. 150-60. See also Arthur J. Ray, *Indians in the Fur Trade: Their Role as Trappers, Hunters, and Middlemen in the Lands Southwest of Hudson Bay,*

1660–1870 (Toronto, 1974), Chap. 4, and Robert-Lionel Séguin, *Le Costume civil en Nouvelle-France*, Musée national du Canada Bulletin no. 215 (Ottawa, 1968). The most comprehensive treatment of Indian trade goods deals with the post-Conquest period: Patricia Miquelon, "Fur Trade Goods of the Montreal Traders, 1760-1821," National Historic Sites Service, unpublished in-house report, 1970.

14. See Edouard-Zotique Massicotte, *Montréal sous le régime français: repértoire des arrêts, édits, mandements, ordonnances et règlements conservés dans les archives du palais de justice de Montréal* (Montreal, 1919), and *ICS*.

15. Henri Têtu and Charles-O. Gagnon, eds., *Mandements, lettres pastorales et circulaires des éveques de Québec*, 2 vols. (Quebec, 1887), I: 535-37. Experimental lifting of the ban on brandy trading was authorized in the 1725 dispatches lost with the *Chameau* and in the 1726 dispatches. In 1727 definitive permission was given with much wringing of royal and ministerial hands. See AC, B 48: 765-66, Ministre à Vaudreuil, Versailles, 15 mai 1725; 49: 658v-60, Mémoire du roi, Versailles, 14 mai 1726; 50: 507v-58v, Mémoire du roi, Versailles, 29 av. 1727; S. Dale Standen, "Charles, Marquis de Beauharnais de la Boische, Governor General of New France, 1726-1747," Ph.D. dissertation, University of Toronto, 1975), p. 131.

16. François Vachon de Belmont, "Histoire de l'eau-de-vie en Can-

ada, d'après un manuscrit récemment obtenu de France," in *Collection de mémoires et de relations sur l'histoire ancienne du Canada, d'après des manuscrits récemment obtenus des archives et bureaux publics en France*, Historical Documents, 1st ser., Vol. II (Quebec, 1840). Vachon de Belmont's explanation accords well with some modern theories of Indian personality and adds substance to André Vachon's "L'eau de vie dans la société indienne," *CHAAR*, 1960, pp. 22-32. Many would give it only qualified approval or none at all. For the variety of modern hypothesizing, see Joy Leland, *Firewater Myths: North American Indian Drinking and Alcohol Addiction* (New Brunswick, N.J., 1976).

17. Adair, "Evolution of Montreal," p. 29.

18. "Congés de traite accordés en 1717," *Bulletin des recherches historiques* 29 (1923): 271-74; "Congés et permis de traite déposés ou enregistrés à Montréal sous le régime française," *RAPQ, 1921-22*, pp. 189-225; "Congés de traite sous le régime français au Canada," ibid., *1922-23*, pp. 196-265.

19. PAC, MG 18 E 29, Collection Charlevoix, "Longue lettre adressé par un jesuite et daté de Québec, 28 octobre 1705 3e lettre."

20. Ibid., "tirés des Mémoires de Mrs. Raudot et de Champigny, M. Raudot fils Lett. 13." In the version in AC, C11A 122: 82-83, the "three words" are added and "Ils continuent" is changed to the past tense, both in Charlevoix's

hand. The two collections were evidently once part of a single collection and merit a scholarly sorting out.

21. Beauharnois to the Minister, Quebec, 16 Oct. 1737, in Reuben G. Thwaites, *The French Regime in Wisconsin*, in *Collections of the State Historical Society*, Vols. 16-18 (Madison, Wis., 1902-1908), 17: 274-76.

22. Ibid., 18: 5-6, Minister to Beauharnois, Versailles, 28 April 1745.

23. Ibid., 17: 473-74, La Galissonière to Minister, Quebec, 24 Oct. 1747.

24. Dechêne, *Habitants et marchands*, pp. 169, 177-88, 217-22; Gratien Allaire, "Les Engagements pour la traite des fourrures – évaluation de la documentation," *RHAF* 34 (1980): 3-26, pp. 18-22.

25. E.g., AQ-Montréal, Etude C.J. Porlier, registre 642, "Registre des engagements de voyageurs pour les pays d'en haut qui doivent hyverner cette présent année 1740."

26. Hubert Charbonneau, Bertrand Desjardins, and Pierre Beauchamp, "Le comportement démographique des voyageurs sous le régime français," *HS/SH* 21 (1978): 120-33.

27. Allaire and Dechêne (n. 24 above) tend toward the acceptance of the extant records of voyages as a suitable basis for quantitative work, accepting that "les répertoires des notaires peuvent être considérés comme de véritables registres d'enregistrement des allées et venues dans l'Ouest" (Dechêne, *Habitants et marchands*, p. 217). Others fear the sources are too fragmentary

for establishing useful figures.

28. Charlevoix, *Journal*, pp. 89-90.

29. On Montreal, n. 24 above; on Quebec, Chap. 7, n. 25.

30. AQ-Montréal, Etude Raimbault fils, obligations, 9 sept. 1728; Etude J.C. Porlier, obligation, 15 juin 1736; Etude Raimbault fils, acte de société, 11 juin 1731; AQ-Québec, Etude Dulaurent, obligation, 15 sept. 1743; AQ-Montréal, Etude Raimbault fils, acte de société, 19 mai 1727.

31. Burpee, *Journals of La Vérendrye*, pp. 435-36 (Report of La Vérendrye, 31 Oct. 1744).

32. Dechêne, *Habitants et marchands*, pp. 203-14, where the author vigorously asserts the reciprocity of credit between Montreal and La Rochelle and hence the "horizontal" nature of that relationship, but see Chap. 7 above.

33. Miquelon, *Dugard of Rouen*, pp. 49, 69, 172-89.

34. That Dugard's factors carried considerable amounts under the heading of current accounts owing for their first three years at Quebec (1732-34) and then dropped the category from their annual statements suggests that tolerating this form of debt owed by merchants of substance was the price of opening business. See AN, 62AQ40, comptes de gestion à Québec, 1730-38. Only debt by notes and obligations is discussed in *Dugard of Rouen*, pp. 77-79. See also ibid., pp. 208-10.

35. Much of the information in Dechêne, *Habitants et marchands*, pp. 161-70, from the late seventeenth and early eighteenth centuries is borne out by the 1747 contract to exploit La Baie in n.

45 below. The same document makes a distinction between the price of furs as set by the Montreal merchants and the Quebec price in terms that suggest transportation costs made the difference.

36. Yves F. Zoltvany, *Philippe de Rigaud de Vaudreuil, Governor of New France, 1703–1725,* Carleton Library (Toronto, 1974), pp. 143-48. See Chap. 9, n. 12.

37. The inner workings of the fur trade, especially in the French period, remain as much a mystery as does most of Canadian business history. Remarks in this section are intended to direct attention to, rather than to solve, a central problem: the division of benefits among officers, outfitters, voyageurs, officials, and the state and changes thereof over time. The *congés* are discussed in Dechêne, *Habitants et marchands,* pp. 177-78; Zoltvany, *Vaudreuil,* pp. 116-19, 174-75; Standen, "Beauharnais," pp. 183-86; and Allaire, "Les Engagements," pp. 3-26, which includes a list of *registres de congés* published and unpublished. My comments on the *congés* are based upon the published registers (see n. 18 above).

38. AC, C11A 77: 94, Beauharnois à Maurepas, Québec, 5 sept. 1742; AQ-Montréal, Etude Raimbault fils, 7 juin 1727, obligation of Commandant Denys de La Ronde's partnership to Charles Nolan Lamarque for 23,510 livres to exploit Chagouamigon and 14 juin 1731, obligation of Commandant Nicolas Antoine Coulons de Villiers's partnership to Louis de La Corne for 16,357 livres to exploit La Baie.

39. *Historical Collections. Collections and Researches Made by the Michigan Pioneer and Historical Society* 34 (Lansing, 1905): 51-53, 59-61, 73-85, 138-40, 157-61, 161-63, 211-12 (Detroit from 1727); Geoffrey S. Simpson, "Quebec and Paris: The French Search for the Western Sea in Canada, 1660-1760," Ph.D. dissertation, Cambridge University, 1972, p. 116; Champagne, *Les La Vérendrye,* pp. 109-16, 481-90; Thwaites, *French Regime in Wisconsin* 18: 10-15, 135-38 (Sioux companies), 165-67, 187 (La Ronde); AC, B 58: 470, Mémoire du roi, Versailles, 12 mai 1733; Zoltvany, *Vaudreuil,* p. 151.

40. Standen, "Beauharnais," pp. 190-91, 242 n. 96; Zoltvany, *Vaudreuil,* pp. 178, 190; Dechêne, *Habitants et marchands,* pp. 182-83.

41. Dechêne, *Habitants et marchands,* pp. 192-93, 206, quoting AC, B 48: 906-7, Maurepas à Vaudreuil, 11 août 1725.

42. Standen, "Beauharnais," pp. 186-94; AC, C11A 49: 334, Dupuy à Maurepas, Québec, 20 oct. 1727; B 52: 504, Mémoire du roi, Versailles, 14 mai 1728; 53: 536, Maurepas à Beauharnois et Hocquart, Compiègne, 2 mai 1729.

43. AC, C11A 50: 23, Beauharnois et d'Aigremont à Maurepas, Québec, 1 oct. 1728; Donald J. Horton, "Gilles Hocquart, Intendant of New France, 1729-1748," Ph.D. dissertation, McGill University, 1974, pp. 66-72; Standen, "Beauharnais," pp. 346-67.

44. AC, B 74: 93, Mémoire du roi, Fontainebleau, 30 av. 1742; fol. 60, Maurepas à Beauharnois, Fontainebleau, 20 av. 1742 (quotation); AC, C11A 77: 94-97, Beau-

harnois à Maurepas, Québec, 5 sept. 1742; Standen, "Beauharnais," pp. 368-72.

45. Thwaites, *French Regime in Wisconsin* 17: 451-55, "1747: Lease for the post at Green Bay"; 18: 7-10, "1747: Partnership to Exploit La Baye."

46. Ibid., 18: 25.

NOTES TO CHAPTER NINE

1. AC, B 52: 504, Mémoire du roi, Versailles, 14 mai 1728 is an excellent example.

2. PAC, MG 5, A-1 25: 111-18 (A.E. vol. 342), "Mémoire sur les points qui doivent etre examinez et decidez par des Commres du Roy, et du Roy de la Gde. Brete. joint à l'instruction remise au Comte de Broglie le 28e mai 1724"; Charles Jenkinson, *A Collection of Treaties*, 3 vols. (London, 1785), II: 34-35.

3. AC, C11E 2: 16-29, "Mémoire pour Servir à Regler Les Limites Entre la Nouvelle france La Nouvelle Angleterre et l'acadie autrement Nouvelle Ecosse" (Bégon, 8 nov. 1713); fols. 90-93, "Limites de la nouvelle france et de la nouvelle angleterre" (Aubery, jan., 1720); PAC, MG 5, A-1, 24: 33-52 (A.E. vol. 334), "Angre. Janer 1720, Memoire general sur les limites de l'Acadie."

4. Examples are Versailles: PAC, MG 5, B-2, 4: 116-262 (A.E. vol. 17), "Mémoire historique sur ce qui à esté stipulé par la paix conclue à Utrecht le lle Avril 1713 . . . Fait en 1724 Decemb 31 par M. le Dran, chef du Depôt des Affares. etrangeres" (hereafter Le Dran's memorandum); Canada: *NYCD* v: 827-28, Beauharnois to Burnet, Montreal, 20 July 1727.

5. Re domino concept: *RAPQ, 1947-48*, pp. 291-92, Vaudreuil au duc d'Orléans, fév. 1716; AC, C11E 10: 102, Beauharnois à Maurepas, Québec, 13 oct. 1727; for utterance in a private merchant's letters, see Dale Miquelon, *Dugard of Rouen: French Trade to Canada and the West Indies, 1729-1770* (Montreal, 1978), p. 142.

6. Marcel Giraud, *Histoire de la Louisiane française*, 4 vols. (Paris, 1953-74), I: 321-26.

7. *NYCD*, V: 217-29, "Conference of Governor Hunter with the Indians," Albany, 7-21 Aug. 1710.

8. Ibid., pp. 437-47, "Conference of Governor Hunter with the Indians," Albany, 27 Aug.-2 Sept. 1715; pp. 484-94, "Conference between Governor Hunter and the Indians," Albany, 13-17 June 1717 (quotation, p. 488).

9. Thomas E. Norton, *The Fur Trade in Colonial New York, 1686-1776* (Madison, Wis., 1974), Chap. 3; AC, C11A 28: 3, Vaudreuil et Raudot au ministre, Québec, 14 nov. 1708. Iroquois traders or Iroquois hunters? Reexamination of the G.T. Hunt thesis is long overdue.

10. Verner W. Crane, *The Southern Frontier, 1670-1732* (Durham, N.C., 1928), pp. 158-61; *NYCD*, V: 372-76, "Conference with the Five Nations at Onondaga," 21-22 Aug. 1713 (date of quotation).

11. Yves F. Zoltvany, *Philippe de Rigaud de Vaudreuil, Governor of New France, 1703-1725*, Car-

leton Library (Toronto, 1974), pp. 133-43; François-Emile Audet, *Les Premiers Établissements français au pays des Illinois: la guerre des Renards* (Paris, 1938), pp. 77-83; Louise P. Kellogg, *The French Régime in Wisconsin and the Northwest* (Madison, 1925), pp. 285-86; *ICS*, p. 129, "Edit de Sa Majesté qui defend . . ." (the amnesty); AC, B 36 pt. 6: 380v-383v, Pontchartrain à Vaudreuil et Bégon, Marly, 3 mai 1714; fols. 377v-378, Pontchartrain à Louvigny, Marly, 1 mai 1714.

12. Zoltvany, *Vaudreuil*, pp. 143-48; *ICS*, Lettres patentes, mars 1716 (coureurs), Déclaration, 28 av. 1716 (*congés*).

13. Crane, *Southern Frontier*, Chap. 8 (quotation at p. 179). Crane discounts Franco-Spanish intrigue as a cause of the rebellion.

14. Zoltvany, *Vaudreuil*, pp. 162-63; A. Jean E. Lunn, "Economic Development in New France, 1713-1760," Ph.D. dissertation, McGill University, 1942, pp. 450-54; Kellogg, *French Régime in Wisconsin*; Lyle M. Stone, *Fort Michilimackinac, 1715-1781: An Archaeological Perspective on the Revolutionary Frontier* (East Lansing, 1974). Forts did change locations, and there were undoubtedly auxiliary posts that are lost sight of (see D. Chaput in *DCB* II: 562) and nameless private posts that usually escape mention or detection. AC, C11A 124: 49-52, "M. le Mis de Vaudreuil 12 8bre 1717 sur les postes et congés" is useful for dates and strategic implications. See also enumeration of garrisons in "Estat des soldats destaché dans les postes outa8an" in C11E 13: 140v-41v.

15. Geoffrey S. Simpson, "Quebec and Paris: The French Search for the Western Sea in Canada, 1660-1760," Ph.D. dissertation, Cambridge University, 1972, p. 41.

16. Harold Hickerson, "Ethnohistory of Chippewa in Central Minnesota," in *Chippewa Indians*, American Indian Ethnohistory: North Central and Northeastern Indians Series (New York, 1974), IV: 55. Dakota dominance beyond Lake Superior, the Dakota-Ojibwa alliance and its later dissolution, and Ojibwa expansion are further treated in Hickerson's "Ethnohistory of Mississippi Bands and Pillager and Winnibigoshish Bands of Chippewa," *Chippewa Indians* II, and his "Ethnohistory of Chippewa of Lake Superior," *Chippewa Indians* III. William W. Warren, "History of the Ojibways, Based upon Traditions and Oral Statements," Chap. 8 of Warren and Edward D. Neill, *History of the Ojibway Nation* (1895; reprint of 1957 ed., Minneapolis, 1970) discusses the importance of firearms in righting a pre-contact imbalance of power.

17. *ICS*, p. 148, "Lettres patentes de Sa Majeste pour la réunion du pays des Illinois au gouvernement de la Louisiane," 27 sept. 1717.

18. Zoltvany, *Vaudreuil*, pp. 168-69; *NYCD* V: 588-91, "Mr. Durant's Memorial relative to French Post at Niagara," New York, 1 July 1721 (first quotation); pp. 576-81, Burnet to Lords of Trade,

New York, 26 Nov. 1720 (second quotation); p. 564, "Conference between Col. Schuyler and the Indians," 1 Sept. 1720; pp. 528-29, "Intelligence of a French Fort at Niagara," 6 July 1719 [*sic*].

19. Zoltvany, *Vaudreuil*, p. 170.

20. S. Dale Standen, "Charles, Marquis de Beauharnais de la Boische, Governor General of New France, 1726-1747," Ph.D. dissertation, University of Toronto, 1975, p. 131.

21. AC, C11A 28: 3, Vaudreuil et Raudot au Ministre, Québec, 14 nov. 1708.

22. *NYCD* v: 576-81 at p. 577, Burnet, New York, 26 Nov. 1720.

23. Ibid., pp. 430-31, Colonel Heathcote to Governor Hunter, Scarsdale, 28 July 1715.

24. Ibid., pp. 506-7, Colonel Schuyler to Governor Hunter, Albany, 5 Feb. 1718.

25. Crane, *Southern Frontier*, Chaps. 8, 9, 11; *NYCD* v: 591-630, "State of the British Plantations in America in 1721"; Lords of Trade to the King, 8 Sept. 1721.

26. *NYCD* v: 484-94, "Conference between Governor Hunter and the Indians," Albany, 13-17 June 1717; pp. 657-81, "Conference between Governor Burnet and the Indians," Albany, 27 Aug.-14 Sept. 1722.

27. Crane, *Southern Frontier*, pp. 179-83; Patricia Dillon Woods, *French-Indian Relations on the Southern Frontier, 1699-1762*, Studies in American History and Culture No. 18 (Ann Arbor, Mich., 1980), Chaps, 4, 5, 7, 8.

28. Norton, *Fur Trade in New York*, Chap. 9, for Burnet's western policy.

29. Zoltvany, *Vaudreuil*, pp. 198-99; Standen, "Beauharnais," pp. 120-29.

30. *NYCD* v: 800-801, "Deed in Trust from three of the Five Nations of Indians to the King," Albany, 14 Sept. 1726. English attitudes regarding their land transactions with Indians were bizarre in that they considered their purchase of land as effecting a transfer of sovereignty over such land. The two transactions are in law, of course, utterly distinct. The trust deeds were perhaps more "normal" transactions. The resulting protectorates did not imply full sovereignty and entailed no transfer of ownership. Was there, in fact, anything in these transactions inimical to the Iroquois other than the use that might be made of such documents by designing Englishmen?

31. This expression in various forms appears intermittently, at least from the time of William III and Louis XIV's letters to end the Iroquois war after Ryswick. For example, in 1726 the headmen reported to Burnet that they had heard "the Six Nations were to be cut off" (*NYCD* v: 789, "Conference Between Governor Burnet and the Indians," Albany, 7 Sept. 1726), but Burnet explained that the emperor (Charles VI) was the intended adversary.

32. See Norton, *Fur Trade in New York*, Chap. 8, for a history of the trade and efforts, especially Burnet's, to stop it.

33. "Etat des differentes sortes de Marchandises qui composent les cargaisons des vaisseaux destinez pour la Colonie du Canada, pour la consommation des habitans"; "Etat . . . pour la traitte avec les

Sauvages . . ." in J. Savary des Bruslons, ed., *Dictionnaire universel de commerce: contenant tout ce qui concerne le commerce qui se fait dans les quatre coins du monde*, 3 vols. (Amsterdam, 1726-32), III: 324-26. See also n. 35 below.

34. Norton, *Fur Trade in New York*, p. 126.

35. Canada, Assembly of the Province of, *Edits et ordonnances: revus et corrigés d'après les pièces originales déposées aux archives provinciales*, I (Quebec, 1854): 302, Arrêt, 25 juin 1707, p. 395, Arrêt, 11 juil. 1718, p. 401, Arrêt, 4 juin 1719; *ICS*, p. 117, Edit 6 juil. 1709, p. 131, Déclaration 6 mai 1715, p. 150, Arrêt, 11 juil. 1718, p. 151, Arrêt, 4 juin 1719, p. 153, Arrêt, 2 juin 1720, p. 157, Règlement 23 juil. 1721, p. 163, Arrêt, 15 mai 1722, Arrêt, 28 jan. 1722, p. 171, Déclaration, 22 mai 1724, p. 183, Ordre de Sa Majesté, 14 mai 1726, p. 191, Arrêt, juil. 1731. Many of these statutes specify beaver pelts only because they are concerned to protect the beaver monopolist's rights. The loophole regarding other furs is only indirectly closed by regulations prohibiting the import of foreign manufactures or prohibiting travel.

36. C.H. McIlwain, "Introduction," in Peter Wraxall, *An Abridgement of the Indian Affairs Contained in Four Folio Volumes, Transacted in the Colony of New York, from the Year 1678 to the Year 1751*, ed. C.H. McIlwain (1915; reprinted, New York, 1968) p. lxvii.

37. Standen, "Beauharnais," pp. 264-66.

38. Donald J. Horton, "Gilles Hocquart, Intendant of New France, 1729-1748," Ph.D. dissertation, McGill University, 1974, p. 159.

39. Quoted in Zoltvany, *Vaudreuil*, p. 166, from AC, C11A 43: 99-100, Vaudreuil au Conseil de Marine, Québec, 4 nov. 1720.

40. The Dutisné dispatches are in AC, C11A 56: 251-71v.

41. Quoted in Standen, "Beauharnais," p. 139, from AC, C11A 49: 49, Beauharnois et Dupuy à Maurepas, Québec, 25 oct. 1727. On Beauharnois's character, see Standen, "Beauharnais," pp. 214-16, 466-76.

42. Quoted in Standen, "Beauharnais," p. 271, from AC, C11A 54: 356v, Beauharnois à Maurepas, Québec, 23 mai 1731.

43. AC, B 48: 741, Maurepas à Vaudreuil, Versailles, 1 mai 1725; 49: 656, Mémoire du roy à Beauharnois et Dupuy, Versailles, 14 mai 1726, 50: 506, Mémoire du Roy à Beauharnois et Dupuy, Versailles, 29 av. 1727; AC, C11A 48: 418, De Lignery à De Liette, La Baye, 15 juin 1726. For Beauharnois, see his numerous dispatches, including that in n. 42 above.

44. Quoted in Standen, "Beauharnais," pp. 277-78, from AC, C11A 65: 143-43v, Beauharnois au Ministre, Québec 17 oct. 1736.

45. The most recent treatment of the Fox wars is in Zoltvany, *Vaudreuil*, and Standen, "Beauharnais," which works also serve as guides to the documents. Kellogg, *French Régime in Wisconsin*, and Audet, *Premiers établissements français*, are of little use for explanation. "Ouachala," *DCB* II: 502, gives evi-

dence of cross currents in the Fox tribe and external pressures. The reference to 1692 is from Warren and Neill, *History of the Ojibway Nation*, p. 419.

46. Simpson, "Quebec and Paris," pp. 117-47 (quotation, p. 130); "Pierre-François-Xavier Charlevoix," *DCB* III: 103-9.

47. In spite of all that has been written about him, La Vérendrye remains unfinished business for the historian. The authoritative bibliographical essay by Y.F. Zoltvany in "Pierre Gaultier de Varennes et de La Vérendrye," *DCB* III: 246-54, to which the provocative Smith (below) should be added, is to be consulted. The present narrative is based primarily on Antoine Champagne, *Les La Vérendrye et le poste de l'Ouest*, Cahiers de l'Institut d'Histoire no. 12 (Quebec, 1969), Simpson, "Quebec and Paris," Standen, "Beauharnais," and Lawrence J. Burpee's collection of documents, *Journals and Letters of Pierre Gaultier de Varennes et de La Vérendrye and his Sons* (Toronto, 1927). The itineraries for the La Vérendryes' overland explorations in 1738 and 1742-43 described in Champagne, *Nouvelles Études sur les La Vérendrye et le poste de l'Ouest*, Cahiers de l'Institut d'Histoire no. 17 (Quebec, 1971) should be studied in the light of G. Hubert Smith, *The Explorations of the La Vérendryes in the Northern Plains, 1738-43*, ed. W. Raymond Wood (Lincoln, Neb., 1980).

It is sometimes alleged that La Vérendrye made a fundamental error in turning southwest from the Saskatchewan to the Missouri, thus delaying the opening of the Canadian West. That there can be no wrong route to a mythical goal (the Western Sea) and that the Canadian West had no northern definition before the surveying of the boundary are the obvious ripostes in addition to the line of argument in the present narrative.

48. Burpee, *Journals of La Vérendrye*, p. 57, Report of La Vérendrye (1730) from AC, F3 11: 474-89.

49. Ibid., pp. 268-69, La Vérendrye to Maurepas, Quebec, 1 Oct 1737, from AC, C11E 16: 345-47.

50. Ibid., pp. 436, Report of La Vérendrye, 31 Oct. 1744, from AC, C11E 16: 467-82.

51. Standen, "Beauharnais," p. 268, quoting AC, C11A 54: 385, Beauharnois à Maurepas, Québec, 1 oct. 1731.

52. Simpson, "Quebec and Paris," p. 166, quoting AC F3 11: 224, Mémoire du Roy, Versailles, 19 av. 1729.

53. See "Le problème financier de La Vérendrye," Appendice Premier, in Champagne, *Les La Vérendrye*, pp. 479-98.

54. Burpee, *Journals of La Vérendrye*, p. 225, Report of La Vérendrye, 2 June 1736 from AC, Moreau de St. Méry, 10: 348.

55. Champagne, *Les La Vérendrye*, p. 125, quoting AC, C11E 16: 286-88, Beauharnois au Ministre, Québec, 15 oct. 1732. On war, see Champagne, Standen, "Beauharnais," and Hickerson in *Chippewa Indians*, Vols. II, III, and IV. Champagne convincingly rejects the idea that the Lake of the Woods massacre was Dakota revenge for J.-B. La Vérendrye's participation in a

1734 war party (*Les La Vérendrye*, pp. 186-87). Hickerson's contention that the Ojibwas broke their alliance with the Dakotas because of the massacre (*Chippewa Indians*, III: 42) is so simplistic that it underscores the need for deeper study. As a signal event, the massacre may end up on the scrap heap with Champlain's lucky shot of 1609.

56. Simpson, "Quebec and Paris," p. 268, quoting BN, FF 13373 (b) Bonnécamps à Castel, Québec, 3 nov. 1750.

57. On the Anglo-American westward movement, see Douglas E. Leach, *The Northern Colonial Frontier, 1607-1763*, Histories of the American Frontier (New York, 1966), and Walter Stitt Robinson, *The Southern Colonial Frontier*, Histories of the American Frontier (Albuquerque, 1979).

58. Wraxall, *Abridgment*, p. 219 n.

59. Clarke's activities are amply demonstrated in *NYCD* VI: 98-242, of which see "Deed to His Majesty of the Land around Irondequoit" at p. 204. See also Norton, *Fur Trade in New York*, pp. 179-82.

60. *NYCD* VI: 172-79, "Conference between the Lieutenant-Governor Clarke and the Six Nations," Albany, 12?, 16? Aug. 1740.

61. Ibid., p. 210, Lt. Gov. Bull to Lt. Gov. Clarke, Charlestown, S.C., June 1741.

62. Ibid., pp. 211-12, Oglethorpe to Clarke, Frederica, 12 July 1741.

63. Robinson, *Southern Frontier*, pp. 142-43.

64. Standen, "Beauharnais," pp. 293-300; Woods, *French-Indian Relations*, pp. 95-161.

65. Standen, "Beauharnais," pp. 299-307, 406-11, 440.

66. Ibid., p. 302.

67. *NYCD* VI: 232-42.

NOTES TO CHAPTER TEN

1. Peter Kalm, *Travels into North America*, trans. J.R. Forster (1772; reprinted, Barre, Mass., 1972), 2 Aug. 1749.

2. "Mémoires sur les Plans des Seigneuries et Habitations des Gouvernements de Québec les Trois Rivières et Montréal, par Gédéon de Catalogne, ingénieur, novembre 7, 1712," in W.B. Munro, ed., *Documents Relating to the Seigneurial Tenure in Canada, 1598-1854* (Toronto, 1908).

3. Fernand Braudel, *Afterthoughts on Material Civilization and Capitalism*, trans. P. Ranum (Baltimore, 1977), p. 7.

4. On population see Georges Langlois, *Histoire de la population canadienne-française* (Montreal, 1936), pp. 75-77, 244; A. Jean E. Lunn, "Economic Development in New France, 1713-1760," Ph.D. dissertation, McGill University, 1942, pp. 443-44; for Montreal, Louise Dechêne, "La Croissance de Montréal au XVIIIe siècle," *RHAF* 27 (1973): 163-80; and Richard C. Harris, *The Seigneurial System in Early Canada, A Geographical Study* (Madison, Wis., 1968), pp. 89-100, on which the description of distribution is based. No population figures are exact;

uncertainty and divergent opinions must be tolerated.

5. De Catalogne, "Mémoires," in Munro, *Seigneurial Documents*, p. 145.

6. Harris, *Seigneurial System*, p. 189; Pierre Deffontaines, "The *Rang*-Pattern of Rural Settlement in French Canada," in Marcel Rioux and Yves Martin, eds., *French Canadian Society*, Carleton Library (Toronto, 1964); Jean-Claude Marsan, *Montreal in Evolution* (Montreal, 1981), pp. 26, 32; G.P. de T. Glazebrook, *A History of Transportation in Canada* (Toronto, 1938), pp. 101-8.

7. Roland Sanfacon, "La construction du premier chemin Québec-Montréal et le problème des corvées (1706-1737)," *RHAF* 12 (1958): 3-29.

8. Max Derreau, "A l'origine du 'rang' canadien," *Cahiers de géographie de Québec* I (1956): 47; B.H. Slicher van Bath, *The Agrarian History of Western Europe, 1500-1850* (London, 1963), p. 57.

9. Harris, *Seigneurial System*, pp. 117-21; Chevalier de La Pause, "Relations et mémoires du chevalier de La Pause," *RAPQ, 1933-34*, p. 211; Louise Dechêne, *Habitants et marchands de Montréal au XVIIe siècle* (Montreal and Paris, 1974), pp. 264-300; Pierre Goubert in Fernand Braudel and Ernest Labrousse, eds., *Histoire économique et sociale de la France* (Paris, 1970), II: 146-47; P. Goubert, *The Ancien Régime: French Society, 1600-1750* (New York, 1974), pp. 113-15.

10. James A. Henretta, *The Evolution of American Society,*

1700-1815: An Interdisciplinary Analysis (Lexington, Mass., 1973), pp. 15-18; James T. Lemon, *The Best Poor Man's Country: A Geographical Study of Early Southeastern Pennsylvania* (New York, 1976), p. 167. The first New England farms had been 20 acres, increased to 200 to 300 in the late seventeenth century, and shrank to less than 100 in the eighteenth. Larger farm size did not lead to more land in cultivation but to a more extensive agriculture. Henretta states that the farmer would plant only 12 acres a year; Lemon estimates 35. Bettye Hobbs Pruitt, "Self-sufficiency and the Agricultural Economy of Eighteenth-Century Massachusetts," *WMQ* 3rd ser., 41(1984): 333-64, p. 338, states that the median size of "improved acreage" in Massachusetts in 1771 was twenty acres.

11. Harris, *Seigneurial System*, pp. 169-92, differentiates between *côte* and straggling village, which, for the purpose of this book at least, seems an unnecessary nicety. The argument in Allan Greer, "Habitants of the Lower Richelieu: Rural Society in Three Quebec Parishes, 1740-1840," Ph.D. dissertation, York University, 1980, that because families scattered among many *côtes*, that unit *ipso facto* was not "the fundamental social unit" (p. 165) is convincing only to the extent that it reminds us that the *côte* did not have the cohesion of later times. See also Goubert, *Ancien Régime*, pp. 78-94.

12. Goubert, *Ancien Régime*, esp. pp. 88-116.

13. De Catalogne, "Mémoires,"

in Munro, *Seigneurial Documents*, pp. 107, 110. See also Harris, *Seigneurial System*, p. 112.

14. AC, C11A 26: 150-71v, Raudot père au Min., Québec, 10 nov. 1707 (quotations); Harris, *Seigneurial System*, pp. 34-40, 65, 105-8; Lunn, "Economic Development," pp. 32-36, 65-66; "The Arrêts of Marly, July 6, 1711," in Munro, *Seigneurial Documents*, pp. 91-94.

15. Harris, *Seigneurial System*, pp. 117-38; Dechêne, *Habitants et marchands*, pp. 247-50.

16. Dechêne, *Habitants et marchands*, pp. 312-14; Greer, "Lower Richelieu," p. 170.

17. Cf. Goubert in Braudel and Labrousse, *Histoire économique et sociale*, II: 130-34.

18. Harris, *Seigneurial System*, pp. 78, 81. My 43 l. corresponds to Harris's 33 l. Harris incorrectly calculates the habitant's milling cost from the mill's net profit rather than its total revenue.

19. Greer, "Lower Richelieu," p. 136.

20. Harris, *Seigneurial System*, pp. 81-97.

21. Louis Franquet, *Voyages et mémoires sur le Canada par Franquet* (Quebec, 1889), p. 157. See also "Louis Lepage de Sainte-Claire," *DCB* III: 390-91.

22. Slicher van Bath, *Agrarian History*, p. 21. Greer, "Lower Richelieu," pp. 140-45, confirms the insignificance of the *domaine*.

23. Emmanuel Le Roy Ladurie, Hugues Neveux, and Jean Jacquart, *L'Age classique des paysans, 1340-1789*, Vol. II of Georges Duby and Armand Wal-

lon, eds., *Histoire de la France rurale* (N.p., 1975), p. 431.

24. Seigneurial privileges and revenues have been examined in Harris, *Seigneurial System*, pp. 63-87, from which the estimate of profitability is taken, and Dechêne, *Habitants et marchands*, pp. 247-54, in which the mill is pronounced unprofitable.

25. Dechêne, *Habitants et marchands*, pp. 255-58; Goubert in Braudel and Labrousse, *Histoire économique et sociale*, II: 128-29; Greer, "Lower Richelieu," pp. 103-28.

26. AC, C11A 7: 144, De Meulles à la Cour, Québec, 28 sept. 1685, quoted in Dechêne, *Habitants et marchands*, p. 306.

27. Nicolas-Gaspard Boucault, "Etat présent du Canada," *RAPQ, 1920-21*, pp. 1-50, p. 20.

28. Fernand Braudel, *Capitalism and Material Life, 1400-1800* (New York, 1975), pp. 71-72.

29. Kalm, *Travels*, 12 Aug., 23 Sept. 1749; Boucault, "Etat présent," pp. 20-21; AC, C11A 67: 97-107, Hocquart[?], "Détail de toute la colonie" (1737).

30. Kalm, *Travels*, 29 Aug., 1 Aug. 1749.

31. De Catalogne, "Mémoires," in Munro, *Seigneurial Documents*, p. 151.

32. Hocquart[?], "Détail de toute la colonie."

33. Kalm, *Travels*, 31 Aug., 13 Sept. 1749.

34. Franquet, *Voyages et mémoires*, p. 181.

35. Lemon, *Best Poor Man's Country*, pp. 154-56; Braudel, *Capitalism*, pp. 78-83; Braudel and Labrousse, *Histoire économique et sociale*, II: 440-45.

36. Dechêne, *Habitants et mar-*

chands, pp. 324-30. These ratios, with all their limitations of time, place, and number, are to be preferred to the theoretical, global estimates presented in Harris, *Seigneurial System*, p. 153, and Jean Hamelin and Fernand Ouellet, "Les rendements agricoles dans les seigneuries et les cantons du Québec, 1700-1850," in Claude Galarneau and Elzear Lavoie, eds., *France et Canada français du XVIe au XXe siècles*, Cahiers de l'Institut d'Histoire no. 7 (Quebec, 1966), pp. 81-120. One must share the scepticism of E. Labrousse on hearing the latter paper (ibid., p. 142) and heed the advice of F. Braudel (*Capitalism*, p. 79). Until more case studies have been done, contemporary testimony may be the best evidence of all.

37. It is this delicate balance that makes rough generalizations regarding yield ratios liable to be completely misleading. See n. 22 above.

38. Kalm, *Travels*. The principal criticisms are at the following dates: 11 July, 28 July, 12 Aug., and 23 Sept. 1749. The mistake of imputing to Kalm our criticism of the facts he presents in a neutral tone can easily lead to misinterpretation.

39. De Catalogne, "Mémoires," in Munro, *Seigneurial Documents*, p. 130 (first quotation), p. 140 (second quotation), pp. 145-48.

40. Kalm, *Travels*, 11 July, 12, 25, 29 Aug.; 23 Sept. 1749; Boucault, "Etat présent," p. 20; La Pause, "Relations et mémoires," pp. 211-12; "Vaudreuil et Raudot au Ministre, Québec,

14 nov. 1709," in "Correspondance entre M. de Vaudreuil et la cour, 1709-10," *RAPQ, 1942-43*, p. 419; Slicher van Bath, *Agrarian History*, pp. 62-63, 70; Dechêne, *Habitants et marchands*, pp. 307-10; R.L. Séguin, *La Civilisation traditionnelle de l'habitant aux 17e et 18e siècles: fonds matériel* (Montreal, 1967), pp. 151-69, 642-50.

41. Kalm, *Travels*, 23 July 1749.

42. Ibid., 12 Aug., 29 Sept. 1749.

43. Ibid., 12 Aug., 7, 23, 29 Sept. 1749; La Pause, "Relations et mémoires," pp. 211-12. Biennial rotation would have been suitable for a land-rich, underpopulated colony where it was not a hardship to leave *more* land fallow. It can give higher yields than triennial, which was only an improvement where it was necessary to keep more land under cultivation to feed more people. See Slicher van Bath, *Agrarian History*, pp. 19-20, 58-59, and David Farmer, "Grain Yields on Westminster Abbey Manors, 1271-1410," *Canadian Journal of History* 18 (1983): 331-47. Kalm's remark, *Travels*, Sept. 23, 1749, suggests peas may have been segregated on poorer soil. Pennsylvanian extensive-land-use rotations in Lemon, *Best Poor Man's Country*, pp. 150, 169-70, suggest other possibilities that might be found.

44. "Messers Raudot au Ministre, Québec, 8 oct. 1708," in Munro, *Seigneurial Documents*, pp. 33-34; Kalm, *Travels*, 23 Sept. 1749. De Catalogne refers to poor lands that have been made productive by manuring ("Mémoires," in Munro, *Seigneurial Documents*,

pp. 121, 122). François Ruette d'Auteuil refers to the manuring of old lands ("Mémoire à son Altesse Royale, Monseigneur le Duc d'Orléans . . . sur l'état présent du Canada, 12 déc. 1715," *RAPQ*, 1922-23, p. 61). Franquet mentions want of it as a possible reason for declining fertility (*Voyages et mémoires*), p. 181. See also Dechêne, *Habitants et marchands*, p. 305, and Harris, *Seigneurial System*, p. 39.

45. Lemon, *Best Poor Man's Country*, p. 173.

46. Slicher van Bath, *Agrarian History*, p. 10; Jacques Jacquart in Duby and Wallon, *France rurale*, II: 216.

47. De Catalogne, "Mémoires," in Munro, *Seigneurial Documents*, pp. 109, 110, 128, 135, 136-39, 141-42; Kalm, *Travels*, 12 Aug. 1749; Dechêne, *Habitants et marchands*, p. 305.

48. Kalm, *Travels*, 28 July, 12 Aug., 7 Sept. (quotation), 25 Sept. 1749; Dechêne, *Habitants et marchands*, 299-300, 310-14. The excision of Kalm's references to fences by his eighteenth-century translator, Forster, and the only partial rectification of this omission in the revised edition by Adolph B. Benson must occasion a *cri de coeur* for a new and scholarly edition of Kalm. The illustration of fencing in the Dover edition (New York, 1966) II: 410 is tantalizing. Do unpublished drawings remain in Sweden or Finland? What "allied documents" remain to be unearthed?

49. Lunn, "Economic Development," pp. 443-44; Dechêne, *Habitants et marchands*, pp.

314-20; Harris, *Seigneurial System*, pp. 155-58.

50. "Ordonnance qui fait défense aux Habitants des Côtes de Montréal d'avoir plus de deux chevaux ou Cavales et un Poulin chacun; du tresième juin, mil sept cent neuf," in Canada, Assembly of the Province of, *Arrêts et règlements du Conseil supérieur de Québec et ordonnances et jugements des intendants du Canada* (Quebec, 1855), p. 273; AC, C11A 33: 15, Vaudreuil et Bégon au Ministre, Québec, 12 nov. 1712; De Catalogne, "Mémoires," in Munro, *Seigneurial Documents*, p. 146; Franquet, *Voyages et mémoires*, p. 27; Kalm, *Travels*, 8 July (quotation), 11 Oct. 1749; Dechêne, *Habitants et marchands*, pp. 318-19. See Séguin, *Civilisation traditionnelle*, pp. 155-56, 648, and Slicher van Bath, *Agrarian History*, p. 70, on horses and harrows, and the latter, pp. 22, 60-64 on feeding horses.

51. Boucault, "Etat présent," pp. 14-16; Kalm, *Travels*, 25 Aug. 1749; Lunn, "Economic Development," pp. 58-61.

52. Kalm, *Travels*, 4 Sept. 1749 near Baie St. Paul; De Catalogne, "Mémoires," in Munro, *Seigneurial Documents*, pp. 135-36.

53. De Catalogne, "Mémoires," in Munro, *Seigneurial Documents*, p. 105; Kalm, *Travels*, 7, 12, 29 Aug.; 12, 19, 25 Sept. 1749; Dechêne, *Habitants et marchands*, pp. 320-22.

54. Goubert in Braudel and Labrousse, *Histoire économique et sociale*, II: 92, 97, 98, 100-18, 150-58; Lemon, *Best Poor Man's Country*.

55. Goubert, *Ancien Régime*, p. 69. Cf. Lemon, *Best Poor Man's Country*, p. 180; Henretta, *Evolution of American Society*, pp. 5-6, and "Families and Farms: *Mentalité* in Pre-Industrial America," *WMQ* 35 (Jan. 1978): 3-32; Dechêne, *Habitants et marchands*, pp. 338-45; Harris, *Seigneurial System*, pp. 37-42; and the all-important caveat to self-sufficiency, Pruitt, "Self-sufficiency and Massachusetts." Only after we have seen how similar the Canadian rural folk were to their neighbours in their attachment to family and subsistence and their divorce from liberal individualism and the market will we be able to proceed to a perception of their uniqueness.

56. Braudel, *Capitalism*, pp. 83-85.

57. Administrators were keenly aware of the need for a market to develop the agricultural and commercial sectors; witness, *inter alia*, AC, C11A 22: 143, "Produit de ce qu'un minot de bled pris a Québec pour le commerce peut rendre a son retour en Canada, Duplessis, Québec, 8 nov. 1708," and ibid., 30: 4, Vaudreuil et Raudot au Ministre, Québec, 14 nov. 1709. Slicher van Bath regards market stimulus as the *sine qua non* of improved practice. See his *Agrarian History*, p. 14, and his "Agriculture in the Vital Revolution," in E.E. Rich and C.H. Wilson, eds., *Cambridge Economic History of Europe* (Cambridge, 1977), V: 71.

58. Dechêne, *Habitants et marchands*, pp. 330-34, 342, 521. See also De Catalogne's comments on the effects of distance from markets, "Mémoires," in Munro, *Seigneurial Documents*, pp. 99, 101-3, 106-8.

59. The temptation to produce a year-by-year table of good and bad harvests or to work out yields per head of population as well as other manipulations must be resisted as the data present not only gaps but also internal contradictions. Only spotty references to the size of harvests can be culled from AC, C11A vols. 19-33, covering the years 1700-12. Lunn's verbal descriptions of harvests in "Economic Development," pp. 94-101, are not consistent with her statistics, pp. 443-44, on which my Table VI is based. To these should be added further related statistics, pp. 445-49. The *Inventaire des ordonnances des intendants de la Nouvelle-France*, ed. P.G. Roy (Beauceville, 1918), Vols. I-III, add mysteries as well as clarifications. The price curve for wheat in Jean Hamelin, *Economie et société en Nouvelle-France* (Quebec, 1960), pp. 58-62, is one of the more reliable guides to the fortunes of the wheat economy, although the absence of a table of values from which the curve has been constructed limits the curve's use to other researchers, a failing of most Canadian works making use of graphics. While monetary perturbations that might affect the price curve can be accounted for, it is less easy to sort out market influences. Nevertheless, it indicates peak prices that, with the possible exceptions of 1710 and 1730, are scarcity peaks. It might be necessary to define "scarcity" differently for the period of

"subsistence plus" harvests up to the mid-1720s and the period of greater market orientation thereafter.

60. C. Bacqueville de la Potherie, *Histoire de l'Amérique septentrionale*, IV (Paris, 1722): 176.

61. Dale Miquelon, *Dugard of Rouen: French Trade to Canada and the West Indies, 1729-1770* (Montreal, 1978), pp. 87-88; Hamelin, *Economie et société*, pp. 64-71; Gratien Allaire, "Les Engagements pour la traite des fourrures – évaluation de la documentation," *RHAF* 34 (1980): 8.

62. Goubert, n. 54 above.

63. Lunn, "Economic Development," p. 85.

64. Lunn, "Economic Development," pp. 52-83.

65. AC, C11A 30: 271, Srs. Raudot au Ministre, Québec, 14 nov. 1709.

66. AC, C11A 79: 270, Beauharnois et Hocquart au Ministre, Québec, 15 sept. 1743. Measures taken in the years 1736-38 can be traced in the letters of Beauharnois, Hocquart, and Honoré Michel (ibid., vols. 66-70) as well as the "Extrait des registres du conseil supérieur de Québec, 9 avril 1737" (ibid., 68: 267-69) and the relevant ordinances in Roy, *Ordonnances*, Feb. 4, 1737-Jan. 4, 1739.

67. Donald J. Horton, "Gilles Hocquart, Intendant of New France: 1729-1748," Ph.D. dissertation, McGill University, 1974, p. 263.

68. De Catalogne, "Mémoires," in Munro, *Seigneurial Documents*, p. 146; Franquet, *Voyages et mémoires*, p. 186 (quotation); AC, C11A 33: 15, Vaudreuil et Bégon au Ministre, Québec, 12 nov. 1712, Pontchartrain's marginalia (quotation).

69. AC, B 59: 442-43, Maurepas à Beauharnois et Hocquart, Versailles, 24 av. 1733, quoted in Horton, "Gilles Hocquart," p. 178, n. 7.

70. Material on apprenticeship is based on Peter Moogk, "The Craftsmen of New France," Ph.D. dissertation, University of Toronto, 1973, and his "Manual Education and Economic Life in New France," in James Leith, ed., *Facets of Education in the Eighteenth Century*, Vol. 67 of *Studies on Voltaire and the Eighteenth Century* (1977): 125-68, and "Apprenticeship Indentures: A Key to Artisan Life in New France," *HP*, 1971, pp. 65-83. On numbers, see n. 4 above and n. 70, Chap. 6 above.

71. Moogk, "Apprenticeship Indentures," p. 65.

72. "Louis Prat," *DCB* II: 531; Lunn, "Economic Development," pp. 243-46, 473-76.

73. Miquelon, *Dugard*, pp. 83-84.

74. Ibid., pp. 166-70. As tonnages are approximate, so too are these figures. The company's last ship, *Astrée*, a hard-luck vessel that lay in the stocks for four years and made only three voyages, may have cost as much as 300 livres a ton, an exception to the trend indicated as a result of special circumstances.

75. The discussion of lumber and masts is from Lunn, "Economic Development," pp. 219-30.

76. Ibid., pp. 468-70.

77. See biographies of the eighteenth-century intendants in *DCB*, vols. II-IV, and esp. Hor-

ton's dissertation, "Gilles Hocquart," which is lucid but overcritical.

78. The present discussion is based primarily on Lunn, "Economic Development," pp. 280-341; Albert Tessier, *Les Forges de Saint-Maurice, 1729-1883* (Trois-Rivières, 1952), pp. 1-89; and Cameron Nish, *François-Etienne Cugnet: entrepreneur et entreprises en Nouvelle-France* (Montreal, 1975).

79. On techniques of production, see Lunn, "Economic Development," pp. 290, 374, and André Bérubé, "Rapport préliminaire sur l'évolution des techniques sidérurgiques aux Forges du Saint-Maurice, 1729-1883," [Parks Canada] Travail inédit no. 221 (Quebec, 1976).

80. Nish, *Cugnet*, p. 59.

81. At the time and since, the building of a large stone house, the "grande maison," has been roundly criticized. But given that it housed the ironmasters, the bookkeepers, visiting partners and officials, a chaplain and numerous workers, and provided offices and fireproof storage for provisions and dry goods sold to workers, it is difficult to argue that it was unsuitable to the operations of such an undertaking. See Jean Belisle, "Le Domaine de l'habitation aux Forges du Saint-Maurice," [Parks Canada] Travail inédit no. 307 (Quebec, 1978), p. 307; and Luce Vermette, "La Vie domestique aux Forges du Saint-Maurice," [Parks Canada] Travail inédit no. 274 (Ottawa, 1977), pp. 28-34.

82. Marie-France Fortier, "La Structuration sociale du village industriel des Forges du Saint-Maurice," [Parks Canada] Travail inédit no. 259 (Quebec, 1977), p. 259; Vermette, "La Vie domestique," pp. 2-3, 111, 122-23; Tessier, *Les Forges*, pp. 88-89.

83. The quotation is from Lunn, "Economic Development," p. 330. The remainder of the paragraph is based on Belisle, "Le Domaine," and Vermette, "La Vie domestique."

84. The subject is dealt with at length in Jacques Mathieu, *La Construction navale royale à Québec, 1739-1759*, Cahiers d'histoire no. 23 (Quebec, 1971) and Lunn, "Economic Development," pp. 253-79.

85. Horton, "Hocquart," pp. 198-99.

86. PAC, MG 28 L 3, Collection Baby, fols. 829-833, Havy et Lefebvre à Pierre Guy, Québec, 19 mai 1746.

87. Paul-Emile Renaud, *Les Origines économiques du Canada: l'oeuvre de la France* (Mames, France, 1928), pp. 284-88; Hamelin, *Economie et société*, pp. 75-100; Marc Gaucher, Marcel Delafosse, and Gabriel Debien, "Les Engagés pour le Canada au XVIIIe siècle," *RHAF* 13 (1959): 247-61, 402-21, 550-61; 14 (1960): 87-108, 246-58, 430-40, 583-602; Moogk, "Craftsmen."

88. Moogk, "Craftsmen," pp. 140-47.

89. AC, C11A 67: 189, "Signallements de quatre soldats," Québec, 17 oct. 1737.

90. Moogk, "Craftsmen," pp. 148-52.

91. AC, C11A 61: 226, Beauharnois et Hocquart au Ministre, Québec, 19 oct. 1734.

92. Claude Le Beau, *Avantures du S. C. Le Beau, avocat en parlement, ou voyage curieux et nouveau, parmi les sauvages de l'Amérique septentrionale*, 2 vols. (Amsterdam, 1738); "Claude Lebeau," *DCB* II: 373-74.

93. Moogk, "Craftsmen," pp. 103-38.

94. Ibid., p. 79, quoting Ruette d'Auteuil, "Mémoire à son Altesse royale . . . (12 décembre 1715)," *RAPQ, 1922-23*, p. 63.

95. AN, AD vii 2a "Règlement au sujet des Engagez et Fusils qui doivent être portez par les navires marchands aux colonies," 16 nov. 1716; "Ordonnance du roy au sujet des engagés," 15 fev. 1724.

96. Michael W. Flinn, *The European Demographic System, 1500-1820* (Brighton, 1981); Pierre Chaunu, *Histoire, science sociale: la durée, l'espace et l'homme à l'époque moderne* (Paris, 1974); Peter Laslett with Richard Wall, *Household and Family in Past Time* (Cambridge, 1972); Goubert, *Ancien Régime*.

97. Jacques Henripin and Yves Peron, "The Demographic Transition of the Province of Quebec," in D. V. Glass and Roger Revelle, eds., *Population and Social Change* (London, 1972), pp. 213-32, propose corrections to the fundamental Jacques Henripin, *La Population canadienne au début du XVIIIe siècle: nuptialité, fécondité, mortalité infantile*, Institut national d'Etudes démographiques, Travaux et documents no. 22 (Paris, 1954).

98. The Canadian adult is believed to have consumed twelve *minots* of wheat a year. See Lunn, "Economic Development," p. 448. One hundred grams of present-day whole grain hard spring wheat and the same weight of rye contain respectively 14 and 12.1 grams of protein. In addition, the wheat contains a bonus of niacin. See Bernice K. Watt and Annabel L. Merrill et al., *Handbook of the Nutritional Contents of Foods* (1963; reprinted, New York, 1975). Roger Saucier, "L'Histoire de l'hygiène du régime français," thèse de D.E.S., Université d'Ottawa, 1969, provides some general ideas on food, clothing, and shelter. Braudel, *Capitalism*, provides the essential European background.

99. Peter Moogk, *Building a House in New France: An Account of the Perplexities of Client and Craftsman in Early Canada* (Toronto, 1977); Georges Gauthier-Larouche, *L'Evolution de la maison rurale laurentienne* (Quebec, 1967), p. 19. Belisle, "Le Domaine" and Vermette, "La Vie domestique," especially p. 274, present material from which a few numerical estimates can be ventured, but housing, like clothing, has yet to be studied statistically. The St Maurice research suggests above-average affluence, such as glass windows, locks, and perhaps the textiles.

100. Kalm, *Travels*, 12 Aug. 1749.

101. Ibid., first and second quotations, 5 Aug.; third quotation, 19 July; fourth quotation, 24 July 1749.

102. AQ, Registre de la prévôté de Québec 95: 10r, quoted in Saucier, "L'hygiène," pp. 81-82.

103. Kalm, *Travels*, July 17, 1749.
104. John J. Heagerty, *Four Centuries of Medical History in Canada*, I (Toronto, 1928); Pierre-Georges Roy, "Les Epidémies à Québec," *Bulletin des recherches historiques* 49 (1943): 204-15; Edouard Desjardins, "Les Epidémies de fièvre pestilentielle survenues en Nouvelle-France," *L'Union médicale du Canada* 102 (1973): 2254-63; AC, C11A

19:1-42 (5 oct. 1701), 21: 5-39 (15 nov. 1703).
105. Roy, "Les Epidémies," pp. 207-8.
106. Flinn, *European Demographic System*, pp. 91-101, on the neglect of mortality; Andrew B. Appleby, "Nutrition and Disease: The Case of London, 1550-1750," *Journal of Interdisciplinary History* 6 (1975): 1-22, on autonomy of disease.

NOTES TO CHAPTER ELEVEN

1. AC, C11A 18: 99, Champigny au Ministre, 15 oct. 1700.
2. Quoted in T.B. Bottomore, *Elites and Society* (New York, 1964), pp. 20-21.
3. Roland E. Mousnier, *The Institutions of France under the Absolute Monarchy, 1598-1789*, Vol. I, *Society and the State*, trans. Brian Pearce (Chicago, 1979): 1-27; for Canada, Fernand Ouellet, "La Formation d'une société dans la vallée du Saint-Laurent: d'une société sans classes à une société de classes," *CHR* 62 (1981): 407-50, and "La Noblesse canadienne en 1767: un inventaire," *HS/SH* 1 (1968): 127-37; and for a more environmental view, Louise Dechêne, *Habitants et marchands de Montréal au XVIIe siècle* (Montreal and Paris, 1974), p. 351.
4. Charles Loyseau, *Des Ordres et simples dignités*, in *Les Oeuvres de Maistre Charles Loyseau, avocat en parlement, contenant les cinq livres du droit* (Lyons, 1701), p. 51.
5. Ibid.
6. Jean Domat, *Les Lois civiles dans leur ordre naturel*, 2nd ed., 3 vols. (Paris, 1697), I: xxv.

7. Canada, Assembly of the Province of, *Edits et ordonnances* . . . (Quebec, 1854), pp. 433-34, 25 juin 1710, 276-77, 30 juin 1710; AC, B 41: 535v, Conseil de Marine à Vaudreuil, Paris, 24 mai 1719, fol. 544, Conseil de Marine à Louvigny, Versailles, 24 mai 1719.
8. *Edits et ordonnances*, pp. 352-54, règlement, 27 av. 1716.
9. AC, C11A 26: 167-68, Raudot père au Ministre, Québec, 10 nov. 1707.
10. W.J. Eccles, *The Canadian Frontier, 1534-1760*, Histories of the American Frontier (New York, 1969), Chap. 5.
11. AC, B 72: 382, Mémoire du Roi, Marly, 12 mai 1741.
12. Canada, Assembly of the Province of, *Arrêts et règlements du Conseil supérieur de Québec, et ordonnances et jugements des intendants du Canada* (Quebec, 1855), pp. 275-76, ordonnance, 25 juin 1710; AC, C11A 34: 4, Vaudreuil et Bégon au Ministre, Québec, 15 nov. 1713; "Correspondance entre M. de Vaudreuil et la Cour," *RAPQ, 1947-48*, p. 242 (Mémoire du roi, Versailles, 19 mars 1714); P.G. Roy, *Inven-*

taire des ordonnances des intendants de la Nouvelle-France (1705-1759) conservés aux Archives provinciales de Québec, Vols. I-III (Beauceville, 1918), pp. 365-66, ordonnance, 19 av. 1734. Bégon's relevant ordinance of 8 Aug. 1708 is not extant in PAC, MG 8, A6.

13. Jean-Baptiste de La Croix de Chevrières de Saint-Vallier, *Catéchisme du diocèse de Québec*, fac. of 1701 ed. (Montreal, 1958), pp. 454-59, and *Rituel du diocèse de Québec* (Paris, 1703), pp. 378-80 (quotation, p. 379). On infrequency of communion, see *Rituel*, p. 186.

14. Cornelius J. Jaenen, *The Role of the Church in New France*, Frontenac Library (Toronto, 1976), p. 57; Gordon Dixon, "The Episcopate of Mgr. de Saint-Vallier, 1688-1727," M.A. thesis, University of Saskatchewan, 1980, p. 83; Henri Têtu and Charles-O. Gagnon, eds., *Mandements, lettres pastorales et circulaires des évèques de Québec*, 2 vols. (Quebec, 1887, 1888), I: 206.

15. Auguste Gosselin, *L'Eglise du Canada depuis Monseigneur de Laval jusqu'à la conquête*, Vol. I, *Monseigneur de Saint-Vallier* (Quebec, 1911).

16. Mathieu-Benoît Collet and Nicolas-Gaspard Boucault, "Procès verbaux sur la commodité et incommodité dressés dans chaque des paroisses de la Nouvelle-France," *RAPQ, 1921-22*, pp. 262-380; Gosselin, *L'Église du Canada depuis Laval*, I: 364-65; Jaenen, *Role of the Church*, p. 90.

17. Micheline D'Allaire, *L'Hôpital-Général de Québec, 1692-*

1764 (Montreal, 1971), pp. 149-55 (quotation, p. 152).

18. Ibid., Chap. 1.

19. Saint-Vallier, *Catéchisme*, p. 177.

20. Ibid., pp. 179-80.

21. Ibid., p. 185.

22. Têtu and Gagnon, *Mandements*, II: 22-23, 15 oct. 1742.

23. Dechêne, *Habitants et marchands*, pp. 402-6.

24. Peter N. Moogk, "Rank in New France: Reconstructing a Society from Notarial Documents," *HS/SH* 8 (1975): 34-53. The quotation, p. 41, is from Claude de Ferrière (1770). Contrary to Moogk's contention, the *douaire* of 1,000 livres, p. 44, indicates considerable respect for the rustic seigneur, since it places him among the honourable employments, which neither his paltry display of wealth nor his real power would indicate.

25. AC, C11A 67: 97 [Hocquart?] "Détail de toute la colonie," 1736. The refrain is constant, for example Saint-Vallier's similar comment, "M. Bégon connait aussi bien que moi la disposition de leurs esprits, peu portés à se soumettre et à reconnaitre leurs supérieurs temporels, de même que les spirituels [10 Sept. 1726]," in Gosselin, *L'Eglise du Canada depuis Laval*, I: 392.

26. See above, Chap. 2 at n. 15.

27. M. Trudel, *L'Esclavage au Canada Français: histoire et conditions de l'esclavage* (Quebec, 1960).

28. Ibid., tables, pp. 84-85, 89, 96.

29. Francis Parkman, *The Old Regime in Canada* (Boston, 1874), p. 395.

30. Fernand Ouellet, "Propriété seigneuriale et groupes sociaux dans la vallée du Saint-Laurent (1663-1840)" in *Mélanges d'histoire du Canada français offerts au professeur Marcel Trudel* (Ottawa, 1978), pp. 183-213, pp. 185-88.

31. Ibid., pp. 192-94. A decision to end ennoblement appears not to have been connected to any specific edict envisaging Canada but was in line with French policy in general. In August 1715, all patents of nobility given for money subsequent to 1689 were suppressed. This was reflected in Canada by a spate of confirmations of nobility in 1717. See AC B 39 at fol. 194. The last Canadian ennoblement indicated in P.G. Roy, *Lettres de noblesse, généalogies, érections de comtés et baronnies insinuées par le Conseil souverain de la Nouvelle-France* 2 vols. (Beauceville, 1920), is that of François Hertel de Rouville in April 1716 (II: 163). A specific order to cease the granting of seigneuries (later countermanded) occurs in AC B 36: 338, Mémoire du roi, Versailles, 19 mars 1714, and ibid., fol. 304, Mémoire du roi, Paris, 15 juin 1716 refers to an order of 1713.

32. W.J. Eccles, "The Social, Economic, and Political Significance of the Military Establishment in New France," *CHR* 52 (1971): 1-21; Fernand Ouellet, "Officiers de milice et structure sociale au Québec (1660-1815)," *HS/SH* 12 (1979): (pp. 37-65), pp. 44-45; AC, C11G 8: 196v, "Ordonnance pour l'établissement d'un cadet dans chacune des 28 compagnies des troupes de Canada," Marly, 8 mai 1731.

33. Claude de Bonnault, "Le Canada militaire: état provisoire des officiers de milice de 1641 à 1760," *RAPQ, 1949-50*, pp. 261-527.

34. Quoted in Dechêne, *Habitants et marchands*, p. 383.

35. Donald J. Horton, "Gilles Hocquart, Intendant of New France, 1729-1748," Ph.D. dissertation, McGill University, 1974, p. 225.

36. Ibid.

37. Dechêne, *Habitants et marchands*, p. 384.

38. See above, Chap. 4 at n. 85.

39. Ouellet, "Propriété seigneuriale et groupes sociaux," pp. 188-89; Terence A. Crowley, "Government and Interests: French Colonial Administration at Louisbourg, 1713-1758," Ph.D. dissertation, Duke University, Durham, N.C., 1975, Chap. 3.

40. See biographies in *DCB* of persons whose names appear in the list of appointees in J. Delalande, *Le Conseil souverain de la Nouvelle-France* (Quebec, 1927) pp. 117-27.

41. Richard C. Harris, *The Seigneurial System in Early Canada, A Geographical Study* (Madison, Wis., 1968), p. 44.

42. Allan Greer, "Habitants of the Lower Richelieu: Rural Society in Three Quebec Parishes, 1740-1840," Ph.D. dissertation, York University, 1980, pp. 422-23.

43. Ibid., p. 102.

44. Ouellet, "Propriété seigneuriale et groupes sociaux," pp. 189-90, 194.

45. Chevalier de La Pause, "Relations et mémoires du chevalier de La Pause," *RAPQ, 1933-34*, p. 212.

46. Louis Franquet, *Voyages et mémoires sur le Canada par Franquet* (Quebec, 1889), pp. 31-32.

47. Dechêne, *Habitants et marchands*, esp. pp. 389-91, 407-13; Ouellet, "Officiers de milice," p. 46. It seems to the present writer that historians miss the point, assuming that if *la vie noble* had any attraction for merchants, they should then have been practising it. This ignores the fact that its virtues represented not the means but the object of social promotion, possibly of such elevation that a given merchant might not aspire even to these outward manifestations. In a society of orders, every order practised its own virtues, and at a crucial moment, probably when the aspiring individual had reached the apex of his own order, he renounced one way of life for another, perhaps at great psychic cost. See my *Dugard of Rouen* (Montreal, 1978), pp. 165-66.

48. The reference is, respectively, to L. Dechêne and F. Ouellet in the works cited above.

49. Ouellet, "Propriété seigneuriale et groupes sociaux," p. 190.

50. Allana G. Reid, "The Development and Importance of the Town of Quebec, 1608-1760," Ph.D. dissertation, McGill University, 1950, p. 281. The assertion that "the king ordered no commercial request to be considered unless it had first passed through the syndic's hands" is a rather expansive interpretation of the ministerial "ought" (AC, B 48: 891-94, Ministre à Chazel, Versailles, 11 août 1725).

51. Peter N. Moogk, "In the Darkness of a Basement: Craftsmen's Associations in Early French Canada," *CHR* 57 (1976): 399-439.

52. Ouellet, "Officiers de Milice," pp. 47-48; Vaudreuil au Ministre, Québec, 25 oct. 1710, "Vaudreuil et la Cour," *RAPQ, 1946-47* (quotation); Dechêne, *Habitants et Marchands*, pp. 448-49; Moogk, "Rank in New France," pp. 44-45.

53. Louis XIV, *Memoires for the Instruction of the Dauphin* (New York, 1970), p. 35.

54. Dechêne, *Habitants et marchands*, p. 386; on *fidélité* and clientage, see Mousnier, *Institutions of France*, Vol. I; Yves Durand, "Clientèles et fidélités dans le temps et dans l'espace," in Yves Durand, ed., *Hommages à Roland Mousnier: clientèles et fidélités en Europe à l'époque moderne* (Paris, 1981), pp. 3-24.

55. John F. Bosher, "Government and Private Interests in New France," *Canadian Public Administration* 10 (1967): 244-57; Crowley, "Government and Interests."

56. S. Dale Standen, "Politics, Patronage, and the Imperial Interest: Charles de Beauharnais's Disputes with Gilles Hocquart," *CHR* 60 (1979): 19-40.

57. AC B 37: 166v-176v, Ministre à Bégon, Marly, 10 juil. 1715.

58. Crowley, "Government and Interests," pp. 77-78 (first quotation), pp. 216-17 (second quotation); Guy Frégault, "Politique et politiciens," *Le XVIIIe siècle canadien: études* (Montreal, 1968), (pp. 159-241), pp. 176-77. Robe and sword distinctions cannot be taken too far as the lines were constantly being crossed in the same extended families. See "Jacques Raudot," *DCB* II: 554-

61, and "Gilles Hocquart," *DCB* IV: 354-65.

59. Frégault, "Politique et politiciens," p. 178. "Political class": my reference is not to Marx but to Mosca.

60. S. Dale Standen, "Charles, Marquis de Beauharnais de la Boische, Governor General of New France, 1726-1747," Ph.D. dissertation, University of Toronto, 1975, pp. 182-86, 331, 355; Frégault, "Politique et politiciens," pp. 171-79, 198-200; "Jacques Raudot"; on Bégon, see Chap. 4 above at n. 70.

61. AC, C11D 4: 61v, "6 obre 1701 . . . Mémoire de ce qui regarde les intérests du Roy touchant Lestablissement que Sa Majesté a dessein de faire dans Sa province de Lacadie" (first quotation); Beauharnois et Hocquart au Ministre, Québec, 10 oct. 1734, *Historical Collections. Collections and Researches Made by the Michigan Pioneer and Historical Society* 34 (Lansing, 1905): 118-19 (second quotation); AC, C11A 19: 64v, Champigny au Ministre, Québec, 7 nov. 1701, 20: 79, "Etat de distribution," 1702 (third quotation).

62. *Michigan Historical Collections* 34: 54-55, Marquise de Vaudreuil to the Minister, n.p., n.d.

63. Jean-Claude Dubé, "Clients des Colbert et des Pontchartrain à l'intendance de Québec," in Yves Durand, ed., *Hommages à Roland Mousnier: Clientèles et fidélités en Europe à l'époque moderne* (Paris, 1981), pp. 199-212; "Michel Bégon," *DCB* III: 57-63; Yves Zoltvany, *Philippe de Rigaud de Vaudreuil, Governor of New France, 1703-1725*, Carleton Library (Toronto, 1974),

pp. 24-25; Horton, "Gilles Hocquart," pp. 7, 26, 40; Standen, "Beauharnais," pp. 27, 481.

64. François Ruette d'Auteuil, "Mémoire sur l'état présent du Canada, 1712," *RAPQ, 1922-23*, (pp. 36-51), p. 38.

65. Helen Nolan, "The Port of La Rochelle, 1715-1745," M.A. thesis, University of Ottawa, 1969, pp. 117-18.

66. Zoltvany, *Vaudreuil*, pp. 54-56, 66-67, 71-74, 88, 96-110; Frégault, "Politique et politiciens"; "Jacques Raudot"; Micheline D'Allaire, *Montée et déclin d'une famille noble: les Ruette d'Auteuil (1617-1737)* (Ville LaSalle, Que., 1980), Chap. 3.

67. "Michel Bégon"; Standen, "Beauharnais," p. 106; Kathryn Young, "Michel Bégon and the Direction of Economic Policy in French Canada from 1712 to 1726," M.A. thesis, University of Manitoba, 1984, pp. 103-13.

68. This treatment of Beauharnois's governorship is based on Standen, "Beauharnais," supplemented as regards the Intendant Depuy with Jean-Claude Dubé, *Claude-Thomas Dupuy, Intendant de la Nouvelle-France, 1678-1738* (Montreal, 1969).

69. "Claude-Thomas Dupuy," *DCB* II: 212.

70. Quoted in Standen, "Beauharnais," p. 227.

71. Quoted in Horton, "Gilles Hocquart," (1974), p. 93. See also Standen, "Beauharnais," pp. 345-46.

72. In addition to Standen and Horton, cited in nn. 70 and 71, see the biographies of these nine men in *DCB*, Vols. III and IV.

73. Standen, "Beauharnais," pp.

346-57. In AC B 65: 404-4v, Ministre à Hocquart, Versailles, 16 av. 1737, Maurepas alludes to conversations "vive voix" with the Intendant in which he appears to have laid down ground rules for economy.
74. Standen, "Beauharnais," pp. 358-62 (quotation, p. 362), 373-74; Horton, "Gilles Hocquart," pp. 154-55.
75. Standen, "Beauharnais," pp. 366-67. Hocquart does not appear to have specifically recommended leasing any posts other than Niagara, Frontenac, and Temiskaming. He rejected this policy for Detroit, recommending, however, that the right to trade be transferred from the commandant to *congé* holders, the policy ultimately determined upon by Maurepas for Detroit and Michilimackinac. See AC, C11A 67: 308, Hocquart au Ministre, Québec, 7 oct. 1737.

76. AC, C11A 78: 47-48, Hocquart au Ministre, Québec, 15 oct. 1742; see also fol. 298, "Projet de règlement fait par le Sieur Michel, commissaire ordonnateur . . . 3 sept. 1742, 77: 329, Hocquart au Ministre, Québec, 16 sept. 1742; AC, B 72: 382, Mémoire du roi, Marly, 12 mai 1741.
77. AC, C11A 77: 94-97, Beauharnois au Ministre, Québec, 5 sept. 1742; 76: 272-77, "Mémoire sur quelques parties de Depenses de Canada qui pourroient considérablement diminués en prenant les arrangemens proposés, Varin, 16 fév. 1741"; 80: 241-41v, Hocquart au Ministre, Québec, 30 oct. 1743.
78. Quoted in Crowley, "Government and Interests," p. 283. The present brief treatment of Louisbourg clientage and corruption is based on Crowley, pp. 37, 66-69, 91-94, 120-21, 126, 219-23, 283-95.

NOTES TO CHAPTER TWELVE

1. AC, B 78: 48, Ministre à Champigny et Ranché, Versailles, 17 mars 1744.
2. PAC, Collection Baby, fols. 524-27, Havy et Lefebvre à Guy, Québec, 7 oct. 1744.
3. AN, 62 AQ 31, Havy à Dugard, La Rochelle, 5 août 1758.
4. "Mandement pour les prières publiques, 29 août 1744," in Henri Têtu and Charles-O. Gagnon, eds., *Mandements, lettres pastorales et circulaires des éveques de Québec*, 2 vols. (Quebec, 1887, 1888), II: 34-36.

5. Quoted in Geoffrey S. Simpson, "Quebec and Paris: The French Search for the Western Sea in Canada, 1660-1760," Ph.D. dissertation, Cambridge University, 1972, p. 134, n. 38.
6. "Histoire et sciences sociales: La longue durée," *Annales ESC* 13 (1958): 725-53.
7. Hugh Honour, et al., *L'Amérique vue par l'Europe*, Catalogue d'une exposition au Grand Palais, 17 sept. 1976-3 jan. 1977 (Paris, 1976).

THE CANADIAN CENTENARY SERIES

A History of Canada in Nineteen Volumes

The Canadian Centenary Series is a comprehensive history of the peoples and lands which form the Dominion of Canada.

Although the series is designed as a unified whole so that no part of the story is left untold, each volume is complete in itself. Written for the general reader as well as for the scholar, each of the nineteen volumes of *The Canadian Centenary Series* is the work of a leading Canadian historian who is an authority on the period covered in his volume. Their combined efforts have made a new and significant contribution to the understanding of the history of Canada and of Canada today.

W.L. Morton (d. 1980), Vanier Professor of History, Trent University, was the Executive Editor of *The Canadian Centenary Series*. A graduate of the Universities of Manitoba and Oxford, he was the author of *The Kingdom of Canada; Manitoba: A History; The Progressive Party in Canada; The Critical Years: The Union of British North America, 1857-1873;* and other writings. He also edited *The Journal of Alexander Begg and Other Documents Relevant to the Red River Resistance*. Holder of the honorary degrees of LL.D. and D.LITT., he was awarded the Tyrrell Medal of the Royal Society of Canada and the Governor General's Award for Non-Fiction.

D.G. Creighton (d. 1979), former Chairman of the Department of History, University of Toronto, was the Advisory Editor of *The Canadian Centenary Series*. A graduate of the Universities of Toronto and Oxford, he was the author of *John A. Macdonald: The Young Politician; John A. Macdonald: The Old Chieftain; Dominion of the North; The Empire of the St. Lawrence* and many other works. Holder of numerous honorary degrees, LL.D. and D.LITT., he twice won the Governor General's Award for Non-Fiction. He had also been awarded the Tyrrell Medal of the Royal Society of Canada, the University of Alberta National Award in Letters, the University of British Columbia Medal for Popular Biography, and the Molson Prize of the Canada Council.

Ramsay Cook, Professor of History, York University, co-author with R.C. Brown of *Canada 1896-1921*, volume 14 of the series, is the Executive Editor of *The Canadian Centenary Series*, 1983.